Writers and their Background

JOHN DRYDEN

John Dryden by Sir Godfrey Kneller
(National Portrait Gallery)

JOHN DRYDEN

EDITED BY EARL MINER

OHIO UNIVERSITY PRESS · 1972

In memoriam
Edward Niles Hooker
and
John Harrington Smith

Contents

ILLUSTRATIONS

DRYDEN, BY SIR GODFREY KNELLER C. 1698
Frontispiece

THE ARCHANGEL MICHAEL, BY GUIDO RENI
Facing p. 102

The Contributors

WILLIAM FROST
Professor of English, University of California, Santa Barbara, U.S.A.

JEAN H. HAGSTRUM
John C. Shaffer Professor of English and Humanities, Northwestern University, U.S.A.

K. G. HAMILTON
Darnell Professor of English, University of Queensland, Australia

ARTHUR W. HOFFMAN
Professor of English, Syracuse University, U.S.A.

JOHN LOFTIS
Professor of English, Stanford University, U.S.A.

GEORGE deF. LORD
Professor of English, Yale University, U.S.A.

EARL MINER
Professor of English, Princeton University, U.S.A.

EUGENE M. WAITH
Douglas Tracy Smith Professor of English, Yale University, U.S.A.

MICHAEL WILDING
Senior Lecturer in English, University of Sydney, Australia.

Writers and Their Background

John Dryden

The study of literature is not a 'pure' discipline for the simple reason that works of literature are affected by the climate of opinion in which they are produced. Writers, like other men, are concerned with the politics, the philosophy, the religion, the arts, and the general thought of their own times. Some writers, indeed, have made their own distinguished contributions to these areas of human interest, while the literary achievement of others can be fully appreciated only by a knowledge of them.

The present series has been planned with the purpose of presenting such writers in their intellectual, social and artistic context, and with the belief that this will make their work more easily understood and enjoyed. Each volume contains a Reader's Guide to the writings of the author concerned, a Bibliography, and a Chronological Table which sets out the dates of the author's life and publications alongside the chief events of historical, intellectual and literary importance of his lifetime.

The editor, Earl Miner, writes in his preface: 'If ever a writer was versatile, Dryden was the one. His dramatic creations include tragedy, comedy, tragicomedy of both kinds, heroic play, masque, opera, and the oratorio. His range in nondramatic poetry or in prose is equally comprehensive, and he spoke the simple truth at the end of his life when he said that, as ideas crowded in upon him, his only difficulty lay in deciding whether to embody them in "verse or to give them the other harmony of prose". Given such variety, then, and so large a canon of works, Dryden, if any writer can, benefits from interpretations by critics of differing viewpoint and of differing convictions.'

discipline since works of
pinion in which they are
ned with the politics, the
eral thought of their own
e their own distinguished
t, while the achievement
owledge of them.

:h has been planned with
eir intellectual, social and
this will make their work
olume contains a chapter
s of the author concerned,
ting out the main dates of
the chief events of con-

:now well only his major
:nowledge Dryden as an
, 'it is hardly too much to
and he gave them speech'.
ted to Dryden's contribu-
the development of prose
is the first of the Moderns,
lled him, who (in another
lish poetry brick and left it
riter whose work marked
sical humanism, on which
which was emerging from
ok, which has been written

by a body of experts and edited by one of our most distinguished Dryden scholars, will be welcomed by many who wish to know more about the genius of a man whose writings throw such a clear light on a crucial period of our political, intellectual and literary history.

R. L. BRETT

General Editor's Preface

THE STUDY of literature is not a 'pure' discipline since works of literature are affected by the climate of opinion in which they are produced. Writers, like other men, are concerned with the politics, the philosophy, the religion, the arts, and the general thought of their own times. Some literary figures, indeed, have made their own distinguished contributions to these areas of human interest, while the achievement of others can be fully appreciated only by a knowledge of them.

The present volume is one in a series which has been planned with the purpose of presenting major authors in their intellectual, social and artistic contexts, and with the conviction that this will make their work more easily understood and enjoyed. Each volume contains a chapter which provides a reader's guide to the writings of the author concerned, a Bibliography, and Chronological Tables setting out the main dates of the author's life and publications alongside the chief events of contemporary importance.

Most students of literature, even if they know well only his major satires and a few shorter poems, would acknowledge Dryden as an important figure. For as T. S. Eliot observed, 'it is hardly too much to say that Dryden found the English speechless and he gave them speech'. The truth of this remark, however, is not limited to Dryden's contribution to the growth of the English Language or the development of prose style. In many other respects as well, Dryden is the first of the Moderns, the Father of English criticism, as Johnson called him, who (in another of Johnson's memorable phrases) 'found English poetry brick and left it marble'. But more than this, Dryden was a writer whose work marked the transition from the Old Christian and classical humanism, on which our culture was founded, to the new society which was emerging from the crisis of the seventeenth century. This book, which has been written by a body of experts and edited by one of our most distinguished Dryden scholars, will be welcomed by many who wish to know more about the genius of a man whose writings throw such a clear light on a crucial period of our political, intellectual and literary history.

R. L. BRETT

Editor's Preface

IF EVER writer was versatile, Dryden was the one. His dramatic creations include tragedy, comedy, tragicomedy of both kinds, heroic play, masque, opera, and the oratorio. His range in nondramatic poetry or in prose is equally comprehensive, and he spoke the simple truth at the end of his life when he said that, as ideas crowded in upon him, his only difficulty lay in deciding whether to embody them in 'verse or to give them the other harmony of prose'. Given such variety, then, and so large a canon of works, Dryden, if any writer can, benefits from interpretations by critics of differing viewpoint and of differing convictions. My collaborators will share with me the hope that in working together we may have seen more sides of Dryden than can be seen very steadily by a single person. But they will also share with me a sense of having left out very much that we all know to be in Dryden. Music, philosophy, science, relation with the moderns on the continent and at home, figurative language, diction, and other linguistic features, rhetoric—the list expands rebukingly. The fact that the essays here often return to poems such as *Absalom and Achitophel* may suggest that most of us see Dryden too narrowly, but it may also suggest that among the subjects dealt with we have included those of high importance to understanding Dryden.

I regard the present essays as a kind of conversation about Dryden. No doubt the pace of the dialogue is even slower than that of Dryden's on dramatic poesy, but the essayists are speaking to each other, to readers, and to others who have and will speak their mind on Dryden— and the essayists are concerned to say what they think is important. In Dryden's own spirit, they respect their author and they seek the best earlier criticism as a guide. But also in Dryden's spirit, they recognize that the only excuses for writing something are the conservative ones of making clear what has been implicit and unexpressed in the experience of reading Dryden, and the radical one of saying things that had not been said but that nonetheless seem true. None of us wishes for the conversation to stop with this book, or for talk about literature to replace reading. But any writer as important as Dryden is worth our reflections, our attempts at insight into him as a means to insight into ourselves, and even our disagreements.

In his search for a new language and new forms to create in art the vision of man as it emerged in the seventeenth century, Dryden created something enduring. What endures is the poetic conception of mankind *in history*, with the present moment at once historical and poetic, the past a valued point of reference, and the future a matter of hope. Before Dryden no important English poet, perhaps none anywhere, had given man dignity for being part of that present in time shared with other men and women—and part, too, of a historical civilization. Although we cannot turn today from the events that most stir us in the world to read about them in contemporary poetry, we can find events like them treated by Dryden and discover the uses of his vision in our own day. Like other great poets, Dryden teaches us a new way of understanding how to make of ourselves and our world what Virgil described as a race and an enduring city (*et genus et mansuram urbem*).

I am grateful to my collaborators for the quality of their work and for their putting up with editorial harrying. My friend Alan Roper has been good enough to vet my work. And Mr Richard Barber of G. Bell & Sons Limited has assisted our enterprise in many ways. Rather late in the writing of this book, Mr Barber observed that I seemed not to have assigned the 'On Reading Dryden' chapter to anyone. I have paid for that oversight by having to write it as well as another essay, and undertaking the Chronology, Bibliography, and Index. At the same late stage, illness prevented one of the potential contributors from completing his essay. To compensate for that, I have encouraged others to define their topics generously.

Except where noted, dates record performance for plays, for non-dramatic works, publication. Years of Dryden's life are given in parentheses under the year.

	The main events of the life of Dryden and immediate family	Main events of literary and intellectual importance	Main events of historical importance
1631 (1)	19 Aug. (NS): Dryden born at Aldwinckle All Saints in Northamptonshire	Stow, *Annals of England*	No Parliament 1629–40 Thirty Years' War in Progress
1632 (2)		Locke, Spinoza born Shakespeare 2nd folio	Money raised for Charles I by sale of monopolies and other schemes
1633 (3)		George Saville (Halifax), Pepys, Wentworth Dillon (Roscommon) born Donne, *Poems* Herbert, *The Temple* Quarles, *Divine Poems* Cowley, *Poetical Blossoms*	Charles I exacts levies without Parliament Laud becomes archbishop
1634 (4)		Robert South born	Ship Money controversy begins Strafford active in Ireland
1635 (5)		Edward Stillingfleet, Thomas Sprat, and ?Sir George Etherege born Académie Française founded P. Corneille, *Medée* Selden, *Mare Clausum* Quarles, *Emblems*	
1636 (6)		Joseph Glanville, Boileau born P. Corneille, *Le Cid*	Bishops hold offices of state First Bishops' War (to 1639)

1637 (7)	Milton's *Comus* published Thomas Traherne born? Hobbes, *Art of Rhetorique* Descartes, *Discours de la Méthode*	Scotland protests imposition of Prayer-Book Prynne, Lilburne, other radicals punished Hampden refuses to pay Ship Money
1638 (8)	Davenant, *Madagascar* Milton, *Lycidas* Quarles, *Hieroglyphics*	Charles I invades Scotland 50,000 English colonists in North America
1639 (9)	Racine born P. Corneille, *Horace, Cinna*	Strafford returns to England to strengthen royal cause Last judicial torture in England
1640 (10)	Wycherley, Aphra Behn born Selden, *De Jure Naturali* Donne, *LXXX Sermons* Jonson, 1st folio, vol. i Milton, *Of Reformation* Bay Psalm Book P. Corneille, *Polyeucte*	April–May: Short Parliament Second Bishops' War Nov.: Long Parlia- ment sits, arrests Strafford, Laud Dec.: Root-and- Branch Petition presented to Parlia- ment
1641 (11)	Thomas Rymer born Georges de Scudéry, *Ibrahim* The Episcopacy or Smectymnuus Con- troversy	Star Chamber, High Commission (of Church) abolished May: Strafford executed Nov.: Grand Remonstrance to Charles I from Parliament
1642 (12)	Isaac Newton born Theatres closed Hobbes, *De Cive* P. Corneille, *Le Menteur*	First Civil War (to 1646) Navy deserts the King Charles I situates in Oxford

1643 (13)		Browne, *Religio Medici* Milton, divorce tracts (to 1645) Newspapers appear in England	Parliament raises funds by excise 1 Sept.: First Battle of Newbury Covenant between Scotland and Parliament
1644 (14)		William Penn born Milton, *Of Education*, *Areopagitica*	Jan.: Scots invade England July: Parliamentary forces defeat Royalists at Marston Moor Dec.: Self-Denying Ordinance (prevents holding military and parliamentary posts at the same time)
1645 (15)		Milton, *Poems* Howell, *Epistolae Ho-Elianae* Waller, *Poems* Boehme's works first translated into English	Jan.: Laud executed March: New Model Army formed (22,000 out of 80,000 Parliamentary troops) June: New Model decisively defeats Royalists at Naseby
1646 (16)	About this time Dryden enters Westminster School as a King's Scholar	Browne, *Vulgar Errors* Crashaw, *Steps to the Temple* Suckling, *Fragmenta Aurea* H. Vaughan, *Poems*	Parliament extorts money from Royalists, oppresses Independents
1647 (17)		John Wilmot (Rochester) born Beaumont and Fletcher, *Comedies and Tragedies* Cowley, *The Mistress* More, *Philosophical Poems* La Calpranède, *Cléopatre*	Cromwell, Independents sieze the King and control of the army Levellers emerge as force in politics and the army Nov.: Charles flees to Isle of Wight
1648 (18)	Dryden recalled in 1693 that he had translated Persius, Satire III, as a school exercise about this time	Hooker, *Laws of Ecclesiastical Polity*, books vi and vii Herrick, *Hesperides* *Eikon Basilike* (sixty editions in first year) Society of Friends begins to form	May–Aug.: Second Civil War Aug.: Scots invade England Dec.: Col. Pride purges the Long Parliament, leaving the 'Rump'

1649 (19)	'Upon the Death of the Lord Hastings' (Dryden's first published work)	Donne, *Fifty Sermons* Lovelace, *Lucasta* Milton, *Tenure of Kings and of Magistrates, Eikonoklastes* Mme. de Scudéry, *Le Grand Cyrus* (10 vols. to 1653)	Third Civil War (to 1651) 30 Jan.: Charles I executed Feb.: House of Lords abolished May: Cromwell invades Ireland Sept.: Cromwell's massacre at Drogheda Oct.: Lilburne the Leveller browbeats the court and goes free
1650 (20)	18 May: Dryden admitted as pensioner to Trinity College, Cambridge	Baxter, *Saints' Everlasting Rest* Hobbes, *Human Nature, De Corpore Politico* Taylor, *Rule and Exercises of Holy Living* (. . . *Holy Dying*, 1651) H. Vaughan, *Silex Scintillans*	July: Cromwell invades Scotland
1651 (21)		Cleveland, *Poems* Davenant, *Gondibert* Hobbes, *Leviathan* H. Vaughan, *Olor Iscanus*	First Anglo-Dutch naval war (to 1654) Charles II crowned at Scone Sept.: Charles II escapes after Battle of Worcester
1652 (22)		Thomas Otway, Nahum Tate born Herbert, *Remains*	Parliament and Cromwell's Council of State vie for power
1653 (23)		Nathaniel Lee born? Walton, *The Compleat Angler* Urquhart, tr. Rabelais, bks. i and ii Molière, *L'Étourdi*	April: Cromwell dissolves Rump Parliament July: the nominated Barebones Parliament sits Dec.: Cromwell becomes Lord Protector
1654 (24)	March: Dryden receives BA, Cambridge University June: death of Dryden's father, Erasmus Dryden	Orrery, *Parthenissa* H. Vaughan, *Flores Solitudinis*	Sept.: First Protectorate Parliament sits

1655 (25)	Dryden possibly in the service of the Protectorate about this time	Fuller, *Church History* Stanley, *History of Philosophy* (complete 1662) Fanshawe, tr. *Lusiad* Wallis, *Arithmetica Infinitorum*	Aug.: Cromwell imposes rule by Major-generals Cromwell vindictively fines royalists
1656 (26)		Cowley, *Poems* Davenant, *Siege of Rhodes* performed Drummond, *Poems* Pascal, *Lettres Provinciales*	Sept.: Second Protectorate Parliament sits Unpopular Major-Generals and heavy Cavalier fines dropped Cromwell completes devastation of Ireland
1657 (27)			April: Blake defeats Spanish fleet at Santa Cruz
1658 (28)		?Allestree, *The Whole Duty of Man* Phillips, *New World of Words*	Protectorate in financial straits 3 Sept.: Cromwell dies, son Richard succeeding
1659 (29)	*Heroique Stanza's* on Cromwell	Chamberlayne, *Pharonnida* Lovelace, *Posthume Poems* Suckling, *Last Remains* P. Corneille, *Oedipe*	May: Richard Cromwell falls Rule by generals
1660 (30)	*Astraea Redux* on the Restoration	Pepys starts *Diary* (1 Jan., ends 31 May 1669) Harrington, *Political Discourses* Donne, *XXVI Sermons* Oct.: Theatres opened Bunyan imprisoned (to 1672) Lely begins 'Windsor Beauties' series	March: Monk occupies London and declares a 'free Parliament' 29 May: Charles II enters London on his birthday Execution of regicides excepted from Act of Oblivion; Milton somehow spared

1661 (31)	*To his Sacred Majesty*	Boyle, *The Sceptical Chymist*; 'Boyle's Law' Glanville, *Vanity of Dogmatising* (rev. 1665) Waller, *On St James's Park* Molière, *Les Facheux*, etc. Lely becomes court painter	Jan.: Fifth Monarchy Men revolt; they and Quakers persecuted May: Cavalier Parliament sits (to 1679) Anglican Church restored Repressive 'Clarendon Code' enacted through 1665 to destroy Dissent
1662 (32)	*To My Lord Chancellor* (Clarendon) Dryden elected 'Original Fellow' of Royal Society	Butler, *Hudibras*, pt. i Fuller, *Worthies of England* Prayer-Book (present form) 15 July: Royal Society given charter Molière, *L'École de femmes*	Anglican persecution of Dissent severe till 1667 Charles II marries Catherine of Braganza Many Presbyterian clergymen lose their livings
1663 (33)	Feb.: *Wild Gallant*, Dryden's first play, is acted 1 Dec.: Dryden marries Lady Elizabeth Howard (aet. ca. 25)	Butler, *Hudibras*, pt. ii May: Theatre Royal opens Shakespeare third folio (with apocrypha)	Clarendon survives impeachment Scotland submits to Restoration settlement
1664 (34)	Jan.: *The Indian Queen* (heroic tragedy) with Sir Robert Howard May: *The Rival Ladies* (tragi-comedy)	Cotton, *Scarronides* Etherege, *The Comical Revenge* Evelyn, *Sylva* Waller, *Poems*	Dutch and English vie over trade in many parts of the world; English seize New Netherlands in America
1665 (35)	Spring: *The Indian Emperour* (heroic play)	Howard, *Four Plays* Marvell, *Character of Holland* Hooke, *Micrographia* La Rochefoucauld, *Maximes*	Feb.: Second Anglo-Dutch War (ends 1667) June: The Great Plague in London
1666 (36)	At Charlton to avoid the plague, Dryden writes *Of Dramatick Poesie* (pub. 1668, rev. 1684) and plays 6 Sept.: Son Charles born (Westminster School, Trinity College, Cambridge, priest at Rome) 16 Oct.: Dryden loans Charles II £500	Bunyan, *Grace Abounding* Tillotson, *Rule of Faith* Boileau, *Satires* Molière, *Le Misanthrope*, etc. *Bibliotheca Fratrum Polonorum* (major Socinian writings) published in Amsterdam, ca. 1655–58	2–6 Sept.: The Great Fire of London

1667 (37)	Feb.: *Secret-Love or the Maiden Queen* (tragi-comedy) *Annus Mirabilis* Aug.: *Sir Martin Mar-All* (comedy) with Newcastle Nov.: *The Tempest* (adaptation of Shakespeare) with Davenant	Milton, *Paradise Lost* (in ten books) Sprat, *History of the Royal Society* Molière, *Tartuffe* Racine, *Andromaque*	Dutch invade Thames and Medway July: Treaty of Breda ends war with Holland inconclusively Aug.: Clarendon compelled to resign
1668 (38)	Early in year son John born (Westminster School, Christ Church, Rome) 13 April: Dryden succeeds Davenant as poet laureate 17 June: Dryden receives Lambeth MA at request of the King June: *An Evening's Love* (comedy)	Cowley, *Works* Denham, *Collected Poems* Orrery, *Mustapha* Etherege, *She Wou'd if She Co'ud* Shadwell, *The Sullen Lovers* La Fontaine, *Fables*, pt. i Molière, *Amphitryon*, etc. Grimmelshausen, *Simplicius Simplicissimus*	Jan.: Triple Alliance (England, Holland, Sweden) against France May: France ends war against Spain
1669 (39)	2 May: Son Erasmus-Henry born (Charter-house, Douay, priest, fifth baronet) June: *Tyrannick Love* (heroic tragedy) 18 Aug.: Dryden succeeds James Howell as historiographer royal	Oxford University Press is housed in the Sheldonian Theatre and is founded on its modern lines Wallis, *Mechanica* Racine, *Britannicus* Bossuet, *Oraison funèbre de la reine d'Angleterre*	License of the court is at its peak Charles II pursues secret agreement with France
1670 (40)	Dec.: *The Conquest of Granada* pt. i (heroic play)	Congreve born Milton, *History of Britain* Pascal, *Pensées* Molière, *Le Bourgeois Gentilhomme*, etc. Racine, *Bérenice*	May: Secret Treaty of Dover Second Conventicle Act; Anglican persecution of Dissenters once again severe
1671 (41)	Jan.: *The Conquest of Granada*, pt. ii (heroic play)	Milton, *Paradise Regain'd, Samson Agonistes* *Westminster Drollery* and similar collections appear	Sham treaty signed with France

1672 (42)	Ca. April: *Marriage A-la-mode* (heroic, comic play), perhaps written in 1671 *Of Heroic Plays* prefixed to *The Conquest of Granada . . . in Two Parts* Nov.: *The Assignation* (comedy)	Addison, Steele born *The Rehearsal*, performed Marvell, *The Rehearsal Transpros'd* Wycherley, *Love in a Wood*	2 Jan.: Exchequer suspends payments (many bankruptcies) 17 March: Third Anglo-Dutch War William of Orange emerges as a power during revolution and French invasion
1673 (43)	Ca. May: *Amboyna* (anti-Dutch tragedy)	Davenant, *Collected Works* Milton, *Poems* (1645 ed. rev.) Molière, *Malade Imaginaire* Racine, *Mithridate*	29 March: Test Act excludes Catholics from office June: James Duke of York resigns as Lord High Admiral because of Test Act Dutch make treaties against France James marries Mary of Este
1674 (44)	Ca. Jan.: *The Mistaken Husband* (anonymous comedy) said to have been touched up by Dryden	Milton, *Paradise Lost* (in twelve books) Rymer, tr. Rapin on Aristotle Boileau, *Lutrin*, *Art Poétique* Malebranche, *Recherche de la verité* Basile, *Il Pentamerone*	Danby in effect creates a Tory party, Shaftesbury a Whig or 'Country Party' Whigs in French pay (to ca. 1678) Marriage proposed for William and Mary
1675 (45)	Nov.: *Aureng-Zebe* (heroic play); in the Prologue Dryden declares himself 'weary' of dramatic rhymed verse and henceforth turns to blank verse	Wycherley, *Country Wife* Rebuilding of St Paul's on Wren's design	Renewed persecution of Dissenters (to 1679) Shaftesbury's Green Ribbon Club formed
1676 (46)		Cotton, *Compleat Angler*, pt. ii Etherege, *Man of Mode* Shadwell, *The Virtuoso*, etc. Leibniz completes the differential calculus	James openly shows his Catholicism

1677 (47)	*The Author's Apology for Heroic Poetry and Poetic License* prefixed to *The State of Innocence* (an aborted dramatization of *Paradise Lost*, date of writing uncertain) *Heads of an Answer to Rymer* written on the blank leaves of a copy, now lost, of *The Tragedies of the Last Age* Dec.: *All for Love* (Dryden's first blank-verse tragedy)	Aphra Behn, *The Rover* Wycherley, *The Plain Dealer* Tate, *Poems* Rymer, *Tragedies of the Last Age Consider'd* Racine, *Phèdre* Spinoza, *Ethics*	Feb.: Shaftesbury committed to Tower for a year by the Lords England allied with Holland 4 Nov.: Marriage of William and Mary
1678 (48)	*Mac Flecknoe* substantially in its present form March: *The Kind Keeper* (comedy)	Bunyan, *Pilgrim's Progress*, pt. i (pt. ii 1684) Butler, *Hudibras*, pt. iii Cudworth, *True Intellectual System of the Universe* Mme de La Fayette, *Princesse de Clèves*	Popish Plot (to 1681) Sept.: Treasonable letters found among papers of James's secretary Oct.: Mysterious death of Protestant justice Godfrey Nov.: Exclusion of James from succession proposed Dec.: Danby impeached
1679 (49)	Jan.: *Oedipus* (tragedy) with Nathaniel Lee Spring: *Troilus and Cressida* (adaptation of Shakespeare's tragedy) with Preface to printed version, *The Grounds of Criticism in Tragedy* 18 Dec.: Dryden beaten in Rose Alley by hired toughs	G. Burnet, *History of the Reformation*, pt. i South, *Sermons* (vol. vi, 1715), etc. Licensing Act expires	Jan.: Cavalier Parliament dissolved Innocent Catholics executed May: First bill to exclude James May: Habeas Corpus Act Sept.: James and Monmouth exiled Oct.: Meal Tub Plot (concocted by Catholics)

1680 (50)	March: *The Spanish Fryar* (comedy) *Ovid's Epistles* tr. by Dryden *et al.*, with a Preface by Dryden on the art of translation	Bunyan, *Life and Death of Mr Badman* Roscommon, tr. Horace, *Art of Poetry* Purcell appointed organist at Westminster Abbey Filmer, *Patriarcha* Fenelon, *Dialogues sur l'Eloquence*	Some court figures desert to Whigs Oct.: Whig Parliament sits Nov.: Halifax sways the Lords to kill the Exclusion Bill
1681 (51)	*Absalom and Achitophel* Epistle dedicatory to published *Spanish Fryar* treats tragicomedy and affective theory	T. Burnet, *Theory of the Earth* (Latin version: English published 1684–90) Hobbes, *Behemoth* Marvell, *Miscellaneous Poems* Oldham, *Satyrs upon the Jesuits*, etc.	March: Third Whig Parliament sits in Oxford March: Louis XIV changes financing from Whigs to Charles II 28 March: Charles II dissolves Parliament The Tory Revenge (to 1685)
1682 (52)	*The Medall* *Mac Flecknoe* *Absalom and Achitophel*, pt. ii, with Nahum Tate *Religio Laici* Dec.: *The Duke of Guise* (tragedy), with Nathaniel Lee	Bunyan, *The Holy War* Otway, *Venice Preserv'd* Creech, tr. Lucretius Ray, *Methodus Plantarum Nova* Leibniz founds *Acta Eruditorum* (Leipzig)	Whig Plots of Insurrection and of Assassination (of the King) Sept.:Tories seize control of London Nov.: Shaftesbury flees
1683 (53)	Boileau's *Art of Poetry*, tr. by Sir William Soame and Dryden Dryden's 'Life of Plutarch' prefixed to *Plutarch's Lives*, tr. by various hands		April: Rye House Plot (to assassinate King and James) June: Rye House and Insurrection Plots betrayed Tories call in municipal charters (to 1684)
1684 (54)	*Miscellany Poems* ('first miscellany') compiled with Tonson the publisher 'To the Earl of Roscommon' 'To the Memory of Mr Oldham'	Oldham, *Remains* Creech, tr. Horace, Theocritus Roscommon, *Essay on Translated Verse*	James reappointed Lord High Admiral Twenty years truce proclaimed between France and Spain

1685 (55)	*Sylvae* ('second miscellany') with Dryden's translations from Lucretius, Horace, etc., and with a Preface on translation and portraits of Lucretius, etc. *Threnodia Augustalis* (on the death of Charles II, accession of James II) June: *Albion and Albanius*, music by Grabu, first English opera entirely in music, with a Preface on the theory of the opera	Fontenelle, *Discours sur la Pluralité des Mondes*, etc.	6 Feb.: Charles II dies; James II ascends with great initial popularity 6 July: Monmouth's rebellion quelled at Sedgemoor Oct.: Louis XIV revokes the Edicts of Nantes (leading to dragooning of Huguenots) Last hanging of a witch in England
1686 (56)	Ode on the death of Anne Killigrew	Browne, *Works* Ray, *Historia Plantarum*	July: James II seeks to control Church by a Court of High Commission Catholics appointed to army and courts; other high-handed acts
1687 (57)	*The Hind and the Panther* *On the Marriage of . . . Mrs Anastasia Stafford* (surviving version is incomplete) *Song for St Cecilia's Day*	Norris, *Miscellanies* Newton, *Principia Mathematica* Wallis, *Institutio Logicae*	Rochester and Clarendon dismissed from office 27 April: James II proclaims a Declaration for general toleration; Dissenters released from prisons James II interferes with Oxford College affairs
1688 (58)	*Britannia Rediviva* (on the birth of a son to James and Mary)	Halifax, *Character of a Trimmer*, etc. La Bruyère, *Caractères* Perrault, *Parallèles des anciens et des modernes*	10 June: Son born to Mary 19 Dec.: William of Orange enters London 25 Dec.: James II flees to France
1689 (59)	Dec.: *Don Sebastian* (tragedy)	Cotton, *Poems on Several Occasions* Selden, *Table Talk* Purcell, *Dido and Aeneas*	13 Feb.: William and Mary proclaimed sovereigns 1 Aug.: Oath of Allegiance in effect Bill of Rights, Toleration Act James II in Ireland: civil war

1690 (60)	Oct.: *Amphitryon* (comedy)	Locke, *Essay Concerning Human Understanding* Petty, *Political Arithmetick* Huygens, *Traité de la Lumière* Academy of Arcadians founded by Crescimbeni, *et al.*	William III defeats James II at the Battle of the Boyne in Ireland Whigs seek to exclude Tories from office William III separates from the Whigs Penal laws, persecution of Catholics (to 1698)
1691 (61)	Ca. May: *King Arthur* (opera), revised from an earlier version now lost; music by Henry Purcell	Wood, *Athenae Oxoniensis* Boyle lectures (for preserving Christianity) founded	English armies on continent (to 1697) July: English forces win decisive victories in Ireland Ireland again devastated Heavy taxes imposed for continental wars
1692 (62)	*Eleonora* (on the death of the Countess of Abingdon) April: *Cleomenes* (tragedy)	Bunyan, *Works* Jonson, second folio L'Estrange, *Fables of Aesop* Southerne, *The Wives Excuse* Phalaris controversy (over authenticity of ancient letters)	Modern systematic taxation, national debt devised Namur lost to France; William III defeated at Steinkirk, etc. French plan invasion of England Feb.: Massacre of Glencoe at orders of William III; Scotland seethes
1693 (63)	*The Satires* (Juvenal by Dryden *et al.*, Persius by Dryden) with a long prefatory 'Discourse' on satire, the epic, major Roman satirists *Examen Poeticum* ('third miscellany') with Dryden's translation of *Metamorphoses*, i, etc. 'The Character of Polybius' prefixed to *The History of Polybius*, tr. Sir Henry Sheer	Congreve, *Old Bachelor* Locke, *Thoughts Concerning Education* Rymer, *A Short View of Tragedy*	Whigs and Tories struggle for supremacy In spite of William's unpopularity, funds are voted for war

1694 (64)	Jan.: *Love Triumphant* (tragicomedy), Dryden's last play 'To my Dear Friend Mr Congreve' 'To Sir Godfrey Kneller'	Congreve, *Double Dealer* Fox, *Journal* Kneller begins 'Hampton Court Beauties'	Bank of England founded Dec.: Triennial Act (confirming parliamentary supremacy) 28 Dec.: Queen Mary dies
1695 (65)	Preface, 'Parallel of Poetry and Painting,' prefixed by Dryden to his tr. of C. A. du Fresnoy, *De Arte Graphica*, deals with central issues of mimetic theory	Blackmore, *Prince Arthur* Congreve, *Love for Love* Milton, *Poetical Works* (first annotated ed., by P. Hume) Tillotson, *Works*	Licensing Act not renewed Aug.: William retakes Namur; other victories Coinage, taxes pose difficult financial problems
1696 (66)	'An Ode, on the Death of Mr Henry Purcell' Dryden continuing his translation of Virgil	Brady and Tate, tr. *Psalms* Suckling, *Works* Bayle, *Dictionaire historique et critique*	Currency reformed Jacobites plot to kill William III Habeas Corpus Act suspended Catholics persecuted
1697 (67)	*The Works of Virgil* (*Pastorals, Georgics, Aeneis*) published by subscription; the dedication and postscript to the *Aeneis* deal with Virgil and long-standing interests in translation and criticism	Collier, *Essays* Congreve, *Mourning Bride* Dampier, *Voyages* Defoe, *Essay upon Projects* Vanbrugh, *Relapse, Provok'd Wife*	Treaty of Ryswick ends war with France to English advantage Debate over a standing army
1698 (68)	*To Mr Granville* *To My Friend* (Pierre Motteux)	Collier, *Short View of the Immorality and Profaneness of the English Stage* Milton, *Collected Prose Works* A. Sidney, *Discourses Concerning Government*	William III reaches secret agreement with Louis XIV on dividing Spain after death of present King Anti-William Parliament sits (to 1700)
1699 (69)		Farquhar, *Constant Couple*, etc. Garth, *Dispensary* Fénelon, *Telemaque*	European manoeuvring over title to territories of the Netherlands English army reduced

1700 (69)	Fables Ancient and Modern (tr. from Ovid, Chaucer, Boccaccio; also *To . . . the Dutchess of* *Ormond, To my Honour'd* *Kinsman, Alexander's* *Feast,* 'Monument of a Fair Maiden Lady', and the splendid Preface) Prologue, Epilogue, Song, and *Secular Masque* for John Fletcher, *The* *Pilgrim*, as revised by Vanbrugh Wed., 1 May (3 a.m.) Dryden dies of degenera- tive diseases, mind clear to the end 9 May: Almost a state funeral with Latin oration by Garth, Horace's 'Exegi monumentum aere perrenius' ode set to grave music, a great procession, and burial in Westminster Abbey	Congreve, *Way of the* *World* Halifax, *Miscellanies* Motteux, tr. *Don* *Quixote*	Parliament and King quarrel over for- feited Irish estates April: King and Whigs give in to Tories on Irish issues and Parliament is pro- rogued William III confronts grave problems in England and as usual carries on
1703	16 April: Son John dies in Rome		
1704	Nine posthumous poems published in *Poetical* *Miscellanies, The Fifth Part* 20 Aug.: Son Charles drowns in Thames		
1710	3 Dec.: Son Erasmus- Henry dies		
1714	Summer: Lady Elizabeth Dryden, long infirm, dies		
1717	*The Dramatick Works*, carefully edited by Congreve, who prefixes a short but warm 'character' of Dryden		

1: On Reading Dryden

EARL MINER

IN THE centennial year of Dryden's death, 1800, and a decade after
publishing his edition of Shakespeare, Edmond Malone published an
edition of Dryden's prose works. Dryden's poems had been printed
steadily throughout the eighteenth century, and his plays less often.
Malone perceived that there were reasons for bringing together many
scattered pieces of prose.

> The great author of the following works has long had the honour
> of being ranked in the first class of English Poets; for to the names
> of Shakespeare, Spencer, and Milton, we have now for near a
> century been in the habit of annexing those of Dryden, and his
> scholar, Pope. The present publication will shew, that he is equally
> entitled to our admiration as a writer of Prose; and that among
> his various merits, that of having cultivated, refined, and improved
> our language is not the least.

So his 'Advertisement' begins, and four or five pages later, he adds: 'The
prose of Dryden has been so long and so justly admired for its copious-
ness, harmony, richness, and variety, that to adduce any testimony in its
favour seems unnecessary.' To gain such praise from a man who had
devoted much of his life to the study of Shakespeare is to pass the highest
test of estimation in English literature. When Dryden wrote *All for Love*
in 'imitation of Shakespeare', he spoke of drawing that bow of Ulysses
which only its Shakespearean owner could draw. All but a few mis-
guided critics are aware that Dryden's play is not equal to *Antony and
Cleopatra*. But there is no other playwright who has sought to meet
Shakespeare on his ground and remained a living author.

I

Dryden's Reputation

At the present time, nearly two centuries after Malone, and three after Dryden himself, Dryden is no longer as much read. Prose fiction, which was of little account in the seventeenth century, has become the novel. After sharing with Milton the role as model for practising poets in the eighteenth century, Dryden gradually came to be linked, as he had not been in the eighteenth century, with Pope. Authors and books have multiplied many times over, and the cult of the modern, which once assisted Dryden, has now placed him in the realm of a classic, just as it will those few authors among our contemporaries who will seem worth preserving. There is nothing curious or malign in such developments, and our great English classics are simply not read as widely as teachers and critics like to presume. If they were not taught in schools and universities, many would almost cease to be known. What is curious is that Dryden, whose sense of England was so eager and so profound, should be so much less honoured in his own country than in other English-speaking countries.

Does Dryden tell English readers what they already know so well that they need no reminder? Or does he tell men with names like Malone, Scott, Christie, Sutherland, and Kinsley (and others in parts more remote) what they feel a need to know about England? Why is Dryden 'glorious' to Scott and humdrum, failing to enhance life, to F. R. Leavis? We must ask such questions, even if we do not have the answers. One thing about Dryden that needs no question is what happens to those who read his works attentively. His limitations, which we shall come to, do not prevent the student of his poems and plays from recognizing their vigour and newness of kind, or the translations as the finest of their kind. His poems are more difficult than Donne's, essentially less so than Spenser's or Wallace Stevens'. But if we are willing to hazard as much of ourselves, of our hopes, and of our civilization as Dryden was willing to, we shall be renewed. There is no reason for English or any other readers to fear Dryden, or to fear for themselves in risking their values in the encounter. Even in satire, with the exception of *The Medall*, Dryden is the most affirmative of poets.

Most readers of this book will possess more than nodding acquaintance with Dryden, and if they choose to read about him they must have a sense of his importance. This and the following chapters must aim therefore to articulate what readers have experienced, to suggest fresh things present in works previously read, and to open unfamiliar doors in that palace of many rooms that makes up the Dryden canon. Beginning with Edmond Malone's comment in 1800, we may consider the vicissitudes of Dryden's reputation. What generations of men and women have differently or commonly found in his works makes some presumption of value for what claims importance for our own lives.

When Garth, a physician and a Whig, pronounced his Latin oration at Dryden's funeral, he welcomed Dryden in effect to a new age of taste and energies that had been forming since the Revolution of 1688. The varying estimates of Dryden in the experience of successive generations tell us a great deal about the literary ideals of those generations and something about Dryden's writing as well. The place to begin is no doubt at the close of Dryden's life: what was thought of him and what was being read? Our problems in answering such questions are well illustrated from a report published in the *Acta Eruditorum* (Leipzig, 1696), informing us with no doubt that on 1/10 December the chief of English poets ('poetarum Anglicorum princeps') had died (50). In July, 1700, the same journal had better information and published it along with a review of *Fables*. In reviewing Dryden's career, the author depicts a different Dryden from the one thought of today. It is a Dryden who should be praised for *All for Love*, for *Oedipus* written with Nathaniel Lee, and for more such plays ('plura illis dramata'). *Of Dramatick Poesie* is mentioned, and to it are added Dryden's translations of Virgil, Juvenal, Lucretius, and others. And of course the *Fables* is discussed at length, with *Palamon and Arcite* receiving last attention (321–5). By June, 1704, the same journal wrote of that most splendid John Dryden, greatest of English poets ('de splendidissimis Johannis Drydeni, summi Anglorum Poetae'), this time mentioning his talents as a satirist and making much of his being buried between Chaucer and Cowley, the one representative of epic, the other of lyric ('medio loco inter Chaucereum & Coulaeum, insignes Anglorum Poëtas, Epicum alterum, alterum Lyricum', 283–5). In this not particularly clear picture, the prominent features include Dryden's eminence, his significance as a practitioner and theorist of serious drama, his importance as translator—particularly in *Fables*—his superiority in satire, and above all his poetry's occupying a space between the epic and the lyric. There have been worse descriptions.

For most of the eighteenth century, poets and critics regarded Dryden as a classic like Milton, and between them these two seventeenth-century poets dominated the choice of poetic styles. By the death of Pope in 1745, however, a new genius had been recognized, and the game of Milton-Dryden-Pope was started, with the last king (or knave) in the pack, Donne, to be added by T. S. Eliot some two hundred years later. One thing that must be emphasized to begin with is that as men these poets could excite genuine depth of feeling. As Pope lay dying, Bolingbroke broke down while trying to describe his goodness. Congreve's infuriatingly brief memoir of Dryden makes one thing perfectly clear: 'I loved Mr Dryden.' In dealing with Dryden (or Donne or Pope) we have to do with fallible human beings, but their reality includes as well human goodness and those particles of divine fire, poetic genius.

Between the death of Pope and the appearance of Johnson's *Lives of the English Poets* (1779–81), Pope's reputation suffered the slump that so often comes after almost unquestioned preëminence. Dryden and Milton were spared at this juncture, partly because of the factor just mentioned, and partly because they were classics, as Dryden himself might have put it, of the last age, seemingly beyond time. But the challenge to Pope grew more radical, and he was beginning to be denied status as a true poet. Hence Dr Johnson was led to raise the question explicitly: Is Pope a poet? And to reply decisively: If Pope be not a poet, where is poetry to be found? In some ways Johnson's *Life of Pope* proves more interesting to study of Dryden's reputation than does the *Life of Dryden*. Toward the end of his *Life of Pope*, Dr Johnson stole a critical page from Dryden's own comparison of two poets and substituted Pope and Dryden for Homer and Virgil, Juvenal and Horace, or Ovid and Boccaccio. It must come as a surprise to every reader following the comparison to discover that the accumulating balance, as it were, of literary virtues somehow is laid aside, and Dryden is preferred:

if the reader should suspect me, as I suspect myself, of some partial fondness for the memory of Dryden, let him not too hastily condemn me, for meditation and inquiry may, perhaps, show him the reasonableness of my determination.

Meditation and inquiry are owed every writer, and would afford reasons for increased admiration of Pope, Wordsworth, or Yeats. Yet as the eighteenth century was drawing to its close, and as different tastes were formed once again, it was not necessary to ask: Is Dryden a poet?

Thanks in large measure to the work of Upali Amarasinghe, Dryden's reputation has been charted for the period from Dr Johnson to the accession of Victoria. As he shows, the reaction to Joseph Warton's *Essay on the Genius and Writings of Pope* (1756) was so adverse that Warton delayed publication of his edition till 1797, when the new taste was more firmly established.[1] The importance of Pope (and Milton) to the fortunes of Dryden resides less in reason than in the critical tendency to associate Dryden with some other writer. The blessings of contradiction in the history of taste are many and real, as we shall see. But from Warton to Victoria the important poetic revolution, believed by the eighteenth century to have been effected by Dryden and refined by Pope, came to seem an orthodoxy to be questioned. During much of this period, Dryden tends to be associated with Milton at Pope's expense, but from about 1820 it was with Pope, and in large measure to Pope's advantage. Reflection would show that such shifts represent not only the constant obsolescence of the 'new' or 'modern', but also responses to differing but genuine elements in the three poets. In following Dryden's reputation, we shall necessarily be saying as much about the responders as about our poet.

Malone's ordering of the English poets would have seemed understandable to the major Romantic poets. Omitting Blake for the moment, it is clear that Coleridge and Wordsworth regarded Milton as an author

[1] For more details on Dryden's reputation, see the biographical studies in the Bibliography of this book and Mark Van Doren, *The Poetry of John Dryden*, New York 1920, ch. vii and Upali Amarasinghe, *Dryden and Pope in the Early Nineteenth Century*, Cambridge 1962, 35 ff. and Index. Both named are most valuable. Amarasinghe shows that Warton's doubts involved no hostility to Pope.

superior to Dryden by a good margin, and Dryden to Pope by the same. Leigh Hunt had a kind of conversion about 1815 from his antipathy to Dryden, and he transferred his enthusiasm to Keats. After *Lamia*, Keats replaced his enthusiastic and not altogether salutary emulation of Milton with a close reading of Dryden, which brought, as is well known, very beneficial, and radically assimilated, results. Scott represents the earlier enthusiasm for 'Glorious John' (*The Pirate*, ch. xiv), 'the great High Priest of all the Nine' (*Old Mortality*, ch. xxx). Without denigrating Pope or Milton when speaking of Dryden, Scott simply ignored them, much to the benefit of common sense and equable understanding. Byron best represents the later taste, for without depreciating Dryden, he eloquently argued for 'the Christianity of English poetry, the poetry of Pope' (*Journal*, 24 Nov. 1813). Opinion also included the general public and the editors of the great quarterlies and reviews. As Amarasinghe says of the general response, 'the bounding vigour and negligent ease of Dryden proved more congenial to the Romantic taste of the time, while the more disciplined and complicated richness of Pope's art was the more attractive to conservative interests'.[1] Dryden was fortunate to have Coleridge on his side, and Pope unlucky to have Richard Jeffrey. As early as this we can observe that Dryden inspires those poets who read him, and possesses a considerable appeal to the intelligentsia outside England, whereas Pope's virtues have held greater appeal to editors and dons, especially in England.

Upali Amarasinghe's fine study almost totally misses another adventure in Dryden's reputation, a belief in cultural collapse or division that runs from Blake straight onto T. S. Eliot. In this dogma of the Fall of Poetry, a demonology was required, along with an angelology. The brighter spirits proved, in a happy revaluation of the sixteenth century, to be the Elizabethan poets (as later, the Metaphysical). Blake was the prophet, in the guise of the historian, of this new Fall. He held that a deep, perhaps irremediable, malaise had infected modern culture. (It is curious how the problems suffered by these prophets are conveniently explained by putting the blame on someone well before their own time.) How had it all come about? The fault lay with the philosophers and

---

[1] *Dryden and Pope*, 215.

scientists: 'Mock on, mock on, Voltaire, Rousseau,' with Newton receiving his share of scorn.[1] What was widespread and often obscure in
Blake was given focus by the earlier Keats. In *Sleep and Poetry* he
branded an 'impious race' that stifled lyricism and brought 'a schism' in
culture. His archvillain was 'the name of one Boileau'.[2] Before long
Dryden and Pope (in our century, Milton) were substituted as the
demons causing the 'schism', the cultural flaw, the curse of prose on
poetry, and the 'dissociation of sensibility'. (Let us blame anybody but
ourselves for our problems.) Blake and the younger Keats had ushered
in an era of critical dogma whose demonic images have only recently
been broken.

Quoting Keats on that terrible schism, James Russell Lowell said
flatly, 'Dryden was the author of that schism'.[3] If a single man can alter
the course of history so radically, he must be worthy of considerably
greater attention than most people have given him. Lowell found that
life has its complexities, however, and was deeply attracted by Dryden,
believing with justice his essay on Dryden to be his finest critical work.
Lowell initiated the line of critics to whom Dryden proves irresistible,
and whose explicit reasons for their love often make the poet seem in-
tolerable. (By way of unfortunate compensation, Lowell was brutally
harsh with Pope.) One such person, Macaulay, a phrase-maker whose
smiles are more refrigeratory than his frowns, said that most of Dryden's
writings 'exhibit the sluttish magnificence of a Russian noble, all vermin
and diamonds, dirty linen and inestimable sables'.[4] In brief, Dryden was
a finer poet than Pope! Arnold has been the greatest of our critics who

---

[1] From Blake's earlier poems, see e.g. 'You don't believe' and *The
Everlasting Gospel*; from the later, *Milton* and much of the visionary
writing. In delineating such ancestry of T. S. Eliot's now exploded no-
tion of a 'dissociation of sensibility', I draw on my 'Double Truth of
Modern Poetic Criticism' in *Sense and Sensibility in Twentieth-Century
Writing*, ed. Brom Weber, Carbondale and Edwardsville 1970, 16–25.

[2] *Sleep and Poetry*, ll. 201–2, 181, and 206.

[3] 'Dryden', *My Study Windows*, London, n.d., Scott Library ed., 265.
In spite of this, Lowell's essay provides the best nineteenth-century
criticism of Dryden after Scott.

[4] 'Dryden's *Works*,' *Edinburgh Review*, January 1828, 34–35; cited by
Amarasinghe.

have explored the paradox of a great writer whose virtues are unbearable and whose faults retain glory. In *The Study of Poetry*, it transpires that Dryden (and poor tag-along Pope) had 'admirable talent', and Dryden 'such energetic and genial power'. In addition to these nice gifts, Dryden provided us with 'the true English prose'. Yes, Dryden and Pope are genuine classics. But they are 'not classics of our poetry, they are classics of our prose'.[1]

Dr Johnson's question, 'Is Pope a poet?' had now been given a new answer and extended to provide a new literary history. So effective did the Arnolds prove that, with some important exceptions,[2] literary historians of the last century reiterate talk of the prosaic or the artificial. And yet, along with Lowell, the author of *The Scholar-Gypsy* felt a real engagement with Dryden and indeed could not forget him. Dryden was in custody. Much the same thing holds for a later book, Mark Van Doren's *Poetry of John Dryden* (New York, 1920), one of the best Ph.D. dissertations produced in English. Its conceptions and values do not match its phrasing, however. (So many of us writing about Dryden want to emulate his prose style without necessarily exercising our minds equally.) When we read (207) that the first stanza of the Killigrew Ode is indeed musical and 'its grammar is regal', we may well think that a poet who can endure in spite of praise of his grammar in a lyric poem will endure through any kind of admiration.[3] It is no wonder that Sir Herbert Grierson could say of Van Doren's book that it 'writ larger Arnold's sentence'.[4] In fact, the telling quotations, pro and con, in Van Doren and Eliot often derive from Lowell, just as Lowell's adaptation

---

[1] *Essays in Criticism*, 2nd series, London 1888, pp. 37, 41–42.

[2] For example, George Saintsbury, as in *A Short History of English Literature*, 1898 *et seq.*, VII, i–iii, and elsewhere.

[3] Yet Van Doren was dealing with a poet whom he felt to be largely unknown. In his Preface (v), he states his purpose as 'an effort to brighten the most neglected side [i.e., poetry] of the greatest neglected English poet'. Again, Dryden's was 'a poetic personality always important and never more freshly so than now'. If what is implied by this is right, the end of the last century and beginning of this brought Dryden's low-water mark.

[4] *Cross-Currents in English Literature of the XVII Century*, 1965, 322.

of the Keatsian 'schism' influenced Eliot's formulation of a 'dissociation of sensibility'.

To T. S. Eliot, Milton and Dryden were the two 'most powerful' poets of the seventeenth century, each driving poetic possibilities into extremes, thereby dissociating a sensibility previously whole. Their sin was nothing less than 'a dazzling disregard of the soul'.[1] Once a critic makes such a discovery, it would be hard to know what he would find next. It might have been better if he had exercised the courage of Scott, who flatly declared, 'I will not castrate John Dryden'.[2] Yet Eliot's uneasy but genuine admiration of Dryden and Milton led him back in print to Dryden as often as to any other poet. In fact, he kept *finding* Milton and, I believe, more often than any other English poet, Dryden. Eliot's example of the importance of Dryden (and Milton) in under-standing ourselves and our poetic generation has proved far more beneficial than such leaden panegyrical precepts as that Dryden's poetry, while unfortunately only stating, states *immensely*. Nothing else in Eliot's criticism bears as radical a mark of indebtedness as his *Dialogue on the Drama* does to *Of Dramatick Poesie*, and I shall leave to others any comparison between them.

Another, less troubled stream of critical assessment of Dryden also takes its start in the last century and has continued into this, rising full current in our own generation. This includes the discussion of two topics that had not been joined since the eighteenth century, the texture of Dryden's poetry in its rhythmic and imagistic characteristics and Dryden as a literary-historical (rather than cultural) phenomenon. Saintsbury was among the first to revive the old view in its double terms. Often referring to Dryden along with Milton (so unwittingly exerting an in-fluence on Eliot) as a prosodist and prose stylist, he also regarded 'The Age of Dryden' as something distinct and irreplaceable in value.[3] His stylistic admiration was echoed most emphatically by Gerard Manly Hopkins. Writing to Bridges on 6 November 1887, Hopkins asked, 'What is there in Dryden?' Since Bridges evidently did not know,

---

[1] 'The Metaphysical Poets' [1921], *Selected Prose*, ed. John Hayward, Harmondsworth, 1963, 113.
[2] Quoted in *The Times Literary Supplement*, 23 July 1971, 865.
[3] See note 2, p. 8.

Hopkins answered: 'Much, but above all this: he is the most masculine of our poets; his style and rhythms lay the strongest stress of all our literature on the naked thew and sinew of the English language.'[1] Given Hopkins' own strong poetic rhythms, the praise is very high indeed. Given the imagery, it appears that he, too, will not emasculate John Dryden.[2] Hopkins entertained doubts whether Dryden chose 'thoughts . . . by nature poetical'. But 'under a kind of living fire they are powerfully charged and incandescent'.

The other, historical, view held by Saintsbury was explored in part by the two best of Dryden's editors who followed Scott. Although a 'Whig' historian whose work on Shaftesbury was 'marred only by . . . excessive partiality' (*Dictionary of National Biography*), W. D. Christie edited Dryden with industry and with a mind well stocked with the classical poets and the history of the Restoration. George R. Noyes, also a man of interests divergent from his Dryden studies, similarly brought a cool and yet engaged temper to bear on Dryden's poetry.[3] Richard Garnett pleasantly confirmed Saintsbury's historical conception in *The Age of Dryden* (1895), as did A. W. Verrall again in his *Lectures on Dryden* (1914). Little that is essential to Dryden in either book is missing from a wider-ranging study, Saintsbury's own *Dryden* (1881) in the English Men of Letters series.

A survey of Dryden's reputation cannot be thought complete without some attention to the last forty years. To alter the phrase of Dryden's Crites, the past four decades have revealed almost a new Dryden to us, although a poet too often brightened more by the scholar's lamp than by the common human sun. Choosing representative men, I begin with Louis I. Bredvold. When *The Intellectual Milieu of John Dryden* appeared in 1934, it was the first serious intellectual study of Dryden. None of the subsequent de-Bredvoldizing of Dryden can alter that remarkable achievement. A few years later (1939), the Clarendon Press brought out

[1] Amarasinghe is surely right (171) to see in this a link between 'the characteristic achievement of [the mature] Keats . . . [and] that of Hopkins'.

[2] *The Note-Books and Papers of Gerard Manly Hopkins*, ed. Humphry House 1937, 88.

[3] For Christie's two editions and Noyes' edition, see the Bibliography.

Hugh Macdonald's painstaking *John Dryden: A Bibliography of Early Editions and of Drydeniana*. Quite apart from its numerous scholarly virtues (and some omissions), Macdonald's study provided at long last what had been desired but never achieved by editors: an understandable order to Dryden's various canon.[1] Whatever 'pure' criticism may affect to believe, the biographies of writers prove interesting, even with Dryden, the last great English writer of whom so little is known. Both the interest and the frustration are reflected in James M. Osborn's *John Dryden: Some Biographical Facts and Problems* (1st ed., 1940) and in Charles E. Ward's *Life of John Dryden* (1961). These books are limited by the paucity of fact, but at the very least they have done away with those false 'facts' on which critics have so often erected their Spanish castles (as for instance Dr Johnson's dating of *Mac Flecknoe* to suggest that it derived from Dryden's pique at having been replaced by Shadwell as Laureate in 1688).

Three more landmarks must conclude this survey. In 1956 Edward N. Hooker and H. T. Swedenberg, Jr., published the first volume of The California Edition of *The Works of John Dryden*, the first attempt since Scott to present Dryden whole. It has been a source of gratification to all concerned that in the past few years this careful edition has gathered something of its subject's energy. Another edition of outstanding accuracy and concise commentary, *The Poems of John Dryden*, was edited by James Kinsley and published in four volumes by the Clarendon Press in 1958. Since modern standards of editing do not allow the shortcuts of former days, Kinsley's singlehanded achievement is remarkable. Finally, a critical revaluation of Dryden has come at last. After the long delayed rehabilitation of Donne, after the reappreciation of Pope stimulated by the Twickenham edition, and along with new work on Milton, Dryden has benefited from studies of his poetry and drama. The new works employ a more modern critical methodology, bringing Dryden at last into our century. One swallow makes no summer, but the first new-style critical study by Arthur W. Hoffman has

[1] Macdonald has what may be an unbeatable footnote (246 n. 2) on Thomas Creech; perhaps its character can be explained by the older *Who's Who* entry on Macdonald himself, 'Secretary to the Lord Chancellor's Visitors in Lunacy'.

been followed by others. *John Dryden's Imagery* (1962) deserves Bred-vold's claim as to priority, since Hoffman takes Dryden seriously in that crucial poetic realm announced by his title. At present the new interest in Dryden shows no sign of ending. But when new experience brings its inevitable changes of view, it will be perfectly clear that between about 1825 and 1925 the criticism of Dryden was a species of allegory about poets' and critics' difficulties with their own age. We need not worry about Dryden as a classic, much less about that aspect of Arnold's critical problems, when Dryden is once more a living part of our literary experience.

II

The Living Dryden

Writers live only as they are read, and for earlier writers there are two kinds of life, defined by which of their works are popular and which classical or read by the audience of the few, however fit. The story of Dryden's reputation, even briefly told, tells of what has been current through nearly three centuries of momentous change in experience and taste. We can see that to most of the eighteenth century, Dryden appealed most in his political and satiric poems, in the narratives including the translation of Virgil, in his poems of address, and in his plays. To most of the nineteenth century, his appeal lay rather in his odes and other lyric verse, in his elegies, and in his *Fables*. In those two centuries and this, his prose has been thought miscellaneous but as much beyond praise as imitation. In this century, we have largely lost the plays performed in the eighteenth century and the *Fables* so highly esteemed in the nineteenth. But *Mac Flecknoe* and *Absalom and Achitophel* have again come to seem central, and the odes with a few other lyrics have earned popularity. The verse addresses, or epistles, have been revalued lately, and someone indeed is always rediscovering something in his spacious literary canon. As much of Dryden, then—perhaps rather more—is generally known as of other writers who come in the same class of great English poets: Donne, Pope, Wordsworth, Keats, Browning, and Yeats.

Like the consensus of time, the individual reader's feeling of what is important in a given author more likely suggests critical evaluation than chronological placement. In other words, a chronological approach profits the ordinary reader less than beginning with what is most accessible. The unconscious business of criticism is the constant reordering of genres, which articulate and stress selected forms of human experience. The predominance of lyric poetry since the Romantics is one such re-ordering, and that alteration in taste directs attention first of all to Dryden's lyric poems. For many readers, *A Song for St Cecilia's Day*, *Alexander's Feast*, and 'To the Memory of Mr Oldham' provide the best entry into his *oeuvre*.

Dryden's music is not that of the lute so much as the orchestra. It is less that of the chamber than of the public hall and forum. His passion is public and outward-looking rather than private and inward. As in his other poems, so in his lyrics Dryden is concerned with what men and women share rather than what constitutes unique, separate possession. So public in mode is his poetry that the elegy for Oldham can be misread as an outpouring from an intimate, 'ontological' experience rather than a view of life formed on time, history, and collective wisdom. In other words, Dryden like every writer hazards or celebrates some part of himself that he considers essential and in ways he deems important. Dryden was far from believing with Donne that one little room is an everywhere, and he did not fall like Shelley on the thorns of generalized life and bleed. Because he lived in dangerous times, and because he felt himself part of them, matters literary merged with matters political and religious. On such bases we appreciate *Mac Flecknoe* and *Absalom and Achitophel*, because we venture that part of ourselves that Dryden risked. Englishmen have long and wisely fought with words rather than with pike and gun. Surely the English epic would properly begin, 'Words and the man I sing.' In that cause Dryden was brave and comprehensive. In ways finally inextricable, *Mac Flecknoe*'s devastating humour turns on art, politics, religion—and personality. In *Absalom and Achitophel* the biblical story and state of near revolution merge to create Dryden's art of politics.

The rest of the current Dryden includes *All for Love* and two major pieces of prose, *Of Dramatick Poesie* and the Preface to *Fables*. The tragedy is one of very few from the generations after Shakespeare and

Webster that still are read by numerous readers. Dryden put into it a part of himself that can be discovered only with difficulty in the other works previously mentioned. In it, he honoured the claims of love and private will against that world which believes that its generals and rulers hold public trust. Its disciplined yet lyric verse holds few resemblances to the argumentative couplets of his heroic plays or the looser, rougher medium of all his subsequent tragedies, from *Oedipus* onward. He could admit the claim of private will only by ordering and compacting the dazzling language and exuberant experience of *Antony and Cleopatra*. Love and death, creation ripened to decay, and fruitful life ended by the march of the legions finally fuse in the remark by Cleopatra's servant: 'Beneath the fruit the Aspic lies.'

Among the admirers of Dryden's prose we must include those who do not know what to make of his poems. Some admirers also make claims for modernity that are not borne out by common sense or its avatars, students. If one could write as well as Dryden, it would be a pleasure to draw a portrait of his prose after his manner of criticism. I shall only suggest that Dryden appears always to be discovering the modern prose paragraph, and almost always to ignore it in favour of the old rhetorical period. Yet the inimitability of his style entails much more than procedure: a great prose style requires unusual gifts of thought, feeling, and imagination.

Apart from this popular group of works, Dryden also lives as a classic read by the few. The state of current criticism reveals that this further reach of his works includes, beside some other things, four chief groups: his *Fables*, his poems of address, some of his plays (with their incomparable prologues and epilogues), and some of his translations. The *Fables Ancient and Modern* best satisfies our need for the richly told story. Much of what is told is dark with human limitation and suffering but, in his search through narrative for what constitutes the good life, affirmation is no less important. With an eye resolutely cast on the divine comedy, Dryden yet somehow manages to direct attention to the lesser human comedy, to which the best reaction, as he well understood, is mingled laughter and sympathy. Such qualities will be found in his depiction of Cymon, as yet a 'Fool of Nature', because love of Iphigenia has not yet quickened his earthy spirit.

> *It happen'd on a Summers Holiday,*
> *That to the Greenwood-shade he took his way*   }
> *For* Cymon *shun'd the Church, and us'd not much to Pray.*
> *His Quarter-Staff, which he cou'd ne'er forsake,*
> *Hung half before, and half behind his Back.*
> *He trudg'd along unknowing what he sought,*
> *And whistled as he went, for want of Thought.*   (79–85)

Here is England, lovely when the sun shines, and here is man, laughable in his own restricted world until love and thought reclaim him to Dryden's and our sense of what being human entails. Cymon whistling in ignorance, and we baffled by the contradictions and flux of daily life, need to discover our purposes in love, in the bloody furies of strife, and in reflective peace. Dryden assists us in a mellow style that he somehow fashioned to convey his view of life when he experienced the harassments of an alien society and of an old age ridden by disease. As readers recognized in the experience of the last century, which told them more of human limitations than our official views allow today, Dryden's *Fables* tell stories of ourselves, our hopes, and our sorry limitations.

Dryden's plays present life's conflicts, as most plays do, but in ways of their own. His repeated concern with outer order and inner insistence on identity and passion finds comic, heroic, and tragic expression. In the late plays, in some ways the best though least familiar, the outer order takes on fatal weight. With its incest theme to assist in dramatic irony and fatal pressure, *Don Sebastian* shows Sebastian and Almeyda seeking to define themselves against a world far larger than themselves in ways that yet allow for their moral freedom and responsibility. Self-definition proves tragic, when the recurrent questions are answered. Who is king? Who is friend, who enemy? Who is parent, child? Who is beloved, sister? When the characters learn, they suffer, but by affirming justice they are able to prove themselves to be themselves, free in a recognizably moral world.

Dryden leads to the affirmation from an early uneasiness expressed by that disturbing creature, Dorax. A convert to Mohammedanism out of spite, until his re-conversion by friendship, he spoils our ideals. He hopes Almeyda perished in battle: 'I hope she dy'd in her own Female calling,/Choak'd up with Man, and gorg'd with Circumcision' (I, i,

143–4). He sickens us more than does violation of the incest taboo. As
for the mob, the common man,

> . . . *I wou'd use 'em*
> *Like Dogs in times of Plague, out-laws of Nature,*
> *Fit to be shot and brain'd; without a process,*
> *To stop infection, that's their proper death.*   (I. i, 161–4)

And this, too, proves worse than the actually constructive behaviour of
the foolish rabble. Such speeches come from the mouth of Dorax, let it
be said (and he is the one major character in the play restored to place
and health). But they form part of Dryden's design by exposing their
own dark colours and by setting off that which is brighter, as for example Sebastian's restraining Almeyda from suicide.

> *Death may be call'd in vain, and cannot come;*
> *Tyrants can tye him up from your relief:*
> *Nor has a Christian priviledge to dye.*
> *Alas thou art too young in thy new Faith;*
> Brutus *and* Cato *might discharge their Souls,*
> *And give 'em Furlo's for another World:*
> *But we, like Centry's, are oblig'd to stand*
> *In starless Nights, and wait the pointed hour.* (II. i, 565–773)

Almeyda replies that what lies beyond is not so clear.

> *Divines but peep on undiscover'd Worlds,*
> *And draw the distant Landscape as they please:*
> *But who has e'er return'd from those bright Regions,*
> *To tell their Manners, and relate their Laws?*

This difference of opinion must be reconciled, and so also must the more
affirmative views with Dorax's bitter reductions.

No part of Dryden's work requires greater rehabilitation than his
comedies. Depreciated by Dryden himself, who posed as a tragedian or
epic poet, they were in fact more popular than his tragedies and provide
great fun along with seriousness. The staple comic themes employed by
Dryden are intrigue, badinage, and farce in nearly equal proportions.
All three have bothered critics who insist on the dignities and proper
rites of life. Sex lies at the centre of the three elements, precisely be-

cause sex thumbs its nose at solemnity. The sober are right to feel alarm when sex mocks sobriety, but they should see that Dryden laughs not only at the rude gesture but also at those making it. He seldom subscribed to 'that Fairy Way of writing' in romantic comedy like *Twelfth Night*. He agreed with Aristotle that laughter arose from what was base or ugly—or from love. The tension in the appeal and the ridicule works itself out as the comic characters challenge the 'Laws divine and humane' (risked by Sebastian and Almeyda) only in the end to withdraw from the singeing fire and affirm once more the patterns of social order. For the affirmation to work, the comic threat must be real and funny.

The Dryden-Newcastle *Sir Martin Mar-All* (acted 1667) is mostly farce and language, scarcely an idea per act, yet even this proved hilarious when performed at the Hampstead Festival in 1963. For once the snigger with which Restoration comedy is often received had been dropped for direct approach. *The Spanish Fryar* (1680) was Dryden's most popular comedy, well organized as it is about a splendid comic figure and well buttressed by English anti-popery. But *Marriage A-la-mode* (?1672), in which intrigue and badinage play a larger role than farce, has come to be the best known of his comedies. Its two 'gay couples' follow appetite toward forbidden fruit, only to retreat as usual. Dryden likes his role as master of the revels, using his lords and ladies of misrule in such ways that in the end he can set the conservative, hierarchical, and indeed normal world back on its stable feet.

Setting aside the other comedies that fit such patterns, we must make exception for Dryden's *Amphitryon* (1690), his greatest comedy and one of the greatest comedies in English. The story of Jupiter's visiting Alcmena in the guise of Amphitryon and so siring Hercules was old when Plautus wrote his play, and when Molière wrote *his* he seized much of what had been done before, especially by Rotrou. Dryden borrows from Molière and Plautus, but by multiplying the intrigue plots he provides more of the ironic reflections that so mark the play. Plautus introduced the droll Sosia but kept the dignity of the father of the gods. Molière's version possesses a lovely, almost free verse and although it lowers the dignity of Plautus's milieu considerably, it maintains 'le *decorum* de la divinité', as he puts it. Dryden makes the gods repulsive.

Such sensual forces of inscrutable will and power intervene and make a mess of human life.

As in *Don Sebastian*, questions are raised about human identity. Who is Amphitryon? And who Sosia? Wives and acquaintances must ask, and so must the individuals concerned. Instead of incest and fate, external intervention threatens any simplicity or happiness of answer. The answers come in terms of Dryden's funniest comic figure, Sosia, who combines something of Charlie Chaplin's long face with something of W. C. Fields's cunning. And the answers come, at the other end of the scale, from the nearly tragic Alcmena. Molière had kept her from the stage after Jupiter's self-revelation, lest the comedy be hazarded. Dryden brings her back for that very purpose and in so doing shifts from Amphitryon to her as the comic centre. As early as the second act she had declaimed against man's estate:

> *Ye niggard Gods! you make our Lives too long:*
> *You fill 'em with Diseases, Wants, and Woes,*
> *And only dash 'em with a little Love;*
> *Sprinkl'd by Fits, and with a sparing Hand.*
> *Count all our Joys, from Childhood ev'n to Age,*
> *They would but make a day of ev'ry life.*   (II. ii)

This is spoken when she thinks she has her husband back, but in reality she is addressing that niggard Jupiter. So fraught with double ironies is this play. When the two Amphitryons confront the other characters, she says 'my Heart will guide my Eyes/To point, and tremble to its proper choice' (V. i), and she does choose her husband. Poor abused Amphitryon rejects her, at which time Jupiter speaks with *human* tenderness for the first time in the play, and that quality deceives her. The *deus ex machina* offers the coldest of comforts, and Sosia's wisecracks are no adequate chorus. As Mercury says in an aside at the end, '*Amphitryon* and *Alcmena*, both stand mute, and know not how to take it' (V. i). Nothing so stark faces any of Dryden's other dramatic characters. This funniest of Dryden's comedies is also his bleakest play.

Unlike Dryden's finest comedies and tragedies, such heroic plays as his double *Conquest of Granada* have no mute moments. They deal not with the reason of life but with the reasons and arguments. Dryden seeks to delineate the boundaries of love and grandeur or *la gloire* by those un-English means, style and show. Duets of debate, pirouettes on punctilios, and high-astounding assertions make up the text. I can imagine *kabuki* actors bringing these plays to life by using the requisite art, but I doubt whether I shall ever see them performed adequately by American or even English actors. The plumed helmet that designated the hero is not contemporary dress, and we can only take ourselves very much more or very much less seriously than do Almanzor or Aureng-Zebe. The heroic plays have settings that provide chronological primitivism and cultural primitivism with energies of empire and struggles for power. Irredeemably exotic, they are also the first clear words from an England learning to lisp her imperial slogans. They seek to make the maximum possible claims upon the world. If Dryden's other plays deal with life as we know it only too well, the heroic plays go on holiday to castles in Spain or to the either Indies of spice and mine.

Dryden's translations range from a few very strict versions to many that are so paraphrastic as almost to be his own poems. The least known of his finest translations are unquestionably his version of Virgil's *Georgics* and sections from Lucretius' *De Rerum Natura*. Dryden was always transforming or translating something with his own alchemy, and later in life his exile in his own land made translation as much a poetic as a financial necessity. Engagement with other times was possible when that with his own age was not. And yet it was in the last ten or fifteen years of his life that he also perfected his art of complimentary address (or verse epistle), showing in it as well as in prologues and epilogues an unusual capacity for catching the accent of various voices and moods. He opens his poem to Congreve, 'Well, then; the promis'd hour is come at last', and ends, 'And take for Tribute what these Lines express: / You merit more; nor cou'd my Love do less.' A different voice speaks in that lovely mythopoeic address to the Duchess of Ormond, 'O true *Plantagenet*, O Race Divine' (l. 30), and yet another speaks in the conclusion to his cousin John Driden of Chesterton.

> . . . *O true Descendent of a Patriot Line,*
> *Who, while thou shar'st their Lustre, lend'st 'em thine,*

> *Vouchsafe this Picture of thy Soul to see;*
> *'Tis so far Good, as it resembles thee:*
> *The Beauties to th' Original I owe;*
> *Which, when I miss, my own Defects I show:*
> *Nor think the Kindred-Muses thy Disgrace;*
> *A Poet is not born in ev'ry Race.*
> *Two of a House, few Ages can afford;*
> *One to perform, another to record.*   (195–204)

And here are voices at random from the fore- and afterpieces of his plays.

> *Much Time and Trouble this poor Play has cost* . . .
> *A pretty task! and so I told the Fool* . . .
> *I'm thinking, (and it almost makes me mad,)* . . .
> *Lord, how reform'd and quiet we are grown* . . .
> *When* Athens *all the* Grecian *state did guide* . . .
> *True Wit has seen its best days long ago* . . .
> *Look round the Habitable World, how few* . . .

Such voices speak alive across three centuries, and it is a pity to apply to them such names as Neoclassicism, or Baroque, Restoration, Renaissance, or Realism. Real experience of so many kinds is created by Dryden, and he did so many things so well, that it sometimes seems as if he could do anything. But he was not that greatest of authors, the divine one, and his genius like his personality was altogether human in possessing limitations.

III

Dryden's Literary World

'If you stand closer, you will be more taken.' So, in English, the motto prefixed to *Absalom and Achitophel*. That is true of Dryden as of other writers: close observation reveals their virtues better than does casual regard. Looking closely also reveals irregularities and warts, and the faults of writers are not always their least endearing features. From Dr Johnson onward it has been common to speak of Dryden's unevenness, and its cause, carelessness. Dryden is not one of your *t*-crossers, and unlike Pope he seldom revised what he once had published. This failing may seem to some less reprehensible than its opposite extreme, but it certainly reflects a similar tendency in all his writing to shift about —in tone, in subject, or in approach. Dryden's prose digresses with uncommon grace, 'never wholly out of the way or in it' being his description of a preface. *The Hind and the Panther* represents the shift of front in extreme form, but even the number of turns in *Absalom and Achitophel* is remarkable. Some of this results from careless association of ideas, but often it is a diversity and fullness of experience brought to focus by an esemplastic mind.

Dryden's most serious limitation is a version of his strength and that of other poets in his century. The strength is breadth and force of intellectual powers. The limitation is depreciation of certain kinds of feeling, or deadening of sensitivities of certain kinds. Dryden's strain of indelicacy or coarseness can be found in Shakespeare, Donne, and Marvell by those who wish to look, and Milton betrays himself by his humourlessness almost as badly as by his humour. But leaving these other great writers aside for other seasons, Dryden often seems to possess more strength of passion than delicacy of feeling. The couplet on transubstantiation in *Absalom and Achitophel* (ll. 118–19), the presentation of Antony's wife and children in *All for Love* (III), and Dryden's dyspeptic bother over Luke Milbourne and Sir Richard Blackmore at the end of the Preface to *Fables* seem to me three serious examples of insensitivity in three of his greatest works. And this limitation, with to be sure its obverse strength, seems to me to govern larger and remoter tracts than those where it has a specifiable presence. To extend Hopkins's remark, Dryden is the most masculine of a century of masculine poets. Because seventeenth-century writers, and Dryden not least, have attracted so many distinguished female students, we must assume that the masculinity, fault and virtue, is a real quality possessing the appeal of reality, just as Jane Austen's feminine qualities lack no appeal to men.

Dryden's other limitations, being slight, may be passed by as we return to qualities neutral or positive. Dryden's love of his sons, his preference for portrait over landscape painting, and his preference for the human voice over musical instruments are not inevitable, but their common element is the attraction of the human. Like Johnson and Milton, he was also a brave man. Truth has seldom been less well served than by accusations that Dryden trimmed to political and religious winds. The 'evidence' has long since been exploded, but some people have liked thinking better of themselves than of Dryden, and so a word must be said. *The Medall, The Hind and the Panther*, the epistle dedicatory and 'Prologue' to *Don Sebastian* show Dryden taking great risks. Beaten by hired toughs on one occasion and later threatened with the punishment for high treason (hanging, drawing, quartering) for being 'reconciled to Rome', Dryden never faltered. That era we name the Renaissance or seventeenth century, and which we may sentimentalize over, was a dangerous unsentimental time that called for stronger nerves than I suspect in myself or most of my contemporary men of letters.

Dryden's engagement with his world was impelled by mind, passion, and will. The recreation of that engagement involved an imaginative version of it in what may be called the public mode. The lack of delicacy mentioned earlier is more common in public poetry than in the private poetry of a George Herbert. On the other hand, a greater, larger if ruder energy is required to sustain longer works with wider views. We are seldom in doubt about Dryden's values, although some critics have taken characters (often villains in plays) or have divorced pronouncements wedded to contexts as if they were Dryden's personal views. That equivalent of Milton's Satan problem vanishes in Dryden if we stand closer and if we also regard the larger movements and ends to which he drives. These are consistently moral and affirmative, with whatever variety and divagation on the way. Everyone feels movement in Dryden's style, 'The long majestic March, and Energy Divine', as Pope put it. I believe it true that his decasyllabic line usually seems somehow shorter than that of any other major English poet. How so rapid a poet could yet prove so allusive and so innovative of new forms of literary structure is a question very difficult to answer. Among the few certainties is that the verse paragraph and not the line is not the basic unit in Dryden. The fullest significance lies in Dryden's larger ordonnances, in those total harmonies that admit of some discords.

The divine energy and the larger harmony derive from a vision of life more radically historical than that of other English poets. He combines three historical views: the cyclical-universal, the progressive, and the providential. The cyclical presumes that mankind is uniformly the same everywhere. Whatever differences may exist, a set of phenomena highly similar would lead to like ends in two different historical periods. The plots against David and against Charles II illuminate each other in *Absalom and Achitophel*, and medieval history illustrates the succession of poets in the poem to Congreve. As the latter poem shows, in the trope of 'the kingdom of letters', political and literary history also parallel each other, and numerous metaphors, analogies, and allusions may tie diverse elements together. Dryden's faith in the possibility of human progress sets him apart from his great predecessors in poetry and contributes to his sometimes hard-bought affirmations. The strong millenial cast of mid-century Puritan thought seems to have shifted the attention of even the unchialistically minded to the future. Systolic and diastolic pressures work between Dryden's conservativism and his optimism. He believed order essential, but only as a dynamic order constituent of a larger harmony. The dynamism resides partly in his style and partly in the imagination which creates the style.

Dryden's providential view owes a more direct debt to his mid-century experience. As the chronological table shows, he lived to observe all three revolutions of the century as well as some aborted ones. But he believed in the constancy of God's relation to His creatures, of eternity to time, of heaven to earth.[1] Poetic expression makes the belief historical by allusiveness and by stress on crucial 'historical' moments. Often the allusion takes the form of so-to-speak retrospective typologies. Like some writers before him, he appropriates the divine to the human, fashioning an allusive triumvirate out of David, God, and Charles II. If Charles is David, he is also a type of Christ and God the Father. The historical nature of such typologies is yet another inheritance from the Puritan revolution. And, with Milton, he inherits a

---

[1] Glossing his 'half the *Orb* of *Round Eternity*', the last line of his pindaric, 'The Muse', Abraham Cowley noted: 'There are two sorts of *Eternity*; from the *Present backwards* to *Eternity*, and from the *Present forwards* . . . These two make up the whole *Circle* of *Eternity*, which the *Present Time* cuts like a *Diameter*, but Poetry makes it extend to all *Eternity to come*, which is the *Half-Circle*.' Dryden would certainly have agreed, even if Cowley's grasp of 'the *Present Time*' was not always firm.

concern with the grandest moments. The crucial times in his providential view are creation and judgment, both of which he often treats. Curiously, however, he seldom gives the Fall of Man more than a glance. Between these grand moments, time moves chronologically, historically in Dryden's works (until the *Fables*), even when he treats events not yet at their end. It seems that time's forward movement is a chief basis of his stylistic energy and clarity, giving life and comprehensibility to grand moments and to a nexus of typology and metaphor.

Dryden's variety and variability discussed earlier have their complement in imagery, simile, metaphor, parallel, analogy, and typology. The comparisons implied by such devices enable him to bring together, by great force of mind and imaginative grasp, realms that have claim to be distinct. By such means the diversity becomes articulate harmony, and things 'divine and humane' come together. Dr Johnson's criticism of *Annus Mirabilis* becomes a species of praise when the true fire is struck: that poem was said 'not so much [to] impress scenes upon the fancy as deduce consequences and make comparisons' (see ch. 8, below). By comparison, the immediate became intelligible through the remote, the contemporary through the classical, literature through politics, poetry through painting, politics through religion, and so on with seeming universal transference of values. For Dryden the older timeless or universal emblems took on time. The sun, oak, lion, gold, phoenix, and so on still represented the king. But the 'Monarch Oakes' of *Mac Flecknoe* recall the Boscobel forest where Charles II hid after the Battle of Worcester. And immediately following (11. 29–30) we learn of the false prince Shadwell that '*Heywood* and *Shirley* were but Types of thee, / Thou last great Prophet of Tautology'. As we come to see, Shadwell is not only the anti-Christ of wit but also shares equally antitypically in the Christological roles of priest and king.

The 'consequences' that Johnson spoke of in Dryden's poetry include explicit inferences and significant comments.

> *All humane things are subject to decay,*
> *And, when Fate summons, Monarchs must obey.*
>
> (*Mac Flecknoe*, 1–2)

The drive of his style does not permit him to develop, even if he would, the shimmering aphoristic brilliance of Pope, but in *Religio Laici* there is one instance of a poem so dominated by 'consequences' that 'comparisons' vanish in discourse of mind. However, between the earliest and the latest of his poems, the two elements usually work together, to function as surrogate of plot. In poems such as *Absalom and Achitophel* action is provided less by plot than by interactions both between parallel elements and between these elements, the characters, and the 'consequences'. The imagined significance and relation proves more important than the *done*. Great deeds metamorphose into great words and analogies.

To my view, the creative force among these elements is 'comparison'. Dryden constantly draws together elements that might otherwise be thought discrete or likely to fly apart. He found a new version of that great trope of the century, *discordia concors*, those agreeing discords that lead to his favourite conception of harmony. (Harmonia was the daughter of Venus and Mars, love and war.) The sensibility which associated those elements which Dryden brought together is very much his own. It manifests itself in songs and satires, narratives and religious confessions, odes and plays, and also in criticism. In this sense Dryden's imagination was esemplastic in a high degree. And yet Dryden's awareness of the separate identity of those elements he brings together enables us to set the limits of his literary world. His achievement falls short of those of two other seventeenth-century writers, Shakespeare and Milton. Only his scale compares to theirs, but his unity amid diversity is one held together by the imagination, mind, and will of his art. Setting aside his plays as more complicated instances, we are led to compare Dryden with Milton. By some miracle not possible to Dryden, and *a fortiori* to other poets of the century except Shakespeare, Milton succeeds in doing more than bring diverse elements into full relationship. Milton manages somehow to assimilate them, making them so far one that we find it impossible to say what, in *Paradise Lost* for example, is real and what mythic. Of that ultimate reach Dryden was not capable.

Dryden's affirmation deserves final stress. Everyone knows that he wrote two satires and that satiric touches abound elsewhere. Yet even his satiric poetry (always excepting *The Medall*) enlarges and finally ennobles. In satire or panegyric, he constantly moves from the lesser to the higher: all literary forms 'Like mounting Larkes, to the New Morning sing . . . As harbinger of Heav'n'. If Shadwell could be compared to prophet, priest, and king, Anne Killigrew can atone for the poets' second fall (11. 66–67) and lead the poetic vanguard as the 'harbinger of Heav'n'. The here and now does not seem so much to lie *sub specie aeternitatis* as to be lifted to supernal realms. Dryden knew Anne Killigrew was no saviour and Charles II no David, but he was generous enough to regard such men and women in terms of the supernal classes to which their best virtues pointed.

Such generosity, such graciousness explains the strong appeal of Dryden to those who know him well. It also explains his connections with most of the really important and good people of his age. Among the few for whom there is no certain evidence that he knew personally, there are Hobbes, Boyle, Hooke, Locke, and Newton. (There is a moral there for some old notions of Dryden.) The evaluation of Dryden does seem to be very like that given by Edmond Malone, and if a suitable motto must be found, the last three lines of the poem to Driden of Chesterton provide it.

> *For ev'n when Death dissolves our Humane Frame,*
> *The Soul returns to Heav'n, from whence it came;*
> *Earth keeps the Body, Verse preserves the Fame.*

Dryden's three orders of time—mortality, immortality, and eternity—are here along with three of the grand Christian and humanist commonplaces. And both triads have been made one. Perhaps the chief virtue of the lines is that, being true to John Dryden, they are also true of him.

2: Dryden's Comedies

JOHN LOFTIS

DRYDEN BEGAN writing comedies soon after the Restoration, earlier than the other principal dramatists of his time, before the conventions of the 'comedy of manners' were established by Etherege and Wycherley in the late 1660s and the mid 1670s. When Dryden began writing comedies, a repertory of new plays had not been developed after the long intermission in theatrical production. The two companies of actors relied perforce on Renaissance plays—above all, on the plays of the dramatists whom Dryden in *Of Dramatick Poesie* of 1668 isolated for special attention: Beaumont and Fletcher, Jonson, and Shakespeare. These dramatists, more than any others, were his masters; and if in the thirty years that separate his first comedy from his last he followed and responded to contemporary developments, his work throughout his career has an affinity with Renaissance drama.

His comedies of London life, *The Wild Gallant*, *Sir Martin Mar-all*, and *The Kind Keeper*, resemble in their citizen characters and boarding house scenes the realistic comedy of Middleton and Brome as well as of Jonson; and they include characters who resemble Jonsonian humours. His tragicomedies from *The Rival Ladies* to *Love Triumphant* have a complication and resolution of potentially tragic action approximating a pattern followed in plays by Shakespeare and Beaumont and Fletcher. His lifelong predilection for tragicomedy, a form that he repeatedly defended in his critical writings, would seem to derive from his admiration for the Renaissance dramatists. Although he was the first great neoclassical critic writing in English, he was not so completely convinced by the arguments of the French theorists and of their

English disciple, Thomas Rymer, that he was willing to give over the use of juxtaposed scenes with contrasting emotional impact.

He did not often write comedies of manners as that term is now usually understood. The plays of Etherege and Wycherley, of his own generation, and those of Congreve, Vanbrugh, and Farquhar, of the following, have shaped our conception of that sub-genre, with its distinctive conventions of plot, locale, character types, dialogue, and satirical objectives. The plays of those five dramatists follow the conventions with remarkable if not complete consistency. The best plays of Dryden do not follow them comprehensively enough for the conventions to be very useful in critical discussion. His affinities with Etherege and Wycherley—in the conduct of dramatic dialogue and in the probing analysis of relationships between social classes and between the sexes—are numerous and important, but the affinities are most apparent in isolated scenes of his tragicomedies, in which remote locales and action of potentially serious import produce an effect reminiscent of Beaumont and Fletcher. He was a man of his times, in writing comedy as in everything else, but he went his own way, experimenting with many forms of comedy, largely avoiding the satirical comedy of fashionable London life in which his most famous contemporaries excelled.

The variety of his comedies suggests the variety of Restoration drama and the range of literary sources from which it derived. He was a learned man, the most learned in the traditional sense of the major dramatists of the later seventeenth century. He knew the classical drama of antiquity, often referring to it in critical essays and basing one of his best comedies, *Amphitryon*, on a story transmitted by Plautus. He was well informed about the French drama written during his own lifetime, reading new plays as they appeared as well as the established masterpieces. He was familiar with that type of the Spanish *comedia* known as the cloak and sword play, imitating at a considerable distance its formal qualities in *The Rival Ladies* and *An Evening's Love* and once at least, in *The Assignation*, taking suggestions for a plot from Calderón.[1] He knew the Italian *commedia dell'arte*, referring to it in

[1] James Urvin Rundle, 'The Source of Dryden's "Comic Plot" in *The Assignation*,' *Modern Philology*, XLV, 1947, 104–11.

dialogue in *The Kind Keeper* (I. i) and basing one of his most popular comedies, *Sir Martin Mar-all* (written with the Duke of Newcastle), on two French plays that in turn are closely based, both of them, on a single Italian play in that form. He took episodes and even stretches of dialogue in his plays from foreign as well as earlier English drama, drawing freely on the work of his predecessors—to such an extent, indeed, that from the 1660s until the last decade of his life he was subjected to charges of plagiarism.

There are few more eloquent tributes to the range of his literary culture than Gerard Langbaine's ill-tempered catalogue, in *An Account of the English Dramatick Poets* of 1691, of his alleged literary thefts. Langbaine provides a comprehensive account of Dryden's reading as it is relevant to his plays. Langbaine is sometimes wide of the mark in specifics, and he fails to mention some works that Dryden demonstrably knew, but the *Account* is nevertheless an inquiry, written by a very well informed contemporary, into the literary background of Dryden's plays. It provides a sobering reminder to us that he knew many books of which the modern memory is dim.

In Dryden and Langbaine, whatever the obscure personal reasons for their quarrel, we would seem to have an opposition of Renaissance and post-Renaissance literary attitudes: an opposition similar to that allegorically expressed only a little later by Swift in *The Battle of the Books*, in the debate between the spider and the bee. Within the Renaissance conception of literary property which Dryden held, he was not guilty of plagiarism in his liberal use in his plays of the work of his predecessors. Shakespeare and Jonson in England, Calderón and Moreto in Spain, Pierre and Thomas Corneille in France, among many others, provided honourable precedents for his own practice. Dryden praised Jonson in *Of Dramatick Poesie* for his use of the work of his predecessors, and we may apply to Dryden himself his own conclusion about Jonson: 'what would be theft in other poets is only victory in him'.

Dryden wrote, or wrote part of, a dozen comedies. He began with a comedy of London life, *The Wild Gallant* of 1663, a form to which he returned in *Sir Martin Mar-all* of 1667 and *The Kind Keeper* of 1678. Alone among the dozen plays these three have English locales and characters, and in the second and third of them the locales and characters seem to have been determined, not by Dryden, but by other persons: the Duke of Newcastle for *Sir Martin* and King Charles II himself for *The Kind Keeper*. The tragicomedies, by far the most important group of the plays, have settings in the Mediterranean countries. The first of them, *The Rival Ladies* of 1664, Spanish in setting and characters, follows at an amused distance the conventions of the currently popular 'Spanish Plot'. *The Rival Ladies* was a qualified success, and in *Secret Love* of 1667 Dryden altered his dramatic strategy, devising the pattern of tragicomedy he would thereafter follow: a two-plot pattern, with differentiation of social rank as well as of mood between the largely independent plots, only one of which includes events potentially tragic in outcome. In *An Evening's Love* of 1668, *Marriage A-la-Mode* of 1672, *The Assignation* of 1672, *The Spanish Fryar* of 1680, and *Love Triumphant* of 1694, Dryden worked variations on the pattern, in some plays giving primary emphasis to the comic plot, in others to the serious. These plays represent over half his production in comedy, much more than that if proper allowance is made for the quality of several of them. And traces of his distinctive pattern of tragicomedy may be seen in the two famous comic plots he reworked: *The Tempest* of 1667 (written with Davenant) including much that is original though it is based on Shakespeare, and *Amphitryon* of 1690, again including much that is original, though it is based on Plautus and Molière.

The locales of Dryden's comedies have a functional relationship to dramatic structure and tone. Without exception, the tragicomedies are set in remote places, removed from the pressing realities of English life; without exception a London locale in his comedies is accompanied by a deflation of spirit, in which the action, if not 'all cheat' (in the phrase he applied to Jonson), is largely just that. He did not, except tentatively in his first play, employ his remarkable gift for repartee, perhaps his most impressive gift as a dramatist, in his comedies of London life. The work of his left hand, these three plays are inferior to his best tragicomedies, just as they are inferior to the best plays of his great contemporaries, who achieve an actuality lightened by conversational wit, in which expressions of affection are not always excluded.

Dryden's comedies have suffered in reputation with critics from his own depreciatory references to them. 'Neither, indeed, do I value a reputation gained from comedy,' he wrote in the Preface to *An Evening's Love*, 'so far as to concern myself about it any more than I needs must in my own defence: for I think it, in its own nature, inferior to all sorts of dramatic writing. Low comedy especially requires, on the writer's part, much of conversation with the vulgar: and much of ill nature in the observation of their follies.'[1] And in the Dedication of *Aureng-Zebe* he wrote that 'some of my contemporaries, even in my own partial judgment, have outdone me in comedy'.[2] We are more likely to agree with him in the latter observation than in the former, and yet both of them may unfairly prejudice the case against him. Modern students have been inclined to take him at his word. David Nichol Smith, for example, used the remark in the Preface to *An Evening's Love* as warrant for confining to a single paragraph his comments on the comedies in an essay devoted to Dryden's plays.[3] This is not to say that his comedies have been ignored;[4] rather that, in the intensity of our preoccupation with Etherege, Wycherley, and Congreve, his comedies have received less attention than they deserve—and less than he in other critical statements would seem to claim for them.

'Wit's now arriv'd to a more high degree,' Dryden wrote not long before *Marriage A-la-Mode* appeared; 'Our native language more refin'd and free'.[5] If in 1671, before the best plays of Etherege and Wycherley had been written, the couplet was boastful hyperbole, it would have become more nearly an accurate judgment by the time Dryden died in 1700. If Shakespeare be left out of account, it is not self-evident that the *comedy* of the earlier seventeenth century is superior to that of the later part of the century. Congreve's accomplishment may equal Jonson's; Dryden's comedies are arguably better than those of Beaumont and Fletcher, which they so often resemble.

[1] Watson, I 145.
[2] Watson, I 191.
[3] Nichol Smith, *John Dryden*, Cambridge 1950, 26.
[4] They are the subject of a recent comprehensive study by Frank Harper Moore, *The Nobler Pleasure: Dryden's Comedy in Theory and Practice*, Chapel Hill, N. C. 1963, to which I gratefully acknowledge an obligation.
[5] Epilogue to *The Conquest of Granada*, Part Two: Watson, I 167.

Dryden alludes in the Prologue to *Marriage A-la-Mode* to a character in Beaumont and Fletcher's *The Scornful Lady*. That comedy depicts a gentleman's stratagems to win a lady whom he has alienated, her love for him notwithstanding, by a public show of affection. Because in plot and in stretches of wit dialogue, the play anticipates Dryden's own pre-occupation with dialogue and episodes turning on antagonism between the sexes, it provides a meaningful subject for comparison with Dryden's own work. Described by Eugene M. Waith as 'the best comedy written by Beaumont and Fletcher in collaboration', *The Scornful Lady* has a plot which, again in Waith's words, consists 'mainly in the brilliant battle of wits' between the two chief characters, the Elder Loveless and the reluctant lady.[1] The play well illustrates what Dryden had in mind when, in *Of Dramatick Poesie*, he described the 'chase of wit' as a special excellence of Fletcher.[2] He emulated the accomplishment, and in several of his plays, including *Marriage A-la-Mode*, he may be thought to have surpassed it.

Reading the latter play along with *The Scornful Lady*, we can see that Dryden's claim, 'Wit's now arriv'd to a more high degree,' was not without some foundation. Dryden's analysis of the vagaries of sexual affection is more probing, and it is much more susceptible to a generalized application to humanity at large, than is Beaumont and Fletcher's. If they occasionally provide an intimate glimpse into the divided mind of the lady, who out of caprice risks the loss of the man she loves, they more frequently confine themselves to banter arising from the ludicrous situations to which Loveless' disguises and stratagems give rise. One seeks in vain in *The Scornful Lady* for lines comparable to many in *Marriage A-la-Mode* in which relaxed conversation conveys profundity of psychological insight with economy and precision of statement. In elegance of style which is yet dramatically appropriate, Dryden is surely superior. His play was written some sixty years closer to our own time, after the important linguistic changes of mid-century; that is after all what he had in mind when he wrote that 'Our native language' was 'more refin'd and free'. The credit for his achievement was parti-

[1] Waith, *The Pattern of Tragicomedy in Beaumont and Fletcher*, New Haven 1952, 101.
[2] Watson, I 60–61.

ally attributable, as he implied more than once, to the age in which he lived. Yet to read *The Scornful Lady* and *Marriage A-la-Mode* one after the other is perhaps to experience an impression that there was indeed improvement with the passage of time in seventeenth-century comedy. It is certainly to experience a sense of movement into something like the modern world. One is reminded of the aptness of Norman N. Holland's phrase, 'the first modern comedies', to describe the best of those written in the Restoration.[1]

Our disappointment with Dryden's comedies of London life is intensified by the expectations we take to them. If in the best of his tragicomedies he surpassed Beaumont and Fletcher, he did not in his London comedies equal, much less surpass, Ben Jonson. Reminiscences of Jonson abound in *The Wild Gallant, Sir Martin Mar-all*, and *The Kind Keeper*, but these plays cannot sustain comparison with *The Alchemist* and *Bartholomew Fair*, nor can they sustain comparison with the best London comedies written in his own time. It is curious that he was not impelled by the successes of Etherege and Wycherley to a more sustained effort in the satirical vein they had opened. Presumably he had them in mind when in the Dedication to *Aureng-Zebe* he wrote that he had been surpassed in comedy by some of his contemporaries. Yet after his relative failure in *The Wild Gallant* and his early successes in tragicomedy, he turned to the life around him only in response to commands he could not refuse. The comic scenes of his best tragicomedies, *Secret Love, Marriage A-la-Mode*, and *The Spanish Fryar*, reveal that he possessed in abundance the specialized gifts for close and witty analysis of social and emotional antagonisms needed for success in the kind of comedy Etherege and Wycherley wrote. The Sicilian or Spanish locales of his plays often seem loose disguises for the London of his own time. Yet the remote places provide an insulation against mundane actuality. His London comedies are different in impact from his own tragicomedies and from the best comedies written by his contemporaries.

The Wild Gallant, like *Sir Martin Mar-all* and *The Kind Keeper*,

---

[1] Holland, *The First Modern Comedies: The Significance of Etherege, Wycherley and Congreve*, Cambridge, Mass. 1959.

seems not to be altogether Dryden's own work. So much is implied in
his Preface to the play: 'The plot was not originally my own: but so
altered by me (whether for the better or worse, I know not) that, who-
ever the author was, he could not have challenged a scene of it.'
Dryden apparently did not know the identity of the author, who was
probably, in view of the early date of *The Wild Gallant*, someone who
had been active before the theatres were closed in 1642. Presumably
Dryden worked from an old manuscript: perhaps, as has been suggested
one by Richard Brome.[1] In any event, the supposition that he rewrote
a Renaissance play would account for the resemblances of *The Wild
Gallant* to the comedies of Massinger, Middleton, Shirley, and Brome
as well as to those of Fletcher and Jonson. If it was not successful with
its first audiences and is now little read, it nevertheless repays attention for the clarity with which it reveals the continuity in English comic
tradition of the seventeenth century: the derivation of Restoration
comedy in themes, character types, and plots from patterns well established before the civil wars. In his critical essays Dryden said little
about the earlier comic dramatists other than Beaumont and Fletcher
Jonson, and Shakespeare. '*Heywood* and *Shirley* were but Types of
thee,' he wrote about Shadwell in *Mac Flecknoe*, and his contempt seems
to have encompassed most of the earlier dramatists. *The Wild Gallant*
is the more significant in his development for the evidence it provides of
a link between his own work and the generality of Jacobean and
Caroline realistic comedies of English life. Yet it has much about it to
remind us of the Restoration. If it resembles Dryden's later comedies—
in its Jonsonian humours, its boarding house scenes, its sexuality, and
its improbable episodes—it approximates more fully than the two later
ones the form which the comedy of manners assumed.

For all its farcical situations, *The Wild Gallant* turns on the central
antagonisms of Restoration comedy: between social classes, between
the generations, and between the sexes. Not surprisingly in this play
produced less than three years after the Restoration, the social antagonisms have political overtones. Loveby's casual allusion (I. ii) to a

[1] Alfred   Harbage,   'Elizabethan-Restoration   Palimpsest,'   *Modern
Language Review*, XXXV, 1940, 307–9.

tradesman named Tribulation might have reminded his first audiences
of Jonson's Tribulation Wholesome, but it would also have reminded
them that many Dissenters of the City had supported Parliament during
the civil wars. Citizens and citizens' wives, like many before and after
them in seventeenth-century comedy, are the destined victims of
young gentlemen, richer in wit than in ready money. Bibber, the tailor
whose love for a joke makes him an easy target, is a type of the Restoration would-be wit, aspiring to a social level above his reach, and Loveby,
'the wild gallant', is an impecunious and free-living true-wit, a fore-
shadowing of such a character as Congreve's Valentine, who like
Loveby is finally saved by the resourcefulness of his lady. Sir Timorous,
'a bashful knight' and victim of town sharpsters, is the familiar figure of
the maladroit squire, one who can be awarded to a clever girl who lacks
the fortune needed for marriage to a true-wit. The Restoration practi-
cality in marriage settlements is fully apparent: the clearheaded young
are not too much in love to forget the need for a fortune, nor do they
cross class lines in choosing a mate.

Lord Nonesuch has the conventional role of a father determined to
marry his daughter, Constance, to a rich man, a role that as in many
another comedy leads his daughter to a defensive stratagem—here a
pretended pregnancy—so that she may marry the man of her choice.
(It is a mark of the early date of the play that Dryden, contrary to the
neoclassical principle that a character's personal qualities should
be commensurate with his rank, portrayed a lord, even one with
a name proclaiming his atypicality, as such a simpleton as this one.)
Constance loves Loveby, but like Angelica in *Love for Love* she is reluctant to admit her love for a man who has been profligate with his
favours and his money. Like Angelica, she undertakes on her own initi-
ative stratagems to aid her beloved, who is ignorant of her affection
for him. Like other heroines of Restoration comedy, Angelica included,
she is a reluctant mistress, in whom affection is not incompatible with a
willingness to enjoy a triumph over her lover. When after she has
secretly supplied Loveby with money, he, in ignorance of the source
of his wealth, boasts to her and her cousin Isabelle about a pretended
inheritance (II. i), the two girls draw him into yet more extravagant
lies, in a conversational duel of wits. The scene is in what proved to be

one of the richest comic veins of the age, one that Dryden himself late:
exploited with distinction. Yet he did so in his tragicomedies rather than
in his later London comedies.

The Wild Gallant did not succeed on the stage to Dryden's expecta
tions, and he is defensive about it in his Preface and in the Epilogue he
wrote for a revival. 'This motley garniture of fool and farce', he called
it in the Epilogue: excessively severe perhaps but not altogether in
accurate as a description of the play, which is indeed a mixture of
comic styles.

The inferiority of *Sir Martin Mar-all* and *The Kind Keeper* to most of
Dryden's plays may be explained by the fact that he did not have a
free hand in them. Samuel Pepys referred to *Sir Martin* in his Diary
16 August, 1667, as 'made by my Lord Duke of Newcastle, but, as
everybody says, corrected by Dryden', a statement consistent with
what can be inferred from the play itself, which retains strong traces of
Newcastle's hand, even as it reveals in its excellences the professional
skill of Dryden. If the radical superiority of the play to Newcastle's
unaided work argues for Dryden's part in it, the presence of situations
and character types taken over from obscure plays by Newcastle as
well as one episode borrowed from an old play that Newcastle but not
Dryden could be presumed to know provides convincing evidence that
the Duke's part in the collaboration was more than nominal.[1] *Sir
Martin* is intermittently a farcical comedy of situation (vulnerable to
the criticism of farce that Dryden included in his Preface to *An Even
ing's Love*), and so is *The Kind Keeper; or, Mr Limberham*, in which
Dryden's collaborator seems to have been the King himself. In a letter
of July 1677 Dryden remarked that 'the Kings Comedy lyes in the Sudds
. . . it will be almost such another piece of businesse as the fond Hus
band, for such the King will have it, who is parcell poet with me in the
plott; one of the designes being a story he was pleased formerly to tell
me'. Dryden refers, Charles E. Ward has explained, to *The Kind
Keeper*, which resembles Tom D'Urfey's *A Fond Husband*.[2] Even if the

[1] Moore, *The Nobler Pleasure*, 53–57; John Loftis and Vinton A. Dearing, ed., *Works*, IX 357–64.
[2] Charles E. Ward, ed., *The Letters of John Dryden, with Letters Addressed
to Him*, Durham, N. C. 1942, 11–12, 47.

King's collaboration was confined to casual suggestions, Dryden was limited by them in writing the play, which can no more be regarded as representing his natural taste in comedy than *Sir Martin*.

Unlike *Sir Martin*, one of the most popular of all Dryden's plays during his lifetime, *The Kind Keeper* did not succeed on the stage, a fact to which Dryden refers with a certain bitterness in his Dedication, attributing its failure to resentment of the sharpness of his satire on 'keeping' mistresses. This would seem to be less than a comprehensive explanation of the play's failure, the reasons for which, entangled as they may be with Restoration politics and personalities, we can probably never know. Dryden praises the play in his Dedication: 'I will be bold enough to say, that this comedy is of the first rank of those which I have written, and that posterity will be of my opinion.' Posterity has not been of his opinion (though the play has numbered George Saintsbury among its admirers),[1] and, in the light of Dryden's reference to it in the letter of July 1677, it is hard to believe that his praise of it was altogether sincere. Perhaps his remark was a politic tribute to the King.

The Kind Keeper and *Sir Martin Mar-all* are alike in respects other than their settings in London boarding houses. Continuity of plot is subordinated in both plays to disjunctive episodes turning on audacious acts of misrepresentation and trickery; both plays have 'humours' characters, including in *The Kind Keeper* the distinctly Jonsonian type of the 'hypocritical' and 'fanatic' Dissenter; both plays portray the mundane realities of London life rather than the social affectations of the fashionable. Dryden includes a reference to *The Alchemist* in the dialogue of *The Kind Keeper* (I. i), and the mad stratagems by which the principal character, Woodall, carries out his simultaneous intrigues with the women of the boarding house are heaped one on another like the stratagems of Face and Subtle to bilk their greedy patrons. The loose-jointed plot, dependent on such a palpable absurdity as a father not recognizing his own son, is resolved by the simple device of revealing that the putative daughter of the landlady is in reality the rich heiress whom Woodall's father has picked out for his lecherous son.

---

[1] S-S, VI, 3–4. My quotations from Dryden's plays are taken from this edition.

King Charles's taste in comedy, it would appear, was not fastidious, nor was that of the Duke of Newcastle. Exposition and continuity of plot are if anything more casual in *Sir Martin* than in *The Kind Keeper*, and the indifference to plausibility of event is scarcely less extreme. Yet *Sir Martin* less frequently approaches the sordid than *The Kind Keeper*, which in its depiction of a father unwittingly aiding his son in whore-mongering can repel even readers who relish the uninhibited treatment of sexual subjects. It is not difficult to discover qualities in the two plays that would have won the earlier a prominent place in the repertory and removed the later from the stage after a short opening run.

A passage in the Preface to *An Evening's Love* would seem to ex-press Dryden's attitude toward such comedies as *Sir Martin Mar-all* and *The Kind Keeper*. He will ignore undiscriminating applause, he in-insists in what must be described as a petulant tone, from a public which is insensitive to 'wit on the poet's part, or any occasion of laugh-ter from the actor besides the ridiculousness of his habit and his grimaces'.

> But I have descended, before I was aware, from comedy to farce; which consists principally of grimaces. That I admire not any comedy equally with tragedy is, perhaps, from the sullenness of my humour; but that I detest those farces which are now the most frequent entertainments of the stage, I am sure I have reason on my side. Comedy consists, though of low persons, yet of natural actions and characters; I mean such humours, adventures, and de-signs as are to be found and met with in the world. Farce, on the other side, consists of forced humours and unnatural events. Comedy presents us with the imperfections of human nature. Farce entertains us with what is monstrous and chimerical: the one causes laughter in those who can judge of men and manners, by the lively representation of their folly or corruption; the other produces the same effect in those who can judge of neither, and that only by its extravagances.[1]

A curiously strong indictment of 'low comedy' to come from a man who just four years earlier had scored a popular success with *Sir Martin Mar-all*, which abounds in 'forced humours and unnatural events', and yet a statement of personal preferences that helps to ex-plain the direction his career took.

[1] Watson, I 145–46.

After this emphatic expression of his antipathies, he describes later in the same Preface the form of comedy he prefers.

> I will not deny but that I approve most the mixed way of comedy; that which is neither all wit, nor all humour, but the result of both. Neither so little of humour as Fletcher shows, nor so little of love and wit as Jonson; neither all cheat, with which the best plays of the one are filled, nor all adventure, which is the common practice of the other. I would have the characters well chosen and kept distant from interfering with each other; which is more than Fletcher or Shakespeare did: but I would have more of the *urbana, venusta, salsa, faceta,* and the rest which Quintilian reckons up as the ornaments of wit; and these are extremely wanting in Ben Jonson. As for repartee in particular; as it is the very soul of conversation, so it is the greatest grace of comedy, where it is proper to the characters.[1]

We can be sure that he meant what he said because for the rest of his life, except in the single instance of *The Kind Keeper,* in which the King was 'parcell poet' with him 'in the plott', he wrote comedies to which this description is applicable.

Dryden wrote tragicomedies at a time when the mixed form was controversial. As early as *Of Dramatick Poesie* he provides an analysis of conflicting opinion on the subject, expressing through one of his interlocutors, Lisideius, the opinion that 'mirth and compassion' are 'things incompatible'[2] and expressing through another, Neander, his own contrary opinion.[3] On few of the subjects treated in *Of Dramatick Poesie* may we feel such confidence as here that we are in touch with a studied conclusion Dryden had reached. Lisideius's arguments in opposition to tragicomedy and Neander's in defence of it are closely and circumstantially applicable to *Secret Love*, on which Dryden was at work at about the time he wrote the essay. The play illustrates Neander's proposition that 'a scene of mirth mixed with tragedy has the same effect upon us which our music has betwixt the acts'. Unlike *The Rival Ladies*, in which several plot lines are interwoven, *Secret*

---

[1] Watson, I 148–49.
[2] Watson, I 45–46.
[3] Watson, I 58.

Love has two largely independent plots, with separate groups of characters, who, as Lisideius derisively put it, 'keep their distances, as if they were Montagues and Capulets, and seldom begin an acquaintance till the last scene of the fifth act'. Far from regarding the separation of the groups of characters as a defect, Dryden regarded it as a valuable formal device which enabled him to present persons of exalted rank without foregoing scenes of irreverent mirth. His convictions on this subject led to the remark in the Preface to *An Evening's Love* that he 'would have the characters well chosen, and kept distant from interfering with each other; which is more than Fletcher or Shakespeare did'. Those Renaissance dramatists were not subject to the kind of censure Dryden sustained for *Secret Love*. In the final scene of that play, Dryden wrote in his Preface, 'Celadon and Florimell are treating too lightly of their marriage in the presence of the Queen, who likewise seems to stand idle while the great action of the drama is still depending', a situation that Dryden was compelled 'to acknowledge . . . as a fault, since it pleased His Majesty, the best judge, to think so'. King Charles insisted that even stage monarchs be accorded the privilege of their rank. Dryden found it convenient to keep royalty out of his comic scenes, in which he indulged his gift for 'repartee', which he regarded 'as the greatest grace of comedy, where it is proper to the characters'.

Dryden's concentration on tragicomedy resulted in his choice of characters of higher rank than those who appear in the plays of Etherege and Wycherley. In the threefold division of society to which he referred in the Prologue to *Marriage A-la-Mode*, 'the town, the city, and the court', he gave primary attention in the tragicomedies to the court (as in the London comedies he gave it to the city), largely ignoring the town—fashionable society, but not of its highest reaches. The other dramatists always kept royalty out of their plays and for the most part even the nobility. Dorimant of *The Man of Mode* may have 'had in him several of the Qualities' of the Earl of Rochester, as John Dennis asserted,[1] but in the play he is not identified as a nobleman. One of the

---

[1] 'A Defence of Sir Fopling Flutter,' in Edward Niles Hooker, ed., *The Critical Works of John Dennis*, 2 vol Baltimore 1939–43, II 248.

reasons for the distance we perceive between Dryden's plays and most comedies of manners lies in Dryden's minimal attention to the social group that from the time of James Shirley to that of Oscar Wilde has provided the richest subjects for the display of snobbery, affectation, and ambition.

Dryden dedicated *Marriage A-la-Mode* to the Earl of Rochester, who, Dryden said, read and criticized it in manuscript and recommended it to the King, who in turn 'by his approbation of it in writing, made way for its kind reception'. Dryden writes with scorn of 'City' folk in his Prologue, and he includes in the play a caricature of a social climber, Melantha—not in her case a 'cit' but a fashionable lady of wealth who aspires yet higher, to an association with royalty. She is of lower social rank than the other three principal characters of the comic plot, and it is not coincidence that unlike them her conversation is marred by her bungling fondness for French words. 'Wit seems to have lodged itself more nobly in this age, than in any of the former', Dryden writes in his Dedication, and the Sicilian setting of the play notwithstanding, he seems to have provided in his comic scenes an improved version of the conversation he heard from the Court wits.

If the tone of the serious plot is different, necessarily so because decorum forbade banter in the presence of royalty, Dryden's social assumptions as they appear in the sequence of events are again aristocratic. The train of events leading to the denouement is set in motion by the discovery of Leonidas and Palmyra, who had been reared in obscurity. The discovery comes about, not through the agency of an informer, but from the undisguisable circumstance that they are of noble appearance and bearing. 'Behold two miracles!' the usurping King exclaims on first seeing them (I. i):

Of different sexes, but of equal form:
So matchless both, that my divided soul
Can scarcely ask the gods a son or daughter,
For fear of losing one.

And Leonidas, unabashed and resourceful amid the new splendours of the court, reveals the magnanimity that is a natural consequence of his royal birth. The plot moves as though by divine plan to a restoration of legitimate succession. Dryden after all wrote the play only a dozen years after legitimacy had prevailed over usurpation in England.

The serious and the comic plots of *Marriage A-la-Mode* illustrate Dryden's juxtaposition of Renaissance dramatic patterns and Restoration attitudes and preoccupations. Along with the analysis of sexual passion in the conversation of his worldly young lovers, an analysis that in its concern for accuracy in physiological and psychological detail can scarcely be paralleled in earlier English drama, he includes a serious plot reminiscent of dramatic romances produced in the reigns of Elizabeth I and James I. What Samuel Johnson said about Shakespeare, that his 'comedy pleases by the thoughts and the language, and his tragedy for the greater part by incident and action',[1] is applicable to the two plots of this single play, just as it is applicable also to the two plots of *Much Ado About Nothing*. Yet if we can find precedents in Shakespeare, and even more of them in Beaumont and Fletcher, for the improbable incidents of tragedy narrowly averted, we cannot find in the verbal duels of Benedict and Beatrice or anywhere else precedents for such an uninhibited comment on the workings of the male mind during sexual intercourse as Rhodophil's patient explanation to Doralice (III. i) that in his effort to enjoy her after three years of marriage he has imagined her to be 'all the fine women of the town—to help me out'.

Dryden examines more audaciously than had any English dramatist before him the irreconcilable tension between the urge for variety of sexual gratification, on the one hand, and the need, which in its origin is both psychological and social, for constancy. The specifics of his conversational review of the subject may owe something to the libertine philosophy of which his patron, Lord Rochester, was a distinguished exponent,[2] but his conception of the subject is not bound by seventeenth-century speculations in moral philosophy or by the habits of life of the Court wits. In answer to a question from Palamede about his wife, Rhodophil professes ignorance (I. i): 'Ask those, who have

[1] *Preface to Shakespeare*. In Arthur Sherbo, ed., *Johnson on Shakespeare*, Yale Edition of the Works of Samuel Johnson, VII, New Haven 1968-69.
[2] On Restoration libertinism, see Dale Underwood, *Etherege and the Seventeenth-Century Comedy of Manners*, New Haven 1957, 2–40.

smelt to a strong perfume two years together, what's the scent.' The seventh commandment of the Old Testament and the modern phrase about 'the seven year itch' alike testify to the strength of the temptation to which Rhodophil is subjected, a temptation not reduced by the fact that he had married a beautiful woman whom he had loved. Should he take a mistress, as Palamede suggests, the remedy could like 'cordials' be but temporary, for, as Palamede adds, 'as fast as one fails, you must supply it with another'. The licence of the Restoration Court enabled Dryden to speak frankly on the subject, but the authority with which he addressed it derived from his humanity rather than from anything he learned from other people.

Despite their longings, the two couples do not commit adultery, and the play closes with a reaffirmation of the marriage tie: not a very vigorous reaffirmation, but still an acknowledgment that social anarchy would ensue if matrimonial law should be abandoned. How seriously, we may ask, are we to take the couples' change of heart? Is it more than a conventional termination of the comic plot? Does the final agreement of Rhodophil and Palamede to respect each other's matrimonial rights constitute an answer to the famous question (*'Why should a foolish marriage vow . . .?'*) with which the play begins? It is scarcely a convincing answer, and its force is weakened by the exhortations to erotic delight that have preceded it. The account of a sexual embrace in the song of the fourth act (IV. ii), reporting instructions exchanged in an effort to reduce differences in the timing of the male and female approaches to ecstasy, is not consonant in emotional impact with a celebration of marital fidelity. Our susceptibility to sexual stimulation conveyed in language as graceful as Dryden's is such that we cannot quickly recover a devotion to the principle of monogamy. The play is erotic in its impact, let us acknowledge it, and our pleasure in it has a sexual as well as an intellectual basis. Yet the eroticism is not incompatible with the exploration, by way of the fable of two couples whose affections are mismatched, of the perennial tension between impulse and obligation. In this play Dryden refuses to make an emphatic moral judgment, a circumstance that troubles us less in the twentieth century than it troubled Jeremy Collier in the seventeenth, Samuel Johnson in the eighteenth, or Lord Macaulay in the nineteenth century.

Jocelyn Powell's perceptive discrimination, in an essay about Etherege, between 'comedy of experience' and 'comedy of judgment'[1] can help us to an understanding of *Marriage A-la-Mode*. The comic plot of Dryden's play depicts the vagaries of sexual love, with analytical attention—unclouded by moral judgment—to the minute discriminations of passion. If we seek for a convincing sign of authorial disapproval of promiscuity, we will be disappointed. To be sure, the impact of the comic plot is softened by that of the heroic plot. Love assumes many forms, and the constancy and devotion of Leonidas and Palmyra provide a reminder that the emotion is not always a matter of lust and a roving fancy. Yet the heroic plot scarcely constitutes a judgment on the intrigues of the uninhibited couples, whose forthright reports of the state of their affections articulate the experience of common humanity.

If the moral and emotional attitudes dramatized in the two plots are complementary, there is nevertheless an extraordinary difference between them, so great a difference that it is remarkable that the two plots can coexist in harmony. The reputation of the play testifies to the fact that audiences and readers have found them compatible. There are fewer thematic and episodic parallels between the two plots than between those in *Secret Love*, that one of Dryden's plays which most closely resembles *Marriage A-la-Mode*. In *Secret Love*, the heroic action, like the comic, portrays the fortunes in love of a young couple, but with the difference from *Marriage A-la-Mode* that the heroic couple themselves suffer from vagaries of affection. When Philocles belatedly discovers that he is the beloved of the Queen, he is briefly tempted by the prospect of grandeur to abandon Candiope, his own lady. The Queen herself in the earlier play, like Florimel in the comic plot, reveals jealousy of a rival. *Secret Love* resembles many Renaissance and Restoration comedies portraying the parallel courtships of a serious and a witty couple, but the same cannot be said about *Marriage A-la-Mode*, in which the obstacles confronting Leonidas and Palmyra are political and dynastic, irrelevant to their affections, which remain constant. Rather than seek thematic links between the two plots, we should

[1] Powell, 'George Etherege and the Form of a Comedy,' in John Russell Brown and Bernard Harris, eds., *Restoration Theatre*, 1965, 43–69.

recall Dryden's musical analogy in *Of Dramatick Poesie*. 'A scene of mirth mixed with tragedy has the same effect upon us which our music has betwixt the acts . . .':[1] something less than an exhaustive account of the matter but one which places emphasis where it belongs, on the calculated and harmonious alternation of mood. Dryden's carefully planned contrasts of mood convey a sense of design or pattern which is itself a source of aesthetic pleasure.

In the Dedication of *Marriage A-la-Mode* Dryden referred to it as 'perhaps . . . the best of my comedies', a judgment in which critics and makers of anthologies in the twentieth century have on the whole concurred. Whether it is in fact superior to *Secret Love*, among his earlier comedies, or *The Spanish Fryar* and *Amphitryon*, among his later, is a question that need not engage us. Its excellencies are like those of *Secret Love*; they are different from, but not necessarily superior to, those of the two later plays. In any event, *Marriage A-la-Mode* represents in Dryden's career a climactic working out of a pattern of tragicomedy in which he projects the intrigues of eminently credible young lovers, whose attitudes toward love and marriage would seem to be those of the inner circle of Charles II's Court, against a background action of political intrigue and improbable adventure. Dryden continued to write comedies with plot lines firmly separated from one another, in which contrasts of mood and sometimes of theme are prominent; but he did not again write a play in which emphasis is so neatly divided between an heroic world of romantic love and a commonplace world of sexual passion, nor did he again provide such gifted conversationalists as three of the young lovers in this play.

In the Dedication of *The Spanish Fryar*, Dryden returns to the subject of tragicomedy. His defence of his two-plot pattern is not so unqualified as it is, in Neander's remarks, in *Of Dramatick Poesie*. We may surmise that in the dozen years since that essay was published neoclassical opinion had hardened against it. Rymer had published his influential *Tragedies of the Last Age*, and Dryden as well as other dramatists and critics had been receptive to Rymer's argument for French formalist principles. Soon after the appearance of *The Tragedies of the*

---

[1] Watson, I 58.

Last Age, Dryden had written *All for Love*, that one of his plays in which
he observed neoclassical precept most consistently. Whatever the
reason for the modification of his opinions, in the Dedication of *The
Spanish Fryar* he rests his case on his own and on his audiences' preferences rather than on a reasoned exposition of the advantages of the
mixed form. The play includes two actions, he writes:

> but it will be clear to any judicious man, that with half the pains I
> could have raised a play from either of them; for this time I satis-
> fied my humour, which was to tack two plays together; and to
> break a rule for the pleasure of variety. The truth is, the audience
> are grown weary of continued melancholy scenes; and I dare
> venture to prophesy, that few tragedies, except those in verse
> [rhymed verse], shall succeed in this age, if they are not lightened
> with a course of mirth; for the feast is too dull and solemn without
> the fiddles.

Dryden reverts to his musical analogy, but this time in a prudential
appeal to taste, in opposition to the rules, and this time his remarks have
a defensive ring.

Throughout the Dedication Dryden gives primary attention to the
'melancholy scenes', a circumstance relevant to our reading of *The
Spanish Fryar*. For the serious much more than the comic plot commands attention, to such an extent that the comic scenes are likely to
seem merely interludes in tragic action. In the relationship between the
two plots as in much else apart from its denouement, *The Spanish Fryar*
indeed resembles the tragedy *Don Sebastian* more closely than the
tragicomedy *Marriage A-la-Mode*. That it does so is an indication of
the gravity of the subjects treated satirically in the comic scenes as well
as those alluded to in the heroic action. In tone, characters, sequence of
events, and even in subdued echoes of Shakespeare's *The Merchant of
Venice*, the comic plot anticipates that of *Don Sebastian*. And the serious
plot hints at the tragic theme which is dominant in the later play,

> That unrepented crimes of parents dead,
> Are justly punished on their children's head,

as Dorax in the final speech of the tragedy puts it. In the opening and
expository scene of *The Spanish Fryar*, Pedro explains of Leonora that
'Her father's crimes/Sit heavy on her, and weigh down her prayers.'

Leonora's relationship with Torrismond is clouded by her dead father's usurpation of his father's throne. The tragic potential of *Don Sebastian* is present in this earlier play. Dryden chose to mute it in an adroitly contrived denouement.

The serious action of *The Spanish Fryar*, with which the play opens and closes, has a more apparent relevance to the conditions of seventeenth-century political life than those of the earlier tragicomedies. There is a fairy tale quality about the dynastic complications depicted in *Marriage A-la-Mode*, a remoteness from historical reality scarcely lessened by the presence of the comic scenes, with their striking psychological realism. In *The Spanish Fryar*, for all its medieval setting in Aragon, the struggle for political power is played out so convincingly as frequently to recall the recent history of England. The allusions to the imprisonment of King Sancho by a usurper could scarcely have failed to put the audience in mind of the imprisonment of King Charles I, and Raymond's account of the King's entrusting him with the care of his son and heir Torrismond (IV. ii)

Till happier times shall call his courage forth,
To break my fetters, or revenge my fate,

would have recalled Charles I's prudent concern that his own sons escape from his enemies. It is a curious tribute to the liveliness of the political themes of the play that after the Revolution, when Queen Mary commanded a performance of it, she was embarrassed by the lines about inherited sin to which I have already referred, lines that seemed to describe her own situation (I. i):

Her father's crimes
Sit heavy on her, and weigh down her prayers.
A crown usurped; a lawful king deposed,
In bondage held, debarred the common light.[1]

This fortuitous bit of political allegory, pertaining to events still in the future when Dryden wrote the play, suggests the force of Dryden's serious plot as well as the difficulties inherent in the dramatic portrayal of conflicts involving royalty.

[1] John Loftis, *The Politics of Drama in Augustan England*, Oxford, 1963, 22 n.

Queen Mary's motive in commanding a performance of *The Spanish Fryar*, which had been barred from the stage during her father's reign, was presumably political: to display publicly her hostility to Catholicism. Dryden must have had a similar motive when, two years after the revelations of an alleged Popish Plot, he wrote the scenes in which the avaricious and hypocritical Friar Dominic appears. The incongruity of Dominic's position as priest with his pious rationalization of his role as pander provides Dryden's most effective comic resource—and it is one which in 1680 would have had political voltage. There is no reason to assume that he had wavered in his loyalty to the principle of legitimate succession in England, which at that time meant the right of succession of the Catholic Duke of York.[1] There would have been political advantages in indicating that the Tories as well as the Whigs could be critical of Catholic duplicity. Dryden wrote *Absalom and Achitophel* the following year, and if the poem is much more explicit about the constitutional issues raised in the Exclusion Controversy, it is not incompatible in its political burden with *The Spanish Fryar*. The primary action of the play as of the poem reaffirms legitimacy, and the play like the poem glances satirically at self-serving politicians who manipulate the emotions of the common folk. 'I have no taste/Of popular applause;' Torrismond declares (I. i), and there is reason enough to believe that he speaks for Dryden:

> *the noisy praise*
> *Of giddy crowds, as changeable as winds;*
> *Still vehement, and still without a cause;*
> *Servant to chance, and blowing in the tide*
> *Of swoln success.*

Such sentiments were scarcely less applicable to the England of 1680 than the criticism of Catholicism implicit in the character of Friar Dominic.

The degeneracy epitomized in the Friar reinforces the tone of calculating sensuality pervading the scenes of Lorenzo's courtship of Elvira.

[1] Louis I. Bredvold, 'Political Aspects of Dryden's *Amboyna* and *The Spanish Friar,*' in *Essays and Studies in English and Comparative Literature by Members of the English Department of the University of Michigan,* Ann Arbor 1932, 119–32; Moore, *The Nobler Pleasure,* 158–62.

A young colonel whose lust has been intensified by the enforced absti-
nence of a military campaign, Lorenzo undertakes with Dominic's
paid assistance the seduction of Elvira, the young, beautiful, and receptive wife of the impotent moneylender, Gomez, who is sixty years
old. Apart from the detail of Dominic's calling, the character relationships and sequence of events—at least prior to the unexpected discovery that Lorenzo and Elvira are brother and sister—parallel those
in many another Restoration comedy. Yet there is no other witty
couple who can provide an ameliorating note of half-idealized love.
Lorenzo and Elvira are articulate in Dryden's more relaxed manner, but
the willingness of Elvira to be seduced precludes a conversational duel,
and the nature of their relationship, before the late introduction of the
theme of incest averted, enforces an unremitting attention to the consummation of adultery.

The comic scenes lack the conversational wit of those in *Secret
Love, An Evening's Love,* and *Marriage A-la-Mode,* and they are less
important in relation to the serious plot. Yet they are remarkably
funny—and they must have been strikingly so when they could be seen
on the stage. It is easy to imagine what a gifted actor could have made
of the role of Friar Dominic, described by Pedro (I. i) as a

> reverend, fat, old gouty friar,—
> With a paunch swoln so high, his double chin
> Might rest upon it; a true son of the Church;
> Fresh-coloured, and well thriven on his trade,—

a description that helps us to understand why the character has seemed
to many readers to be a redaction, in priestly garb, of Sir John Falstaff. Dominic is a tribute to Dryden's versatility as a comic dramatist
as well as to his clearheaded awareness of the claims of the flesh in
opposition to those of an idealized code of conduct, claims of the flesh
including but not restricted to the imperious needs of sexual love. It is
idle to assess the resemblances of Dominic to Falstaff: they are members of a famous brotherhood, to which Cervantes's Sancho Panza also
belongs, men in whom a conflict between earthly and spiritual desires
is almost non-existent, so strong is the commonsensical awareness of
the simple need of a man to live comfortably in a difficult and dangerous

world. Love and lust are facts of life, and Dryden in this play makes ample acknowledgment of them, but they are less important in the totality of experience than a reading of English drama would lead one to believe. Dryden enlarges, almost in an Elizabethan manner, the spectrum of his comic targets. The variety of the targets as well as the nature of Lorenzo's intrigue to seduce Elvira results in dialogue very different from the repartee of *Marriage A-la-Mode*, and it results also in a deflation of mood.

Yet it is the serious plot which controls the play. Dryden writes with pride about it in his Dedication, commending the diction, which is indeed vigorous and free of the bombast that, as he acknowledges, had sometimes appeared in his heroic plays. We may feel less confidence in accepting his praise of the denouement, in which against all expectation the protagonist and his wife end in happiness and prosperity and the seeming villain reveals himself as prudent and even benevolent. 'The dagger and the cup of poison are always in a readiness;' Dryden remarks in his Dedication, 'but to bring the action to the last extremity, and then by probable means to recover all, will require the art and judgment of a writer; and cost him many a pang in the performance.' Dryden's terms are well chosen, and insofar as they mean that he has managed the action adroitly, they are accurate. Passages early in the play may be seen in the retrospect afforded by the fifth act to prepare for the revelations of the events by which catastrophe was averted. Bertran's enigmatic response to the Queen's half-articulated command to kill the imprisoned King and his suspicion that she may be using him as a tool to prepare the way for Torrismond (III. iii) provide plausibility for Bertran's ruse of falsely pretending to kill the King. So also the Queen's doubts and hesitations in her complicity in the projected crime provide plausibility for her later most sincerely experienced remorse. The vacillating and weak-willed Queen may not seem an appropriate wife for Torrismond, but, like the Queen in *Secret Love*, she provides a not unconvincing study in a mind torn by conflicting desires.

The tragicomic movement of the main plot is well contrived. So much we must concede. The next step in an evaluation of it brings us to decision on problems common to the form of tragicomedy, a form that has always been more popular in the theatre and with readers than with critics. The problems are too familiar, and too generalized in their application to the drama of many generations, to repay much attention here. We may acknowledge at once that Dryden's denouement inhibits an exploration of the consequences of sin: actual sin in the case of the Queen, who had indeed hinted to Bertran that she wished him to kill the King; a contemplation of sin in the case of Bertran, who had apparently refrained from the murder as much out of prudent calculation as moral compunction. And curiously the comic action proceeds analogously. Because Lorenzo and Elvira are revealed to be brother and sister, their sin remains merely one of thwarted intention. Whatever Dryden thought of Thomas Rymer's doctrine of 'poetical justice,' he manipulated the events of this play to provide a delight arising from unexpected turns of plot.

Less than a year before *Amphitryon; or, The Two Socia's* was performed in 1690, Dryden had defended himself in the Preface to *Don Sebastian* against the charges of plagiarism Langbaine made in *A New Catalogue of English Plays* of 1687. 'The *materia poetica* is as common to all writers', Dryden wrote in the Preface to *Don Sebastian*, 'as the *materia medica* to all physicians.' As if to illustrate that proposition, he turned in *Amphitryon* to one of the oldest of all comic stories, best known in the versions of Molière and Plautus but with a literary ancestry extending into antiquity far beyond Plautus: 'were this comedy wholly mine,' Dryden writes to his patron in his Dedication, 'I should call it a trifle, and perhaps not think it worth your patronage; but when the names of Plautus and Molière are joined in it, that is, the two greatest names of ancient and modern comedy, I must not presume so far on their reputation, to think their best and most unquestioned productions can be termed little.' Dryden joins an acknowledgment of literary indebtedness to a conventional compliment to his patron, and by implication he reaffirms his conception of literary property. Plautus had drawn on the writings of his predecessors; Molière—as well as Rotrou and others—had drawn on Plautus. Could anyone who knew and admired the classical tradition in comedy censure Dryden for emulating his distinguished predecessors?

Amphitryon was published too late for Langbaine to consider it in its proper alphabetical order in *An Account of the English Dramatick*

Poets, but he included an entry for it in his Appendix of late additions
to that work. Dryden's literary borrowings for the play presented an
awkward subject to Langbaine, and his comments reveal an ambiguity
in evaluation, a grudging admiration for Dryden's accomplishment
undercut by the use of a depreciatory metaphor. Referring to Dryden's
acknowledgment of his sources, Langbaine justly adds that he has
taken more from Molière than from Plautus:[1] 'but however it must
with Justice be allowed, that what he has borrowed, he has improv'd
throughout; and *Molliere* is as much exceeded by Mr *Dryden*, as *Rotrou*
is outdone by *Molliere*.' A handsome compliment—but one qualified
in what follows: 'The truth is, our Author so polishes and improves other
Mens Thoughts, that tho' they are mean in themselves, yet by a *New
Turn* which he gives them, they appear Beautiful and Sparkling: Herein
resembling Skillful Lapidaries, that by their Art, make a *Bristol* Stone
appear with almost the same Lustre, as a Natural Diamond.'[2] Langbaine is more accurate in his descriptive remarks than in his critical
evaluation. The 'other Mens Thoughts' that Dryden used were scarcely
'a *Bristol* Stone,' nor is his play a counterfeit diamond, but he nevertheless borrowed more liberally for *Amphitryon* than for any other play he
wrote.[3] Yet it is his own play, in his distinctive style, directed in many
particulars to an English audience of 1690.

Dryden exploits the eroticism inherent in his subject more forth-
rightly than had Molière,[4] but he is scarcely gross. Although *Amphitryon*
is as singlemindedly preoccupied with seduction as *The Kind Keeper*, it
has an ameliorating classical setting unlike the London milieu of the
other play, which is all too convincing to permit an escape into fantasy.
The quality of fantasy in *Amphitryon*, the vicarious experience it provides of sexual fulfilment, constitutes a special attraction of the subject.

[1] N. B. Allen, *The Sources of John Dryden's Comedies*, Ann Arbor 1935,
concludes (266) that 'only about two per cent of the play contains
material from Plautus, whereas nearly fifty per cent of it is from
Molière'.
[2] Langbaine, *An Account of the English Dramatick Poets*, Oxford 1961,
sig. oov–oo2r.
[3] Allen, 236.
[4] S-S, VIII 2.

If Charles Lamb's famous defence of Restoration comedy as existing in a self-contained and amoral world of its own is applicable to any late seventeenth-century play, it would seem to be applicable to this one, in which the king of the gods employs divine powers to enjoy a wife devoted to her husband, whose love for her husband ironically intensifies Jupiter's pleasure in her embraces. The adulterous relationship has a natural consequence, but with the supreme felicity of his divinity, Jupiter can interpret Alcmena's pregnancy as a favour granted to her.

Yet for all its classical setting, its eroticism, and its sustained gaiety, *Amphitryon* is an audacious play, a comical study of a grave situation arising from the self-indulgent intrusion of the great into the affairs of their inferiors. The opening scene establishes a conception of Jupiter as despotic, and it suggests as well the vulnerability of common folk to the abuse of power. In an expository conversation, Jupiter explains to Mercury and Phoebus the plan he has ordained. (The mock logic of the passage, in Dryden's best philosophical style, reminds us that not long before he had written *The Hind and the Panther*.) 'Fate is,' Jupiter declares,

> . . . what I,
> By virtue of omnipotence, have made it;
> And power omnipotent can do no wrong. . . .

When he has told Mercury and Phoebus about his intention to enjoy the wife of Amphitryon, he silences their objections with a further revelation:

> . . . yet thus far know,
> That, for the good of humankind, this night
> I shall beget a future Hercules,
> Who shall redress the wrongs of injured mortals,
> Shall conquer monsters, and reform the world.

Dryden had the warrant of classical mythology for all this, and he stops short of a sustained parallel with human affairs. He nevertheless glances at recent English history.

If the first audiences saw a double meaning in the play, they would probably have thought of Jupiter as representing Charles II (and perhaps James II also), famous for the prodigality of his favours and famous too for his generosity to his mistresses and illegitimate offspring. The Epilogue, spoken by Phaedra of easy virtue, would seem to be an ironic lament for the Restoration Court:[1]

> When the sweet nymph held up the lily hand,
> Jove was her humble servant at command;
> The treasury of heaven was ne'er so bare,
> But still there was a pension for the fair.
> In all his reign, adultery was no sin;
> For Jove the good example did begin.

Acceptable sentiments two years after the Revolution, affectionate criticism of the late King for those who chose to find it, in the vein of half-disguised topical allusion recurrent in the play. Mercury describes in the opening scene a quarrel between Jupiter and Juno that would have put audiences in mind of the matrimonial relations between Charles and Queen Catharine. 'She threatened to sue him in the spiritual court for some matrimonial omissions; and he stood upon his prerogative; then she hit him on the teeth of all his bastards,' among whom Mercury himself was numbered. It tells much about the atmosphere of political liberality of William III's reign, in comparison with the early years of Charles II's, that a Roman Catholic dramatist who had been closely associated with the Restoration Court could treat the familiar habits of royalty jestingly. 'These are a very hopeful sort of patriots,' says Sosia in indignation against his master (II. i), 'to stand up, as they do, for liberty and property of the subject: There's conscience for you!' Gibes at the slogans of the Revolution were permissible when spoken by a serving man of ancient Thebes, who was confronted on stage by a god who had assumed his likeness.

The topical allusions testify to the inventiveness of Dryden's re-shaping of the familiar story. So also does the structural pattern of the play, which approximates to the pattern of the tragicomedies more closely than may at first appear. Again Dryden introduces separate groups of characters, of different rank, engaged in largely independent intrigues, though they are frequently together on stage; and again he uses contrasts in mood and personality in successive scenes, develop-

[1] Allen, *Sources of Dryden's Comedies*, 235–6.

ing thematic and episodical parallels among them. The heroic dimension of Jupiter's courtship of Alcmena is sustained by an eloquent blank verse appropriate to the king of the gods. Jupiter's lines represent Dryden's best vein of dramatic poetry, never bombastic, often ironic, and occasionally in the love scenes lyrical, expressing a tenderness undercut by our awareness of his true identity. Amphitryon sometimes speaks in blank verse, but not consistently and not with the eloquence the god can command. As in the tragicomedies Dryden turns from the verse of the heroic characters to a conversational prose when the lesser characters talk with the deflation of everyday life about their own affairs and the affairs of their betters. Phaedra returns us to a credible world when she ventures the opinion (III. i) that Amphitryon has picked a quarrel with Alcmena because she has drained him of sexual energy and he is ashamed to admit it. Phaedra, who has no parallel in Plautus or Molière, is a variant of the type figure of the coquette, more covetous and less libidinous than most of them, but still a character who can play a love game with Mercury in the manner of Dryden's earlier comic heroines. Mercury's courtship of her, in which he is aided by his supernatural powers and hindered by the physical appearance he has assumed, provides a humorous parallel to the main action, reinforcing the eroticism of it. Unlike Jupiter's relationship with Alcmena, Mercury's with Phaedra is to continue after play's end, under conditions specified in a celestial version of the Restoration 'proviso' (V. i). And Sosia's aversion to his wife and his reluctance to perform his husbandly duties, as well as his suspicion of Mercury, provides a contrast to the ardours and suspicions of his master Amphitryon.

Amphitryon's and Alcmena's sequence of experiences, as they are confused and troubled by Jupiter's intrusion into their lives, is not unlike that of the protagonists of the tragicomedies, who find themselves in difficult or desperate circumstances, which are then resolved in a final turn of unexpected events. Their plight is grave indeed, leading in fact to Amphitryon's threat (III. i) to divorce Alcmena. Yet the reader or spectator, informed from the beginning of the true relationships among the characters, cannot feel a concernment comparable to that evoked by the tragicomedies, partly because he is already informed that the troubles are transitory, and partly because the tragic potential of the situation is obscured by the cynical comments on it of the secondary characters. Dryden suggests though he does not emphasize the pathos latent in the predicament of Alcmena. 'A simple error is a real crime,' she says poignantly (V. i), 'And unconsenting innocence is lost.' If Dryden develops more fully than Plautus and Molière those possibilities which Alcmena's puzzlement presents for examining the ambiguities of emotion and even of knowledge based on personal experience, he yet stops short of such a full exposition of her doubts as that of Heinrich von Kleist in the early nineteenth century. Dryden resolves her problems—and Amphitryon's—with a reversion to classical myth when Jupiter offers such consolation as he can in his announcement that she will become the mother of Hercules. Mercury's response to the congratulations offered Amphitryon after Jupiter's announcement would seem to articulate Dryden's doubts about the nature of the divine favour granted: 'Keep your congratulations to yourselves, gentlemen. 'Tis a nice point, let me tell you that; and the less that's said of it the better. Upon the whole matter, if Amphitryon takes the favour of Jupiter in patience, as from a god, he's a good heathen.'[1]

Like Shakespeare in *The Comedy of Errors* at the beginning of his career, Dryden at the end of his own career turned to a play of Plautus. *Amphitryon* is his penultimate comedy, followed some four years later by *Love Triumphant*, which derives in part from Beaumont and Fletcher's *A King and No King*.[2] Although more influential than anyone else in establishing neoclassicism in England, Dryden retained his affinities—in the choice of literary sources, subjects, and dramatic forms—with his Renaissance masters. For this reason, perhaps, his comedies have often seemed to be apart from the main line of development in the Restoration. They are indeed different from the comedies of Etherege, Wycherley, and Congreve. Whether the best of them are inferior to the best written by Etherege and Wycherley, as Dryden implied in the Dedication of *Aureng-Zebe*, would seem to me to be an unanswerable question—or at least a question to which the answer

---

[1] In my interpretation of *Amphitryon*, I am much indebted to the editor of the present volume.

[2] Allen, *Sources of Dryden's Comedies*, 150.

would turn on preconceptions concerning human nature and the nature of comedy. Neoclassicism even today has not lost all its force in dramatic criticism, and we are still inclined to undervalue Dryden's plays because of his predilection for the mixed form of tragicomedy. If we can take them for what the best of them are, superb dramatic entertainments combining romantic adventure with acutely observed scenes from familiar life, and if we can suspend our neo-Aristotelian conceptions of what comedy should be, we are likely to think that he understated the claim for his own work.

3: Dryden and the Tradition of Serious Drama

EUGENE M. WAITH

IT HAS seemed easy in recent years to understand why Restoration audiences enjoyed the witty and licentious comedies of Etherege, Dryden, Wycherley, and others, for, we are apt to say, weren't the rakes and 'visard masks' in the audience precisely the kind of people presented on-stage? If they were, however, it has seemed very odd indeed that they patronized at the same time serious plays which upheld the most rigorous standards of conduct in love as in war. Serious drama in that period was never far from the heroic mode, and to some critics it is nearly incredible that heroic plays could have been tolerated—much less liked—by audiences then or at any time.[1] Yet literate Frenchmen and Englishmen in the seventeenth century not only attended heroic plays with pleasure but devoured at length the heroic romances of Madeleine de Scudéry, Gauthier de la Calprenède, and Lord Orrery.[2] Montague Summers, with characteristic panache, wrote that 'An essential preliminary for the consideration of the Heroic Play

---

[1] Thomas J. Fujimura has an excellent summary of the various formulations of this problem and of the main solutions offered in 'The Appeal of Dryden's Heroic Plays', *PMLA*, LXXV, 1960, 37–40. His own solution, a drastic one, is that the seeming ideals of love and honour represent, in fact, 'a passional commitment to sex and self-aggrandizement' (40). See Anne T. Barbeau's comments on Fujimura in her sensitive study, *The Intellectual Design of John Dryden's Heroic Plays*, New Haven and London 1970, 8.

[2] Among English readers Dorothy Osborne is especially interesting on this subject: see Dorothy McDougall, *Madeleine de Scudéry: Her Romantic Life and Death*, 1938, 121–30.

of the Restoration is an intimate knowledge of the Heroic Romance. He who has not read at least his *Polexandre, Cassandre, Cléopâtre,* and *Faramond,* his *Ibrahim, Artamène, Clélie* and *Almahide,* whether in the original or in the English translations, to which the dramatists so often turned, is simply neither equipped nor competent to write upon the Restoration theatre.'[1] And he went on to hint at his own equipping in 'some old-world garden' or 'at a winter fireside'. Given the exhausting length of the works he mentions, it is his 'at least' which is most crushing to the unequipped. Yet there can be no doubt that, however overstated, Montague Summers' case has merit. Dryden drew heavily upon these romances in his plays, and an understanding of both his comedies and his serious drama is increased by even a slight familiarity with a few of the works on that formidable list.

The appeal of heroic romance (and of heroic drama) to Dryden and his contemporaries can be explained in several ways. Whether or not ladies and gentlemen in the Restoration period were, as we like to think, similar to the characters in contemporary comedy—and whether or not they behaved unheroically in private life—the better educated among them shared the veneration of the classics which seventeenth-century scholars inherited from their humanist predecessors; the authority of Aristotle, as Baxter Hathaway reminds us, was 'gaining rather than losing strength'.[2] To one brought up on the classics the claims of the heroic could never be weak. What seems more strange today is that a love of Homer and Virgil might lead to a love of La Calprenède; yet we know that Dryden, in giving the literary ancestry of his hero, Almanzor, names Homer's Achilles, Tasso's Rinaldo, and La Calprenède's Artaban.[3] As the heroic tradition had previously broadened to

---

[1] *Dryden: The Dramatic Works,* ed. Montague Summers, 6 vol 1931–32, I, xl.

[2] 'John Dryden and the Function of Tragedy,' *PMLA,* LVIII, 1943, 665.

[3] Watson, I 163. George R. Noyes writes: '. . . the heroic plays were fundamentally romantic in tone. It would be hard to frame a definition of romanticism that should include *Marmion* and exclude *The Conquest of Granada*': *The Poetical Works of Dryden,* 2nd ed Cambridge, Mass. 1950, xxv.

include the great knights of medieval romance, so it now accommodated
with equal ease the heroes of contemporary romance, who, in certain
respects, were an amalgamation of classical and medieval types. To
relish the latest romance was to be fashionable, but in a very conservative way.

The fashion had roots that were not entirely literary, however. The
chief writers of romances were *précieux* and *précieuses*, whose taste had
been formed in the famous 'Chambre Bleue' of the Marquise de Rambouillet. That *préciosité*, hilariously mocked by Molière for its later
excesses, was initially a serious and largely successful movement for
the refinement of both manners and letters is now well known, thanks
to the work of many French scholars.[1] As the great evils to be avoided
were boorishness and insensitivity, both moral and aesthetic, so the
ideals to which the *précieux* aspired included a standard of behaviour
and an intellectual and artistic cultivation not far removed from the requirements of Castiglione's courtier. The concept of the gentleman in
England, admirably described by Ruth Kelso, was closely related to the
ideals of sixteenth-century Italy and seventeenth-century France,
though Elizabethan formulations gave less importance to courtesy.[2] By
Dryden's time, thanks largely to the importation of *précieux* ideals, this
outward manifestation of inner nobility had been added, so that conduct becoming a gentleman implied some of the polish for which the
French were famous. That the splendid heroes of the French romances
both spoke and demeaned themselves like highly cultivated gentlemen was part of their attraction.

By a strange irony, the term *honnête homme*, used to designate the
urbane product of the best French society, came by the latter half of
the century to mean a man whose politeness was no guarantee of his
morals—a rake, it might be, with excellent manners. Such a man was, of
course, a perversion of the *précieux* ideal, but even allowing for the

[1] See, for example, René Bray, *La Préciosité et les précieux*, Paris 1960;
orig. 1948; J.-E. Fidao-Justiniani, *L'Esprit classique et la préciosité*,
Paris 1914.
[2] *The Doctrine of the English Gentleman in the Sixteenth Century*, University of Illinois Studies in Language and Literature XIV, Urbana,
Ill. 1929.

perversion, one must recognize the idealistic basis of the respect for politeness as an indication of humanity and consideration. 'Ein Mensch ist kein Tier,' as one of Brecht's characters remarks in an even more ironical context.

The emphasis on courtesy in seventeenth-century France serves to remind us of the persistent influence of the chivalric romances, in which we hear courtesy praised almost as often as bravery. A surprising number of characteristics of the heroes of those romances continued to be the *desiderata* for the ideal man in both France and England and, all the more, for their fictional representations. In addition to valour and courtesy the seventeenth-century hero, like his medieval forebear, was expected to be loyal and honourable, desirous of glory, capable of an idealized love, liberal, and, most important of all, great-minded.

The pastoral romance which became the bible of the *précieux*, Honoré d'Urfé's *L'Astrée* (1608–24), presented innumerable exemplary instances of all these virtues and directly inspired the prolific Madeleine de Scudéry, whose romances appeared, instalment after instalment, throughout the middle twenty years of the century. Her models, she wrote in the address to the reader in *Artamène, ou le Grand Cyrus* (1649), were Heliodorus and 'le grand Urfé', whose way was the only one to arrive where one wanted to go: 'à la Gloire' (sig. i4ᵛ). In the light of such testimony it appears that Jacques Debu-Bridel was guilty of only slight exaggeration when he entitled an article, 'La Préciosité: conception héroïque de la vie'.[1] With the longing for elegant conversation in the salons went a desire to ennoble life.

To suggest that English readers of romances and the spectators in the English theatre shared this desire is to risk, once again, the incredulity of those who believe that Restoration society was invincibly frivolous. Yet there is evidence in the literary and dramatic traditions of the day that heroic premises were acceptable in several different forms. Panegyric poetry, for example, properly described by Ruth Nevo as 'a species of heroic poetry',[2] was written by some of the best

[1] *Revue de France*, XVIII, 1938, 195–216.
[2] *The Dial of Virtue*, Princeton, N.J. 1963, 27.

poets of the period. Despite the obvious risks in speculating about how readers 'must have' responded to anything, it is probably safe to say that no one thought of taking literally the sort of compliments found in some of Denham's and Cowley's poetry, where the king is made a hero, if not a god (Nevo, 28ff.). On the other hand, there was a sense in which the king—not James or Charles, but the king as vicegerent of God in traditional belief—belonged in the company of heroes and gods. Extravagant praise of him might, therefore, function in more than one way. It might, certainly, call attention to the discrepancy between the actual and the ideal, in which case it would function as a kind of satire. But it might be interpreted as encouraging him to be more like the ideal image of himself, or as building a kind of temporary bridge from the actual to the ideal, asserting the possibility that such nobility might be achieved. To Davenant and Hobbes one of the chief purposes of heroic poetry was to inspire and reform rulers.[1]

In the masques performed at the courts of James I and Charles I courtly compliment assumed an even more striking form. James, enthroned in the middle of the hall, was repeatedly addressed from the stage by his own name or as Arthur, Albion, or Neptune, and was made the ultimate source of the harmony with which every masque ended. Charles was similarly glorified, but, unlike his father, also participated in some of the masques, appearing as 'Philogenes', the lover of his people, or as the British Hercules. On these occasions the sovereign, as well as many of the nobility of both sexes, assumed roles which were often heroic. Though the authors of the masques wisely relieved the noble masquers of the duty of memorizing lines, and hence of 'acting' in the fullest sense of the word, the court was provided with the most vivid images of familiar persons momentarily transformed into heroes and gods. In France, where such things were done in an even grander manner, the sun-king was eulogized in Corneille's spectacular *Andromède* by the sun himself, who was persuaded by the Muse of tragedy to

[1] See Sir William Davenant, Preface to *Gondibert* in *Critical Essays of the Seventeenth Century*, ed. J. E. Spingarn, 3 vol Bloomington, Ind. 1957; orig. 1908, II, 14, 45; Thomas Hobbes, 'Answer to Davenant's Preface', Spingarn, II, 54–55.

arrest his chariot in mid-flight in order to contemplate the miracle that was Louis XIV.

Somewhat analogous transformations and impersonations occurred in the social world of the French salons. By the magic of an anagram Catherine de Vivonne, the Marquise de Rambouillet, became Arthénice to some of her friends, and in *Le Grand Cyrus* she was recognized as a Persian lady, Cléomire, while the Prince de Condé was Cyrus himself, and the author appeared as the poetess Sappho. To unfriendly critics the affectation of such names, the self-delusion of such roles, was merely ridiculous, but for those in the circle it was a pleasant game not unrelated to their programme of ennobling life.

In the dedication of *Le Grand Cyrus* to the Duchesse de Longueville that lady is given as idealized a character as Mlle de Scudéry gives her in the romance itself in the person of the heroine, Mandane. In a very similar way Dryden idealizes those to whom he dedicates his heroic plays, placing them in the world of his heroes, and in one notable instance, the dedication of *The Conquest of Granada*, claiming his patron as the inspiration of his play. Though it may be hard to recognize the future James II in this portrayal of a heroic figure, it is easy to accept the proposition that such an ideal prince is both the model for future heroes of fiction and, as Davenant and Hobbes believed, the imitator of past heroes.[1] Dryden's eulogy of the then Duke of York is altogether pertinent to the relationship between heroic drama and those for whom it was written:

Heroic poesy has always been sacred to princes, and to heroes. Thus Virgil inscrib'd his *Aeneids* to Augustus Caesar; and, of latter ages, Tasso and Ariosto dedicated their poems to the house of Este. 'Tis, indeed, but justice that the most excellent and most profitable kind of writing should be address'd by poets to such persons whose characters have, for the most part, been the guides and patterns of their imitation. And poets, while they imitate, instruct. The feign'd hero inflames the true, and the dead virtue animates the living. Since, therefore, the world is govern'd by precept and example, and both these can only have influence from

---

[1] See my discussion of Dryden's dedications in 'The Voice of Mr Bayes', *Studies in English Literature*, III, 1963, 335–43.

those persons who are above us; that kind of poesy which excites to virtue the greatest men is of greatest use to humankind.

'Tis from this consideration that I have presum'd to dedicate to your Royal Highness these faint representations of your own worth and valor in heroic poetry.[1]

Dryden extends the compliment to his audience in the Epilogue to *The Conquest of Granada*, where he vaunts the superiority of the plays of that day to those of the preceding era:

> *If love and honor now are higher rais'd,*
> *'Tis not the poet, but the age is prais'd.*
> *Wit's now arriv'd to a more high degree;*
> *Our native language more refin'd and free.*   (ll. 21–24)

Dryden's interest, and that of his contemporaries, in the heroic world of serious drama is not alien to their other literary concerns or to their view of themselves as gentlemen living in a witty, civilized society. If there were any doubt that Dryden's high opinion of heroic poetry remained constant throughout his life, one need only turn to the first sentence of the dedication of his translation of the *Aeneid*, published three years before his death: 'A heroic poem, truly such, is undoubtedly the greatest work which the soul of man is capable to perform' (Watson II 223). John Heath-Stubbs says, 'it is to the ideal of Epic or Heroic verse (in his age the two terms were synonymous) that, I think, all his work really points'.[2] It is not surprising, then, that all his serious drama is tinged with the heroic.

Some will question whether he was ever seriously interested in the drama. Admirers of Dryden who are unsympathetic to his plays like to remind us that Dryden wrote them only to make money. There are

1 *Selected Dramas of John Dryden*, ed. George R. Noyes, Chicago and New York 1910, 3; all quotations from *The Conquest of Granada* are taken from this edition; quotations from the text of the play are from Part I unless otherwise noted.

2 'Dryden and the Heroic Ideal', in *Dryden's Mind and Art*, ed. Bruce King, Edinburgh, 1969: New York 1970, 3. See H. T. Swedenberg's important article, 'Dryden's Obsessive Concern with the Heroic' in *Essays in English Literature of the Classical Period . . .*, ed. D. W. Patterson and A. B. Strauss, *Studies in Philology* Extra Series 4, 1967, 12–26.

several well-known comments that can be cited to support this view of a reluctant play-wright, notably one from 'A Parallel of Poetry and Painting' (1695), where he says that *All for Love* was the only play he wrote for himself (Watson, II 207). Even in the dedication of *Aureng-Zebe* (1675), when he was at the height of his success as a playwright, he protests his unfitness for this employment and wishes he had time to write an epic instead.[1] In the dedication of *The Spanish Fryar* (1681) he repents of his stylistic excesses in *Tyrannic Love* and *The Conquest of Granada* (Watson, I 276), and in the Preface to *Don Sebastian* (1690) complains wearily of the necessity of returning, once again, to the stage (11. 17–18, 34–36).[2] Though there is no reason to doubt Dryden's sincerity in these comments, there is no way of knowing whether he felt equally unenthusiastic during the composition of each of his more than twenty plays, in many of which there are extended passages of characteristically vigorous writing. Certainly the essay *Of Dramatick Poesie* and the prefaces to the plays testify to his continuous absorption in the problems of dramatic composition. The important questions to ask are how well Dryden succeeded, having, for whatever reasons, decided to write drama, and what were the distinctive qualities of the drama he wrote. After all, even Shakespeare, according to Pope, wrote 'for gain, not glory'. Dryden's occasional blasts at the theatre and even his acts of contrition should not deter us from a careful consideration of work which bulks so large in his writing career, and to which he devoted so much of his criticism.

At the core of the heroic ethos, informing alike epic and romance, was an admiration for the greatness of mind or soul of which man is capable. Corneille refers to the 'grandeur d'âme' of his heroes, whose pursuit of 'la gloire' is well known.[3] Called in English by many names, of which

---

[1] *Aureng-Zebe*, ed. Frederick M. Link, Lincoln, Neb. 1971, 9; all quotations from the play are taken from this edition.

[2] *John Dryden: Four Tragedies*, ed. L. A. Beaurline and Fredson Bowers, Chicago and London 1967, 285; all quotations from *Don Sebastian* are taken from this edition.

[3] See Arthur Kirsch's illuminating comments on Corneille and Dryden in *Dryden's Heroic Drama*, Princeton, N.J. 1965, 46–65; also my *Ideas of Greatness*, 1971, 177–93.

'magnanimity' was one of the commonest, the concept was so elastic that it was stretched to cover ethical positions which may at first seem quite unrelated. Frequently magnanimity was seen as a kind of fortitude, the basic ingredient of primitive heroism, as in this definition published in 1595:

> Now then, Magnanimitie is a certaine excellencie of courage, which aiming at honour, directeth all his doings thervnto, and specially vnto vertue, as the thing that is esteemed the efficient cause of honour; in respect wherof, it doth all things that are vertuous and honourable with a braue and excellent courage, and differeth from valiantnesse or prowesse, in that prowesse respecteth chiefly the perils of warre, and magnanimitie respecteth honour.[1]

This sort of magnanimity is precisely the virtue Abdalla, in *The Conquest of Granada*, ascribes to Almanzor:

> *This, sir, is he who for the elder fought,*
> *And to the juster cause the conquest brought;*
> *Till the proud Santo, seated in the throne,*
> *Disdain'd the service he had done to own:*
> *Then to the vanquish'd part his fate he led;*
> *The vanquish'd triumph'd, and the victor fled.*
> *Vast is his courage, boundless is his mind,*
> *Rough as a storm, and humorous as wind:*
> *Honor's the only idol of his eyes;*
> *The charms of beauty like a pest he flies;*
> *And, rais'd by valor from a birth unknown,*
> *Acknowledges no pow'r above his own.* (I 247–58)

'Magnanimity' also designated a much more self-effacing greatness, however, as can be seen in a work published in 1586. Here, though magnanimity is related to fortitude, it is a distinct quality, defined as 'generositie or noblenes of hart,' of which it is said:

> We learne that this vertue maketh him that possesseth hir, good, gentle, and curteous, euen towards his greatest enimies, against

---

1 Jaques Hurault, *Politicke, Moral, and Martial Discourses*, tr. Arthur Golding, 1595, 287.

whom it suffereth him not to vse any couin or malice . . . causing him further to make choice of and to finish all honest matters
of his owne will, and for their loue, not caring at all for mortall and
corruptible things, that he may wholy apprehend and take hold of
those things that are diuine and eternall.[1]

When the hero of *Don Sebastian* takes part of the blame for the rebellion of his officer, Dorax, his magnanimity, in this sense, over-
whelms the offender, who protests: 'O stop this headlong Torrent of
your goodness' (IV. ii, 906). A moving scene of mutual forgiveness
follows. Such 'generositie or noblenes of hart' is a more spiritual kind
of greatness than Almanzor's valiant aid to the defeated, occasioned by
the 'proud Santo's' disdain. The ending of *Don Sebastian* confirms the
impression of a spiritual greatness. Don Sebastian, having discovered
that he has unwittingly married his half-sister, renounces his wife and
his kingdom, and plans his withdrawal from the world to a 'Solitary
cell'. 'O Truly great!' Dorax comments, and even Muley-Zeydan, the
Moorish king, is moved to tears, 'not squeez'd by Art, / But shed from
nature' (V. i, 555ff., 659–661). Don Sebastian's withdrawal is made to
seem the moral victory of one who has risen above considerations of
self.

These glimpses of the courageous, proud Almanzor and of the generous, compassionate, self-abnegating Sebastian may serve to indicate the
range of Dryden's depiction of heroic greatness. In the early examples
of his serious drama the emphasis falls on the more self-assertive kind,
carried, in at least one instance, to the point of truly evil megalomania.
In the later plays the emphasis shifts to generosity and transcendence.
Both kinds of greatness are present, however, in early and late plays.
The Indian Emperor, the first heroic play of Dryden's unaided composition, ends with the departure of Guyomar, an important secondary
character, into the wilds beyond the mountains, away from the part of
Mexico conquered by the Spaniards. At the end of *Tyrannic Love*
Porphyrius declines the offer of the imperial throne to live in retire-
ment with Berenice. And just as these motifs of renunciation are soun-

[1] Pierre de la Primaudaye, *The French Academy*, tr. Thomas Beard, 1586,
289, 298.

ded in plays where the dominant tone is heroic self-assertion, so in
Don Sebastian, which ends on so pathetic a note, there are, earlier
numerous echoes of Almanzor's exuberance in the behaviour of the
rebellious Dorax. The changing emphasis reflects a gradual shift o
sensibility during Dryden's long career and also, perhaps, some of the
changes in his personal life.

Although *The Indian Queen*, of 1663/4, presenting in rhymed coup
lets the trials and triumphs of Montezuma, was, as the editors of the
California Dryden state, 'the first fully formed heroic play to be acted
in London',[1] Dryden and his brother-in-law, Sir Robert Howard, with
whom he collaborated, cannot be called the inventors of the form
however it is defined. Even if the term is restricted to plays written in
heroic couplets, an earlier example exists in the Earl of Orrery's *Alte
mira* or *The General* (both titles were used), written in 1661 and per
formed in Dublin in 1662, though not in London till after *The India
Queen*. If the term is used more loosely, Davenant's 'opera', *The Sieg
of Rhodes*, put on in 1656 and again, in an augmented version, in 1661
may be cited, remembering that Dryden, in his essay, 'Of Heroi
Plays', published with *The Conquest of Granada*, said: 'For heroic play
. . . the first light we had of them on the English theatre was from th
late Sir William Davenant' (Watson, I 157). But there were precedent
for the kind of drama Dryden and Howard were attempting long be
fore *The Siege of Rhodes*. The king and his court, during their exile, ha
been favourably impressed by French serious drama, which was heroi
in theme and written in rhyming couplets. The most distinguished ex
amples prior to 1660 were the brilliant plays of Corneille, glorifyin
that 'grandeur d'âme' which he considered the most essential quality o
the tragic hero. In England certain heroes of Marlowe's and Chapman'
were conspicuous examples of extraordinary greatness, and Beaumon

---

[1] *The Works of John Dryden*, Berkeley and Los Angeles 1956–   , VIII
283; the Commentary on *The Indian Queen* in this volume contains an
excellent brief account of the origins of the Restoration heroic play
(284-9). See also my *Ideas of Greatness* and other works on this subject
listed in the Bibliography. All quotations from *The Indian Queen, The
Indian Emperor*, and *Tyrannic Love* are taken from the volumes of this
as yet incomplete edition.

and Fletcher had promulgated a fashionably heroic ethos derived from romance, borrowing in two instances from d'Urfé, the idol of the *précieux*. In the reign of Charles I several playwrights closely associated with the court had continued to mine the vein of heroic romance, giving ever more space to the presentation of the ideal love portrayed by d'Urfé and his imitators.[1]

Influenced to some extent by these earlier plays, French and English, and taking most of their plot from three French romances (*Works*, VIII, 289), Dryden and Howard composed their play, which was an instant success.[2] It was adorned with painted scenery, a novelty in the English theatre, and the heroine was adorned with 'wreaths' of feathers brought from Surinam by Aphra Behn. The action, in the exotic setting of Mexico, had enough surprising reversals and nice dilemmas to test the most heroic mettle. And beyond these superficial attractions the play had more solid dramatic virtues in its two principal characters, Zempoalla, the 'Indian Queen', and Montezuma—roles which were brilliantly conceived and interestingly juxtaposed. The usurping queen, torn by the conflict between her boundless ambition and her unreciprocated love for Montezuma, is given ample opportunity to display her fiery nature, although the poetic force of her lines is rarely adequate to the occasion. Too seldom is she allowed to express her lively contempt for virtue in such a couplet as:

> *Honor is but an itch in youthful blood,*
> *Of doing acts extravagantly good.*　　(III. i, 96–97)

---

[1] See Alfred Harbage, *Cavalier Drama*, New York 1964; orig. 1936, 7–71. On English heroic drama before the Restoration see my *Ideas of Greatness*, 35–176 and *The Herculèan Hero*, London and New York 1962, 60–151.

[2] There is no general agreement about the division of labour between them. Harold J. Oliver argues powerfully that Howard should be given the principal share of the credit: *Sir Robert Howard*, Durham, N.C. 1963, 61–79; but the resemblance of the play in regard to characterization and design to Dryden's later plays, as well as its dissimilarity to other Howard plays, inclines me to agree with the editors of the California Dryden, (VIII, 283, 284, 298) that the shaping force was mainly Dryden's.

Though Montezuma repels her advances and remains faithful to the virtuous heroine, he is not himself a model of virtue in all respects. He is introduced in a situation which anticipates the opening of *The Conquest of Granada* and delineates in a few strokes a variety of heroic character which appealed strongly to Dryden. Like the hero of romance on whom he is modelled, Montezuma is initially presented as an invincible warrior of unknown origins—a mysterious stranger who brings victory to whomever he befriends. Having helped the Peruvian Inca to defeat Zempoalla's Mexicans, he is shown in the first scene deserting to the other side when the Inca refuses to give him his daughter. The more strictly virtuous characters, though they admire Montezuma, are critical of his 'wilde distempers' and unreasonable rages, likening his mind to a limitless sea (I. i, 59–62, 66–67). His heroic greatness is unquestioned, but like Hercules or Achilles, he is more courageous than forgiving, more concerned with personal honour than the common good.

The arrangement of characters which defines this greatness by a series of contrasts between Montezuma and more conventionally virtuous characters as well as more obviously wicked ones is typical of Dryden's plays. Not only does it add to the interest of each situation in which these characters appear, but it sets up a dialectic which justifies Anne T. Barbèau in discussing the heroic plays as 'plays of ideas', where the political and philosophical theories of his time are dramatized.[1] In the best plays the schematization is not so rigid as to destroy the illusion that the characters are independent beings, though it is sufficiently firm to impose on the plot a coherent pattern of meaning.

In the early plays the schemes do not always function as they should. In *The Indian Emperor* (1665), Dryden's sequel to *The Indian Queen*, the proliferation of contrasting characters is such that in reading it, one is driven to making diagrams to keep the relationships in mind. Zempoalla, now dead, has had a son and two daughters who are involved romantically, but in most cases unsatisfactorily, with Montezuma, his

---

[1] *Intellectual Design*, 3–23; L. T. Beaurline says very well that a 'sense of impassioned design' informs most of Dryden's serious plays: *Four Tragedies*, 4.

two sons, and his daughter. When Cortez arrives on the scene one further complication is added. Since the Indians are warring amongst themselves as well as against the Spaniards, the mismatching of lovers is paralleled by complexity in the political situation. Dryden's manipulations, while they result in several effective scenes, are a little too obviously clever.

In *Tyrannic Love*, the story of the martyrdom of St Catherine of Alexandria by the Emperor Maximin (1669), the scheme fails in a different way. Dryden's intention, as he says in the preface, was to make his wicked tyrant a foil 'to set off the Character of S. Catherine' (ll. 8–9), but the ranting Maximin, madly defying heaven, is the character everyone remembers:

> *But by the Gods, (by* Maximin, *I meant)*
> *Henceforth I and my World*
> *Hostility with you and yours declare:*
> *Look to it, Gods; for you th'Agressors are.*
> *Keep you your Rain and Sun-shine in your Skies,*
> *And I'le keep back my flame and Sacrifice.*
> *Your trade of Heav'n shall soon be at a stand,*
> *And all your Goods lie dead upon your hand.*

Compared to this sort of talk, the quietly-reasonable arguments of St Catherine for Christianity are pallid.

That Maximin's extravagance sometimes borders on absurdity may be, not miscalculation, but evidence that, as D. W. Jefferson puts it, 'heroic virtuosity is an idea to be played with; an opportunity for poetry, but also an opportunity for wit'.[1] There are similar passages in both *The Conquest of Granada* and *Aureng-Zebe*, one of which prompted Colley Cibber's frequently-quoted observation that the poet doubtless in-

---

[1] 'The significance of Dryden's Heroic Plays', in *Restoration Dramatists*, ed. Earl Miner, Englewood Cliffs, N.J. 1966, 27. See also Miner's introduction, 13–14, and his comment on Dryden's capacity for laughing at himself in *Dryden's Poetry*, Bloomington and London 1967, 104. I cannot accept all of Jefferson's conclusions nor Bruce King's more radical contention in *Dryden's Major Plays*, New York 1966, that the heroic plays are to be taken as satires.

tended such extravagances 'to make his Spectators laugh, while they admir'd them'.[1] If the bravura performance of a Dryden hero cannot always be taken quite seriously, neither is it ever purely a laughing matter. In a somewhat analogous way royal panegyric in a poem or a masque is neither to be wholly believed or disbelieved.

Moves back and forth along the paths that lead to belief and disbelief, to laughter and what Dryden called 'concernment', are most obviously called for in plays such as *Secret Love, or the Maiden Queen* (1667), where Dryden, possibly following the example of Etherege in *The Comical Revenge, or Love in a Tub* (1664), pairs a comic plot concerning the witty lovers, Celadon and Florimell, with a heroic-romantic plot in which a queen, in love with one of her subjects, allows him to marry the woman he loves. The sincerity and strength of the queen's love and the nobility of her renunciation are not diminished by the licentious badinage of the comic plot even when it wittily parallels the dialogue of the serious plot. But neither does the cynicism of Jaques and Touchstone destroy romantic values in the Forest of Arden, nor does Shakespeare's Sonnet 130, beginning 'My mistress' eyes are nothing like the sun', make the Petrarchan conventions in some of the other sonnets unacceptable. So obvious a point is worth making only because of the frequent assertion that heroic ideals are especially vulnerable to the attack of laughter. A more persuasive argument is that they are made less vulnerable when the author provides an outlet for the laughter that heroic excesses may provoke. The symbiotic relationship of libertine comedy and heroic romance is demonstrated in Madeleine de Scudéry's *Le Grand Cyrus*, from which Dryden took both the serious plot (intended by the authoress to refer to Queen Christina of Sweden) and most of the comic plot, borrowing additional material for this from 'The Story of the French Marquis' in another of her romances, *Ibrahim, ou l'Illustre Bassa*.[2] In her preface to *Ibrahim* Mlle de Scudéry

[1] *An Apology for the Life of Colley Cibber*, ed. B. R. S. Fone, Ann Arbor, Mich. 1968, 72.

[2] I am indebted to Ned Bliss Allen's careful analysis of Dryden's sources and of his use of them in *The Sources of John Dryden's Comedies*, University of Michigan Publications, Language and Literature XVI, Ann Arbor, Mich. 1935, 74–99. See also Beaurline's perceptive comments in

justifies the levity of this story by reminding her readers 'that a Romanze ought to have the images of all natures'.[1] D'Urfé, whom she admired on this side idolatry, had similarly included in his pastoral romance the libertine Hylas, who scoffs at romantic ideals. Dryden's combination in *Secret Love*, and later in *Marriage a-la-Mode* (1671), followed the main line of heroic romance.

The Conquest of Granada, the first part of which was performed at the end of 1670, and the second part early in 1671, is the first of the four plays on which Dryden's reputation as a writer of serious drama chiefly rests.[2] After his excursion into Roman history in *Tyrannic Love* he turned to Spanish history, radically modified by stories borrowed from French romance, and gave himself the scope of ten acts, the better to achieve variety, a feature of romance which was generally admired. From a letter written by Mrs John Evelyn we know how one spectator at least responded to the romantic ethos:

'Since my last to you I have seen 'The Siege of Granada,' a play so full of ideas that the most refined romance I ever read is not to compare with it; love is made so pure, and valour so nice, that one would image it designed for an Utopia rather than our stage. I do not quarrel with the poet, but admire one born in the decline of morality should be able to feign such exact virtue; and as poetic fiction has been instructive in former ages, I wish this the same event in ours.'[3]

Her delight in the ideals of the play, remote as they seem 'in the de-

the General Introduction to *John Dryden: Four Comedies*, ed. L. A. Beaurline and Fredson Bowers, Chicago and London 1967, 1–16, and in the introduction to *Secret Love*, 25–30.

[1] *Ibrahim*, tr. Henry Cogan, 1652, sig. A4ᵛ. All quotations from *Ibrahim* are taken from this translation.

[2] The others being *Aureng-Zebe, All for Love*, and *Don Sebastian*. I have discussed the first three in *The Herculean Hero*, 152–201, and all of Dryden's serious plays in *Ideas of Greatness*, 203–35, 253–64. See the excellent discussions of the serious plays through *All for Love* in Kirsch, *Dryden's Heroic Drama*, and of those through *Aureng-Zebe* in Barbeau, *Intellectual Design*.

[3] Quoted in *The London Stage 1660–1800, Part I: 1660–1700*, ed. W. Van Lennep, Carbondale Ill. 1965, 177, 180.

cline of morality', is striking, as is the resemblance of her views on instruction to those of Davenant and Hobbes.

The play opens at the court of the Moorish King Boabdelin with a seemingly gratuitous account by the chieftains present of a bullfight held earlier that day, in which a 'stranger', 'a brave unknown', had surpassed even the best of the Moors. This stranger, modelled, like Montezuma in *The Indian Queen*, on the Artaban of La Calprenède's *Cléopâtre*, is, of course, the hero, Almanzor, who is made to seem a creature from another world. Dryden's strategy in this opening becomes clear in the description of Almanzor's encounter with the bull, itself a noble creature, which ranges the bull-ring 'monarch-like', an almost mythical embodiment of untrammelled force. Almanzor's victory over the bull is similar to the slaying of a dragon, by which the prowess of a knight of romance may be revealed.

No sooner is the description completed than the action of the play begins with a battle between two Moorish factions, the Zegrys and the Abencerrages, in the midst of which the stranger arrives, sees that the Abencerrages are losing, and soon kills one of the Zegry leaders. When the king, taking up the Zegry cause, condemns him to death he delivers the most famous lines in the play:

> *No man has more contempt than I of breath,*
> *But whence hast thou the right to give me death?*
> *Obey'd as sovereign by thy subjects be,*
> *But know that I alone am king of me.*
> *I am as free as nature first made man,*
> *Ere the base laws of servitude began,*
> *When wild in woods the noble savage ran.*   (I. 200–9)

The suggestions of a Golden Age add another mythic dimension to the hero, who, up to this point, has not been named. Only now, as the petulant Boabdelin is about to carry out his threat, does his brother enter to reveal that Almanzor is the warrior of fabulous valour, whose assistance he has enlisted against the Spanish besiegers. He then gives the description, already quoted, of Almanzor's vast courage and boundless mind. In no play does Dryden contrive a more effective initial presentation of the hero.

In the essay 'Of Heroic Plays' which he prefixed to the first edition Dryden not only names the literary ancestors of Almanzor but states his preference for a hero who is not perfectly virtuous and not totally committed to 'the point of honour, so much magnified by the French, and so ridiculously aped by us' (Watson, I 164). Despite his large debt to the French, he is wary of over-refinement, and believes that he is following Homer and Tasso in showing 'what men of great spirits would certainly do when they were provoked, not what they were obliged to do by the strict rules of moral virtue' (*ibid.* 164–5). Not that he is uninterested in exemplary characters, for he challenges comparison with the French in his depiction of 'the patterns of exact virtues, such as in this play are the parts of Almahide, of Ozmyn, and Benzayda' (*ibid.* 165).

Almahide, contracted to Boabdelin when Almanzor meets her, becomes instantly the object of his first love. We have been told that 'the charms of beauty like a pest he flies' (I 256), and it is as a pest that he describes her even in his first rapture:

> *I'm pleas'd and pain'd, since first her eyes I saw,*
> *As I were stung with some tarantula.*   (III. 328–9)

But despite this comical bit of self-analysis, there is no doubt in his mind or ours that his love for Almahide is the genuine heroic article, which will largely determine the remainder of his career. In the scheme of the play, as it unfolds after this point, Almahide's influence upon Almanzor is the thematic centre. She first persuades him to accept her fidelity to Boabdelin (V. iii, 212–323). Later, a message from her determines him to fight for Granada and for her husband rather than for himself and his personal honour, when, like Achilles, he is sulking in exile (Part II, II. iii, 1–10).

From this moral platform he is guided to his final position by a supernatural agent, providing the 'enthusiastic parts of poetry' which Dryden defended as among the greatest beauties of heroic poetry (Watson, I 160–1). From his mother's ghost Almanzor discovers his identity as the son of the Spanish general, the Duke of Arcos, and when the continued feuding of the Moorish factions has led to the death of Boabdelin and a Spanish victory, the way is cleared for Almanzor to pledge his allegiance to King Ferdinand and receive the promise of Almahide's hand. Ferdinand, a somewhat shadowy figure in the play, is presented as an ideal king, opposed to the vacillating and passionate Boabdelin. Isabella is a patroness of heroic love (Part II, I. i, 145–54). Both of them represent Christianity, into which, as it now appears, Almanzor was born, and to which Almahide is converted. Thus, with the sanction of religion, the political order coincides with the order of love.

Although Almanzor's achievement of true love appears to coincide with the acknowledgment of powers, both divine and political, 'beyond his own', neither his development nor the definition of true love is made simple. Various sorts of love and ambition in the play are distinguished one from another with some subtlety. That love cannot be equated with unthinking obedience is shown by the effect Almanzor has upon Almahide, balancing, to some extent, hers upon him. She learns to admire in him an energy and independence (V. iii, 198–211) which he does not completely renounce even at the end, telling Ferdinand, in effect, that kingliness is a bond between them:

> *I bring a heart which homage never knew;*
> *Yet it finds something of itself in you:*
> *Something so kingly that my haughty mind*
> *Is drawn to yours, because 'tis of a kind.*
>
> (Part II. V. iv, 153–6)

Almahide, Ferdinand, and providence in one sense shape Almanzor's career, but in another sense, they merely help him to find himself.

What he is and is not becomes clearer through contrast with another sort of love and ambition in Lyndaraxa, whose Hobbesian pursuit of power makes her a faithless lover and an unscrupulous schemer. Her very determination to free herself from all restraints and reach the top by any means offered finally subjects her all the more completely to the caprice of fortune. When she attempts to make use of Almanzor by undermining his devotion to Almahide, the limits of his irregularity are defined by his firm refusal (Part II, III. iii, 59–182).

If Almanzor, in spite of his indubitable development, is most often remembered for that sort of magnanimity called 'a certain excellencie of courage', Ozmyn and Benzayda are characterized from the start by the other sort—the 'generositie or noblenes of hart', which Almanzor occasionally displays. Son and daughter of rival chieftains, these two lovers seem at first to be as star-crossed as Romeo and Juliet. The pattern of their misfortunes is set by a story used by the rhetorician, Seneca the Elder, father of the philosopher, as the basis for an exercise in forensic oratory—the *controversia*. In the case with the mellifluous title, 'Archipiratae filia', the daughter of a pirate chief frees one of her father's captives on condition that he will marry her, but the young man's father threatens to disinherit him if he marries a girl who has proved her unreliability by betraying her father's trust. Student orators were to devise speeches in favour of the marriage or against it.[1] Fletcher and Massinger combine this with another *controversia* to make a tragedy, *The Double Marriage*, distinguished by its extraordinary dilemmas and by the ingenuity with which each person argues for his position. Madeleine de Scudéry, coming upon this story, if not in Seneca, then possibly in a French collection called *Epitomes de cent histoires tragicques* by Alexandre van den Busche (Paris 1581), where it is Epitome 48, makes out of it 'The History of Osman and Alibech' in *Ibrahim* (Part I, Bk. I, 5–13 and Part IV, Bk. IV, 194–204), from which Dryden derives his subplot. For Mlle de Scudéry the agonizing situation of the young lovers becomes the occasion, not for ingenious argument, but the display of signal generosity. Alibech, with tears in her eyes, begs Osman to obey his father, but Soliman, before whom they are pleading their cases, is so 'touched with the pitty of such tender apprehensions' (13) that he gives Alibech a magnificent dowry, which immediately silences the objections of Osman's father. Another ordeal follows, however, when Alibech's pirate-father captures Osman's father, and demands his own daughter as ransom. Osman's father refuses to ask Alibech to return, and both Osman and Alibech offer themselves to her father to rescue his prisoner. Just when the old pirate has them all in his power, the spectacle of so much generosity proves too much for him,

[1] *Controversiae*, I, 6; see *Controverses et suasoires*, ed. Henri Bornecque, Paris 1932.

and with reason and nature 'both of a side' (204), he is moved with compassion. A tearful reconciliation ends the tale.

In *The Conquest of Granada* the fortunes of war put the young lovers at the mercy of first one father and then the other. In the final situation Ozmyn's father is the one who has the other three in his power, and is overcome by their nobility:

> 'Twas long before my stubborn mind was won;
> But, melting once, I on the sudden run;
> Nor can I hold my headlong kindness more
> Than I could curb my cruel rage before.
>
> (Part II, IV. i, 130–3)

In the light of Dryden's later plays it is interesting that the most conspicuous of the 'exact virtues' of which Ozmyn and Benzayda are 'patterns' is compassion. The sensibility manifested in this secondary plot is, as Mrs Evelyn realized, of the sort to be found in 'the most refined romance'.

In *Aureng-Zebe* (1675), Dryden's next serious play, the more rarified sort of magnanimity is more prominent than in *The Conquest of Granada*. The story, taken from recent Indian history, but altered in many details concerns the strife amongst the four sons of the old Emperor over the succession. Only Aureng-Zebe defends his father and seeks no power for himself. Except for the extravagance of his love for Indamora, he is a model of virtuous behaviour, unlike his brother Morat, the son of the Emperor's second wife, Nourmahal. From this fiercely ambitious lustful woman, a worthy successor to Zempoalla, Morat appears to inherit his distinguishing traits. And as Aureng-Zebe is contrasted to Morat, so Indamora and Morat's faithful wife, Melesinda, are contrasted to Nourmahal. The old Emperor, 'who in his youth for glory strove/ Would recompense his age with ease and love' (I. 86–87) by attempting to seduce Indamora, whom he has promised to Aureng-Zebe. The pattern of contrasting characters is reminiscent of Dryden's earlier plays but is made even more evident by the compact structure.

Although Aureng-Zebe is, from the first, so much more regular a hero than Almanzor, even he is lifted to a higher plane of virtue by Indamora, who persuades him to 'stand the blameless pattern of a son' (I. 456) in the face of his father's ingratitude and betrayal. Later in the play she has to show him that his jealous suspicions of her are false (IV. ii, 7–159; V. 447–605). On Morat, who seems in some respects to be an intensification of what is most erratic and wilful in Almanzor, her effect is more startling. When he, like his father, tries to force himself upon her, she not only resists him, but shows him how to express more truly the potential greatness which she has the sympathy to perceive in him. Her analysis of his character is a key passage for the understanding of Dryden's concept of heroism:

> *Yours is a soul irregularly great,*
> *Which, wanting temper, yet abounds with heat,*
> *So strong yet so unequal pulses beat;*
> *A sun which does through vapors dimly shine.*
> *What pity 'tis you are not all divine!*   (V. 91–95)

A turn of the plot later enables him, though mortally wounded, to save her from Nourmahal, and to die at her feet with the words:

> *I leave you not, for my expanded mind*
> *Grows up to Heav'n while it to you is joined;*
> *Not quitting, but enlarged! A blazing fire*
> *Fed from the brand.*   (V. 433–6)

In the dedication of the play Dryden felt obliged to defend Indamora against critics who found her too frail and timorous in her scene with Nourmahal. Though he claims that he has merely given Indamora, in contrast to certain romantic heroines, a 'practicable virtue, mixed with the frailties and imperfections of human life' (ll. 251–3), he reveals that his model for her in the scene of Morat's death was Mandane, the heroine of *Le Grand Cyrus*, who is similarly defended by a dying admirer, and, similarly compassionate, is described as 'this generous and pitiful Princess'.[1] Dryden has made Indamora not less of a romance heroine but a heroine in whom compassion rather than courage is portrayed.

In certain scenes with Indamora and Melesinda there is a veritable fugue on the theme of pity. Both women are spectacularly unfortunate,

---

[1] *Artamenes, or the Grand Cyrus*, tr. F. G., 5 vol 1653–55, Part IX, Bk. I, 7.

but when one is temporarily worse off, the other takes pity on her, displaying that 'noblenes of hart' to which Dryden gives increasing attention. The pathos of these, and several other, scenes in *Aureng-Zebe* is set off by the satirical exuberance of the Emperor, when he berates Nourmahal, and even of Aureng-Zebe, in his attacks of unreasoning jealousy. When Dryden's characters indulge in sarcasm he devises for them a vigorous but polished irony which is equally appropriate to comedy and tragedy, and suggestive of the sort of raillery which was presumably heard in Restoration society. At such moments one is particularly aware that 'the conversation of gentlemen', which Dryden praised Beaumont and Fletcher for imitating (Watson, I 68), was one of his models. An unbroken line seems to extend from the drawing-room to the world of heroes. Boabdelin says to Almanzor:

> *Then sure you are some godhead; and our care*
> *Must be to come with incense and with pray'r.*   (V. iii, 87–88)

The Emperor replies to Nourmahal's insistence on her virtue:

> *In unchaste wives*
> *There's yet a kind of recompensing ease:*
> *Vice keeps 'em humble, gives 'em care to please.*
> *But against clamorous virtue, what defense?*
> *It stops our mouths and gives your noise pretense.*   (II. 263–7)

Aureng-Zebe's relationship to his father is second in importance only to his troubled love-affair. The old Emperor, besotted by his infatuation for Indamora, continues to treat his loyal son with the grossest cruelty till the moment when he sees that Morat, whom he has favoured, means to take his throne and Indamora. When Aureng-Zebe overlooks the unjust treatment he has received and pledges his support against Morat, the old man is so moved by his generosity that he at last confesses his fault and returns his son's love (IV. ii, 171–96).

Such scenes, in which one character recognizes in the other a goodness against which he has perversely struggled, held a special fascination for Dryden. In *All for Love* the scene of which he was proudest was that of the quarrel and reconciliation of Antony and Ventidius in the first act

(Preface, ll. 324-6).[1] Again, in his reworking of Shakespeare's *Troilus and Cressida*, he took special pains with an added scene of quarrel and reconciliation between Troilus and Hector, and called attention in his Preface to the precedents for this kind of scene in Euripides, Shakespeare, and Beaumont and Fletcher (Watson, I 241-2). All three of these scenes of Dryden's point toward the one in *Don Sebastian* where Dorax is overwhelmed by the 'headlong torrent' of the hero's goodness.

Dryden's interest in scenes of reconciliation is clearly in line with his depiction of that magnanimity which makes its possessor 'good, gentle, and curteous, even towards his greatest enimies'. Hence, it is surely no accident that, incorporated in the Preface to *Troilus and Cressida*, where he discusses such scenes, is the essay on 'The Grounds of Criticism in Tragedy' with his famous description of pity as 'the noblest and most god-like of moral virtues' (Watson, I 245). He was influenced, as he says, by Rapin, one of several French critics who not only stressed the importance of stirring an emotional response to tragedy, but recommended pity as the best antidote for pride and hardness of heart. La Ménardière and the Abbé d'Aubignac, who frequented the salons of the *précieux*, considered pity a noble emotion, characteristic of the great of soul.[2] To present on the stage persons capable of such sentiments—able to transcend pure self-regard—is not to impugn their heroism but, rather, to show the sort of greatness for which they stand. Though there is no doubt that Dryden sought to make the characters of *Aureng-Zebe* credibly human, and that in their moments of weakness some of them are objects, rather than agents, of pity, the play as a whole does not reveal what one critic has called a 'subversion of the heroic ethos'.[3] Even Melesinda, the faithful, put-upon wife of Morat, has her moment of greatness when she sacrifices herself on her husband's funeral pyre.

[1] All quotations from *All for Love* are taken from *Four Tragedies*, ed. Beaurline and Bowers.
[2] See my essay, 'Tears of Magnanimity in Otway and Racine', in *French and English Drama of the Seventeenth Century, Papers read at a Clark Library Seminar*, Los Angeles 1972. On Rapin see also Eric Rothstein, *Restoration Tragedy*, Madison, Milwaukee, London 1967, 1-23.
[3] Kirsch, *Dryden's Heroic Drama*, 118-42, esp. 126.

All for Love, or The World Well Lost (1677) is the best of Dryden's adaptations of Shakespeare, and possibly his best play. His abandonment of rhyme in order 'to imitate the Divine *Shakespeare*' (Preface, l. 306), and his remarkable tightening of the structure are too well known to require further comment. The character of Antony is not much altered, though his shifts between a Roman sense of duty and a passionate commitment to Cleopatra are more neatly schematized, as one would expect from a reading of Dryden's earlier plays. The moves of Ventidius and Octavia to break Cleopatra's hold on him, and the countermoves of Cleopatra and Alexas, correspond precisely to the major structural units of the play. Antony's nature is summed up before his first appearance by Ventidius:

> *Virtue's his path; but sometimes 'tis too narrow*
> *For his vast Soul; and then he starts out wide,*
> *And bounds into a Vice that bears him far*
> *From his first course, and plunges him in ills.*   (I. 124–7)

Much of what Shakespeare implies about Antony is made explicit in this description, which recalls Montezuma and Almanzor. In the highly emotional scene with Octavia and his 'two little Daughters' Antony demonstrates a generosity and compassion also indicated by Shakespeare. As Dryden presents them they look forward to Don Sebastian. Impressed by the greatness of Octavia's soul, he at first resists her appeal because he finds himself in a dilemma: 'Pity pleads for *Octavia*;/ But does it not plead more for *Cleopatra*?' (III 339–40). But when his children embrace him his resistance is overcome, and the tearful reconciliation moves even the old soldier, Ventidius, to tears. At a later point in the play this scene is balanced by one in which, again on the verge of tears, Antony is tempted to forgive Cleopatra and Dolabella for what he wrongly suspects to be their unfaithfulness to him (IV, 588–91). Though forgiveness is deferred on this occasion, the capacity for it is once more asserted, and in the climactic position of the end of an act.

Dryden's alterations of the character of Cleopatra, which help to create the more heroic tone of *All for Love*, amount to considerably more than accentuating traits already present. Shakespeare's 'serpent of

old Nile', devious, unpredictable, contrary, and often unqueenly, is exchanged for one of the great ladies of romance, majestic at all times. Her
love is 'noble madness', a 'transcendent passion' (II. 17, 20), and when
she confronts Octavia, even her insults are delivered with a certain
propriety: 'And when I love not him, Heav'n change this Face/For one
like that' (III. 449–50). Dryden feared that his introduction of Octavia
into the Alexandrian scenes might attract too much pity for her, and
thus take away pity from the hero and heroine. Yet at this meeting of
the two women Cleopatra proves herself at least Octavia's equal in
proclaiming her sufferings, for which she says she is not even recom-
pensed by the 'specious Title of a Wife', but, instead, has to 'bear the
branded Name of Mistress' (ll. 460–5).

If familiarity with Shakespeare's Cleopatra makes both the dignity
and the self-pity of Dryden's heroine surprising, even more so is her
aversion to deceit. When Alexas urges her to flirt with Dolabella in
order to make Antony jealous, she protests that her love is so true that
she can neither 'hide it where it is,/Nor show it where it is not' (IV.
89–91), and after a tentative overture, she reveals her love for Antony
so unmistakably that Dolabella says:

> *I find your breast fenc'd round from humane reach,*
> *Transparent as a Rock of solid Crystal.*   (IV. 201–2)

Such straightforward dealing is the boast of Antony and of Almanzor
before him. It is the product of that heroic plainness which Dryden
typically contrasts with the corruption and meanness of a 'world well
lost'. In Cleopatra, as in Antony, it is combined with an exuberance of
feeling, betokening generosity, which is often presented in images of
overflowing water. After Antony's jealousy has been aroused by the
combined contrivance of Alexas, Ventidius, and Octavia, Cleopatra
confesses to Antony that she began a flirtation with Dolabella, but
could not carry it through:

> *. . . I could not counterfeit:*
> *In spight of all the damms, my love broke o'er,*
> *And drown'd my heart again.*   (IV. 520–2)

However clear the moral fault of these lovers is made—as Dryden says
in the Preface, 'our passions are, or ought to be, within our power' (l.

22)—the insistent association in the poetry of bounteous nature with the images of overflow tends to subvert the moral by suggesting growth and fulfilment.

At the end, though Dryden does full justice to the heroic pathos of the double suicide, there is an unexpected calm, approaching serenity. It begins to be felt when the dying Antony is placed in a chair and, asked by Cleopatra how it is with him, replies with an almost comic detachment:

> *'Tis as with a man*
> *Removing in a hurry; all pack'd up,*
> *But one dear Jewel that his haste forgot;*
> *And he, for that, returns upon the spur:*
> *So I come back for thee.*   (V. 365–9)

The strong feeling is controlled by polite self-depreciation. But the quietness of understatement is succeeded by something more positive and more elevated. The final picture of the couple whose love has threatened imperial order suggests that they have established a superior order of their own:

> *See, see how the Lovers sit in State together,*
> *As they were giving Laws to half Mankind.*   (V. 508–9)

In the dedication of *The Spanish Friar* (1680), a play with one comic and one heroic plot, Dryden reproaches himself for the extravagant heroic rant of Maximin and Almanzor, and distinguishes between a 'lofty style', which is 'naturally pompous and magnificant', and a 'swelling puffy style', which only 'looks like greatness' (Watson, I 277). His style in *All for Love*, three years before, was already more restrained than in his early plays, and it became even more so. But the most casual perusal of the heroic plot of *The Spanish Friar* is sufficient to show that a quieter style is not incompatible with the portrayal of the highest aspirations and the most noble self-sacrifice. The play is not one of Dryden's best, however. It was in *Don Sebastian* that he demonstrated how effectively a vigorous but low-keyed style could support the lofty sentiments of heroic characters.

By the time that Dryden wrote *Don Sebastian* (1689), after several years' absence from the theatre, he was in a most unhappy situation.

Having supported the policies of James II, and having become a Catholic, he was removed from his laureateship after the Revolution of 1688, and his pension was cancelled. In the dedication of the play to the Earl of Leicester he extols 'the offices of pity', and, referring to his miserable state, says, 'the lowermost party, to a noble mind, is ever the fittest object of good-will',[1] (a comment which reflects on Almanzor's benefactions). He goes on to say that 'the ruggedness of a stoic is only a silly affectation of being a god', whereas 'To find in ourselves the weaknesses and imperfections of our wretched kind, is surely the most reasonable step we can make towards the compassion of our fellow-creatures' (S-S, VII 303). In the dedication of *Amphitryon* (1690) he praises Sir William Gower for 'natural commiseration', which he relates to 'the settled basis of your good nature and good sense', contrasting 'things of honour', which 'have, at best, somewhat of ostentation in them, and self-love' with 'tenderness . . . which is humanity in a heroical degree' (S-S, VIII 6–7). No doubt Dryden's need of compassion fortified the conviction he shared with many others at the end of the century that it was one of the chief indications of a great mind. His association of reason with compassion, which seems to anticipate eighteenth-century views of good nature, is very similar to what may be found in the romances of Mlle. de Scudéry. As 'reason and nature' combine to make the pirate-chief take pity on his daughter and her husband, so, at the end of *Ibrahim*, reason triumphs over Soliman's anger at his rebellious bassa, now in his power; he weeps, and gives Ibrahim his freedom, thus ending the story with a splendidly magnanimous gesture (Part IV, Bk. V, 228–30).

Don Sebastian, a mammoth play, which had to be cut in performance, contains some of Dryden's best dramatic writing. By passing over the recorded facts about the Battle of Alcazar (1578), in which King Sebastian of Portugal presumably died, and accepting a legend that the king had survived, Dryden gave himself the freedom to invent a totally unhistorical sequel. The principal characters are more complex and more humanly appealing than those in any of his plays, even *All for Love*. The hero, though a great warrior, has already had to face the limitations

[1] S-S, VII 302.

imposed on him by a disastrous defeat, and later he must face the discovery that he has committed incest. Described at the beginning as a model hero, 'Brave, pious, generous, great, and liberal' (I. i, 103), a more mature and steady Aureng-Zebe, he is inexplicably a victim rather than a conqueror. Almeyda, supposed at first to be the sister of one of the defeated Moors, is more nearly the hero's equal in courage than any of Dryden's sympathetic heroines except Cleopatra. She has the energy and verve of Nourmahal but also the settled purpose and devotion of Almahide or Indamora. Though there is no need for her to raise Sebastian's moral sights, she inspires in him a noble passion, which is made blameworthy only by a trick of fate. The resemblance between the two of them—specifically, 'the greatness of their Souls'—is a device of Dryden's, as he says in the Preface (l. 244), to prepare for the discovery of their blood-relationship.

Dorax, as has already been suggested, has something of the irregularity of earlier heroes, but also an even greater capacity for recognizing his own failings. He is a decidedly rough diamond when we first meet him as a renegade who joined the Moors because he considered himself slighted by Don Sebastian. Capable of the grossest comments on Almeyda, whom he distrusts, he can also give a generous account of his former master's virtues. Finally, Muley Moluch is as wilful, cruel, and unreliable as other tyrants in Dryden's plays, and deliberately made so, contrary to the indications of history, 'because I stood in need of so shining a Character of brutality' (Preface, ll. 191–2), but, unlike his predecessors, he is moved by admiration for the hero (I. i, 406–8) and tempted by pity for the heroine (III. i, 247–51).

Dryden took considerable pride in the writing of *Don Sebastian*. For years he had been loosening the style of his dialogue, abandoning the neat closed couplets of his early heroic plays for couplets with frequent enjambment in *Aureng-Zebe*, and then blank verse. Here he achieved a 'roughness of the numbers and cadences' which he considered 'more masterly' than anything he had previously done (Preface, ll. 69–73). The boasts of his hero in the first act, while free of the flourishes which made Dryden ashamed of some of the speeches of Maximin and Almanzor, are still grand enough to suggest heroic scope and to appeal to the spectators' imaginations:

> *. . . if I fall*
> *It shall be like my self; a setting Sun*
> *Shou'd leave a track of Glory in the Skies.*   (I. i, 341–3)
>
> *Not less ev'n in this despicable now,*
> *Than when my Name fill'd Affrick with affrights.*   (ll. 350–1)
>
> *If burnt and scatter'd in the air: the Winds*
> *That strow my dust, diffuse my royalty,*
> *And spread me o'er your Clime.*   (ll. 367–9)

The old extravagance is there, but given form in a more substantial poetic fabric than Almanzor's

> *Obey'd as sovereign by they subjects be,*
> *But know that I alone am king of me.*

Dryden modulates the style of Sebastian's speeches from the bravura of these early ones to the resignation of

> *The world was once too narrow for my mind,*
> *But one poor little nook will serve me now;*
> *To hide me from the rest of humane kinde.*   (V. i, 557–9)

The satiric thrust found occasionally in *The Conquest of Granada* and more often in *Aureng-Zebe* recurs in some of the pithy speeches of Dorax, such as this one:

> *The genius of your Moors is mutiny;*
> *They scarcely want a Guide to move their madness:*
> *Prompt to rebel on every weak pretence,*
> *Blustring when courted, crouching when opprest.*
> *Wise to themselves, and fools to all the World.*
> *Restless in change, and perjur'd to a Proverb.*   (III. i, 407–12)

At other times the verse approaches the naturalness of conversation, and, in the comic scenes, is replaced by prose.

The triumphs of *Don Sebastian* are those of splendid dramatic moments, made so by fine delineation of character and by quiet elegance of style. The intricate plotting, characteristic of Dryden, is overwrought in comparison to *All for Love* or even *Aureng-Zebe*, though it is undoubtedly clever. The low-comic sub-plot, which is, as Beaurline shows, wittily juxtaposed with episodes of the main plot (*Four Tragedies*, 282–3), is less open to objection than the almost comic complication of the two independent attempts to poison Dorax, which result in saving his life, or the oppressive hints and premonitions which carefully prepare for the revelation of incest. Although the tragic precedents for such preparation are obvious, it does not seem altogether in place in the story of Sebastian and Almeyda, whose protestations of heroic love are more easy to accept than their blood-curdling visions of ghosts and recollections of horoscopes. At best, these are the seventeenth-century equivalents of the Freudian dreams which, as we know, it is also easy to overdo. Dryden's stylistic control in *Don Sebastian* is not matched by judgment in the management of the plot.

Despite the excesses of an overlong play, however, the achievement of the great scenes remains. The reconciliation of Dorax and Sebastian, used earlier as an example of one kind of magnanimity, is convincingly based on the interaction of the two characters and on the reappraisal of himself to which a new piece of information forces Dorax. The emotional power of the scene is indubitable. The success of another moving scene, in which Sebastian and Almeyda discover their relationship, has an analogous basis, and the analogy in itself contributes to the effectiveness. At the end of this scene, in his last speech, Sebastian expresses not only the crushing grief of separation but also his concern for Almeyda's grief. Thus the play closes on a note of tenderness, 'which is humanity in a heroical degree'.

With *Don Sebastian* Dryden's most important dramatic writing in a serious vein was over, but in two later plays there are occasional flashes of heroic fire. *Cleomenes, the Spartan Hero* (1692), a play which Thomas Southerne finished because of Dryden's illness, presents the unavailing struggles of a deposed patriot-king, and the last play of all, the tragicomedy, *Love Triumphant* (1694), glorifies generosity, ending with a strange scene in which a wilful king gives up the revenge he could take as he recognizes the virtue of his intended victim. After reading this scene it is no surprise to find, in the dedication of *Love Triumphant*, that the play of Corneille's which Dryden took to be 'the very best' was *Cinna*, which concludes with the unexpected forgiveness of the conspirators by the Emperor Augustus. Both this opinion and

Dryden's contrivance in his tragicomedy proclaim the kind of magnanimity which appealed to Dryden in his later years.

In one respect Dryden's portrayal of the protagonists of serious drama is remarkably consistent throughout this whole career: they are all extraordinary personages, possessed of that special fortitude, or *areté*, which distinguished the heroes of ancient epic. Don Sebastian, though more credible, is no more ordinary than Montezuma or Almanzor. Despite some important shifts of emphasis, he is firmly tied to a traditional depiction of the hero. When the greater tenderness and compassion of which he is capable are assigned to a more nearly average human being—to the man next door, so to speak—a more profound change takes place. When anyone, through the exercise of reason and good nature, may rise to greatness of spirit, the concept of the hero is threatened with extinction. In the domestic tragedies of some of Dryden's later contemporaries and successors this further shift of sensibility is manifested, yet, since the dream of human nobility remains, the transition is not abrupt. *Don Sebastian* and *Love Triumphant* point the way.

4: Dryden's Grotesque: An Aspect of the Baroque in His Art and Criticism

JEAN H. HAGSTRUM

I

The Baroque and Grotesque in Dryden's Theory and Practice

IN THE Church of the Capuchins in Rome, Guido Reni's 'St Michael' portrays the archangel about to plunge his sword, with a powerful thrust, into the body of Satan. The face of St Michael wears an expression of smooth, graceful, detached, and somewhat effeminate calm that we today may find superficial but that the late seventeenth and the eighteenth centuries admired as ideal beauty.[1] In contrast to the victorious angel is the fallen devil, his face bearing suggestions of hair, his forehead wrinkled, his eyes dark and somewhat slanting, his nose pointed, his body muscular and powerful. Although threatening and ominous even in defeat, Satan is far from being the stock-devil of folk legend. He is in fact fully human and looks a little like a middle-aged Italian.

Dryden knew of this painting. In 'A Parallel of Poetry and Painting', written in 1695, he translated a long passage from Bellori, which included a letter by Guido about his 'Saint Michael'. In the letter the painter discusses both his archangel and his devil. The angel he describes in terms that Dryden regularly used to express ideal beauty—an idea of perfection formed in the imagination. The devil—an embodiment of the 'contrary idea of deformity and ugliness'—Guido says he tried to blot from his remembrance.[2]

---

[1] See Jean H. Hagstrum, *The Sister Arts*, Chicago, 1959, xxi, 110, 167–68.

[2] *Essays of John Dryden*, ed. W. P. Ker, Oxford 1900, II, 121.

The painting embodies several baroque features: a conflict between good and evil in which good triumphs, a strong accent on the ideal humanity of the good figure, a subordination of landscape and background, the omission of the monstrous, and the achievement of success in an atmosphere of threatening turbulence. These and other features of the baroque appear almost everywhere in Dryden—in historical poem, heroic drama, satire, opera, and great ode.[1] But the painting—with Guido's letter about it—provides emblem and motto for this essay, not for general stylistic reasons, but because the Satan portrayed—human and plausible and threatening—is precisely the kind of grotesque that Dryden was to develop in the decade of the sixties. Besides, Dryden, like Guido, tended to develop his grotesque as part of an antithesis. Both the grotesque and the contrast that contains it will be the focus of our attention in examining the main literary works of the poet's striking, formative, difficult, and relatively unstudied early years.

Maximillian E. Novak has already called attention to the matter we are studying—'the baroque concept of playing the grotesque against the beautiful'.[2] And Dryden himself stated the same principle, applying it to the theatre: 'Thus in a play, some characters must be raised, to oppose others; and to set them off the better . . . thus, in my *Tyrannic Love*, the atheist Maximin is opposed to the character of St Catherine.'[3] One

---

[1] John Heath-Stubbs says *Annus Mirabilis* has 'verve and baroque extravagance' as well as 'baroque wit' and calls Dryden's heroic ideal 'baroque'. See 'Dryden and the Heroic Ideal' in *Dryden's Mind and Art*, ed. Bruce King, Edinburgh 1969, 4, 23. Robert Etheridge Moore calls Dryden's special quality in the heroic plays 'baroque' and sees in *The Tempest* 'a fascinating illustration of the baroque passion for piling into a single work so wide a diversity of appeals as to land it straight in the lap of the grotesque': *Henry Purcell & the Restoration Theatre* 1961, 17, 183. See also Jean H. Hagstrum, *Sister Arts*, 197–8. Imbrie Buffum regards 1660 as the date for the advent of the baroque into England. If so, Dryden's style in the decade under consideration was abreast of an exciting new development. See *Studies in the Baroque from Montaigne to Rotrou*, New Haven 1957, viii. See also Margaret Bottrall, 'The Baroque Element in Milton', *English Miscellany* I, Rome 1950, 31–42.

[2] *Works*, X 366; a note on *Tempest*, III. ii, 38.

[3] Watson, II 203.

of Dryden's mentors, Ovid, himself a master of the grotesque, led the English poet's awakening 'Invention and Fancy' into an attractive psychological locus for a modern concept of the grotesque: '*Ovid* images . . . the movements and affections of the mind, either combating between two contrary passions, or extremely discompos'd by one . . .'[1]

If the intellectual and stylistic habit of powerful contrast is eminently baroque, then so is the dark and distorted evil which that contrast brings into view. In the 1660s a poet whose eye and imagination were trained to absorb visual effects had these vivid grotesques available to him from the baroque theatre: fauns, satyrs, serpents, dragons, wild men of the forest, Medusas, mermaids, animals with human heads, Silenus, peasants at their feasts, comic masks.[2] Baroque and Mannerist painting contributed the signs of the Zodiac, weird metamorphoses based on Ovid, dreams, caprices, *bizzarrie*, Bacchic scenes, cock-fights, Pan, Polyphemus, emaciated saints, severed heads, and horrendous details of plague, pestilence, illness, and damnation.[3] The walls of a cultivated man's *musée imaginaire* in the late seventeenth century was likely to be hung with all manner of memorable grotesquerie.

In his own infrequent uses and definitions of *grotesque* Dryden appears to be fully conventional. He associates it with the visual:[4] with clowns, the 'Dutch kermis, the brutal sport of snick-or-snee', 'the fine woman [who] ends in a fish's tail'.[5] The term is used to refer to forms, details, and combinations that are heterogeneous, unnatural, false, deformed, hideous, deviant, fantastic, bizarre, extravagant, and laughable. Follow-

[1] *Works*, I 53.
[2] See Margarete Baur-Heinhold, *Theater des Barock Festliches Bühnenspiel im 17. und 18. Jahrhundert*, Munich 1966, *passim*.
[3] Any collection of baroque art will provide examples. See also Raffaelle Carrieri, *Fantasia degli Italiani*, Milan 1939, *passim*.
[4] The grotesque had its origins in fanciful murals, found in Roman *grotte*, combining human and animal motifs with foliage and flowers. See Arthur Clayborough, *The Grotesque in English Literature*, Oxford 1965, I.
[5] 'A Parallel of Painting and Poetry' and 'Dedication of the *Aeneis*' (1697), Watson, II 189, 229.

ing Montaigne, Dryden applied the term to literature and found its equivalent in that lowest form of comedy, the farce.[1] The grotesque could provide pleasures, but these tended to be 'accidental', not essential, unless the imitation was skilful.[2] So great was the prestige of natural and idealized representation in Dryden's scale of literary values that *grotesque* as a term of criticism was pejorative and not very important.

It was far different in his art and that of his contemporaries, where the presence of energetic and unforgettable representations of distorted reality and unnatural nature forced Dryden the critic to come to terms with the grotesque. In returning to a contrast that looks obsessive, between Venus and the lazar, Dryden kept asserting the right of the artist to represent leprous, beggarly, repulsive reality.[3] In 1668 he called *Bartholomew Fair* the 'lowest kind of comedy' but conceded it was art because the low was 'heightened' and intensified: though the 'original be vile', Jonson 'hath made an excellent lazar of it'.[4] And in 1670 he defended his own portrayal of moral monstrosity in *Tyrannick Love*: 'there is as much of Art, and as near an imitation of nature, in a *Lazare*, as in a *Venus*'.[5] In coming to accept critically as subjects of art the beggar as well as the monarch, the tyrant as well as the good king, the monster as well as Venus, Dryden's best teacher must have been himself. For there was a strain of the realistically grotesque in his poetry from the very beginning. The famous small-pox sores on the fair skin of Lord Hastings need not detain us. But the Swiftian portrayal in Dryden's first published poems of the aged as 'Times Offal', with 'Catarrhs,

[1] 'Parallel', Watson, II 190. See Clayborough, *Grotesque*, 3.
[2] See Neander's elaborate definition of humour, in which laughter was associated with the bizarre or fantastic and pleasure with natural imitation: *Of Dramatic Poesy* (1668), Watson, I 72–73.
[3] See the excellent note on Dryden's contrast between the lazar and Venus in his 'Account' of *Annus Mirabilis* (1667) in *Works* I 56, 274–6.
[4] 'Defence of an Essay of Dramatic Poesy' (1668), Watson I, 114–15.
[5] *Works*, X 110. It must have cost Dryden something to admit the grotesque to his critical system, so committed was he to natural and ideal imitation. Robert D. Hume rightly says that imitation was Dryden's 'critical keystone' and that growing realism did not obviate his requirement that art imitate the idea of perfect nature: *Dryden's Criticism*, Ithaca, N.Y. 1970, 217.

Rheums, Aches',[1] presages a preoccupation with the grotesque and ugl
during and beyond his apprentice years.

The grotesque in Dryden breaks out of the lexical confinements of
criticism. It exists in life as well as in art. When men 'fall into' it, the
become fools or knaves on and off the stage. The grotesque can be
psychological and social condition. Dreamers, fanatics, lunatics, lover
who 'rage' like Dido, the rabble who are as 'blind' and 'wild' as th
Cyclops, the 'Ghosts of Traitors' who join 'Fanatick Spectres' o
London bridge for a witches' Sabbath, the much-flattered heroes of
Homer—a race of 'ungodly man-killers' who murder, destroy God
images, and 'never enjoy quiet in themselves, till they have taken
from all the world'—and those 'good salvage Gentlemen' the critics ar
even Dryden himself who resembles them ('He is like you, a ver
Wolf, or Bear')—all these are versions of the grotesque who inhat
that literary-courtly-social-political-religious-learned milieu that Dry
den made so peculiarly the subject of his art.[2] *Impossibile est* the grotesqu
non describere—because men living together were so adept at producir
monstrosities. Dryden may have rhetorically heightened but he did no
create 'the lurid Anglican depiction of Catholics'[3] that appears in h
verse:

> *An hideous Figure of their Foes they drew,*
> *Nor Lines, nor Looks, nor Shades, nor Colours true;*
> *And this Grotesque design, expos'd to Publick view.*

This grotesque Dryden goes on to call an 'Aegyptian Piece' with 'bar
ing Deities', 'perverse', 'unlike', a 'daubing', a 'Monster' 'mishapen
'ugly', like a '*Holland* emblem', full of 'malice' and fit for 'a Fiend'
Dryden's grotesque, broadly considered, is the result of an imperfe

---

[1] 'Upon the Death of Lord Hastings' (1649), ll. 82–83.

[2] For the references in this paragraph, see 'Dedication of Plutarch's
Lives', S-S, XVII 16–17; 'A Short Account of Virgil's Persons, Manners,
and Fortune', S-S, XIII 311; *Astraea Redux*, ll. 45–48; *Annus Mirabilis*,
stanza 223; Dedication of *Examen Poeticum*, Watson, II 167; Second
Prologue of *Secret Love*, ll. 47–48.

[3] Earl Miner's phrase in *Works*, III 445.

[4] These lines and phrases come from the Hind's fable of the Pigeons in
The Hind and the Panther, III 1042–57.

society pressing in on the mind of a sensitive and articulate observer.

The grotesques Dryden created during the 1660s differ from the grotesques of his mature polemical writings in poetry and prose in being less obviously, less consistently the objects of laughter and hatred. That is, Dryden seems to have had feelings about the earlier distortions rather more mixed than he reveals later when his rhetorical and satirical techniques are more refined and his own commitments more single and clear. The probing, inquiring young mind open to all the contemporary currents—naturalistic, sceptical, irreverent, even cynical—is more ambiguously poised, and the grotesque formulation can contain alloys of reason and sense, of attractive power and energy. It happens that the wickedness and folly portrayed in the sixties had a sublime side to it: Dryden's rhetoric in giving the devil his due is often brilliant and blinding.

The grotesques of the sixties fall into three chief categories: the social grotesque, the grotesque of superstition, and the grotesque of power. Each example of these is presented in a contrast that has a positive side. Sometimes these contrasts appear as in the massed opposites of baroque art, sometimes as argument.[1] The word combats range from 'the amatory battledore and shuttlecock' that Saintsbury deplored[2] to the rhymed theology of *Tyrannick Love*. The contrasts are serious or comic, heroic or tragic. The arguments and the discussions, so often dismissed as frigid and unnatural in drama, often had fatal consequences in action: Dryden said, 'on the result [of argumentation and discourse] the doing or not doing of some considerable action should depend'.[3] It will be my aim to describe both the grotesque and the positive value against which it is developed.

---

[1] Bredvold notes Dryden's 'delight in testing certain arguments by throwing them into the arena with their opposites. Such a debate is more than a mere rhetorical exercise; . . . it is the vigorous play of the intelligence': *The Intellectual Milieu of John Dryden*, Ann Arbor, 1934; rprd 1966, 110.

[2] The phrase is quoted by Arthur C. Kirsch in *Dryden's Heroic Drama*, Princeton 1965, 58.

[3] Preface to *The Rival Ladies* in *Works* VIII, 101.

II

The Social Grotesque

Dryden was invincibly a public poet, his chief themes concerned with men and their institutions. It is not surprising, then, that he should early have thought of the grotesque in social terms. This category may be regarded in three sub-divisions: (1) the grotesque of passionate individualism that attacks the order of a good society that must be bound by principles of honour and loyalty; (2) the grotesque of ridiculous folly, which is exposed by a fashionable society in which a sublimely bungling fool cannot operate; and (3) the grotesque of hypocrisy produced by a nominally Christian society that in actuality is fiercely commercial and aggressively imperialistic.

In *The Rival Ladies* and *Secret Love* the grotesque is, typically, developed in an antithesis, but that antithesis lies within the good people. The evil is frustrated by a rigorous individual application of the ethical and social will. The danger represented by the grotesque of lawless passion and individualism remains, as it should in tragicomedies of the 'platonic' variety, a threat only, a threat obviated in the happy denouement.

The response Dryden intended to elicit in *The Rival Ladies* (published, 1664), the second of his plays to be written and the third to be acted, was admiration for the ideal of honour and loyalty. Dryden seems to develop separate ideals for the man and the woman. For the man, the ideal against which the threatening grotesque is developed is loyalty to his word and to the social institution of betrothal. For the woman, it is loyalty to the first passion, the strong implication being that unattached, promiscuous passions forever changing their object constitute peculiarly dangerous and grotesque behaviour in a woman.

It is clear that the ideals of male chivalry and female loyalty and faithfulness are threatened by passions that Dryden twists into the grotesque. Gonsalvo's love of Julia arises like a fire of straw and is bluntly characterized as fury and madness. The fire does not burn itself out but grows as the play proceeds. In the end it is honourably put out by the good, knightly hero, himself a courteous man who respects social law and who quenches his passion out of respect for betrothal and for a rival's prior claims.

Julia's love is more complex in its nature and in its potential dangers. At the beginning she seeks a convent as a temporary asylum because her love is all desire ('Inclination') and offends virtue in its lack of judgment. Her love is like 'the Day-dreams of melancholy Men':

> *I think and think on things impossible,*
> *Yet love to wander in that Golden maze.* (III. i, 56–58)

Toward Gonsalvo her emotions range from grateful friendship and potential love to loathing, at least professed loathing. She is willing to make this concession at the end to Gonsalvo: 'Were I not Rod'rick's first, I should be Yours.' But in the end Julia must remain true to her first passion, which is admittedly 'faulty' but so violent that its object could be changed only with grave danger:

> *My violent Love for him, I know is faulty,*
> *Yet Passion never can be plac'd so ill,*
> *But that to change it is the greater Crime.* (V. iii, 69–72)

An austere and perhaps even cruel ideal! But the fickle Restoration seems to have known from experience the mad folly of allowing *la donna* to be *mobile*. Ferdinand in *The Tempest* laments the female propensity toward variety:

> *Nature has done her part, she loves variety. . . .*
> *. . . No, no their Nurses teach them*
> *Change, when with two Nipples they divide their*
> *Liking.* (IV. i, 106, 109–10)

Variety in love, so often wittily sung to light and delicate airs in Caroline gallantry, was apparently safest as a male privilege; from it women must be guarded at all costs. But in this play male loyalty is a virtue too; as Gonsalvo says, in concluding the play,

> *Beauty but gains, Obligement keeps our Love.* (V. iii, 280)

In *Secret-Love, or the Maiden-Queen* (performed in 1667, published in 1668) we are concerned with the serious plot in verse, not with the pert and high-spirited prose of the comic sub-plot. The grotesque is here, as in the earlier 'platonic' play, developed within the character of the heroine, the queen who has fallen in love beneath her and is the victim of

passion, jealousy, and desires that alternate between love and violence
By her own confession, the Queen goes mad with love and shame: 'C
whither am I fallen?' [V. i, 281] But in the end the distraught monarch
renounces her love, approves the marriage of her beloved Philocles to
her rival Candiope, dedicates her nobler love to her people, and even
attains a rich, sable beauty as duty prevails over disruptive passion:

> *Behold how night sits lovely on her eye-brows,*
> *While day breaks from her eyes!*   (V. i, 430–1)

Philocles, ignorant at first of the Queen's passion for him, must struggle
with ambition and desire when he learns of it:

> *Sure I had one of the fallen Angels Dreams;*
> *All Heav'n within this hour was mine!*   (V. i, 434–5)

In both his 'platonic' tragicomedies of love and loyalty Dryden uses an
enlarging biblical, astronomical, and planetary imagery, showing that
the stakes are high and that the social grotesque of lawless passion
possesses its own kind of menacing dignity.

In *Sir Martin Mar-all* (performed in 1667, published in 1668) Warner
the servant, provides the ideal, and a most unusual one it is, seeming to
anticipate the democratic aspirations expressed by the clever servants of
Beaumarchais and Mozart. Warner is a Truewit, clever, sexually
adequate, articulate, and an aggressive and imaginative master of the
social mores of his society. He wins the lady, the high-spirited Millisent
because, in addition to his demonstrated mental and his promised physical potency, he is revealed at the end as a kinsman of a nobleman. He
is, for all that, a Neander, a new man, and one may think that Dryden
consciously or not, must have put a good bit of himself into the servant
hero who rises in the world through mother-wit, invention in plots, and
skill in music and verse.

Against that social ideal of witty and successful energy, the grotesque
of comic folly is developed in the invincible fool, Sir Martin, who does
indeed 'mar all' attempts by cleverer people to make him win his goal
in love. Like Pope's personified Dulness, Sir Martin's bumbling folly
grows and grows, finally able almost to propel itself. The fool, who rises
like a balloon from abject repentance at the moment of failure to a

blime and impenetrable ambition as he undertakes each new plot, is
ot God's fool embodying the wisdom of simplicity and goodness. He
Nature's fool placed in Restoration society—as Rose says, he 'has a
re way of acting a Fool, and does it . . . naturally' (II. ii, 30–31).
otally incapable of mastering the Way of the World, he cries out, 'I
ink there is a Fate upon me' (V. i, 223). And so in fact there is, for the
an is a wrench in the social machinery of his day, a grotesque created
y the world where cleverness, a good memory, the ability to act, and
ill in the arts open the doors to progress.

Sir Martin is a comic grotesque of the purest variety. Mentally and
cially malformed, a distorted Gothic country figure, he is a throw-
ck to another time and another place, set in a new and glittering
ilieu. When acted by Nokes, he must have been almost unbearably
nusing to Dryden's contemporaries, as a total antithesis to the witty,
ccessful, well-oiled machines of the Restoration beau monde. Pepys
w the play perhaps as many as ten times and judged it to be 'undoubt-
lly the best comedy [that] ever was wrote'.[1]

In placing 'Christian' conquerors on the soil of the New World,
ryden seized an opportunity to develop a stunning variation of the
cial grotesque. Men professing the faith of Western Europe in a lov-
g, forgiving, self-sacrificing God, confront the sun of natural religion
d, bathed in its light, are exposed as avaricious, sadistically cruel, and
tellectually tyrannical. The Spanish conquerors represent what Blake
lled the Abomination of Desolation, religion wrapped in war, and it

[1] *Works*, IX 352. John Loftis concludes, regarding the Newcastle-
Dryden collaboration, that the dramatic superiority of this play is owing
to Dryden but that much of the comedy may have originated with Newcastle. See *Works*, IX 355–6 and n. 30. F. H. Moore believes that Newcastle wrote the first three acts, Dryden the last two, and that then
Dryden went over the whole play, putting it in its final form. But he
credits Dryden with the success of the play. See 'The Composition of
Sir Martin Mar-All', *Essays in English Literature of the Classical Period
presented to Dougald MacMillan*, ed. Daniel W. Patterson and Albrecht
B. Strauss, *Studies in Philology* Extra Series No. 4, Jan. 1967, 27–38.
Reviewing the evidence, I cannot be absolutely certain that the Warner
episodes are peculiarly Dryden's, and my suggestion that he is a Neander especially close to Dryden will have to be regarded as speculative.

is a measure of the intellectual boldness of the young Dryden that he
was able to draw so unvarnished a grotesque of elements present in his
own 'Christian', commercial, and imperialistic culture.

The grotesque is developed against the dreams of the Golden Age
revived by the sight and news of primitive men in the age of American
exploration. In 1662 Dryden described the Indians Columbus had found
as

> . . . *guiltless* Men, *who danc'd away their time,*
> Fresh *as their* Groves, *and* Happy *as their* Clime.[1]

In *The Indian Emperor*, first performed in 1665, Dryden's hero, Cortez
replies to Vasquez's view that all is wild and savage in the New World

> *Wild and untaught are Terms which we alone*
> *Invent for fashions differing from our own:*
> *For all their Customs are by Nature wrought,*
> *But we, by Art, unteach what Nature taught.*[2]   (I. i, 11–14)

[1] 'To My Honored Friend, Dr. Charleton' (1662), ll. 13–14.
[2] Jeffry Spencer has called my attention to a striking parallel to this
passage in the essay 'Of Canniballs', in the *Essays* (I xxx) of 'honest
Montaigne', as Dryden called him:

I find, that there is nothing Barbarous and Savage in this Nation, by
any thing that I can gather, excepting, That every one gives the Title
of Barbarity to every thing that is not in use in his own Country: As
indeed we have no other level of Truth and Reason, than the Example
and Idea of the Opinions and Customs of the place wherein we Live.
There is always the true Religion, there the perfect Government, and
the most exact and accomplish'd Usance of all things. They are Savages
at the same rate, that we say Fruits are wild, which Nature produces of
her self, and by her own ordinary progress; whereas in truth, we ought
rather to call those wild, whose Natures we have chang'd by our Arti-
fice, and diverted from the common Order. . . . neither is it reasonable,
that Art should gain the Preheminence of our great and powerful
Mother Nature. We have so [oppress'd] her with the additional Orna-
ments and Graces, we have added to the Beauty and Riches of her own
Works, by our Inventions, that we have almost Smother'd and Choak'd
her; and yet in other places, where she shines in her own purity, and
proper lustre, she strangely baffles and disgraces all our vain and frivolous Attempts. . . . These Nations then seem to me to be so far Barbarous; as having receiv'd but very little form and fashion from Art

ꞵy the character of Montezuma, a noble savage adhering to the natural
ghts of his natural faith, those grotesques, the evil Christians, are most
ꞁarshly judged as perverted, unnatural creatures.

In *The Indian Queen*, performed in 1663 ('the first fully formed heroic
ꞁlay to be acted in London',[1] a collaboration of Howard and Dryden),
Ꞁontezuma, always larger than life, reveals at the outset both passion in
ꞁs love and also fury in his wars; yet he rises by the end of the play to
ꞁeen and accurate perception, tolerance of the opinions of others,
ꞁenerosity to his foes—qualities becoming a well-tempered, magnanim-
ꞁus hero. In Dryden's own play on the American theme, the *Indian
Ꞁmperour*, Montezuma once again begins faultily: his lion-heart caught
ꞁ the toils of love, he cuts a somewhat pathetic figure, weary of flesh
ꞁnd passion and racked with psychological 'agues and Feavers' (II. i,
ꞁo9). But as before he ends as a noble natural hero, superior in character
ꞁ all save Cortez, and at the close even dramatically superior to him.[2]
Ꞁontezuma's moral stature shrivels almost all around him—the wild
ꞁndian rebels, his own timid and flattering priest, and above all the
ꞁonquering Christians. Courteous, proud, tolerant (with a relativistic
ꞁiew of religions), and loyal to his natural lights, he is the unspoiled,
ꞁatural ideal against which the Christians, lay and clerical, are revealed
ꞁs grotesques. The light that exposes them is the light of his own natural
ꞁather, the sun. What a stunning and noble contrast it is to the hell-fire
ꞁith which the priest threatens the noble savage! Montezuma says to
ꞁe orthodox priest who tortures him:

---

and Humane Invention, and consequently, not much remote from their
Original Simplicity. The Laws of Nature however govern them still,
not as yet much vitiated with any mixture of ours': tr. Charles Cotton,
3 vol 1685–6, I 366–8.
[1] *Works*, VIII 283. This play was written in collaboration with Sir
Robert Howard, but the California editors conclude that Dryden is
'essentially its creator' and speak of the play as his (VII 23).
[2] Arthur Kirsch, in an able analysis of this play, argues that its 'real
hero' is Cortez. *Dryden's Heroic Drama*, 89. See also Kirsch's review of
Works, IX, in which he reaffirms his view: *Philological Quarterly* XLVI,
July 1967, 341. There is little doubt that Kirsch is right about Dryden's
intention. The effect of the concluding act, however, is to elevate
Montezuma and the philosophy that he expresses.

> *Thou art deceived'd: for whensoe're I Dye,*
> *The Sun my Father bears my Soul on high:*
> *He lets down a Beam, and mounted there,*
> *He draws it back, and pulls me through the Air:*
> *I in the Eastern parts and rising Sky,*
> *You in Heaven's downfal, and the West must lye.*[1]

How the Christians shrivel in that natural light—they who preach orthodox doctrine while applying the whip and turning the wheel, who lust for women and for gold, and who profess a frowning Religion and are impelled by 'holy avarice'.[2]

Dryden's social grotesque is a complex and growing concept. In the two 'platonic' plays it takes the form of an interior threat within the character of the good persons, the threat to human order of indulging disruptive sexual fantasies and desires. In the comedy the grotesque is an unconquerable folly that has to be displaced by the new man who rises from a hitherto unrecognized status. And in the Indian plays the grotesque grows within a Christian society that yields to the temptations of gain and the intellectual tyranny that beset it recurringly.

III

The Grotesque of Superstition

It is typical of the probing, tentative, and sceptical mind of the Dryden of the sixties that he should invert his antitheses. We have just beheld a good primitive setting off, in high relief, the social grotesque of Christian villainy. We now consider several socially tempered and benevolent men and women, both pagan and Christian, whose good

[1] V. ii, 43–48. These lines anticipate the majestic opening of *Religio Laici*, where the sun no longer stands for natural religion but for supernatural revelation.

[2] This powerful and satirical oxymoron is uttered to the Christian priest by the grieving and embarrassed Cortez, who runs to take Montezuma off the rack: 'how now, Religion do you Frown? / Haste Avarice, and help him down' (V. ii, 115–16). Whatever may be said about Dryden on English imperialism, his understanding of Spanish behaviour in the New World cannot be faulted.

Foto Alinari

Saint Michael the Archangel by Guido Reni

ness sets off the fierce destructiveness and death-dealing energies of primitive men and women.

On the positive side of this contrast stand three characters from the plays of the decade—the first being Acacis in the *Indian Queen*, a Mexican prince, the son of the usurping Zempoalla, whose violent blood he has not inherited, although his brothers and sisters have, and of a dead father, a mild and gracious ruler from whom he has inherited gentle virtue, noble mildness, and civility. These virtues appear as he releases prisoners, nobly loves the good Orazia, shows chivalry to his rival Montezuma, remains loyal to his friend and his beloved even unto death. His own hand administers that death, and the entire, somewhat ambiguous world of the *Indian Queen* acknowledges the loss of a good and gentle man, charitable and noble, although an Indian pagan.

If Acacis is *homo naturaliter Christianus,* Cortez is the converse, *homo Christiane naturalis*. He possesses the natural virtues of the pagan just as the pagan possesses the Christian virtues of humility and charity. Dryden reveals his scorn of the confinements of religious creed in this period by producing benevolent heroes, baptized and unbaptized. Cortez is, as we have found, hardly a towering hero, and Montezuma upstages him in the final forture scenes of the *Indian Emperour*. But a hero he surely is, courteous as a lover, tolerant as a thinker, faithful to his promises. In the end he regrets deeply the bloody night perpetrated by Christian grotesques and pagan fanatics alike, and he puts an end to the flame, the sword, and the rack.

Berenice, the pagan Roman turned Christian in *Tyrannick Love* (performed 1669), is the third example of the civilized norm, so complexly constituted already of the gentle natural man and the gentle Christian man. Berenice's civility is of sterner stuff than that of the males in the other plays, and her honouring of convention strikes a modern as chilling and perhaps even cruel. She prefers death to the breaking of marriage vows that tie her to a criminal who she hates. She frustrates a plot by her lover, whose love she chastely reciprocates, against the tyrant-husband, whom she loathes—a woman whom her lover describes as 'Too ill a Mistress, and too good a Wife' (V. i, 448). Nevertheless, Dryden gives her a Christian death of beauty and dignity, in full hope of an unsullied union with her lover in the other world. And one would have to say that this heroic woman, this staunch upholder of the virtues of order public and private, this somewhat aggressive instrument of necessary social law, joins Acacis and Cortez as an exemplar of love and loyalty, of the tempered personality whose fires are controlled by the pledged word and responsibility to society.

Against such an ideal Dryden presents the grotesque of wild, savage men and women, of vengeful passions, lawless beliefs, arrogant cosmologies—the grotesque of the elemental superstitions of primitive personality. This grotesque is, like its ideal counterpart, complexly constituted, appearing to be of two kinds: the grandly impressive, the proto-heroic—the stuff of which true heroes could be made if the direction were different and the controls stronger; and the contemptible and loathsome, the ridiculously and dangerously sub-human or monstrous. Zempoalla is of the first variety and the monsters and sailors in *The Tempest* are of the second.

Zempoalla, the Indian Queen, with a few changes in the chemistry of her nature, could have emerged as finely tempered steel. But as Dryden and Howard present her, she is a cauldron of seething, primitive passions that boil in her blood and the blood of her children in the sequel play, the *Indian Emperour*. Zempoalla is a usurper, itself a dreaded role in Dryden's category of crimes. She desires the blood of the great, good man whom her gentle son Acacis wishes to spare. She is as passionate in love as she is violent in blood-lust, wishing to possess and command the person of Montezuma. A woman of dreams as well as rages, she seeks out the darker gods of night and the deep places of the earth and the mind; and she courts the elements, wild animals, and serpents, always associated in Dryden's mind with the older grotesques of superstition and the supernatural evil. When these prove ineffectual, Zempoalla turns sceptic, rejecting them and their priests, shrieking out her impieties, threatening to burn the temples of the tyrants of the sky and earth who insist on leaving the soul in perplexity. Coming to believe that the gods are ruled by fate, whose harsh decrees determine the world's course, Zempoalla now and then reminds one of the Restoration naturalist and unbeliever, to whose arguments Dryden was of course fully exposed. Still, Zempoalla is not a metaphysical unbeliever; she is rather a frustrated believer, whose unbelief is the result of rage rather than ratocination. The pagan queen hates virtue—and this is perhaps the most serious charge the play levels against her—considering it

> . . . *only heat*
> *That reigns in Youth, till age findes out the cheat.*

(III. i, 98–99)

In this grotesque of wild blood and hot brains, Dryden anticipates his Maximin and pushes the grotesque of superstition to the frontiers of the grotesque of power.

Such majesty of evil the grotesques of the Davenant-Dryden *Tempest* do not possess, and we confront now the other type of superstitious grotesque, the bestial, ridiculous, but potentially dangerous low characters, Caliban, Sycorax, and the rabble. The monsters of this Restoration adaptation of Shakespeare do share with Zempoalla primitive passions and superstitions, but they are at the other end of the same category of grotesque.

Caliban is of course pure grotesque, closer than any other creation of this period to the abstract definition from the visual arts discussed earlier. He is a modification of Shakespeare's Caliban, whom Dryden admired as a dramatic creation and whom he characterized as possessing 'all the discontents and malice of a witch, and of a devil, besides a convenient proportion of the deadly sins; gluttony, sloth, and lust are manifest; the dejectedness of a slave is likewise given him, and the ignorance of one bred up in a desert island.'[1] Somewhat demythified, as are almost all of Shakespeare's unnatural or supernatural beings, Caliban remains grotesque, an uneducable human-animal—'What have we here, a man, or a fish?'—[2] lecherous, drunken, abject, doomed to a sub-human existence.

[1] 'Preface to Troilus and Cressida' (1679), Watson, I 253.
[2] II. iii, 160. Maximillian E. Novak concludes that Dryden is essentially right about the nature of his collaboration with Davenant—'that Davenant's role was limited to suggestions for a character like Hippolito, to the writing of some sections concerned with the sailors, and to a general supervision'. See *Works*, X 321. It may be, therefore, that some of the materials we are considering as part of Dryden's vision of the grotesque may be less his than Davenant's. Yet surely, as an intimate collaborator, he was close enough to these scenes to allow us to regard

His sister Sycorax possesses approximately the same 'virtues' as he
brother, and the two together add to the monstrousness of the anti
humanity they represent by committing brother-sister incest. Trincalo
who has learned that this lady had 'a Witch to her Mother' and th
Devil 'for Father', comes upon the two in *delicto* that is uncommonl
flagrante:

> . . . *I found her under an Elder-tree,*
> *upon a sweet Bed of Nettles, singing Tory, Rory, and*
> *Ranthum, Scantum, with her own natural brother.*

(IV. ii, 107, 109

This unlovely, loving pair mingle with the sailors; and of the com
merce of the islanders with the Italians Dryden makes lively and inter
esting drama. The sailors become rabble—grotesques of a sub-humai
variety, true brothers of the island naturals. The satire does not attacl
the lower classes *per se:* as humble sailors on their stout ship, fighting th
storm at the beginning or going home at the end, they are admirabl
enough. But drunken, bawdy, lusting for power, trying to create a stat
and falling apart in the process, choosing a king, and playing at being
dukes and viceroys—they then sink to the dregs of democracy an
would pull down, if they could, all nobility, rank, station, decency, an
order. So the sailors, separated from their rightful leaders and joining
the monsters, become like them—only worse; and the island-creature
also sink lower for their commerce with the rabble:

> . . . *The Monsters* Sycorax *and* Caliban
> *More monstrous grow by passions learn'd from man.*

(IV. iii, 270–1

With this kind of grotesque, essentially serious, Dryden permits him
self to be playful, as in farce. And there is hoyden comedy as Trincalc
courts Sycorax, whose 'dear Blobber-lips' long for the boatswain'
whistle and thirst for his wine (III. iii, 12).

When taken as a whole, Dryden's grotesque of superstition may be
viewed as a modified Horatian monster with a head of some magnifi

---

them as a part of his vision of social evil at this time, particularly since
they fit so snugly with Dryden's values.

cence (Zempoalla's, say, the head of an angry and damned rebel). But the creature ends in a fish's tail—the 'human' beasts of the Enchanted Island.[1]

IV

The Grotesque of Power

The climax of the grotesque Dryden created in the sixties comes at the end of the decade in the character of Maximin, the villain of *Tyrannick Love*. As we have already said, that tyrant is anticipated in Zempoalla, lawless, passionate, and impious. It may be asked why the Indian Queen and the Roman Emperor are not placed in the same category of grotesque. To do so would obscure the essential differences. The American Indies being conquered by Christians stand at a great imaginative and moral distance from imperial Rome being converted to Christianity. One is a place of nature, the other of over-ripe institutions. Though Zempoalla is not a monster like Sycorax, she is closer to the island of natural superstitions than is Maximin. The queen lusts for power and tries to use it, but Maximin's power is wielded within institutions the Restoration would recognize as like its own—a powerful ruler abusing his prerogative, a hater of those familiar Anglo-Saxon institutions, the Senate and mixed government. Zempoalla is an exotic pagan confronting good natural men in her own culture. Maximin is also a pagan who nevertheless resembles Cromwell or a French or Spanish Bourbon and who faces pure and primitive Christian thought and character within his own state. Zempoalla faces a natural order that can be insulted more or less with impunity. Maximin faces a supernatural order against which his impieties are blasphemous.

The positive values against which Maximin's impious love and dangerous exercise of power should be seen come from both within and outside the play. The Prospero of *The Tempest*, a play written only

---

[1] Compare Horace's monster, with a human head, a horse's neck, feathered limbs, and a fish's tail (*Ars Poetica*, ll. 1–5), which Dryden frequently used to exemplify the grotesque. See, e.g., 'Dedication of the *Aeneis*', Watson, II 229; and 'A Parallel of Painting and Poetry', Watson, II 189.

two years or so before *Tyrannick Love*, provides one antithesis. Dryden
and his collaborator waver somewhat in the presentation of his character, but the intention is clear: Prospero is supposed to be a good man
of essentially benign power, trying first to train and then, failing that, to
restrain, the wild, natural man in his charge. Somewhat stiff and calculating in his dedication to safe social conventions for his children and
excessively aware of the danger to them that love can create, he is
nevertheless flexible. Each daughter is treated differently, and his plans
are accommodated to rapidly changing conditions and accidents. All in
all, Prospero is realist ('How much in vain it is to bridle Nature')
generous (he will give Ariel his freedom), modest and even sceptical
about his art ('perhaps my Art it self is false'), humble before mystery
('man's life is all a mist'), and pragmatic about the supernatural (if a
fatal event is good, it is from heaven; if evil, from ourselves).[1] He
anticipates the humanistic, ethical, disciplined, and dignified eighteenth-
century man. Although indubitably wise, he is occasionally a bit stuffy
and often cliché-ridden—an Imlac of the Restoration. And perhaps even
a Voltaire or a Goethe! For this benevolent, demythologized ruler
wants the magical island to become 'a place of Refuge to the afflicted'
(V. ii, 261–2).

It is of course not against Prospero in another play but against Saint
Catherine in *Tyrannick Love* that Maximin, the grotesque of power, is
developed. As one would expect from the lover of verse arguments,
Dryden makes his Christian heroine a formidable dialectician, so successful in debate that her opponent, the pagan philosopher Apollonius,
is converted and therewith carried off to his death. Her religion is in its
essence the purest gospel—severely inward, austere, noble, exalted.
The prohibitions against sin are, as in the Sermon on the Mount
(Matthew 5:27–28), extended deep within to the very innermost psyche
where desires are born. According to the heroine-saint, the Christian
cannot even desire another's goods, and 'we proscribe the least immodest thought' (II. i, 218). Saint Catherine's own modesty is awesome
and super-human, if not inhuman. When the lusting but frustrated
emperor has decreed a bloody end for the saint and her mother Felicia—

---

[1] *Tempest*, III. v, 121, 154, 155–62.

the flesh will be torn away in 'gory Gobbet[s]' until the beating heart is exposed—Catherine worries more about an immodest exposure of her body than about her and her mother's joint torture on the wheel and the spike: 'Let not my body be the Tyrant's spoil' (V. i, 251–307). And yet the queen is a woman of human feeling, as the great temptation provided by her mother's weakness and desire to be spared suffering reveals. Rejecting Maximin's foul lust, his gods, his empire, and his bed, Catherine goes to her death a fully responsible creature, willing her own demise and accepting the immediate consequences of her action (V. i, 281–9). We are fortunately spared, by a Christian *deus ex machina*, from the sight of blood and rent flesh; and Catherine goes to a baroque death, one that could be represented by a great seventeenth-century Italian master in a house of prayer. But not by Bernini perhaps—for in Catherine of Alexandria there is no hint of the sensual, no recollection of that other Egyptian queen Dryden was later to represent on the stage, no combination of Ovidian voluptuousness and Christian sweetness.[1] The baroque of Catherine's climactic death is, rather, that of the purer, milder, blander Bolognese eclectics, the Carracci. It is a pure 'spousal' scene with the heavens radiant and the air filled with music and light and love.

Against so lofty an example of Christian thought and Christian style in life and art, the answering grotesque must, in its own way, be equally 'pure'. No outrageous, outlandish monster will do; only the highest, most dangerous evil, the evil of power. Since Christianity was embedded deep in culture, its solutions being theoretically within the power of every citizen and every leader, the threat to it must be plausibly immediate and real. And so Dryden has made it. If Catherine versifies Tillotson, Maximin recalls Hobbes.[2] Guido's Satan was said to resemble Pope Innocent X; Dryden's Maximin is a Western, even an English, Satan, now and then so close to Dryden himself that the following lines

[1] On Mary Magdalens and Cleopatras that resemble each other in baroque art and on the *madonna volutta*, see Hagstrum, *Sister Arts*, 119–20, 195–6.
[2] Bruce King, *Dryden's Major Plays*, N. Y. 1966, 50–58; see also Louis Teeter, 'The Dramatic Use of Hobbes's Political Ideas', *ELH* III, June 1936, esp. 161–2.

of Maximin might have been spoken by a member of the King's party in *Absalom and Achitophel*:

> *The silly crowd, by Factious Teachers brought*
> *To think that Faith untrue their youth was taught,*
> *Run on in new Opinions blindly bold;*
> *Neglect, contemn, and then assault the old.*
> *Th' infectious madness seizes every part,*
> *And from the head distils upon the heart.*
> *And first they think their Princes faith not true,*
> *And then proceed to offer him a new;*
> *Which if refus'd, all duty from 'em cast,*
> *To their new Faith they make new Kings at last.*
>
> (II. i, 143–52)

Yet, however plausible his ideas, Maximin develops into a bitter, relentless tyrant who accepts no free will but his own, who regards the unfettered conscience as his greatest rival, and who would bind free reason with the hideous chains of intellectual and moral bondage. By the end the tyrant has become a full grotesque, decreeing and describing torture and then calling for 'the sport' to begin. And in his death Maximin, raging at his own gods, roars out what we today would call black humour. The dying villain shakes his fist at his gods, declaring his everlasting emnity.:

> *. . . Henceforth I and my World*
> *Hostility with you and yours declare:*
> *Look to it, Gods; for you th' Aggressors are . . .*
> *Your Trade of Heav'n shall soon be at a stand,*
> *And all your goods lie dead upon your hand.*   (V. i, 593–9)

He and Placidius, next to the Emperor the most wicked of the characters, stab one another. Maximin sits dying upon the body of his *quondam* officer, whom he gratuitously stabs again and again. As the tyrant dies he imagines his own flight heavenward, a grotesque parody of Saint Catherine's martyr journey to bliss:

> *And shoving back this Earth on which I sit*
> *I'le mount——and scatter all the Gods I hit.*   (V. i, 633–4)

In dispatching Hobbes-Maximin, Dryden has created a scene of great grotesque energy, and the Emperor—hideous, bold, leering, and fiercely attractive—brings his half of a powerful baroque contrast to a fitting climax.

Maximin also brings the decade we have been studying to a fitting and summary climax. A grotesque of power, he recalls the grotesque of superstition. Grimly serious, he nonetheless has a touch of comic verve, and this '*Son* of a Thracian *Herds-man, and an* Alane *Woman*' is in his last hours not entirely unrelated to the rabble of *The Tempest* who play at being king and viceroy.[1]

V

Dryden and the Supernatural

Maximin is, as we have seen, a Satan who is fully human. He approaches the magnificent lineaments of Milton's mighty figure in *Paradise Lost*, which had appeared only three years before the publication of *Tyrannick Love*. To achieve the human grotesque of such plausibility and power must have cost Dryden a good deal of energy and even anguish, an anguish born out of his having to face the very disturbing matter of supernatural and metaphysical evil. No study of Dryden's grotesque in the sixties would be complex enough or complete if it ignored the marks of struggle one sees upon the poet in this, the period of his great apprenticeship. These signs appear in many strange and baffling ways: awkwardness and embarrassment in dealing with the supernatural, an excessive and inappropriate merriment in dealing with the diabolical, some infirmity of purpose and unsteadiness of aim in portraying his heroes, the dazzling virtuoso alternations in vigorous argument between equally plausible alternatives, and above all the heightening and lowering the tone with confusing swiftness. The subject is extremely elusive and will have to be dealt with in caution.

Dryden's treatment of the supernatural in general throws light on his handling of the diabolical grotesque in particular. In the preface to

---

[1] Preface to *Tyrannick Love, Works*, X 112. Novak, who notices the grotesque quality in Maximin, relates it in part to the Emperor's plebeian and boorish qualities: *ibid.*, 389.

Tyrannick Love, in which he defends his right to portray the grotesque of evil that Maximin represents, he affirms, somewhat defensively one feels, his own faith in Christianity. He also declares that the drama ought to 'second the Precepts of our Religion' in decently representing 'patterns of piety . . . equally removed from the extremes of Superstition and Prophaneness'.[1] One must of course take Dryden at his word and respect his sincerity. At the same time one cannot ignore the many ironies and incongruities that surround this austerely Christian play, with its super-human ideals of inward purity, played before an audience, in part devout, and in part bawdy and loud, an audience that included scoffers, libertines, and the Merry Monarch himself. It was said that Nell Gwynn, who played the part of the love-martyr Valeria, became the King's mistress during the play's run—a fact which, if true, compounds the ironies, for the play was written to honour Charles's queen, Catherine of Braganza. That Nell as Valeria caught the roving royal eye may be no more than rumour, but it is fact that at the end of this most Christian play Nell spoke a naughty and merry epilogue as she was being carried off by the bearers just after she had stabbed herself for her lost love. Calling the bearer a 'confounded Dog' for taking her away, she rose to speak the lilting lines that begin: 'I am the ghost of poor departed *Nelly*.' Scoffing at her posthumous condition as a love martyr in a religious play, she said:

> *I'm what I was, a little harmless Devil*
> *For after death, we Sprights have just such Natures*
> *We had, for all the World, when humane Creatures.*
>
> (Epilogue, ll. 4–6)

We are suddenly, after the baroque world of Catherine's death, in the land of Restoration gaiety that looks ahead to Pope's Ariel in the *Rape of the Lock*.

   Such sudden change in tone from the sublimely serious to the wittily ridiculous was perhaps one of the young Dryden's concession to his merry and irreverent age. If so, he made it often enough for one to feel that there was something far from uncongenial in the sceptical mockery that is now and then allowed to dissipate the solemnity. We have noticed

---

1 Preface to *Tyrannick Love*, *Works*, X 109.

how Zempoalla and Maximin can suddenly turn and rage against the
gods and their priests. Although the Christian Dryden shared their dislike of priestcraft, he never treated the Christian Trinity with similar
irreverence. And yet the examples that follow scarcely reveal humble
piety before supernatural mystery. In *Annus Mirabilis* God himself
extinguishes the flames that are devouring London:

> *An hollow chrystal Pyramid he takes,*
> *In firmanental waters dipt above;*
> *Of it a brode Extinguisher he makes*
> *And hoods the flames that to their quarry strove.*

(stanza 281)

Dr Johnson, who disliked religion in verse and who wanted grandeur to
be kept general, found the image 'unexpectedly mean', and Sir Walter
Scott deplored the wild mixture of metaphors from candle-snuffing to
falconry.[1] Prospero's supernatural ministrations never put him in the
role of a celestial fire-chief, but he is sufficiently embarrassed to wonder
if 'perhaps my Art it self is false' (*Tempest* III, 154). In *The Indian Emperour* Dryden comes close to parodying *On the Morning of Christ's
Nativity* (ll. 173–220): just as the coming of the Christ child sent the
pagan deities whirring through the air, so in Mexico the new Christian
God will drive away the native deities from their beloved earth, a God
who, in a bitter final irony, turns out to be Gold:

> *A God more strong, who all the gods commands,*
> *Drives us to exile from our Native Lands;*
> *The Air swarms thick with wandring Deities,*
> *Which drowsily like humming Beetles rise*
> *From their lov'd Earth, where peacefully they slept,*
> *And far from Heaven a long possession kept.*
> *The frightened* Satyrs *that in Woods delight,*
> *Now into Plains with prick'd up Ears take flight;*
> *And scudding thence, while they their horn-feet ply*
> *About their Syres the little* Silvans *cry.*
> *A Nation loving Gold must rule this place,*
> *Our Temples Ruine, and our Rites Deface.*   (II. i, 25–36)

[1] Note to ll. 1121–4 in *Works*, I 317.

The contemporary of Hobbes, the member and apostrophizer of the Royal Society, is not at ease in Zion! Dryden's vision of the supernatural reveals, in his earlier years, a curious mixture of embarrassment, distance, and a humour which is wry if not black.

If the portrayals of supernatural good boldly approach the irreverent, the portrayals of cosmological evil go over the border. Dryden of course had inevitably to be concerned with the devil: anyone setting his hand to the creation of grotesques would sooner or later encounter the father of all grotesquerie. The young Dryden was absolutely relentless in reducing the 'black Gentleman' (*Tempest* III. ii, 46) to a comic grotesque. In his 'first attempt . . . in *Dramatique Poetry*', *The Wild Gallant*, performed first in 1662, the hero Loveby has much to do with Satan (who is only one of the *dramatis personae* in disguise). He meets the devil outrageously tricked out 'à l'antique', jokes with him, treats him as an old friend, uses him to flick at churchmen and fanatics, praises him as a 'very honest and well-natur'd fellow', chides him when he does not reveal the source of the unexpected gifts of money. Loveby gets cosy enough to allow the devil to call himself Loveby's 'Genius', and he addresses Loveby as 'my Son', leading him in the end to his beloved Constance and the person who marries them. Evil spirits appear in the play and are mercilessly laughed at, as are those who believe in them. One old fool believes that the females of his household and also he himself are pregnant by the agency of the devil. Surely Dryden is joining the younger wits of the Restoration in laughing at the devil-superstitions of their elders.[1]

Horseplay with the devil and his minions was not new to the drama. But even in devil farces Satan was taken seriously, sometimes carried off by a Vice to the place of torment. Ben Jonson's devil is an ass, not because he is laughable or because he is only someone else in disguise but because he is outwitted in evil by men who are worse than he.[2] Dryden's purpose, however, is not to satirize evil as stupid but to laugh

---

[1] See Preface and esp. the following scenes in *The Wild Gallant*: II. i; II. ii; III. ii; IV. ii; V. ii, iii, iv.

[2] See Alan C. Dessen, *Jonson's Moral Comedy*, Evanston, Illinois 1971, 221–35.

at the devil himself, his very existence. He dethrones Satan from a place of fear in men's minds to an object of their comfortable laughter. In *The Tempest* he and his collaborator continue the gay demythologizing of the supernatural evil being. The Italian nobility on the enchanted island are hungry and thirsty and have a vision of what Gonzalo especially longs for—'Boyl'd/Bak'd, and Roasted' meat. Eight fat, well-fed spirits enter with a cornucopia. Gonzalo, thinking they are devils, cries out, 'O for a Collop of that large-haunch'd Devil'. For a feast at that moment the Christian will risk even damnation: 'if the black Gentleman be so ill-natur'd, he may do his pleasure'. (III. ii, 34–35, 39, 46–47)

Dryden's merry way with Satan and devils makes it difficult to believe we are in the age of Baxter and Bunyan, an age when Satan was very real and very much feared and when orthodox opinion urged that disbelief in supernatural evil was a first and inevitable step to atheism. And of course Dryden's age and the immediately subsequent one reacted strongly. Writing in 1673 Richard Leigh, attacked the supernatural in heroic plays, not only 'Heroes, more lawless than their *Savages*', but also 'notional *creatures, Astrall* Spirits, *Ghosts*, & *Idols*'.[1] Two years before Dryden's death, Jeremy Collier censured Dryden's *An Evening's Love, or the Mock Astrologer* (performed in 1668). Its first act includes a scene set in a chapel, a 'sacred place' to the Christian polemicist but one Dryden desecrated with ridicule of devotion along with the other world, Scripture, and the sanctions of the pulpit. Collier was especially offended at the ridicule of the supernatural evil, the making sport, at the close of the play, with 'Apparitions and Fiends': 'One of the Devils sneezes, upon this they give him the Blessing of the Occasion, and conclude *he has got cold by being too long out of the Fire.*' Granted that Collier's conscience was excessively tender—he was capable of being outraged at the charming opening lines of *Absalom and Achitophel*—and granted too that he came late in the day and may have taken much too seriously the Restoration joke. But is it hard to see why the faithful would wince, since they believed with Collier that the Scriptures provided 'a frightful Idea . . . of hell', described in

---

[1] Quoted by Kirsch, *Dryden's Heroic Drama*, 39.

'all the Circumstance of Terror', as a 'solemn warning'? Dryden had in their eyes 'diverted himself with the *Terrors* of *Christianity*'.[1]

Dryden's ambiguous way with the supernatural has complicated our analysis of his early grotesque. It should not obscure his twofold achievement in the sixties: the casting out of the demonic, allaying the power of the superstitious grotesque by laughing at it and burying it; and transferring evil to the mind of responsible men and to society. He shifted the focus of evil from super-nature to nature, from a *post mortem* hell to present reality. Satan does not cease to exist, only the excessively grotesque and farcically inhuman devil does. Satan is re-born as a human figure, vastly more menacing than the cloven-footed and horned monster of superstitious legend and primitive belief. He becomes the superstitious tyrant, Zempoalla, and that anti-man, the towering grotesque of power, the Emperor Maximin. These grotesques make war, as Satan always has, on humanity itself and the structures it has erected for stability and self-realization. And these grotesques, along with others we have studied, reappear in Dryden's greatest work. The grotesque social fool is born again in Buckingham, Achitophel revives the grotesque of lawless and destructive power, and the grotesque of untamable passion, primitive and unstable, reappears in Antony.

To prepare for that great human achievement—the creation of grotesques that threaten psychological peace and corporate safety—Dryden had to exorcize unnatural silliness, to cleanse the mind of supernatural fears and to allow it to concentrate on real and present dangers. He abandoned or modified the older and cruder grotesques of emblem art, or mannerist and baroque hells, of the distorted fancies of *capricci* and *bizarrie*, and even of Shakespearean magic.[2] The last scene

---

[1] *A Short View of the Immorality and Profaneness of the English Stage*, 61, 191, 193; facsimile of 3rd ed 1698, Munich 1967, with a *Nachwort* by Ulrich Broich.

[2] 'But *Shakespeare's* Magick could not copy'd be, / Within that Circle none durst walk but he.' (Prologue to *Tempest*, ll.19–20). For a somewhat different view of the grotesques in Dryden's *Tempest*, see Willard Farnham's *The Shakespearean Grotesque*, Oxford 1971, 156–9, which studies Caliban's transformation 'from a monstrous underling capable of strange nobilities of spirit into a monstrous underling pure and simple' (159).

(V. ii) of the Dryden-Davenant *Tempest* is eloquent. It is the fate of those 'mishapen creatures' (l. 223), as Gonzalo calls them, the children of a powerful witch, simply to be left behind. Caliban, who is now over his illusion that the drunken sailors were gods and who now, with his sister, admires those 'brave Sprights' (l. 228), the Italian gentlemen, has to submit to rejection, as though there were no room for him and his kind in the new dispensation. And when Sycorax offers to come with her sometime husband and keep him warm in his cabin, Trincalo replies: 'No my dainty Dy-dapper, you have a tender constitution, and will be sick a Ship-board. You are partly Fish and may swim after me. I wish you a good Voyage' (ll. 251–53). And so the grotesques are remanded to the sea, out of sight, out of mind—to that oblivion, in fact, where Guido had wanted to consign the Satan that appeared at the bottom of his painting.

Little in human culture appears to be permanent. And Dryden's attempts to exorcize metaphysical and cosmological evil, transferring the grotesque to the human plane where human reason and will could subdue it, opened up enormous possibilities for realistic, social, psychological, and moral art. But in the Romantic age and in post-Romantic cultures the grotesque of deep, permanent, and universal evil—fatal, deterministic, unassailable—revived and was re-mythologized. To return to the painting which I made the emblem of this chapter, we find that Hawthorne's Miriam in *The Marble Faun* rejects Hilda's love of the dainty and beautiful Saint Michael and calls for a "smoke-blackened fiery-eyed demon, bestriding that nice young angel, clutching his white throat with one of his hinder claws" (Chap. 20). Dryden might have said of Hawthorne and his century, or of Joyce and our century, what he could not have said of the eighteenth century, but what he did say of the seventeenth century as it and his own life came to a close: 'Thy Chase had a Beast in View.'[1]

Dryden's grotesque belongs, as we saw at the outset, in the framework of the baroque. Just as Dryden throughout his life continued to produce versions of the grotesque, so the larger ambiance of the baroque continued to nourish his spirit. In what he termed 'the descrip-

---

[1] *The Secular Masque* (1700), l. 93.

tions or images' of that early 'Historical Poem', *Annus Mirabilis*, the pompous decorations of baroque allegory constantly appear. The heroic plays continue to develop those massive baroque contrasts of light and dark, good and evil, that we have considered to be the essence of the antithesis that contains the grotesque. One great historical satire at least, *Absalom and Achitophel*, unfolds as a grand baroque display, massing its opposed legions as though on the canvas of a Last Judgment. *All for Love* may recall one of the central themes—and even visual arrangements—of seventeenth-century art, Hercules at the Crossroads, and the great odes embody such obsessive baroque subjects as Saint Cecilia and such insistently baroque habits of thought as the virtual deification of authority. Dryden's imagination submits easily to upward-sweeping and curving forms of the plastic baroque, filling his sky with angels who descend and ascend. And the commerce of earth and sky is accompanied by grandiose celebrations of music, poetry and painting, secular and religious, not unlike the exaltation of the icon in the propaganda art of Counter-Reformation culture.[1]

The grotesque, however, although it is developed primarily in connection with—or more precisely *against*—baroque idealization, is also related to that side of Dryden's spirit that has been called neoclassical. At the outset I described Guido's painting as baroque. It is more accurate to call it baroque and neoclassical. Guido imitated Raphael, who in turn had imitated ancient marbles in creating the delicate, lovely, decorous humanity that endeared him to the subsequent centuries. For Dryden's age and the eighteenth century, Guido's and Raphael's much-loved 'air' became a paradigm for graceful, urbane, and fully human reality. Dryden has often been regarded as the founder of English neoclassicism, but he is more properly thought the inheritor, refiner, and propagator of a native strain emanating from Jonson and earlier writers. Of that strain he makes a spiritual countermovement to the exalted, religious, authoritarian, and highly decorated baroque. It cannot be ignored that the baroque of Dryden takes on a special quality by co-existing with a powerful desire to imitate the decorum of the

[1] For further discussion of the baroque elements summarized here, see Hagstrum, *Sister Arts*, 178–81, 190–6, 197–209.

classics, to refine the language, to discipline the imagination, and to transform the brick of crude satire to the marble of Horace. And this society-oriented virtuoso, who worked to develop sweet and sounding numbers and condensed, precise, and worldly speech, was also not unaffected by the neoclassical ambition in his creation of the grotesque. For it was, as we have seen, his accomplishment to transfer the grotesque from the supernatural to the natural sphere—to demythologize it and make it a more human and socially effective literary form.

Viewed broadly, the grotesque has its proper context not in the baroque alone but also in what may be called—if we are permitted to use the term loosely and suggestively—neoclassical empiricism.[1] The grotesque may in fact be the fruit of a union that brought together an imaginative energy that pushed upward toward the sublime, boldly risking the abyss of the bathetic, with an intellectually sharp, civilized, and this-worldly rationality that tried to apply the *frein vital*[2] to all human concerns.

---

[1] I borrow this term (used in connection with literature and art) from my own *Samuel Johnson's Literary Criticism*, Chicago 1967, ch. 1. ('Experience and Reason') and from Donald Greene's cogent article, 'Augustinianism and Empiricism: A note on Eighteenth-Century Intellectual History' in *Eighteenth-Century Studies* I, Sept. 1967, 33–68, esp. 34–36. See also Robert Hume's persuasive discussion in ch. 5 (on neo-classicism) of his *Dryden's Criticism*. For a defence of the use of the term neoclassicism, see James William Johnson, *The Formation of English Neo-Classical Thought*, Princeton 1967, ch. 1.

[2] The French phrase comes from Irving Babbitt, who used it to attack what he regarded as the Romantics' lack of vital control.

5: Dryden's Panegyrics and Lyrics

ARTHUR W. HOFFMAN

JOHN DRYDEN's career as a poet obliged to deal with public figures and public occasions began almost at the moment of the Restoration of Charles II and ended very shortly after James II went into exile, and resumed those Stuart travels that his brother Charles had successfully vowed not to undertake again. Both the beginning and the ending of this long stretch of Dryden's career are associated with dramatic historical events, the return of Charles in triumph and the departure of James in bitter retreat and, as it turned out, final exclusion. The poems clustered around the Restoration begin with the death of Cromwell, which opened the way for the King's return and foreshadowed that event. *Heroic Stanzas* ('. . . to the Memory of . . . Oliver Late Lord Protector . . .'), published in 1659, was followed by three poems in an annual series, poems in praise of the public figures and in celebration of the official events which constituted the Restoration: *Astraea Redux* ('A Poem on the Happy Restoration and Return of His Sacred Majesty Charles the Second'), in 1660; *To His Sacred Majesty* ('A Panegyrick on His Coronation'), in 1661; *To My Lord Chancellor*, in 1662. Dryden returned to the mode of official panegyric in a major way with *Threnodia Augustalis* ('A Funeral-Pindarique Poem Sacred to the Happy Memory of King Charles II'), in 1685, and *Britannia Rediviva* ('A Poem on the Prince Born on the 10th. of June, 1688'), in 1688; it should not, however, be overlooked that he had practised it also in the short form of a prologue addressed to the King and Queen, a prologue addressed to James, Duke of York, and a poem to the Duchess of York, all of these written in the early 1680s and associated with the winding down of the crisis produced by the efforts to exclude James from succession to the throne. There are important differences among the six major poems in this general grouping, but there are reasons for separating them from other poems that Dryden designates as panegyric (e.g. *Eleonora*) as well as poems so thoroughly devoted to the development of a focus of praise that critics usually call them panegyrics (e.g. *To Her Grace the Dutchess of Ormond*). All six poems are focused on issues of government, and among the matters they consider are the head of state and his character, the monarch in relation to his realm, the beginning of a reign with the coronation of a king, the transmission of the king's power to his subjects, the death of a king as end and beginning, and the birth of an heir to the throne.

That Dryden as a poet was bound to deal with these matters may serve to call attention to several dimensions of obligation present in different degrees during the course of Dryden's career. In continuation of Renaissance tradition, Dryden, like Milton, conceives his role as a poet as entailing the responsible consideration of those at the head of society and the issues and events in which theirs is the leading role. Throughout his life, whether in the vein of satire or of compliment, Dryden undertakes to fulfil this traditional social responsibility of the poet. A different dimension of obligation came to bear on Dryden in 1668 when he became Poet Laureate. While the four major poems he had written on affairs of state between 1659 and 1662 had reflected part of Dryden's own conception of his role as a poet, after 1668 poems devoted to such subjects had to be conceived as official poems, expressions of the Poet Laureate. That the Laureateship need not be a deadening condition was established brilliantly in *Absalom and Achitophel* (1681) but, of course, rhetoric of praise had a secondary, though not submerged, role in that poem. The two major occasions when Dryden's Augustan idea of a poet and his tenure as Laureate operated together to define an obligation to praise came in 1685, with the sudden death of Charles II, and in 1688, with the birth of an heir to James II. At the death of Charles, Dryden spoke as laureate for the nation, with a sense of trials successfully combatted and endured, trials the challenge of which the poet had had some considerable share in meeting. At the birth of a Catholic heir to the throne, Dryden was once more writing out of his office and allegiance to the Stuarts, perhaps also out of a special sense of fealty to a co-religionist, but against an ominous background. He knew that in celebrating the birth of James's heir he did not speak for the nation; by 1688 James had alienated most of his subjects, including many Catholics. Dryden performed his official task of celebrating a beginning. It is quite likely that he knew that he might well be announcing an end.

One of the clearest distinctions between the time of Dryden and the time of Pope has to do with the closeness of a major poet to the throne. Maynard Mack, writing about Pope, says, 'The time was past when any serious writer could find his place to stand beside the throne. Dryden had managed this, and in his finest poems speaks as if the establishment, with the monarchy its centre, spoke through him—the last principle of order in a disintegrating world. But for Pope, after the death of Anne, the throne as centre of the dream of the civilized community has become absurd. . . . Dryden's angle of vision was no longer available to a serious poet.'[1] After 1689, when Dryden was dismissed from the Laureateship and isolated from his former mode of participation in society by restrictions enacted against his religious beliefs, his angle of vision toward the throne moved closer to that characteristic of Pope. Pope expresses himself as proud that he had taken up the pen to praise only in the case of Harley, and then only after that statesman's fall from power. Johnson deplores Dryden's facility in the vein of compliment. To be placed 'forever near a throne' expressed a condition that Pope could formulate and employ as an anathema. To be placed near the throne was, for just short of thirty years, twenty-one of those years as laureate, a condition of Dryden's activity as a poet.

In writing *Heroic Stanzas* in memory of Oliver Cromwell, Dryden was not yet functioning in positive relation to the throne, but he was writing about affairs at the centre of society and celebrating the position occupied by the man who had ordered that society in the absence of a monarch. Unlike the three panegyrics soon to follow in the 1660s, this poem is written in quatrains—Davenant's *Gondibert* stanza. What Dryden contrives to do with the ordonnance of the poem is to begin and

---

[1] Maynard Mack, *The Garden and the City: Retirement and Politics in the Later Poetry of Pope, 1731–1743*, Toronto 1969, 234–5.

nd with quiet dignity and solemnity, bringing his reader at both points nto the funeral situation itself, the presence of the body stilled in death ind later the image of dust and a silent urn, while between these two reverentially quiet moments he spreads the extraordinary activity and strength of Cromwell, his intelligence, his discerning judgment of men, out above all his commanding force. Through this middle section of the poem Dryden manages the verse form so that the opening lines of stanzas support the suggestion of decisiveness by abrupt trochaic or spondaic initial feet, sometimes further highlighted by a radically early caesura:

> *He, private, mark'd the faults of others sway,* . . . (33)
> *Peace was the Prize of all his toyles and care,* . . . (61)
> *Swift and resistlesse through the Land he past* . . . (49)[1]

Not only do the quatrains open strongly, but many of them have a re-newed firm beginning, whether as antithesis or parallel continuation, in the opening elements of the third line. When the idea to be expressed is speed and force of movement, as in the quatrain beginning with the last line cited above, Dryden removes most of the indication of end-stops and medial pauses and creates something close to an unimpeded movement through four lines:

> *Swift and resistlesse through the Land he past*
> *Like that bold* Greek *who did the East subdue;*
> *And made to battails such Heroick haste*
> *As if on wings of victory he flew.* (49–52)

There is throughout the poem a relentless Protestant concentration on the individual, on the man. It would be difficult to find another poem so dominated by the pronoun 'he'. And this, of course, is as it must be, since the man is everything and the office nothing. Powerful, complex, traditional systems of symbolism cannot be drawn in because the man is the structure, the beginning and the end of it. 'The King is dead, long

---

[1] *Works*, I 12–13. The two major poems discussed that are not yet pub-lished in the California Edition are *Alexander's Feast* (1697) and *To Her Grace the Dutchess of Ormond* (1700); these poems are cited from the edi-tion of James Kinsley, *The Poems of John Dryden*, 4 vol Oxford 1958.

live the King!' is a theme that cannot be approached. The focus of the
praise is and must be heroic virtue. Perhaps as a consequence, the poem's
figuration involves elements of eccentricity as it touches the motif of
sovereignty or authority. Metaphysical conceits, akin specifically to
those of Cowley, appear:

> *'Tis true, his Count'nance did imprint an awe,*
> *And naturally all souls to his did bow;*
> *As* Wands of Divination *downward draw*
> *And point to Beds where Sov'raign Gold doth grow.*
>
> (73–76)

> *When such* Heröique Vertue *Heav'n sets out,*
> *The Starrs like* Commons *sullenly obey;*
> *Because it draines them when it comes about,*
> *And therefore is a taxe they seldome pay.*   (105–8)

Though stated with admirable clarity and compression, tailored to the
four-line stanza, the conceits mingle cumulatively with figures more
directly classical both in form and in allusive content. Elements of the
traditional symbolic structure can be variously attempted and touched
but in this context he failed to excite its proliferating and extensive
resonances.

The three poems that follow the Cromwell stanzas all express joy at
the return of Charles, but it is the restoration of kingship and the throne
to which they are centrally addressed. 'Justice brought back' translates
the title of the first in the series, and the title signifies not that Charles is
justice, but that the return of 'His Sacred Majesty' marks the resump-
tion of a sanctioned structure of law and the prospect of stable continuity:

> *And now times whiter Series is begun*
> *Which in soft Centuries shall smoothly run* . . . (292–3)

Astraea Redux deals with the physical advent of the King and expresses
the renewed adjustment of subjects to their lawful monarch as well as
of the monarch to the condition of his subjects and country. *To His
Sacred Majesty* is a celebration of the ritual moment of anointment, the
coronation. *To My Lord Chancellor* deals with the ways in which the

power wielded by the King is and should be channelled into the actions that give shape and direction to society and that practically convey his influence and concern to all of his subjects.

These poems are all written in couplets, and Dryden does not avail himself of devices of expansion which became characteristic of his later verse. He does, however, especially in *Astraea Redux* and *To My Lord Chancellor*, possibly as a carry-over from writing in quatrains, employ quite a few run-over or lightly end-stopped couplets which produce the effect of movement continued through four lines and, in at least one case in *To My Lord Chancellor*, (113-18), through six lines. Stricter observance of the closure of the couplet in the coronation panegyric, *To His Sacred Majesty*, creates an effect of couplet stichomythia, but this inclination toward greater inflexibility of form may be related to the ritual character of the occasion. The expansion from couplet to triplet, with the third line often an Alexandrine (a procedure which Dryden learned to use very effectively, and which is characteristic of his later verse) does not appear in these poems. They are the poorer for the lack of this mode of variation and avenue of expression, but they have their own merits.

What some of these merits are could be illustrated from any one of them or from all three, but *To My Lord Chancellor* will serve because it seems to benefit from Dryden's work on the earlier poems and to achieve a certain ease and graciousness of manner which appear again in consummate form in the last decade of Dryden's career in poems such as *To . . . Mr Congreve* and *To Her Grace, the Dutchess of Ormond*. When Dryden is speaking about Charles and to Charles, there is a necessary distance to be preserved and even, for all the mood of rejoicing, some awkwardness of recollected and still-to-be-overcome estrangement. The speaker, with the nation, is not yet purged of guilt for the interregnum, the period now figured as a second deluge: the return of the son refreshes the memory of the beheading of the father. Nervousness and apprehension are commingled with celebration and joy. The manner of address to a king is not new, but partly forgotten and disused. In addressing a poem to Edward Hyde, Earl of Clarendon, Dryden pays tribute to a man whose service to Charles, the father and the son, has been loyal and uninterrupted. He is also addressing a man

who, in his younger days, had been in a modest way a poet and on term
of friendship with Ben Jonson, with Cowley and Carew, and wit
Edmund Waller. In the context of Clarendon's devotion to the King, a
well as his affection for poets, the highest orders of symbolism in rela
tion to the monarch,—both Christian and classical in derivation—
come easily into play, while at the same time the elevation of poetry i
far from incidental:

> *When our Great Monarch into Exile went*
> *Wit and Religion suffer'd banishment:*
> *Thus once when* Troy *was wrapt in fire and smoak*
> *The helpless Gods their burning shrines forsook;*
> *They with the vanquisht Prince and party go,*
> *And leave their Temples empty to the fo:*
> *At length the Muses stand restor'd again*
> *To that great charge which Nature did ordain;*
> *And their lov'd Druyds seem reviv'd by Fate*
> *While you dispence the Laws and guide the State.*   (17–2ℂ

The figuration is classical, the topics linked are poetry and religion, an
the temples left empty seem to stand at once for the shrines of art an
those of faith. The role of the King as God's vicegerent, enacting withi
society functions parallel to and in harmony with those of his Make:
can be expressed in directly Christian symbolism:

> *By you he fits those Subjects to obey,*
> *As Heavens Eternal Monarch does convey*
> *His pow'r unseen, and man to his designs,*
> *By his bright Ministers the Stars, inclines.*   (83–8ℂ

The idea of the secret transmission of power is so placed that the trans:
tive verb ends one couplet, that end being easily and quietly run over t
get to the object, 'pow'r', which begins the next couplet. The adroitnes
of the versification in thus opening one couplet into another is an earl
instance of a kind of skill in verbal maneuver which one comes to ex
pect in Dryden's later poems.

Twelve lines later the god-analogue shifts to a classical context an
once again strikingly figures the relation of the King and his ministe:

> *Shown all at once you dazled so our eyes,*
> *As new-born* Pallas *did the Gods surprise;*
> *When springing forth from* Jove's *new-closing wound*
> *She struck the Warlick Spear into the ground;*
> *Which sprouting leaves did suddenly inclose,*
> *And peaceful Olives shaded as they rose.* (99–104)

From the symbolic expression in these lines it is an easy step to direct discussion of 'the arts of Peace' and to praise of Clarendon for his quiet mastery of the complexities of government. Clarendon, by delegated authority, governs in a realm in which the intricacy and variety of movements and pressures, attractions and repulsions, effects and counter-effects, are akin to the complexly interrelated movements of the spheres in the order of the cosmos. At one remove from the King, here is the traditional symbolic expression of orderly government with the sun as the physical centre and God as the spiritual centre of ultimate order. What Dryden manages to do here with this figure of spacious dignity is to transmute it into an apt expression of the daily successful discharge of the manifold duties of a minister of state, and to associate the consequent calm and quiet achieved in the realm with the stillness of space and majestic order of the stars:

> *Such is the mighty swiftnesse of your mind*
> *That (like the earth's) it leaves our sence behind;*
> *While you so smoothly turn and roul our Sphear,*
> *That rapid motion does but rest appear.*
> *For as in Natures swiftnesse, with the throng*
> *Of flying Orbs while ours is born along,*
> *All seems at rest to the deluded eye:*
> *(Mov'd by the Soul of the same harmony)*
> *So carry'd on by your unwearied care*
> *We rest in Peace and yet in motion share.* (109–18)

The unusual sequence and enjambement in the last three couplets are finely adjusted to the themes of motion and rest which they convey.

Dryden also shows himself capable of developing an extended comparison and amplifying details in support of the whole. He does this perhaps most notably in a context of paradox in which he opposes Clarendon's eminence and equality, his loftiness yet ease of access, and the fact that though secure, he is subject to and a centre of assault. The emphasis falls on a natural phenomenon and features of the order of nature, but the allusions incorporated, especially in the early lines and near the end, extend the whole with major classical symbols of order in which the arts and religion are once again drawn together:

> *In all things else above our humble fate*
> *Your equal mind yet swells not into state,*
> *But like some mountain in those happy Isles*
> *Where in perpetual Spring young Nature smiles,*
> *Your greatnesse shows: no horrour to afright*
> *But Trees for shade, and Flow'rs to court the sight;*
> *Sometimes the Hill submits itself a while*
> *In small descents, which do its height beguile;*
> *And sometimes mounts, but so as billows play*
> *Whose rise not hinders but makes short our way.*
> *Your brow which does no fear of thunder know*
> *Sees rouling tempests vainly beat below;*
> *And (like* Olympus *top,) th'impression wears*
> *Of Love and Friendship writ in former years.*   (133–46)

To My Lord Chancellor is a poem in which the whole interlocking traditional system of symbolism radiating from the King as God's agent in history can be touched and activated.[1] In its figuration, the poem presents the King in direct relation to God, the King as the sun, the stars as the King's ministers; the ranks and relations of orbs and spheres, motions and order of the cosmos as structure and function in the realm; and the King as soul of the nation whose spirits flow through the body politic. Partly, I suppose, because Dryden was in this poem supporting a man who for all his powers was at this point in some actual difficulty,[2] and partly because Clarendon offered Dryden an opportunity to con-

---

[1] For discussion of this traditional system of symbolism as developed by Dryden, see Hoffman, 25–30, 148–56; Roper, 50–103. For more general consideration of the tradition, see Ernst Kantorowicz, *The King's Two Bodies: A Study in Mediaeval Political Theology,* Princeton 1957.

[2] '. . . the Lord Chancellor had aroused envy . . . and a storm had gathered to shatter the calm of his good fortune. To Clarendon's friends the hostility must have appeared formidable . . .' *Works,* I 242.

sider not only justice and the arts of government but also the arts of peace and the ideal of civilized community, the poem manages to so blend its dignified symbolism with a sense of human and social rapport, that love and friendship can be honoured even though they may be rare in the atmosphere of power and high place.

Such were the notes struck by Dryden at the beginning of a reign that was to extend over two dozen years. In 1685 Dryden, as laureate, who himself had a great part in the trials and successes of the reign of Charles II, faced the responsibility of an official poem lamenting the King's death, and he produced a large if not a magnificent poem, the longest of the commemorative poems (eighteen stanzas, five hundred and seventeen lines), written in the pindaric mode. Perhaps in no other poem did Dryden speak so distinctly in his official role. With high seriousness he put on priestly robes for the occasion and brought himself as close as could be to the throne. In *Threnodia Augustalis* he spoke as the priest of Augustus and the servant of kings.

As Scott long ago noticed, the title-page of the poem is most unusual: *Threnodia Augustalis*, A Funeral-Pindarique Poem, Sacred to the Happy Memory of King Charles II, By John Dryden, Servant to His late Majesty, and to the Present King.' The title and identification of the author are designed to ascribe more than conventionally the quality of happiness to what had been, after all, and not very long ago, a dramatically troubled and threatened reign, and in doing so to associate James as closely as possible with his brother. It is even possible that Dryden had already decided not to write a separate poem for the coronation of James, but rather to celebrate the new reign immediately, and to relate it to the memory of Charles, who had fought so stubbornly and so adroitly to secure the continuity of succession. The poem expresses its utmost commitment to Charles and to the throne by continuing the effort to which both Charles and Dryden had already given so much. Even though, at the time of the poem, he had not yet been officially confirmed as the Laureate of the new reign, Dryden insists on the continuity by presenting himself as servant to the present king as he had been to his late brother. The evidence of the poem itself, the disposition of emphases within it, strongly bear out that such are the designs of the title.

For the epigraph of the poem, Dryden chose lines from the ninth book of the *Aeneid*, lines at the end of the episode of Nisus and Euryalus. These lines immediately follow the description of dying Nisus, still fighting to avenge his dead friend, Euryalus, and finally collapsing on his body; in Dryden's translation they are:

> *O happy Friends! for, if my Verse can give*
> *Immortal Life, your Fame shall ever live. (Aeneis, IX, 597–8)*

James had fought for Charles and Charles for James; the allusion honours the two together and intensifies their closeness. Dryden has done and is doing his utmost for both of them.

To say that the poem has a tactical disposition in relation to issues of state is not to say that the lament for Charles is not properly conducted. The priestly speaker expresses the intensely focused emotional impact of a sudden death as well as a sense of implications ominously widening out to a cosmic event. Both of these recognitions figure in the first stanza and offer some illustration of the latitude and varying capacity of the pindaric:

> *Thus long my Grief has kept me dumb:*
> *Sure there's a Lethargy in mighty Woe,*
> *Tears stand congeal'd, and cannot flow;*
> *And the sad Soul retires into her inmost Room:*
> *Tears, for a Stroke foreseen, afford Relief;*
> *But, unprovided for a sudden Blow,*
> *Like* Niobe *we Marble grow;*
> *And Petrifie with Grief.*   (1–8)

Frequent end-stopped lines, slowed further by early spondees, and with the direct recurrence of the word 'Grief', give the effect of hovering over an emotion that cannot as yet find the avenue of its release. As the implications of the event are entered into, however, the lines spread out and move, long line travels on into still longer line to provide the necessary space for depicting the scope and meaning of the death of a king:

> *As if great* Atlas *from his Height*
> *Shou'd sink beneath his heavenly Weight,*

> And, with a mighty Flaw, the flaming Wall
> (*As once it shall*)
> Shou'd gape immense and rushing down, o'erwhelm this nea-
>   ther Ball;
> So swift and so surprizing was our Fear . . .   (29–34)

There is a fine oxymoron, capturing the burdens of a king together with the rightness of regal responsibility in 'heavenly Weight'. The impact of the short parenthesis, chilling as it is, scarcely breaks the threatening motion of collapse, making it impend for a bare moment before sweeping into the unusual length of a fourteener where three verbal components urge it along to the end.

In his priestly role, Dryden movingly prays for Charles at the moment of death, pronouncing a formal Christian benediction, touched in its final line by a suggestion of Elysian fields; the concluding triplet, with the fixity of its anaphora, is more powerful and firmer because of the varying lengths of the rhymed lines that precede it:

> Calm was his life, and quiet was his death.
>   Soft as those gentle whispers were,
>   In which th' Almighty did appear;
> By the still Voice, the Prophet knew him there.
> That Peace which made thy Prosperous Reign to shine,
> That Peace thou leav'st to thy Imperial Line,
> That Peace, oh happy Shade, be ever thine!   (285–91)

Even in the benediction pronounced for Charles, the middle line of the triplet pointedly blesses the succession. There are three other passages of prayer in the poem, including one which culminates by representing Charles as guardian angel of the arts. Solemn as the poem is over much of its length and solemn as this prayer must mainly be taken to be, the lines leading into it are surely among the wryest ever to be written in a funeral panegyric. They can serve to illustrate that even in panegyric, soaring on Pindar's wings, the earth below is not altogether lost to sight, and honest praise derives strength when truths not altogether favourable to the subject have plainly not been shunned. They are lines that Charles would have appreciated:

> *So, rising from his Fathers Urn,*
> *So glorious did our* Charles *return;*
> *Th' officious Muses came along,*
> *A gay Harmonious Quire like Angels ever Young:*
> *(The Muse that mourns him now his happy Triumph sung)*
> *Even* they *cou'd thrive in his Auspicious reign;*
> > *And such a plenteous Crop they bore*
> > *Of purest and well winow'd Grain,*
> *As* Britain *never knew before.*
> *Tho little was their Hire, and light their Gain,*
> > *Yet somewhat to their share he threw;*
> *Fed from his Hand, they sung and flew,*
> *Like Birds of Paradise, that liv'd on Morning dew.*
> *Oh never let their Lays his Name forget!*
> *The Pension of a Prince's Praise is great.*
> *Live then, thou great Encourager of Arts,*
> > *Live ever in our Thankful Hearts;*
> *Live blest Above, almost invok'd Below;*
> > *Live and receive this Pious Vow,*
> *Our Patron once, our Guardian Angel now.*   (368–87)

Amusing as these lines are, they are also rather breathtaking, for while creating allusively an image of Charles as King-God-*pastor*, Dryden grazes the edge of the sardonic suggestion he had made a few years earlier about the Whig sheriff of London, Slingsby Bethel: 'With Spiritual food he fed his Servants well' (*Absalom and Achitophel*, 626). Honorific as the God-analogue is in praise of the King, the figure always includes distance between its two elements, a distance which at times irony opens wider, as here; there is the hand of God, and then there is the hand of Charles.

The most unusual feature of the poem, however, is the extent to which it is devoted to Charles' brother, James. James figures in eleven out of eighteen stanzas as well as by implication in two additional stanzas in which Charles is praised for weathering the Exclusion Crisis and maintaining the succession to the throne. He appears at the end of Stanza I as Hercules taking on the burden of Atlas. Stanza II is entirely devoted to him, half of Stanza VII, almost all of the long Stanza VIII, and

Stanzas XV–XVIII are entirely devoted to James. These features of the poem reflect the unusual character of the title-page. They follow also from the commitment Dryden makes in the epigraph, and that moment of the *Aeneid* is deliberately resumed in the second stanza where the culmination of the tribute to James as a faithful brother appears in the definition of his grief as beyond the measure of a relative, beyond the measure of any bond of physical kinship, and to be defined finally as the grief of 'a Friend'. For all that the poem does in praise of Charles and in praise of James, and for all the dimensions of national roles that the poem in its last four stanzas assigns to James with the Laureate's concentrated determination and concern for the welfare of monarch and nation together, this is also a poem in which love and friendship are written, this time in the brow of kings.

Britannia Rediviva, Dryden's last official panegyric as Laureate, was written in an atmosphere of bitterness and strife. Dryden had hoped that James might develop and continue some of the characteristics of his late brother. In a letter to Sir George Etherege he wrote: 'Oh that our Monarch wou'd encourage noble idleness by his own example, as he of blessed memory did before him for my minde misgives me, that he will not much advance his affaires by Stirring.'[1] By the time Dryden wrote his poem, however, James's arbitrary acts, which seemed designed to fasten Catholic power on the army and on the universities, had badly frightened the nation; just three weeks later an invitation designing a different future was sent to William of Orange, James's successor.

It is ironic that Charles suffered much because he did not have a legitimate son who could inherit the throne, while the birth of a legitimate son and heir to James helped to drive him off the throne. The birth of a son to the King would normally be an occasion of national rejoicing, and Dryden tries to make it so in his poem, but his success is restricted. Even though the poem is in Dryden's mature couplet style with resort to triplet expansion (including a terminal Alexandrine, and with additional hexameter expansions) these devices are seldom put to impressive use, perhaps because they are often most effective in the

[1] Charles E. Ward, ed. *The Letters of John Dryden, With Letters Addressed to Him*, Durham 1942, 27.

release of power generated in the course of fairly long passages in which divergent streams come together, but the cross-currents Dryden must reckon with in this poem dissipate power, or, as he contends with them, cause him to sound shrill or loud rather than strong. In invoking religious sanctions and credentials for the child, the poem is often engaged more clearly in contention than praise:

> *Fain wou'd the Fiends have made a dubious birth,*
> *Loth to confess the Godhead cloath'd in Earth.*
> *But sickned after all their baffled lyes,*
> *To find an Heir apparent of the Skyes:*
> *Abandon'd to despair, still may they grudge,*
> *And owning not the Saviour, prove the Judge.*   (122–7)

In lines directly adjacent, the heir is 'the true Eaglet' who 'safely dares the Sun' (21) and 'Aeneas . . ./Shining with all his Goddess Mother' Grace' (128 and 131).

This saviour-figure is to atone for the nation's crimes, especially for the judicial murders that followed on the testimony of Titus Oates regarding the Popish Plot and for the efforts to exclude James from the throne. Yet for all Dryden's devotion to a cause, and even devoutness at times he clearly understands what would be needed to heal the nation's bitter conflicts and to maintain as King a man such as James so that there might be a throne for his heir to succeed to:

> *By living well, let us secure his days,*
> *Mod'rate in hopes, and humble in our ways.*
> *No force the Free-born Spirit can constrain,*
> *But Charity, and great Examples gain.*
> *Forgiveness is our thanks, for such a day;*
> *'Tis Godlike, God in his own Coyn to pay.*   (298–303)

The lines that Dryden addresses to James at the conclusion of the poem are a remarkable illustration of the use of praise to present a warning:

> *The Name of Great, your Martial mind will sute,*
> *But Justice, is your Darling Attribute . . .*
> *A Prince's favours but on few can fall,*
> *But Justice is a Virtue shar'd by all.*

> *Some Kings the name of Conq'rours have assum'd,*
> *Some to be Great, some to be Gods presum'd;*
> *But boundless pow'r, and arbitrary Lust*
> *Made Tyrants still abhor the Name of Just;*
> *They shun'd the praise this Godlike Virtue gives,*
> *And fear'd a Title, that reproach'd their Lives.*
>
> *The Pow'r from which all Kings derive their state,*
> *Whom they pretend, at least, to imitate,*
> *Is equal both to punish and reward;*
> *For few wou'd love their God, unless they fear'd.*
>
> *Resistless Force and Immortality*
> *Make but a Lame, Imperfect Deity:*
> *Tempests have force unbounded to destroy,*
> *And Deathless Being ev'n the Damn'd enjoy,*
> *And yet Heav'ns Attributes, both last and first,*
> *One without life, and one with life accurst;*
> *But Justice is Heav'ns self, so strictly He,*
> *That cou'd it fail, the God-head cou'd not be.*   (333–4; 337–56)

Dryden began the series of royal panegyrics at the hopeful moment of the Restoration by invoking from classical mythology a myth of the return of the goddess of justice. That was the ideal that Dryden presented for the reign of Charles. At the end of this series of panegyrics Dryden seems to suggest that only by disavowing arbitrary acts and cleaving to justice can this man, for whom Dryden and Charles laboured to maintain the succession, continue on the throne and be succeeded there by his son, the new-born heir. Failing in justice, the God-King James could not be.

II

The drama of Dryden's official panegyrics dealing with monarchs and affairs of state begins with a time of triumph and national exultation but curves downward to its end in a context of imminent defeat and failure, celebrating at the last a birth which ironically is related to the end of the Stuart line on the throne of England. There is another group of

poems, however, in which Dryden can be observed in the act of praise
and their curve of development is different in a number of ways. These
poems range from elegiac to panegyric and they deal with the death of
a young and vigorous satiric poet, the death of a young lady accomplished in both poetry and painting, the death of 'a very young gentleman', with the exemplary life of a late Countess with whom Dryden
had no direct acquaintance, with the death of the greatest musician of
the age, with the marriage at Christmas time of a young lady belonging
to a distinguished Catholic family, and with the presentation of a version of one of Chaucer's poems to a Duchess whose husband had continued into the last decade of Dryden's life a generous patronage which
had been begun by his grandfather.

To write in any adequate way of all these poems would require a
great deal of space. Some of these poems will be dealt with in other
essays in this collection and will be touched on here only to fill in some
features in a sequence of poems of praise. To exhibit the range of
Dryden's capacity and something of the phases of its development in
these poems can perhaps be accomplished by choosing several by way
of illustration. Though many of these poems are occasioned by a death
the subject is variously conceived and managed. Not only are there
differences in conception, and in the management that derives from
conception, but there are developments of a technical sort for operations that are, more or less, within the same conceptual frame.

The poems in this group that will provide the base for comment and
illustration are: *To the Memory of Mr Oldham* (1684), *To . . . Anne
Killigrew* (1685), and *Eleonora* (1692). *To Her Grace the Dutchess of
Ormond* (1700) will be touched on very briefly for some features of its
special mode of panegyric.[1] The first two of these fall within the period
of Dryden's functioning officially as Laureate (*To . . . Anne Killigrew*,
it should be remembered, is directly adjacent to *Threnodia Augustalis*)

[1] The combination may be observed also in Pope's *To Robert Earl of
Oxford, and Earl Mortimer.* Geoffrey Tillotson called the poem 'an
elegy in an epistle' 'Pope's "Epistle to Harley": An Analysis', in *Pope
and His Contemporaries,* ed. James L. Clifford and Louis A. Landa,
Oxford 1949, 69; and M. H. Abrams calls it a 'panegyric': *The Poetry
of Pope: A Selection,* New York 1954, vi.

nd the latter two belong to the decade of Dryden's alienation from the hrone. The last three of these poems *can* be classified as panegyrics; the poem for John Oldham is, as is widely agreed, a fine example of re-tricted classical elegy. When Dryden was treating death in the manner f classical elegy, he felt bound to curtail flights of figuration and also to keep in check directly sensory language which might generate un-pleasant effects—such effects as are thoroughly appropriate to satire and re, paradoxically, one of the risks of panegyric. In the area of pane-gyric, however, he seems to have worked through a number of experi-ments. *To . . . Anne Killigrew* is written in the style which seventeenth-century poets, following Cowley, had come to understand as Pindar's; we can still term it pindaric, but most of the time resort to the lower case eems appropriate. In a pindaric poem as conceived in the seventeenth century, the poet quite deliberately reached for extravagant figuration and allowed himself to luxuriate in a great variety of licence in his verse orm. Stanzas were expected to vary considerably in length and to con-tain within them lines that varied widely in length, while diversities of ine length were woven through the fabric in rhyme. Both *To . . . Anne Killigrew* and *Threnodia Augustalis* exhibit this conception of the pin-daric ode.

In the last decade of his life, however, Dryden undertook to adopt he pindaric mode of figuration—and here, in a qualified way, one could ay Pindar's figuration—to couplet versification. In *Eleonora*, which Dryden clearly regards as a poem in the manner of Pindar, and finally, n *To Her Grace the Dutchess of Ormond*, a poem which critics have rather generally termed panegyric (as Dryden had designated *Eleonora*), he undertakes to adapt this kind of figuration to couplet versification, and even to a form of the verse epistle. Dryden, like his contemporaries, apparently did not understand that the Pindaric strophes were actually strict forms, but both in *Eleonora* and in *To Her Grace the Dutchess of Ormond* he set himself the task of using the figures of praise while re-taining the couplet structure. Such an undertaking had the effect of bringing him, in the last decade of his life, close to the procedures of Donne in his *Anniversaries*, and in the preface to *Eleonora*, of course, he makes direct acknowledgment of the closeness of that relationship.

In the poems chosen for illustration, the Oldham poem is about

Oldham in a way that the Killigrew ode is not about Anne Killigrew
Eleonora is not about the Countess of Abingdon, but rather, as in Donne'
treatment of Elizabeth Drury, about qualities beyond the range of an
mortal woman. Dryden had originally intended calling the poem *Th*
Pattern, and, as Earl Miner has pointed out in his chapter on this poem
Eleonora is the pattern in a dual sense, both as a paradigm *of* a set c
ideal qualities and as a model *for* emulation.[1] The poem addressed t
the Duchess of Ormond, however, finds a new middle ground; clearl
the poem as panegyric is about things that lie well beyond the Duches
or any other mortal, but somehow in the Ormond poem the relation be
tween what is ideal and what is actual has been brought into a new kin
of accommodation, possibly because of the matrix of the verse epistl
An inspection of figuration and couplet versification may shed light o
the processes of development in these poems.

The figures of speech in *To the Memory of Mr Oldham* are few an
unsurprising; they are quietly, almost reticently conventional, an
associated with a pair of apparently standard Virgilian allusions:
footrace for competitive striving (Nisus and Euryalus in the *Aeneid*),
tree bearing fruit for the creative accomplishments of a poet; the suc
cessful military commander (Marcellus in *Aeneid* VI) for the write
who commands language, and the promising young man, early dea
(the young Marcellus of *Aeneid* VI), for the writer not yet arrived at fu
prowess, an allusion standard enough in *locus* though subtle in its dualit
of reference.[2] These figures and allusions are with one exception tailore
to the dimensions of the couplet, and all of the couplets are closed b

[1] Miner, 221. Donald R. Benson, in his article 'Platonism and Neoclassic Metaphor: Dryden's *Eleonora* and Donne's *Anniversaries*', *SP*
LXVIII, 1971, 340–56, contends for the synthetic character (i.e. put
together from manifold expressed similarities, the ideal constructed as
a compendium of particulars) of Dryden's Platonism or Neo-Platonism.
Donne's he sees in terms of more direct, metaphorical predication, experience of the essence, a form of experience of grace. Miner argues
that Neo-Platonism is a less consistent and less important element in
these poems of Donne's than in Dryden's poem; with this view Benson
disagrees.
[2] See the discussion of figuration and allusion in this poem in Hoffman,
92–98.

rather distinct end-stops. The exception is the figure of 'generous fruits'
which quite intelligibly is accorded the expansion of a triplet. Nothing
in this poem—neither the figures of speech, the allusions, nor the versification—is extravagant. The classical allusions are sufficiently honor-
fic, yet quietly so. Nevertheless Oldham is enlarged by the tribute paid
him; the cumulative effect is surprising because the means scarcely seem
adequate to the result.

   The result is obtained partly because some of Oldham's limitations
are *expressed*, and with the clear confidence that the tribute can contain
them, and in the process of stating limitations Dryden pays Oldham in
the coin of true wit, the kind of currency that a fellow poet might be
expected to appreciate, while at the same time maintaining his own
integrity and poetic standards:

> *O early ripe! to thy abundant store*
> *What could advancing Age have added more?*
> *It might (what Nature never gives the young)*
> *Have taught the numbers of thy native Tongue.*
> *But Satyr needs not those, and Wit will shine*
> *Through the harsh cadence of a rugged line.*
> *A noble Error, and but seldom made,*
> *When Poets are by too much force betray'd.*
> *Thy generous fruits, though gather'd ere their prime* ⎫
> *Still shew'd a quickness; and maturing time*   ⎬
> *But mellows what we write to the dull sweets of Rime.* ⎭
>
>   (11–21)

These eleven lines are almost half the poem, and they certainly are not
fully or directly engaged in forwarding the movement of praise. They
begin with a rhetorical question, which in an elegy does not expect an
answer, but they proceed to answer the question in very blunt terms.
Then, having broached the subject of harsh cadence, they illustrate how
rough a pentameter can be made without ultimate breach of the formal
matrix. Finally, while speaking of rhyme as a modest accomplishment,
they slide into a rhyming triplet. All of this is the reverse of fulsome
compliment, but it would be wrong to suggest that it is not compliment
at all. The kinds of things Dryden is doing here with language are the

kinds of things poets care about, and they are done not only as part of talking about Oldham but also *for* Oldham. They are one of the ways of establishing Dryden's closeness to Oldham, emphasizing that, for all their differences, they are 'Cast in the same Poetic mould' (4).

The two explicit allusions to the *Aeneid* are supported by at least one other more covert Virgilian allusion, the final line of the poem in which Dryden expands to hexameter length and closely translates a line that Virgil wrote about young Marcellus. The 'hail and farewel' formula may derive from Catullus' elegy for his young brother, or, as Miner suggests (250), from the Aeneas and Pallas relation, or from both. The poetic matrix in the poem is strongly Virgilian but also more generally classical. The final couplet of the poem is an epitome of the classical model:

> Thy Brows with Ivy, and with Laurels bound;
> But Fate and gloomy Night encompass thee around.   (24–25)

Oldham is made to stand with young Marcellus, with the brother of Catullus, with Nisus and Euryalus, and also, as poet, with Dryden, Virgil, and Catullus. The figuration employed in the poem develops very economically the dimensions of Oldham as natural man subject to fate and Oldham as artist capable of one of the limited victories over time. The circles of the last couplet draw those limits. In the panegyrics the circles are different in their implications as are the methods which lead to them; as symbols they allude to completeness and perfected order and to the spatial and temporal cycles of cosmic order.

Dr Johnson, in writing about the ode to Anne Killigrew, applied Horace's praise of Pindar: '*Fervet, immensusque ruit.*'[1] At the end of the Oldham elegy, the subject *stands*. Everything that has been accomplished in his praise has been done under the most severe restriction. In the panegyrics, especially in the Killigrew ode, the subject acts and moves. She is the focus of persistent and expansive figuration, and in a verse form that allows the figures to be extended almost at will, to dictate line-lengths, and to be played across a freely varying rhyme scheme. In the first stanza of the poem, the speculation concerning the

---

[1] Samuel Johnson, *Lives of the English Poets,* ed. G. B. Hill, 3 vol Oxford 1905, I 439.

precise location of the soul of Anne is twenty-two lines long. It is essentially one continuous, powerfully organized sentence structure which rests on a 'Whether . . . Or . . . Or . . . Whatever' sequence leading into the firm imperatives 'Cease' and 'Hear', with all of these key structural components located emphatically at the beginning of lines. Though this sequence in the first stanza is longer, the fifteen-line sequence in the last stanza is perhaps still more impressive in its '. . long majestic march, and energy divine.':

> *When in mid-Aire, the Golden Trump shall sound,*
>   *To raise the Nations under ground;*
>   *When in the Valley of* Jehosaphat,
> *The Judging God shall close the Book of Fate;*
>   *And there the last Assizes keep,*
>   *For those who Wake, and those who Sleep;*
>   *When ratling Bones together fly,*
> *From the four Corners of the Skie,*
> *When Sinews o're the Skeletons are spread,*
> *Those cloath'd with Flesh, and Life inspires the Dead;*
> *The Sacred Poets first shall hear the Sound,* ⎫
>   *And formost from the Tomb shall bound:* ⎬
> *For they are cover'd with the lightest Ground* ⎭
> *And streight, with in-born Vigour, on the Wing,*
> *Like mounting Larkes, to the New Morning sing.*   (178–92)

There is an astonishingly long sweep of movement to that final verb, 'sing': The structure is 'When . . . When . . . When . . . When . .', four times at the head of the line while the sweep of events in the last Judgment scene is portrayed. 'The Golden Trump' sounds in the first line and hovers over the scene for ten more lines; 'Sacred Poets' are first to hear, and the versification, along with the figuration, sets them most vividly in motion. The unusual tactic of running over the end of a triplet into a subsequent couplet extends the movement, and the doubled act of rising in the resurrection of the poets, their first bounding out of the grave, then rising like larks into the sky, creates an effect of extraordinary vigour, zest, and joy, a truly remarkable imaginative realization of the joyful resurrection. The pacing of the phrases in the

final couplet is especially adroit. The action builds up in a series of sho[r]
phrases until released in the last, longer phrase by the crucial verb, th[e]
verb which the immediacy of the initial 'streight' leads to and whic[h]
completes not only the very long sequence of fifteen lines but als[o]
across the full span of the couplet, the alliterative continuation launche[d]
and sped from 'streight' to 'sing'.

The quality and abundance of figuration in this poem have been [a]
good deal discussed and should be apparent in the stanza just cited. I[n]
the course of the poem, Anne Killigrew is developed into a comple[x]
metaphoric figure by a process of figuration and allusion both classic[al]
and Christian. She is a *'Vestal'*, a 'Saint', an atoning figure, a redeemer, [a]
king, an emperor, a creative and forming principle, and through her th[e]
poem enacts a redemption of sacred poetry from its fallen position as a[n]
art. Through her the subject of poetry itself animates the poem an[d]
generates the energy that rises to the call of resurrection.[1]

In *Eleonora* Dryden undertook to conduct the typical activities [of]
panegyric while writing in couplets. In his dedication of the poem [to]
the Earl of Abingdon, Dryden wrote:

> The Reader will easily observe, that I was transported, by the
> multitude and variety of my Similitudes; which are generally the
> product of a luxuriant Fancy; and the wantonness of Wit. Had I
> call'd in my Judgment to my assistance, I had certainly retrench'd
> many of them. But I defend them not; let them pass for beautiful
> faults amongst the better sort of Critiques: For the whole Poem,
> though written in that which they call Heroique Verse, is of the
> Pindarique nature, as well in the Thought as the Expression; and
> as such, requires the same grains of allowance for it. It was in-
> tended, as Your Lordship sees in the Title, not for an Elegie; but
> a Panegyrique; a kind of Apotheosis, indeed; if a Heathen Word
> may be applyed to a Christian use. And on all Occasions of Praise,
> if we take the Ancients for our Patterns, we are bound by Prescrip-
> tion to employ the magnificence of Words, and the force of Fig-
> ures, to adorn the sublimity of Thoughts. *Isocrates* amongst the
> *Grecian* Orators; and *Cicero*, and the younger *Pliny*, amongst the

---

[1] See Hoffman, 98–128, for a more extensive discussion of this poem,
and the earlier essay by E. M. W. Tillyard in *Five Poems, 1470–1870*,
London 1948, 49–65. See also Miner, 253–65.

Romans, have left us their Precedents for our security: For I think
I need not mention the inimitable *Pindar*, who stretches on these
Pinnions out of sight, and is carried upward, as it were, into
another World.[1]

Dryden is clearly conscious of undertaking something special, and
while he is most careful to explain his view of the style and the rationale
of the figures, he is also aware that a combination of the Pindaric style
of thought and figures with heroic couplets is not the easiest or most
expected match. He is, of course, returning to something he had done
thirty years before in *To My Lord Chancellor*, but the differences in the
versification are very marked. In the earlier poem, there were no triplets, while in *Eleonora* there are seventeen. There is a triplet in the opening verse paragraph (9–11) and a triplet concludes the poem. At one
point there are four triplets in fourteen lines (140–53). At another point
there are two successive triplets (46–51). In several other places triplets
occur quite close together. It should further be observed that often a
triplet is arranged to continue a movement launched and flowing from
couplets immediately preceding. Moreover, Dryden quite frequently
resorts to hexameter lines, and these occur not only as the final Alexandrine in a number of the triplets but are also dispersed through the
basic pentameter couplet structure. Clearly Dryden has resorted to all
of his devices of expansion and has used them rather heavily as one way
of emulating the purported looseness of Pindaric style, but probably
more importantly as ways of accommodating a procession of lofty and
amplifying figures.

The way these procedures work may be considered, for example,
in the opening lines of the poem, though the main figure of speech there
is an analogy which Johnson regarded as containing too much likeness
in its components. The figure seems clearly, like many others in this
poem, to derive from Donne, in this case from 'A Valediction Forbidding Mourning', and the way Dryden adjusts it to his verse form is instructive:

> *As when some Great and Gracious Monarch dies,*
> *Soft whispers, first, and mournful Murmurs rise*

[1] *Works*, III 232.

> *Among the sad Attendants; then, the sound*
> *Soon gathers voice, and spreads the news around,*
> *Through Town and Country, till the dreadful blast*
> *Is blown to distant Colonies at last;*
> *Who, then perhaps, were off'ring Vows in vain,*
> *For his long life, and for his happy Reign:*
> *So slowly, by degrees, unwilling Fame* ⎫
> *Did Matchless* Eleonora's *fate proclaim,* ⎬
> *Till publick as the loss, the news became.* ⎭
>
>   (1–11)

Donne's stanzaic poem handles the main elements of the comparison in two four-line units; 'As virtuous men passe mildly away'[1] is developed through the first stanza and 'So let us melt, and make no noise' is carried through the second stanza. Dryden's comparison is to the death of a king, amplified and extended to convey the importance of the event by having the news gather momentum, force, and volume, the farther it spreads until it descends like a sudden blight, a dismal blare of sound, a fearsome hurricane breaking on remote colonies. There is an interior pause in the third line, but the ends of the lines are run-over so that six lines are traversed before there is an end-stop, and two more lines are grammatically continuous before the opening 'As when' statement is completed. Then a triplet, also a continuous unit, with pronounced enjambement of the first line and only a light stop at the end of the second, relates the comparison to Eleonora and emphasizes the public import of her death. The figure is not designed to take one's breath away by suddenness of wit nor by daring elevation, but to cause one to traverse dimensions from a death-bed to a palace room, from a room to a town, town to a nation and thence to the far reaches of an empire spread over the globe. The limits of the couplet are present as the formal equivalent of boundaries to be crossed, but the usual closure of the couplet is suspended so that the movement may continue, crossing a full sequence of borders to reach the dimensions of its ultimate global extent.

---

[1] Donne's poem is cited from *The Complete Poetry of John Donne*, edited by John T. Shawcross, Garden City, New York 1967, *A Valediction forbidding mourning*, 87–88.

There are also places in the poem where Dryden gathers momentum in launching a figure of some elevation, expands to give the figure the requisite space, then restricts the flow to create concluding emphasis. For example:

> *Sure she had Guests sometimes to entertain,*
> *Guests in disguise, of her Great Master's Train:*
> *Her Lord himself might come, for ought we know;*
> *Since in a Servant's form he liv'd below:*
> *Beneath her Roof, he might be pleas'd to stay:*
> *Or some benighted Angel, in his way*
> *Might ease his Wings; and seeing Heav'n appear*
> *In its best work of Mercy, think it there,*
> *Where all the deeds of Charity and Love*
> *Were in as constant Method, as above:*
> *All carry'd on; all of a piece with theirs;*
> *As free her Alms, as diligent her cares;*
> *As loud her Praises, and as warm her Pray'rs.* (52–64)

This passage is the culmination of a fifty-odd line section devoted to Eleonora's acts and modes of charity. It begins with the genial, almost cajoling suggestion that considering the merits that have been recounted, she must have been singled out for divine, or if not divine, at least angelic visitation. The suggestion of a divine visitation is simply glanced at, insinuated as a possibility, the kind of thing that is warranted by sanctified tradition. Then, with that piece of boldness out of the way, the sufficiently lofty suggestion of an angelic visit is given a special development. The idea of a visit by the divinity has been offered hesistantly, haltingly, with stops at the end of three consecutive lines (54–56), but the angel's visit extends through five lines without endstop. This five-line section records a most amusing angel in its opening oxymoron of 'benighted Angel', an angel somewhat wearied by running errands, settling his wings for a rest, and then conveniently deceiving himself that he has in fact reached his heavenly home because, to a sleepy angelic eye, Heaven itself seems to appear, created in its essential features by the charity of Eleonora. The conclusion of this flight of celestial wit is a triplet insisting firmly that it is all so, carried by a series of phrases picking up and repeating the 'all' and 'as' items and structures of the preceding couplet, emphasizing the declarations half-line by half-line in structures parallel and additive through the whole triplet so that one understands how that angel could indeed have been so deceived and yet scarcely deceived at all.

Some of the difficulty with *Eleonora* derives from its topical organization. As a panegyric, it fails to generate an overall movement and action. '*Fervet, immensusque ruit*', if allowance be made for a few stanzas, can justly be applied to the Killigrew ode as a whole, but not to *Eleonora*. Such movement as Dryden manages in *Eleonora* is chiefly local, though the local movement is at times finely accomplished, incorporating modes and tones of wit that one would scarcely expect the subject could admit.

The devices of expansion which appear in *Eleonora* are all present again in *To Her Grace the Dutchess of Ormond*: the frequent triplets, sometimes in close collocation; the couplets linked by removal of end-stops; the frequent hexameters (though in the Ormond poem hexameters are dispersed through the general fabric of the couplet structure, and there is only one introduced as the final line of a triplet). Dryden's confident and superbly controlled use of these devices contributes to the overall excellence of this poem. But there are, of course, other reasons for this poem's success and distinction in its panegyric dimension besides technical mastery.

In *Eleonora* Dryden created a poem which derives from Donne's *Anniversaries*, and though he borrowed heavily from the eulogistic sections of these poems, Dryden's panegyric remains closest to the meditative mode. The pattern is a pattern for reflection and emulation. In the Ormond poem, however, the woman addressed is alive, active and in motion, and an account can be rendered of things she, together with her illustrious husband, has done, actions she is presently engaged in, and future actions envisaged. The poem is filled with actual and symbolic voyages, the contours of individual movement and of broader historical movements, orbits and cycles of the cosmos, departures and returns, death and birth, and Dryden's long-standing, and perhaps for him, most powerful and happy symbol, renewal and restoration.

What makes panegyric succeed in this poem, however, is that Dryden does not saddle himself with the task of elevating the Duchess and her virtues by themselves, but makes the focus of his praise not only the presence of these virtues in men but also the celebration of such virtues in poetry. As in the Killigrew ode, an important part of the *subject* is poetry. Dryden makes extraordinarily effective use of the fact that the *occasion* he has designed for this poem is the presentation to the Duchess of Chaucer's poem, *The Knight's Tale*, the old poem renewed by Dryden as *Palamon and Arcite*. With all the voyages and returns, what really seems to move Dryden is the idea of poetry brought back. This time he is bringing back from the edge of oblivion a native poet, Chaucer, but as before he is also bringing back Homer and Virgil (and Juvenal), Horace and Persius, Ovid and Boccaccio, many of them in this poem itself, and the others elsewhere in the *Fables* volume. With that idea to celebrate and with a manifest and deep sense of joy in his own continuing and even renewed poetic powers, Dryden makes panegyric joyful, makes it move and attract belief. The following excerpts show the symbolic motif of return and renewal, and in the last passage, the couplet-triplet sequence opens within itself into as fine a structure of this sort as any Dryden ever managed:

> *As when the Stars . . .*
> *. . . move in Measures of their former Dance;*
> *Thus, after length of Ages, she returns,*
> *Restor'd in you . . .*
>
> *As when the Dove returning . . .*
>
> *When at Your second Coming You appear*
> *(For I foretell that Millenary Year) . . .*
> *Bless'd be the Pow'r which has at once restor'd*
> *The Hopes of lost Succession to Your Lord,*
> *Joy to the first, and last of each Degree,* ⎫
> *Vertue to Courts, and what I long'd to see,* ⎬
> *To You the Graces, and the Muse to me.* ⎭
>
> (21, 25–27, 70, 80–81, 146–50)

The woman addressed in this poem is very much alive, most happily revived from past illness, as is the poet who speaks to her in the social

discourse characteristic of the epistle. The return to society of health
and of poetry, the 'Pow'r' that is so movingly celebrated in a human
unison, is the power of God.

III

Lyricism has obviously been entwined in many passages of the poems
discussed as panegyrics and consequently has already been dealt with
in some respects. No one recently has been disposed to write of Dryden
as primarily a lyric poet, and Scott's judgment that Dryden was unsur-
passed in lyric poetry seems either baffling or a mere curiosity in the
history of criticism. Nevertheless, the evident power generated in
Dryden's panegyrics when the true subject becomes poetry itself is also
displayed in diverse ways in poems that are engaged with music,
whether the poems are songs, or whether music itself is the subject or a
great part of the subject.

The verbal artistry of the songs seems simple enough most of the
time and their subjects conventional to the point of banality. Many of
them are love songs, and when they are interesting it is because of
special treatments of emotional and sexual experience in which attitudes are so mixed, qualified, complicated, and stretched under tension
that the reader is unsettled by what is being harmonized for him. The
best of these seem to insist that the reader put together several readings
as the 'simple' music of the poem. They are the kind of songs that could
appeal to a Millamant because they are capable of engaging the problem
of love as passionate urgency ('I find I love him violently'), as conflict,
contest, combat—the 'agon' preliminary to consummation and sexual
union—as absurdity and as reflection extended in time. In this last there is
a consciousness permeated by Suckling and Waller and a tradition voiced
through them that apprehends the future and qualifies in advance the
whole idea of constancy, ranging from the inconstancy of youth and
physical attractiveness on to the final transience of the body which
betrays all to dust.

The vibrations of Dryden's songs can mingle aggression with an
urgency that leads to sexual consummation; a good example is the
fourth song from *An Evening's Love* (1671), the fifth and sixth stanzas:

> DAMON. *Anger rouzes love to fight,*
> *And his only bayt is,*
> *'Tis the spurre to dull delight,*
> *And is but an eager bite,*
> *When desire at height is.*
> CELIMENA. *If such drops of heat can fall*
> *In our wooing weather;*
> *If such drops of heat can fall,*
> *We shall have the Devil and all*
> *When we come together.*   (21–30)

The line that Celimena repeats in its conditional form is limited on first utterance to wooing. When the line is resumed it carries the vividness of the original image derived from Donne, of the sweating closeness of lovers, into the release of the hyperbole which anticipates sexual consummation. This consummation is expressed in a colloquial figure whose idiom, in the cultivated context of this love debate, suddenly generates full power and variety of suggestion. The effective deployment of 'the Devil and all' assures that the last line will give the extraordinary impact of bodies in actual physical collision. Plain colloquial toughness placed in the mouth of the woman—and in pastoral—concludes the song with a superb jolt, violent encounter and union at once.

Startling in a different way is the third song from *An Evening's Love:*

SONG

Calm was the Even, and cleer was the Skie,
    And the new budding flowers did spring,
When all alone went Amyntas *and I*
    To hear the sweet Nightingale sing;
I sate, and he laid him down by me;
    But scarcely his breath he could draw;
For when with a fear he began to draw near,
    He was dash'd with A ha ha ha ha!

2

He blush'd to himself, and lay still for a while,
    And his modesty curb'd his desire;

> *But streight I convinc'd all his fear with a smile,*
> * Which added new flames to his fire.*
> *O* Sylvia, *said he, you are cruel,*
> * To keep your poor Lover in awe;*
> *Then once more he prest with his hand to my brest,*
> * But was dash'd with A ha ha ha ha.*

> 3
> *I knew 'twas his passion that caus'd all his fear;*
> * And therefore I pity'd his case:*
> *I whisper'd him softly there's no body near,*
> * And layd my cheek close to his face:*
> *But as he grew bolder and bolder,*
> * A Shepherd came by us and saw;*
> *And just as our bliss we began with a kiss,*
> * He laughed out with A ha ha ha ha.*

In the previous song, the psychological tension and conflict are finally drawn off into physical climax. There is the successful statement of a splendid power. This song, on the contrary, is teasing and insinuative, and in the first two stanzas, chiefly at the instigation of the woman, passion is aroused only to be dissipated by her peal of silvery laughter. The event, moreover, is being recounted; it is in the past. Involved as she *was*, seriousness abruptly evaporated, and she could see her lover only as ludicrous; in the first two stanzas she is clearly superior and the laughter is at his expense. In the third stanza, however, she has yielded to the point of being equally involved; as the shepherd-intruder passes by, his laughter is at the expense of both. There is a suggestion of frustration and sexual absurdity in the unrealized climax. It is *they* who yield to embarrassment in being observed, they to whose emotions the comic response is chilling. The shepherd laughs at his discovery, but the laughter of the outsider is also in some degree the participating response of the green world. Such is the complex challenge of some of these songs; one wishes for and wonders about the Peter Quince and the clavier that would really succeed in setting them.

The full range of Dryden's lyrical powers is best displayed, however, in *A Song For St Cecilia's Day* (1687) and *Alexander's Feast; or the Power of Musique* (1697). These are poems in which the words not only wait for the music to which they will move but also take on the task of expressing and harmonizing various conceptions of music, among them both the idea of harmony in philosophical, cosmological, and theological ramifications as well as the notion that special rhythms can be the instigators and directors of specific passions. In the preface to *Albion and Albanius* (1685), Dryden wrote: 'it is my part to invent, and the musician's to humor that invention.'[1] James E. Phillips characterizes this statement as containing 'the essence of seventeenth-century theory regarding the relationship of poetry and music.'[2]

It is the concern of literary criticism to look at Dryden's 'invention'. There is a curious link between *Alexander's Feast* and the official panegyrics where the focus is on a public figure. But in the panegyrics the relationship between the poet and the monarch is much more overtly realized and thrust forward as drama, and there is a further difference in that the heroic image of the monarch is qualified and reduced, while the heroic image of the poet is magnified. When all is said that can be said about the glory of Alexander and the scope and splendour of the scene, and when the joys that are there to be enjoyed have been drunk to the intense limit of the excess which makes them heroic, there drifts over the scene a haze of extravagance tinged with bitter wisps of negation, and even a few curls of mockery ('Assumes the God,/Affects to nod,/And seems to shake the Spheres.' [39–41]; 'Fought all his Battails o'er again;/And thrice He routed all his Foes; and thrice He slew the slain'. [67–68]). Dryden–Timotheus–Prospero has 'bedimmed/The noontide sun . . . /And 'twixt the green sea and the azured vault/Set roaring war'.

The poem seems to recognize and portray a power of limitation acting both upon Alexander, whose triumphant occasion this feast is, and upon Timotheus, the 'old' musician who controls and gives shape to the episodes of the occasion. There is a process at work that involves the interaction of two kinds of power, each modifying the other, the

[1] Watson, II 41.
[2] James E. Phillips, 'Poetry and Music in the Seventeenth Century'. *Music and Literature . . . Papers Delivered . . . at the Second Clark Library Seminar*, Los Angeles 1954, 21.

world's conqueror turning in orbit with the imperial musician, a motion roughly analogous to the rotation discerned in double stars, or in a monarch and a laureate. What Timotheus can predicate is to some degree limited by Alexander, and what Alexander does or is represented as doing is to a degree both instigated and governed by Timotheus and the power of his music. The subject and the music, both Alexander and the song, are lofty and ancient in their derivation. 'The song began from Jove' (25) relates both to the myth of Alexander's being the son of Jove himself, but more than that to a whole idea of kingship, as well as to the older conception of music to which Timotheus' playing gives expression. Here are rhythms that inspire in an emperor a sense of godhead, that rouse the martial spirit, that festively celebrate the joys of Bacchus, that slide into the soft Lydian measures attuned to the pleasures of love, or rise frighteningly to invoke hysteria of passion; and Alexander *amens* 'with zeal to destroy' (147), driven by all the ghosts of Grecians unburied to hurl the torch that set Persepolis aflame and left the world that vast monument of broken columns and departed empire.

It may be to the point to cite Dryden's allusions to Alexander in two other places, both of a still later date, both in the *Fables* volume of 1700; in *To My Honour'd Kinsman*, Dryden writes:

> *When once the* Persian *King was put to Flight,*
> *The weary* Macedons *refus'd to fight:*
> *Themselves their own Mortality confess'd;*
> *And left the son of* Jove, *to quarrel for the rest.*   (160–3)

And with special application to the panegyric treatment of princes by poets, he writes in his version of *The Cock and the Fox*:

> *Ye Princes rais'd by Poets to the Gods,*
> *And* Alexander'd *up in lying Odes.*   (659–60)

Alexander's Feast concludes with something close to this sense of the role of the older music and of 'old Timotheus' (167); he has been involved in and has accepted the imaginative task of apotheosis: 'He rais'd a Mortal to the Skies' (169). 'Divine Cecilia' gives expression to a new order of music, a philosophical, cosmological, and theological harmonizing of word, thought, and music. This music does not undertake to raise up man or even monarch as hero and set him among the gods but to bring the divine order from God down through the intervals of the cosmos to touch at one of its limits the intricate harmony of man: 'She [St Cecilia] drew an Angel down' (170).

Dryden's last lyric, *The Secular Masque* (1700), faced man on the stage of historical time and reviewed with extraordinary concision and terse unsolemnity the diverse men and actions of a whole century. As *Alexander's Feast* is not without suggestions of a mock-heroic perspective,[1] so Momus is the figure who pronounces summary judgments on the *saeculum* just concluded:

> MOMUS.   All, all, of a piece throughout;
> Pointing to ⎱
> DIANA.   ⎰ Thy Chase had a Beast in View;
> to MARS.   Thy Wars brought nothing about;
> to VENUS.   Thy Lovers were all untrue.
> JANUS.   'Tis well an Old Age is out,
> CHRONOS.   And time to begin a New.   (86–91)

Both in the concluding stanzas of *Alexander's Feast* and more completely in *A Song For St Cecilia's Day*, St Cecilia stands, unlike Momus, at the edge of or outside the framework of human time. The music associated with her is that of an angelic visitation or of the whole cosmological order within which the passions play and are played on as the variety of instruments, both man himself as he is swept by the music of universal forces and man-made music issuing from the flawed implements of his own making. No individual figure is elevated, no man heroicized in the middle stanzas of this poem; here are only men and their characteristic passions, ebbing and flowing, rising and falling, striking out a particular music and with the instruments developed over the course of man's actual and imaginative history, from the shell to the trumpet or the violin, from Jubal and Hebraic tradition and from Orpheus and classical tradition with all nature moved and following after the divine musician.[2]

---

[1] See Miner's comment that in lines such as 66–68, 84–88, and 109–115 in *Alexander's Feast* the tone of *MacFlecknoe* occurs for almost the last time (269).

[2] For two fine discussions of the poem in its musical settings by Giovanni Baptista Draghi and George Frederick Handel, see Ernest Brennecke,

Dryden invents the poetry for the creation of order out of the jarring
atoms of original potentiality to begin his song and a poetry for the
last judgment to end his praise of St Cecilia. It has become difficult now
to read Dryden's words without having Handel's music sounding in our
ears, but it is well to remember that it is Handel's part 'to humor
[Dryden's] invention'.

Dryden's invention both for creation and last judgment is a worthy
design for the subjects. In the Creation stanza, rhymes, rhythms, and
line lengths are jumbled and only gradually brought into discernible
and, at last, definite order:

> *From Harmony, from heav'nly Harmony*
> > *This universal Frame began.*
> *When Nature underneath a heap*
> > *Of jarring Atomes lay,*
> *And cou'd not heave her Head,*
> *The tuneful Voice was heard from high,*
> > *Arise ye more than dead.*
> *Then cold, and hot, and moist, and dry,*
> *In order to their stations leap,*
> > *And Musick's pow'r obey.*
> *From Harmony, from heav'nly Harmony*
> > *This universal Frame began:*
> > *From Harmony to Harmony*
> *Through all the compass of the Notes it ran,*
> *The Diapason closing full in Man.*

Jr., 'Dryden's Odes and Draghi's Music', *PMLA* XLIX, 1934, 1–34,
and Bertrand H. Bronson, 'Some Aspects of Music and Literature in
the Eighteenth Century', *Music and Literature . . . Papers Delivered
. . . at the Second Clark Library Seminar*, Los Angeles 1954, 30–41.
Important and acute comment on the poem is to be found in John
Hollander, *The Untuning of the Sky: Ideas of Music in English Poetry,
1500–1700*, Princeton 1961, 401–10 and *passim*, and in the course of an
article by Earl R. Wasserman, 'Pope's *Ode for Musick*', *ELH: A Journal
of English Literary History* XXVIII, 1961, 165–9, as well as in an article
by Jay Arnold Levine, 'Dryden's *Song for St Cecilia's Day, 1687*', *PQ*
XLIV, 1965, 38–50, and in Miner, 277–86.

In the stanza of the Last Judgment there is at the outset the unison of the 'Grand CHORUS,' the line lengths start close to accord and move to absolute accord (4,3,4,3,4,4,4,4) and the rhyme scheme moves in a parallel progress (ababccddd), with majestic firmness of rhythm throughout:

> As from the pow'r of sacred Lays
> 　The Spheres began to move,
> And sung the great Creator's praise
> 　To all the bless'd above:
> So when the last and dreadful hour
> This crumbling Pageant shall devour,
> The trumpet shall be heard on high,
> The Dead shall live, the Living die,
> And Musick shall untune the Sky.

This is not the heroic, which is vulnerable to the insidious intrusion of mockery, but the dignified simplicity of the sublime.

Dryden marked his copy of Spenser as offering a suggestion for this St Cecilia's Day poem. The passage he marked was in the Mutability Cantos of *The Faerie Queene* (VII, vii, 12), a stanza in which the gods are ravished by the miracle of music's power. For the conclusion of his *Song for St. Cecilia's Day* he may well have cast his eye over the stanza that concludes the Mutability Cantos, as may the reader in thinking of Dryden's ode:

> *Then gin I thinke on that which Nature sayd,*
> 　*Of that same time when no more Change shall be,*
> 　*But stedfast rest of all things firmley stayd*
> 　*Upon the pillours of Eternity,*
> 　*That is contrayr to Mutabilitie:*
> 　*For, all that moveth, doth in Change delight:*
> 　*But thence-forth all shall rest eternally*
> 　*With Him that is the God of Sabbaoth hight:*
> *O that great Sabbaoth God, graunt me that Saboaths sight.*

6: 'Absalom and Achitophel' and Dryden's Political Cosmos

GEORGE de F. LORD

I

Restoration and The Conservative Outlook

THROUGHOUT HIS career as a political writer Dryden repeatedly used the theme of restoration as his central myth. Beginning with *Astraea Redux* (1660) we can trace through his writings on public affairs, whether they deal with the Stuart Restoration (the central political event of the age in Dryden's imagination), or the re-establishment of the Church, or the return of Justice, or the reformation of poetry, or the re-discovery of historical truths, a remarkable preoccupation with a cosmogonic myth of restoration, recovery, or renewal after exile, defeat, or destruction. Although it assumes a variety of forms, such as Aeneas' flight from Troy and founding of Rome, or the establishment of the Augustan settlement following the Roman Civil Wars, or David's exile and subsequent victory over the plots of Saul or Absalom, or Christ's triumph over the temptations of Satan, the essential myth is the restoration of royal authority after a period of rebellious disorder.

It follows that no contemporary occasion or event is presented in itself, as a unique historical fact, without some counterpart drawn from the past or from Greek and Roman myth or the Bible. In the events of his own times Dryden always saw a recurrence of past events or the re-expression of some archetypal pattern. His view of history is thus inescapably retrospective and cyclical and it dreads anarchy above all things, and, next to anarchy, innovation. The statement of one of our leading contemporary theologians defines perfectly the essence of Dryden's conservative political cosmos:

If . . . we examine the historical movements of political and social renewal, we will find that the 'myth of the eternal return' was operative here as well. Ironically enough, all known movements for a new future were initiated under the banner of the category 're'. We speak of *re*naissance, *re*formation, *re*volution, of *re*vival, *re*newal, and *re*storation, etc. In all these movements men sought not the new of the future but 'paradise lost' or the 'golden age,' the primitive natural condition of man or the original order of things. They sought their future in the past. They connected the renewal of the present with a 'dream turned backward.'[1]

Of all Dryden's poems *Absalom and Achitophel* represents most completely and pervasively his lifelong affinity for seeing the present in terms of the past, and the *Life of Plutarch* shows his approach to history as a model for the future. History, he says,

helps us to judge of what will happen, by showing us the like revolutions of former times. For mankind being the same in all ages, agitated by the same passions, and moved to action by the same interests, nothing can come to pass but some precedent of the like nature has already been produced, so that having the causes before our eyes, we cannot easily be deceived in the effects, if we have the judgement enough but to draw the parallel.[2]

In employing the myth of restoration to defend the status quo in

[1] Jürgen Moltmann, *Religion, Revolution, and the Future*, New York 1969, 24.

[2] Quoted by Miner, 106. Just before this went to press, the editor of the volume drew my attention to a then just published article by Steven N. Zwicker, 'The King and Christ: Figural Imagery in Dryden's Restoration Panegyrics', *PQ* L, 1971, 582–98, which deals with Dryden's use of biblical typology for political poetry. Zwicker also comments on Marvell's treatment of Cromwell as an instrument of divine providence in *The First Anniversary* (see below). The central argument of Zwicker's cogent and persuasive essay seems to be that Dryden, in his poems on the Restoration, uses 'the typological perspective of the Old Testament to enlarge the meaning of the biblical elements of the [poems], to create an image of the King as divine healer and savior, and to postulate a 'sacred history' of contemporary events which would persuade his audience that recent English history recapitulates Old Testament history and reflects eternal Christian realities' (584).

Church and State Dryden was combatting the radical eschatological views derived from the apocalyptic books of the Old and New Testaments, such as the Book of Daniel, the Book of Revelation, the prophecies of Isaiah, and the epistles of St Paul, which proclaimed the establishment of Christ's kingdom on earth by a unique divine intervention in human history, concluding with the destruction and redemption of the world. This vision is at the centre of Christian eschatology. In Dryden's time it found one of its most powerful renderings in Book III of *Paradise Lost*. It also inspired, or was used to justify, many revolutionary political schemes in seventeenth-century England. In the breathing-spell which followed the Restoration Dryden found abundant evidence that political dissidents, by a reckless application of apocalyptic prophecy to contemporary affairs, were a threat to a precariously re-established order. As a leading defender of and spokesman for this order from 1660 to his death in 1700 Dryden devoted his energies and talents to discrediting political innovation by advancing the conservative myth of restoration against the radical myth of apocalypse. In 1660 he established the story of the exiled and restored David as a model for Charles II:

> *Thus banish'd* David *spent abroad his time,*
> *When to be God's Anointed was his Crime.*
> (*Astraea Redux*, 79–80)

The identification and Dryden's practice of scanning history for 'the like revolution of former times' were uncannily validated in 1681 when the Monmouth-Shaftesbury conspiracy against Charles provided an inescapable counterpart to the conspiracy of Absalom and Achitophel against David. In what must have seemed for Dryden a most compelling way, political circumstance provided him with the fable for his greatest poem.

A more secular restoration motif was interwoven, in the body of Dryden's political verse, with the Davidic myth. I am referring, of course, to his ubiquitous Virgilian theme of the establishment of the peace of Augustus after the Roman Civil Wars. In adapting this pattern from history, Dryden cast himself as a new Virgil proclaiming a new Augustan age of peace and prosperity. The role allowed Dryden to dramatize himself not only as a spokesman for the restored order and its Laureate but as the presiding genius of a new literary age which was also a conservative age bent on imitating the classics.

In all ways the Davidic myth and the Augustan myth, as Dryden employed them, served to dampen political ardour and instil obedience, a lesson further reinforced in *Absalom and Achitophel* by telling allusions to the temptation and fall of man in *Paradise Lost*. In contrast to the excitements of apocalyptic myth with the prospect of imminent divine intervention, the conservative myth as Dryden used it was deliberately quiescent and cool. Apocalypse riveted its vision on the immediate future and emphasized the need to act; the conservative myth saw the present in the past and emphasized passive acceptance.

The conservative does not ordinarily entertain large hopes (sometimes, perhaps, because he already has much of what other people hope for). The cyclical view of history feels itself threatened by radical change, even if the innovator is God himself. When considered alongside the myth of apocalypse, the conservative myth seems secular in every sense of the word, especially if the religious element is tempered, as it is in Dryden, by Augustan motifs. In such a cosmos God becomes something of an abstraction, a dim coadjutor to the vicegerent king. This low-keyed, secular quality in *Absalom and Achitophel* and Dryden's other political poems can be more fully understood if in due course we compare it with Marvell's vivid eschatological vision in the poems on Cromwell, with their sense of the imminent pressure of the divine on human affairs.

II

The Restoration Myth from Astraea Redux *to* The Secular Masque

In Dryden's political poems from *Astraea Redux* (1660) to *Absalom and Achitophel* (1681) we find a central myth of renewal and restoration following a crisis of civil war, defeat, destruction, or exile. The contemporary event is always presented *sub specie aeternitatis* by means of analogues usually drawn from classical mythology, Roman history, or the Old Testament. Thus no contemporary event or issue is seen as unique, and the participants in these national dramas are generally reduced to types. Each contemporary event or issue has its counterpart in Augustan Rome, or in the book of Samuel, or in the *Aeneid*. Dryden's good characters in the political poems are especially lacking in individuality. The public-spirited and self-effacing qualities of virtue as Dryden here conceives of it—in striking contrast to the egotism of his dramatic heroes—helps to define the admired monarchs and statesmen and warriors in terms of functions and relationships rather than in terms of extraordinary gifts or *virtù*. This is plainly seen in the case of Barzillai's heroic son (in real life the Earl of Ossory) and of the handful of faithful followers David relies on in the crisis of *Absalom and Achitophel*.

> *Now more than half a Father's Name is lost.*
> *His Eldest Hope, with every Grace adorn'd,*
> *By me (so Heav'n will have it) always Mourn'd,*
> *And always honour'd, snatcht in Manhoods prime*
> *By' unequal Fates, and Providences crime:*
> *Yet not before the Goal of Honour won,*
> *All parts fulfill'd of Subject and of Son;*
> *Swift was the Race, but short the Time to run.*
> *Oh Narrow Circle, but of Pow'r Divine,*
> *Scanted in Space, but perfect in thy Line!*

(831–9)

Individuality entered the picture with Dryden's villains. The catalogue of rebels, dreamers, informers, and plotters includes more eccentric characters than any other English poem except, perhaps, for *The Canterbury Tales*. Wickedness is conceived of as eccentric and egocentric. Each villain is wicked in a special way, while the good are all good in the same way. Because they are incapable of the reciprocal loyalties that link king and subject, master and servant, god and man, or father and son, these villains are very much cut off from others. Their eccentricity is further emphasized by idiosyncrasies of appearance and manner. It is significant that none of the good characters in *Absalom and Achitophel* is given a physical description, while all the evil ones are marked by unforgettable physical features.

It follows that with Dryden's aversion to the idiosyncratic there should be a corresponding aversion to novelty. The central conspirators of the exclusion Crisis are the slaves of the New. Achitophel is 'Restless, unfixed in principles and place,/In power unpleased, impatient of disgrace,' and Zimri is hailed as 'Blest madman, who could every hour employ,/with something new to wish or to enjoy'. Dazzled by ambition or bemused by mad schemes for innovation the rebel leaders are seen as prisoners of the moment. The essence of Dryden's profound mistrust of political alteration is conveyed in one of the most powerful couplets in *Absalom and Achitophel*:

> *All other Errors but disturb a State;*
> *But Innovation is the Blow of Fate.*
>
> (799–800)

With his aversion to innovation Dryden also seems to feel a certain anti-intellectualism. Among David's supporters the only one to whom intellectual brilliance is attributed is 'Jotham of piercing wit and pregnant thought', and even here the emphasis on perspicuousness rather than originality is significant. All the other virtuous characters, including the King, are recognized for their sense of duty and loyalty, not for their brilliance. Dryden's implicit anti-intellectualism is expressed in the much-quoted couplet:

> *Great Wits are sure to Madness near ally'd;*
> *And thin Partitions do their Bounds divide.*
>
> (163–4)

Intellectual brilliance is as dangerous in its own way as the inner light of the spirit, that fallible guide of the sects:

> *Plain* Truths *enough for needfull* use *they found;*
> *But men wou'd still be itching to* expound:
> *Each was ambitious of th' obscurest place,*
> *No measure ta'n from* Knowledge, *all from GRACE.*
> Study *and* Pains *were now no more their Care;*
> Texts *were explain'd by* Fasting, *and by* Prayer:
> *This was the Fruit the* private Spirit *brought;*
> *Occasion'd by* great Zeal, *and* little Thought.
>
> (*Religio Laici,* 409–16)

The devotees of the novel, whether in religion or politics, are doomed to an ephemeral existence:

> *A Thousand daily Sects rise up, and dye;*
> *A Thousand more the perish'd Race supply.*
>
> (*Ibid.* 421–2)

Thus *Religio Laici* indicts the Dissenters whose shifting political allegiances *Absalom and Achitophel* had arraigned in these lines:

> *For, govern'd by the* Moon, *the giddy* Jews
> *Tread the same track when she the Prime renews:*
> *And once in twenty Years, their Scribes Record,*
> *By natural Instinct they change their Lord.*
>
> (216–9)

Dryden's innovative Jews seem to illustrate Santayana's remark that 'those who do not remember the past are condemned to repeat it'.

Perhaps the most striking aspect of Dryden's conservatism is that it permeates every part of his political verse: it is explicitly stated and argued; it is illustrated by a wide variety of examples; and it is represented in the very structure and style of the poems. All these aspects of Dryden's conservatism have been extensively treated by others, and so I would like to concentrate on what seems to me to be an important but rather neglected subject, Dryden's concept of history in the political poems. This, I think, points to a radical issue which divided Conformist and Dissenter, Whig and Tory, Puritan and Anglican throughout the great religious and political crises of the seventeenth century.

To begin with I would like to point out that in *Absalom and Achitophel*, his most important political poem, Dryden showed very clearly his central concern with the relationship of the present to the past. Because the story of David had already been widely used by various pamphleteers to figure forth the story of Charles II, it has often been assumed that Dryden's contribution to the use of myth was mainly a question of greater dexterity and wit. While there is no doubt about the technical superiority of his poem over its models and predecessors, this should not be allowed to blind us to Dryden's real innovation in the use of Old Testament myth—that is in the *amalgamation* of present and past. We do not see the present through an allegory from or an analogy with the past; we see past and present simultaneously. David does not simply stand for Charles II; he does not merely resemble him; David *is* Charles. Dryden is not saying that we can learn lessons from the past. He is everywhere affirming that we can *only* understand the present when it is amalgamated with the past.

At the heart of Dryden's conservatism is the feeling that past, present, and future co-exist. We can see in Dryden those aspects of the Anglican temper defined by James Sutherland:

> To some extent it is possible to see the division between Anglicans and Nonconformists as another aspect of the battle between the Ancients and the Moderns. The Anglican priest naturally felt himself to be the trustee of a venerable ecclesiastical tradition, performing the unvarying offices of the Church and celebrating its time-hallowed ritual.[1]

While Dryden's anticlericalism would have rejected such an assumption of an ecclesiastical role, he undoubtedly regarded himself as the trustee of venerable political and religious traditions and the celebrator of time-hallowed rituals. At the centre of his thought throughout his career was something like what Mircea Eliade has called 'the myth of the eternal return', in which the chief feature is a recurrent restoration and resanctification of the community after losses and violations. This 'primitive' ontological conception Eliade describes thus:

> An object or an act becomes real only insofar as it imitates or repeats an archetype. Thus, reality is acquired solely through repetition or participation; everything which lacks an exemplary model is 'meaningless,' i.e., it lacks reality. Men would thus have a tendency to become archetypal and paradigmatic. This tendency may well appear paradoxical, in the sense that the man of a traditional culture sees himself as real only to the extent that he ceases to be himself (for a modern observer) and is satisfied with imitating and repeating the gestures of another. In other words, he sees himself as real, i.e., as 'truly himself', only, and precisely, insofar as he ceases to be so.[2]

[1] *English Literature of the Late Seventeenth Century*, New York and Oxford 1969, 303-4.
[2] *Cosmos and History*, New York, 1959, 34.

A quick survey of the recurrent rituals of restoration in Dryden's political verse will demonstrate this point. *Astraea Redux*, which proclaims the theme in its title, carries as its epigraph the well-known lines from the most famous of Virgil's *Eclogues* (the fourth), in which the restoration of Justice is hailed:

> *Iam Redit & Virgo, Redeunt Saturnia Regna.*

The restoration of Charles II after a long exile is thus identified with the restored Saturnian Age in which the departed Astraea (Divine Justice) returns to earth. Since Virgil was celebrating the birth of a prophecied redeemer in the fourth Eclogue, and since this eclogue was often regarded as an anticipation of the birth of Christ, the cosmogonic implications of this identification of Charles with the newborn son of the Consul Pollio could scarcely be more powerful. But Dryden extends them even further by including an identification with an Old Testament type as well:

> *Thus banish'd* David *spent abroad his time,*
> *When to be God's Anointed was his Crime.*
>
> (79–80)

Toward its close the poem hails the inception of the new age under this new Augustus (yet another powerful identification):

> *And now times whiter Series is begun*
> *Which in soft Centuries shall smoothly run.*
>
> (292–3)

In the next forty years Dryden's poetry is imbued with this theme of restoration, renewal, and return, culminating in the haunting chorus of the *Secular Masque*:

> *All, all, of a piece throughout;*
> *Thy Chase had a Beast in View;*
> *Thy Wars brought nothing about;*
> *Thy Lovers were all untrue.*
> *'Tis well an Old Age is out,*
> *And time to begin a New.*
>
> (92–97)

The restoration of Charles II with its archetypes of David's return from exile and the investiture of Augustus as emperor, becomes Dryden's central pattern for a long series of restorations. *To his Sacred Majesty, a Panegyrick on his Coronation* celebrates that crown 'Preserv'd from ruine and restor'd by you.' This motif of restoration is combined with Aeneas' escape from Troy and founding of Rome in a passage from *To my Lord Chancellor Presented on New-years-day* (1662):

> *When our great Monarch into Exile went*
> *Wit and Religion suffer'd banishment:*
> *Thus once when* Troy *was wrapt in fire and smoak*
> *The helpless Gods their burning shrines forsook;*
> *They with the vanquisht Prince and party go,*
> *And leave their Temples empty to the fo:*
> *At length the Muses stand restor'd again*
> *To that great charge which Nature did ordain;*
> *And their lov'd Druyds seem reviv'd by Fate*
> *While you dispence the laws and guide the State.*

(17–26)

Of course the conclusion of *Absalom and Achitophel* is the most prominent instance of the restoration theme—in fact here Dryden is emphasizing a *re*-restoration:

> *Henceforth a Series of new time began;*
> *The mighty Years in long Procession ran:*
> *Once more the Godlike* David *was Restor'd,*
> *And willing Nations knew their lawful Lord.*

As a recent critic remarked, the Godlike David is more Godlike than God, whose only function in this poem is to nod affirmatively in response to David's reassertion of his power. These lines combine in an exemplary fashion all the main ingredients of Dryden's restoration myth: divine sanction, inauguration of a new age, the identification of the King as David with undertones of Aeneas, and the re-establishment of the nations' obedience to their lawful lord. In fact, Dryden's attachment to these themes verges on the tedious, and one soon becomes adept at anticipating the exact point at which these plangent heroic notes will come in. One foresees the climax of *Threnodia Augustalis*:

Dryden's strategy is already dictated by past practice, and so the death of Charles is inevitably subordinated in the conclusion of the poem to the succession of his brother:

> . . . *with a distant view I see*
> *Th' amended Vows of* English *Loyalty.*
> *And all beyond that Object, there appears*
> *The long Retinue of a Prosperous Reign,* . . .
>
> . . . *While starting from his Oozy Bed*
> *Th' asserted Ocean rears his reverend Head;*
> *To View and Recognize his ancient Lord again:*
> *And with a willing hand, restores*
> *The* Fasces *of the Main.*
>
> (504–7, 513–17)

Although the myth is most centrally expressed in those numerous poems that deal with the restoration and succession of the Stuart line, Dryden extends it to include a variety of subjects, from Charleton's discoveries at Stonehenge to the Duchess of York's return from a trip to Scotland. Sometimes its use seems perfunctory, as it does in the flattering condescension to the Duchess, but it is more discriminating in the Charleton poem. Dryden wittily combines Dr Walter Charleton's theory that Stonehenge was built by the Danes as a temple for the coronation of their kings with an allusion to Charles' alleged asylum there after the Battle of Worcester and an implied reference to the founding of Rome:

> *These Ruines sheltred once* His *Sacred Head*
> *Then when from* Wor'sters *fatal Field* He *fled;*
> *Watch'd by the Genius of this Royal place,*
> *And mighty Visions of the* Danish *Race.*
> *His* Refuge *then was for a* Temple *shown:*
> *But,* He *Restor'd, 'tis now become a* Throne.
>
> (53–58)

Stonehenge is implicitly identified with the temple of Apollo at Cumae where Aeneas descended into the underworld and saw mighty visions of the *Roman* race. Thus Dryden constantly juxtaposes recent or contemporary events with mythic or historical counterparts in a distinctively Virgilian way. In an equally Virgilian way he establishes a relation between losses and gains in the fate of the royal line and the nation: defeat and flight, exile and wandering, become the swelling prologue to the imperial theme. *Il faut reculer pour mieux sauter.*

Dryden employs the same principle in treating the devastation of London by the Great Fire of 1666. Since the remarkable rebuilding of the city had scarcely begun, there was as yet little tangible reason for hailing London's renewal as he does in *Annus Mirabilis* (1667). Here is no actual equivalent to the Restoration of Charles, and so Dryden's implicit argument seems to be, *because* the city was burned, it will be renewed like the Phoenix:

> 294
>
> *Already, Labouring with a mighty fate,*
> *She shakes the rubbish from her mounting brow,*
> *And seems to have renew'd her Charters date,*
> *Which Heav'n will to the death of time allow.*
>
> 295
>
> *More great then humane, now, and more* August,
> *New deifi'd she from her fires does rise:*
> *Her widening streets on new foundations trust,*
> *And, opening, into larger parts she flies.*

At the height of the Exclusion crisis Dryden again used the legend of Noah and the Flood (another version of the basic theme) which he first alluded to in these opening lines of *To his Sacred Maiesty*:

> *In that wild Deluge where the World was drownd,*
> *When life and sin one common tombe had found,*
> *The first small prospect of a rising hill*
> *With various notes of Joy the Ark did fill.*

The Epilogue to the King . . . at Oxford . . . 19 March 1681 treats the turbulence of the times and the desperate hope for a peaceful solution to the crisis in terms of the same myth:

> *Our Ark that has in Tempests long been tost,*
> *Cou'd never land on so secure a Coast.*

> *From hence you may look back on Civil Rage,*
> *And view the ruines of the former Age.*
> *Here a New World its glories may unfold,*
> *And here be sav'd the remnants of the Old.*
>
> (17–22)

Here Dryden employs one of their favourite weapons against the predominantly Dissenting and Whiggish champions of Exclusion by appropriating to the King's side their customary designation of themselves as the saving remnant.

In an interesting anticipation of Pope's treatment of the *translatio studii* in the *Essay on Criticism* and the *Dunciad*, Dryden in 1684 hails the restoration to England of Greek and Roman learning in Roscommon's *Essay of Translated Verse*:

> . . . *The Wit of* Greece, *the Gravity of* Rome
> *Appear exalted in the* Brittish *Loome;*
> *The Muses Empire is restor'd agen,*
> *In* Charles *his Reign and by* Roscomon's *Pen.*
>
> (26–29)

One concluding example will show how pervasive the theme of restoration is in Dryden's poetry. In a poem of pure compliment welcoming the Duchess of York after one of her sojourns abroad Dryden turns the following dainty conceit:

> *The Muse resumes her long-forgotten Lays,*
> *And Love, restor'd, his Ancient Realm surveys;*
> *Recalls our Beauties, and revives our Plays.*
> (*Prologue to the Dutchess on her Return*
> *from Scotland,* 1682, ll. 30–32)

III

The Rejection of Innovation

Whenever Dryden celebrates a public event, then, he combines it with some classical or mythic prototype and thus endows it with a kind of cosmic regularity and inevitability. A natural correlative to this is in his rejection of the search for novelty and innovation, which I have already glanced at. It is given general force in the Prologue to *The Un-happy Favorite* (1682):

> *Tell me you Powers, why should vain Man pursue,*
> *With endless Toyl, each object that is new,*
> *And for the seeming substance leave the True . . . ?*
>
> (12–14)

The erratic and perverted character of the crowd is emphatically expressed in these lines from *The Medal* (1682):

> *Almighty Crowd, thou shorten'st all dispute;*
> *Pow'r is thy Essence; Wit thy Attribute!*
> *Nor Faith nor Reason make Thee at a stay;*
> *Thou leapst o'r all eternal truths, in thy* Pindarique *way!*
>
> (91–94)

In such a mob doctrines and tenets can only be ephemeral:

> *The common Cry is ev'n Religion's Test, . . .*
>
> *And our own Worship onely true at home.*
> *And true, but for the time, 'tis hard to know,*
> *How long we please it shall continue so.*
> *This side to day, and that to morrow burns;*
> *So all are God-a'mighties in their turns.*
>
> (103, 106–10)

Dryden's most telling indictment of the sects is of course in *Religio Laici* (1682):

> *The* Common Rule *was made the* common Prey;
> *And at the mercy of the* Rabble *lay.*
> *The tender Page with horney Fists was gaul'd;*
> *And he was gifted most that loudest baul'd:*
> *The* Spirit *gave the* Doctoral Degree:
> *And every member of a* Company
> *Was of* his Trade, *and of the* Bible free.
>
> *While Crouds unlearn'd, with rude Devotion warm,*
> *About the Sacred Viands buz and swarm,*

> *The* Fly-blown Text *creates a* crawling Brood;
> *And turns to* Maggots *what was meant for* Food.
> A Thousand daily Sects rise up, and dye;
> A thousand more the perish'd Race supply.
>
> (402–8, 417–22)

Bernard Schilling, among others, has shown how extravagances of style were as much to be avoided as such moral or spiritual extravagances:

> A form that lacks discipline is then appropriate for expressing rebellious sentiments, and suggests how the desire for political and social order led to so much control of literary expression. Behind all the vast structure of rule and law there is a fear lest individual energy, if given any chance at all, will assert itself dangerously. Hence the attack on such displays of energy as eloquence, vigorous figurative language, powerful original thought or speculation, and, worst of all, the force of human imagination, which might lead into a whole complex of dangers suggested by the term 'enthusiasm'.[1]

The conservative myth is celebrated in a style that avoids these pitfalls, a style which by its regularity and sobriety, its balance and rationality, and its irony and good humour enacts the meaning it expresses. In this neoclassical style wit is, in Dryden's phrase 'a propriety of thoughts and words; or, in other terms, thoughts and words elegantly adapted to the subject'.[2] Invention, for Hobbes (and Dryden would have concurred in this), carried little emphasis on creating something new, but was a matter of seeking and recovering something that was lost, a 'calling to mind'.[3] In the preface to *Annus Mirabilis* Dryden describes the function of wit as searching 'over all the memory for the Species or Ideas of those things which it designs to represent'. Thus neoclassical style was undergirded by a neoclassical psychology of

[1] *Dryden and the Conservative Myth: A Reading of 'Absalom and Achitophel'* New Haven and London 1961, 50.
[2] 'The Author's Apology for Heroic Poetry and Poetic License', Watson, I 207.
[3] Quoted in George Williamson, 'The Restoration Revolt against Enthusiasm', *Seventeenth-Century Contexts*, Chicago 1960, 212.

literary creation, and, like both the style and the conservative myth, focussed on the past, seeking what is lost. Ancient truths, the same *hic et ubique*, were to be expressed under the aegis of Homer, Virgil, Aristotle, Horace, and the Bible.

IV

The Restoration Myth and the Defence of the Stuart Settlement

The weight of this formidable neoclassical machinery was employed by Dryden to persuade the moderate sort of people to accept the Stuart settlement. For Dryden the chief enemies of peace in church and state were those who, with the battle cry of 'Popery and Tyranny', were seeking to disturb the succession in the Exclusion Crisis of 1681. It is appropriate that *Absalom and Achitophel*, a poem dealing with threats to the Stuart dynasty and to the principle of succession, should embody in every way the principles that underlie succession—all the conservative, retrospective principles that I have discussed earlier. The exclusive legitimacy of James as heir to the throne is an absolute right, not a relative one, and it is not negotiable. To tamper with it would be to tamper with the Law, which is divinely ordained: it would be to 'touch the ark'. Although Dryden goes to some lengths to present James as a worthy heir, his right to the throne is constitutionally independent of personal merit. I suspect that a corresponding function of the raillery with which Charles' various love-affairs are treated in the opening of *Absalom* is to undercut the notion of personal merit. Dryden enunciates (at least by implication) the doctrine of the king's two bodies —the natural and the politic—dealt with by Kantorowicz.[1] His basic assumption is that Charles, whatever his imperfections as a man, *is* the legitimate monarch, endowed with certain inalienable rights and corresponding responsibilities, chief among them in this crisis being the safeguarding of the succession to the throne.

Just as the Exclusionists would have threatened to destroy the suc-

---

[1] Ernest H. Kantorowicz, *The King's Two Bodies: A Study in Medieval Political Theology*, Princeton 1957.

cession and thereby the orderly continuity on which Church and
State are founded so, in an earlier national crisis of war, plague and
fire, the radical element threatened the continued existence of England
by its apocalyptic interpretation of events. In *Annus Mirabilis* Dryden's
strategy consists of deflecting the linear, eschatological view of events
with which the sects hailed the end of the world in 1666—and sought, in
Marvell's memorable phrase, 'to precipitate the latest day'—into the
familiar cyclical cosmos of loss and renewal. War, plague, and fire
had, as dissenting prophets declared, been a judgment of God for sin,
but the sin, in Dryden's view, was that of the rebellious citizens of
London and not the allegedly profligate King and his court. So Dryden
deftly turned the apocalyptic interpretation of events back upon the
Dissenters and implicitly identified the origins of London's devastating
fire with the career of the regicide dictator he had once celebrated in
Heroique Stanzas:

213

As when some dire Usurper Heav'n provides,
  To scourge his Country with a lawless sway:
His birth, perhaps, some petty Village hides,
  And sets his Cradle out of Fortune's way:

214

Till fully ripe his swelling fire breaks out,
  And hurries him to mighty mischiefs on:
His Prince surpriz'd at first, no ill could doubt,
  And wants the pow'r to meet it when 'tis known:

215

Such was the rise of this prodigious fire,
  Which in mean buildings first obscurely bred,
From thence did soon to open streets aspire,
  And straight to Palaces and Temples spread.

It is hard for me to avoid the idea that Dryden was alluding here to the
Cromwell of Marvell's *Horatian Ode*, who

. . . like the three-fork'd Lightning, first
Breaking the Clouds where it was nurst,

> *Did thorough his own Side*
> *His fiery way divide.*
>
> *Then burning through the Air he went,*
> *And Pallaces and Temples rent:*
> *And* Caesars *head at last*
> *Did through his Laurels blast.*
> *'Tis Madness to resist or blame*
> *The force of angry Heavens flame;*
> *And, if we would speak true,*
> *Much to the Man is due:*
> *Who, from his private Gardens, where*
> *He liv'd reserved and austere,*
> *As if his highest plot*
> *To plant the Bergamot,*
> *Could by industrious Valour climbe*
> *To ruine the great Work of Time.* . . .

(13–16, 21–34)

Nearly all Marvell's details appear in Dryden's stanzas: the obscurity of Cromwell's birth, his portentous role as a Heaven-sent scourge, his sudden attainment of power and his impetuous career, his 'mighty mischiefs', the unpreparedness of his prince, and his rending of 'Palaces and Temples'. On the first of the stanzas quoted above the California edition notes: 'Perhaps a reference to Cromwell, who came from the country and who was an obscure figure until the 1640's. The passage was probably in Gray's mind when he wrote 11, 57ff. of the *Elegy*.'[1] If the three stanzas are taken together, however, we seem also to get a subtle allusion to the hero of Marvell's *Ode* and a rather surprising agreement between these two poets in their way of looking at the 'dire Usurper' as a unique agent of apocalypse. Essential differences only begin to appear as the two poets develop in separate ways their estimate of the mighty mischiefs which are threatening 'the great Work of Time'. The differences are partly due to the circumstances under which the poems were written: in *An Horatian Ode* Marvell has to deal with the King's death as a *fait accompli*; in *Annus Mirabilis* Dryden is trying to

[1] *Works*, I. 307.

ward off a repetition of the dire event predicted by the radical Dissenters. E. N. Hooker describes the polemical purpose of the poem thus:

> . . . *Annus Mirabilis* is, in one sense, a piece of inspired journalism, written to sway public opinion in favor of the royal government, which dreaded a revolution—a revolution which, according to republican propaganda, was to be ushered in by omens and portents, by "wonders" signifying the wrath of God against the King and his party. Because of the mystic properties of the figure '666,' expectations of revolution had centered around the year 1666; years before, William Lilly had prophesied that 'in 1666, there will be no King here, or pretending to the Crowne of England.' Fear was widespread. Pepys, recording a conversation with Lord Sandwich on 25 February 1666, reported: "He dreads the issue of this year, and fears there will be some very great revolutions before his coming back again."[1]

Hooker goes on to enumerate some of the pamphlets which attempted to exploit these fears: *Mirabilis Annus, the Year of Prodigies; Mirabilis Annus Secundus: or the Second Year of Wonders;* and so on. Not only did Dryden turn the enemy's guns upon them, but he adopted and modified the prophecies of the Sectarians about the impending end of the world and made it serve his view of restoration and renewal. Thus the stanza which precedes the passage quoted earlier includes one of Dryden's few eschatological references in the political poems:

> *Yet* London *Empress of the Northern Clime,*
>   *By an high fate thou greatly didst expire;*
> *Great as the worlds, which at the death of time*
>   *Must fall, and rise a nobler frame by fire.*

But once again the eschatological catastrophe has been deflected into the cosmogonic cycle of renewal.

V

The Issue of Biblical Interpretation

Bernard Schilling defines the conservative myth as used by Dryden in these words:

[1] Works, I. 258.

Dryden works from an inherited set of symbols and responses to them that make up a general interpretation of life. This might be called a mythology of order, a set of connected myths, drawing on the literary tradition from Rome through the Renaissance, on the Bible as read in the 17th century, on the political and religious experiences of the mid-century civil war, and on the assumptions of rule and control that dominate neoclassical literary theory.[1]

In this otherwise excellent summary, 'the Bible as read in the 17th century' calls for more definition. To a large extent one of the major issues of the seventeenth century was how to read the Bible. The Brownists, Anabaptists, Familists, Muggletonians, and Independents, as well as the Presbyterians (among others) all had their own ways of reading the Bible, and these often differed as much from each other as they did from the more or less established Anglican views of Dryden. With good reason Dryden was alarmed by the divisive effects the private spirit brought in its various interpretations of the holy text. He was deeply concerned lest such independence of interpretation lead to further upheavals in Church and State. As Schilling observes, 'if conservatism, like classicism, in Oliver Elton's phrase, is the triumph of obedience, Dryden seems to have obeyed naturally. He seems free, with no sense of straining toward what was required by neoclassical authority in art, by the demands of political and religious order.'[2] It was virtually inevitable, then, that after writing *Absalom and Achitophel* and *The Medall* he would next direct his attention to what might be regarded as the issue behind the issue of Exclusion and the Popish Plot —the private spirit in religion which had produced that 'Headstrong, Moody, Murmuring race' whom 'No King could govern, nor no God could please.' Thus in *Religio Laici* (1682) Dryden fortified his conservative myth with pragmatic Anglican underpinnings. The poem is not really about a layman's faith as much as it is about obedience to the Church:

> In doubtfull questions 'tis the safest way
> To learn what unsuspected Ancients say:

[1] *Dryden and the Conservative Myth*, 2.
[2] *Ibid.* 4.

> *For 'tis not likely we shou'd higher Soar*
> *In search of Heav'n than all the Church before:*
> *Nor can we be deceiv'd, unless we see*
> *The* Scripture, *and the* Fathers *disagree.*
> *If after all, they stand suspected still,*
> *(For no man's Faith depends upon his Will;)*
> *'Tis some Relief, that points not clearly known,*
> *Without much hazard may be let alone:*
> *And, after hearing what our Church can say,*
> *If still our Reason runs another way,*
> *That private Reason 'tis more Just to curb,*
> *Than by Disputes the publick Peace disturb.*
> *For points obscure are of small use to learn:*
> *But* Common quiet *is* Mankind's concern.
>
> (435–40)

With such gestures toward tolerance Dryden is bent on enforcing the authority of the Established Church instead of making a confession of a layman's faith. If we compare *Religio Laici* with the *O Altitudo's* of its predecessor, *Religio Medici*, the lack of content in Dryden's poem is as remarkable as its commonsense tone. Here the medium, a style 'Plain and Natural, and yet Majestick', is indeed the message. Part of Dryden's conservative strategy is to ascribe to certain public institutions like the Church and the Monarchy and the Law the authenticity they claim without looking very deeply into the authenticity of the claim. He is adept at begging the question while inducing a mood of agreement.

VI

The Conservative Dryden and the Apocalyptic Marvell

At the heart of the great political and religious conflicts of the English Revolution, then, we find a profound disagreement about the nature of history. At the height of the crisis, in his poems on Cromwell, Marvell turned to the apocalyptic visions of the Gospel according to St John, the Book of Revelation, and the Book of Daniel. He found there the sanctions for a revolutionary Christian orthodoxy, at the same time rejecting the democratic views of the Anabaptists, Levellers, and other separatists as anarchical, and the conservative, cyclical view of history as heretical, secular, and futile—'the vain curlings of the wat'ry maze'. Against the forward eschatological thrust of such revolutionary doctrines Dryden employed a view of history that was retrospective in every sense of the word. As a conservative spokesman in politics Dryden was continually reacting against the initiatives of innovators and radicals, by the force of gravity in conservative and traditional authority (to change the metaphor) pulling their missiles out of a trajectory and into an orbital cycle.

A central myth in which both Dryden and Marvell embodied their political views was, of course, the story of David in the Book of Samuel. This story may well have been *the* central political myth of seventeenth-century England. Perhaps it would not be too much to say that the essential struggle of this revolutionary century was reflected in the struggle for possession of the Davidic myth. Dryden's great coup was to capture the myth for the conservative side, and, as it were, retire it permanently.

Although it was widely employed in the literature of controversy by both radicals and conservatives, until *Absalom and Achitophel* appeared, the myth of David was employed most effectively by Protestant reformers. They habitually identified leading figures with such characters in the story as David himself, Michal, Absalom, Achitophel, Saul, and so forth. Joseph Mazzeo has traced this interpretative tradition back to the early middle ages and the coronation of King Pepin:

> This tradition of Davidic kingship as model kingship which started with Pepin persisted through the Middle Ages into the Renaissance. Thomas Aquinas, for example, in *De regimine principium* gives David as an example of the ideal ruler, one who does what every ruler should and places his reward in God.[1]

Mazzeo cites Kantorowicz (*The King's Two Bodies*) to witness that 'Pepin's anointment as if he were a king of Israel was of great importance for the political evolution of Europe, for it is "the keystone of this

---

[1] *Renaissance and Seventeenth-Century Studies*, New York and London, 1964, 188.

evolution and at the same time the cornerstone of medieval divine right
and *Dei Gratia* kingship".'[1] The use of the myth as a precedent establishing divine right may remind us of the range of interpretations and
applications to which it was subjected.

Mazzeo goes on to trace another traditional interpretation of David
as 'humble psalmist', citing Dante's use of him as an example of *humili-
tas* in *Purgatorio* X, and as the dancer before the Ark, 'who by his self-
imposed humility before the Lord became less a king before such as
Michal but more in the eyes of his Creator', thus providing 'a perfect
exemplum of the favourite Christian paradox of *humilitas-sublimitas,*
supremely manifested in the life of Christ. . . .'[2]

Finally, Mazzeo traces a third tradition of Davidic interpretation
which tends to play down David's humility and to emphasize his role
as a great composer, applying to him 'a well-developed conception of
music as the art of cosmic harmony'.[3] This music, he continues, was 'an
image of that unity in variety which is the essence of a well-ordered
city'.[4] It is this aspect of the Davidic myth that lies behind Marvell's
presentation of Cromwell as Amphion in *The First Anniversary* (1655):

> *The listning Structures he with Wonder ey'd,*
> *And still new Stopps to various Time apply'd:*
> *Now through the Strings a Martial rage he throws,*
> *And joyning streight the* Theban *Tow'r arose;*
> *The flocking Marbles in a Palace meet;*
> *But, for he most the graver Notes did try,*
> *Therefore the Temples rear'd their Columns high:*
> *This, ere he ceas'd, his sacred Lute creates*
> *Th' harmonious City of the seven Gates.*
>
> *Such was that wondrous Order and Consent,*
> *When* Cromwell *tun'd the ruling Instrument;*
> *While tedious Statesmen many years did hack,*
> *Framing a Liberty that still went back;*

[1] *Renaissance and Seventeenth-Century Studies*, New York and London,
1964, 188.
[2] *Ibid.* 191.
[3] *Ibid.* 192.
[4] *Ibid.* 192.

> *Whose num'rous Gorge could swallow in an hour*
> *That Island, which the Sea cannot devour:*
> *Then our* Amphion *issues out and sings,*
> *And once he struck, and twice, the pow'rful Strings.*
>
> (57-74)

It is important to remember that the Davidic myth was not primarily literary in its applications to seventeenth-century political and religious matters in England. Unlike the Virgilian elements in the conservative myth, which always retained a literary flavour and often some savour of intellectual snobbery, the Davidic myth sprang in part from a popular cultivation of the Bible. It was a way of interpreting contemporary issues in an oral tradition derived from pulpit, parliament, and other arenas of discussion and debate. Some of the bizarrer instances of this widespread practice Louise Fargo Brown examines in *Baptists and Fifth Monarchy Men*. In the projected uprising of 1665 'the organization of the conspirators was as nearly as possible along biblical lines. The forces were to be divided into three bands, according to the precedent established by Abraham, Gideon, and David.'[1] 'A . . . proclamation . . . outlined the government of the coming state. Christ was to be the supreme legislative power; the Scriptures, the body of the law, a Sanhedrim of Godly men was to be the chief magistracy, having control of the militia.'[2] On another occasion Venner, the radical mystagogue who led the uprising, and his associates were compared to Korah, Dathan, and Abiram, thus providing a precedent for Dryden's identification of the despicable Titus Oates as Corah.[3] Captain John Vernon understandably irritated Henry Cromwell, commander-in-chief of the forces in Ireland, when he preached a sermon comparing Henry to Absalom, remarking 'that Absalom grasped at unlawful power, and that such men might pretend to be for the saints, but that it was as Pharaoh was for Joseph, and Herod for John the Baptist'.[4] Henry cashiered

---

[1] *The Political Activities of the Baptists and Fifth Monarchy Men in England during the Interregnum*, Washington 1912, 112.
[2] *Ibid.* 112.
[3] *Ibid.* 113.
[4] *Ibid.* 155.

another officer of his command for intimating that he was trying
'Absalom-like, to steal the affections of his father's people away from
him . . .'[1] John Canne, the journalist, referred to the restoration of the
Rump in the spring of 1659 as 'the work of an overturning Providence
which had subverted the throne of iniquity and defeated the combinations of Achitophels, thereby encouraging the saints to hope that the
day of redemption was drawing nigh'.[2] Thus Dryden, in his satirical
attacks on 'a thousand dreaming saints', attacked the abuses of apocalyptic scriptural interpretation of contemporary events, above all in
that central Old Testament myth, the story of David. As my quotations
from contemporary sources show, he did not have to debase this use
of the myth—the more far-out sectarians had obligingly done that for
him already. But in representing apocalyptic Christianity only by members of the lunatic fringe (however numerous) and playing off against
them his cool, rational, established, secular Christianity, Dryden
ignored a far nobler apocalyptic version of the Davidic myth. Against
Dryden's aging and worldly David, who can only restore the *status
quo ante*, we need to place the apocalyptic David Marvell represented
in the *First Anniversary*, a unique hero who might become the final instrument of divine intervention in history:

> . . . *'Tis he the force of scatter'd Time contracts,*
> *And in one Year the work of Ages acts;*
> *While heavie Monarchs make a wide Return,*
> *Longer and more Malignant than* Saturn:
> *And though they all* Platonique *years should raign,*
> *In the same Posture would be found again.*
>
> *Hence oft I think, if in some happy Hour*
> *High Grace should meet in one with highest Pow'r,*
> *And then a seasonable People still*
> *Should bend to his, as he to Heavens will,*
> *What we might hope, what wonderfull Effect*
> *From such a wish'd Conjuncture might reflect.*

[1] *The Political Activities of the Baptists and Fifth Monarchy Men in England during the Interregnum*, Washington 1912. 167.
[2] *Ibid.* 183.

> *Sure, the mysterious Work, where non withstand,*
> *Would forthwith finish under such a Hand:*
> *Fore-shortned Time its useless Course would stay,*
> *And soon precipitate the latent Day.*

> (13–18; 131–40)

VII

Dryden, Marvell and Moderation

The death of Cromwell and the ignominious collapse of his son demolished Marvell's millenarian hopes, however cautious, and tempered
his belief in 'the power of providence to change the course, and thus
the meaning of history'.[1] Yet Marvell was to see the hand of providence
in the restoration of Charles II, and if he did not hail the event with
Dryden's enthusiasm he accepted it as a return to the traditional form
of a mixed monarchy with its balance of royal prerogative and parliamentary privilege. Sooner than Dryden Marvell was to see a threat to
this balance in the extension of power on one side at the expense of the
other. For Marvell the chief danger was the encroachment of royal
power on the rights and privileges of parliament and the increasingly
arbitrary conduct of affairs by the King, who was (according to the
usual fiction) the victim of bad ministers. This view was advanced as
early as 1667 in the conclusion to *The Last Instructions to a Painter* with
its double plea to the King to assume his responsibilities and to replace a
corrupt and self-seeking ministry with loyal friends in the House of
Commons:

> *Bold and accurst are they that all this while*
> *Have strove to isle our* Monarch *from his* Isle,
> *And to improve themselves, on false pretense,*
> *About the* Common-Prince *have rais'd a Fense. . . .*
> *But they whom, born to Virtue and to Wealth,*
> *Nor Guilt to Flatt'ry binds, nor Want to Stealth;*
> *Whose gen'rous Conscience and whose Courage high*
> *Does with clear Counsells their large Soules Supply;*

[1] John M. Wallace, *Destiny his Choice: The Loyalism of Andrew Marvell*,
Cambridge 1968, 102.

> *That serve the* King *with their Estates and Care,*
> *And as in Love on* Parliaments *can stare,*
> *(Where few the Number, Choice is there lesse hard);*
> *Give us this* Court *and rule without a Guard.*
>
> (965–8, 981–8)

Such virtuous supporters of the King are remarkably like Barzillai, Dryden's ideal courtier:

> *The Court he practis'd, not the Courtier's art:*
> *Large was his Wealth, but larger was his Heart:*
> *Which well the Noblest Objects knew to choose,*
> *The Fighting Warrior, and Recording Muse.*
>
> (825–8)

Dryden, however, persistently represented any attempt by the parliamentary opposition to check the extension of royal power as a usurpation, and he failed to see, or he ignored, the dangers emanating from Charles' entente with Louis XIV. Even before 1670 Marvell seems to have been alert to the autocratic tendencies of the regime. As Wallace says, 'politically, the farsightedness of *The Last Instructions* makes *Annus Mirabilis* look myopic'.[1] Here one may raise the question as to whether the inveterate tendency of conservatives like Dryden to look to the past may blind them to the present and to probabilities in the future.

Yet if we would understand Dryden's moderation it is important for us to see how closely it resembles in principle the moderation of Marvell, a chief spokesman for the opposition. 'God send us moderation and agreement,' Marvell wrote in 1671, and this prayer 'may stand as an epigraph to all his efforts during the last years of his life'.[2] But the prayer might equally well represent Dryden's political position at the time of writing *Absalom and Achitophel*: 'If I happen to please the more moderate sort, I shall be sure of an honest Party; and, in all probability, of the best Judges; for the least Concern'd are commonly the least

---

[1] John M. Wallace, *Destiny his Choice: The Loyalism of Andrew Marvell*, Cambridge 1968, 173.
[2] *Ibid.* 184.

Corrupt.'[1] He shared with Marvell a deep aversion to the 'parti-color'd mind' and a habitually pragmatic approach to political questions. With equal firmness they rejected republican government of any kind and clove to the idea of monarchy, in the support of which Marvell was as unyielding (in *The Last Instructions*) as Dryden was in *Absalom* or *His Majesties Declaration Defended* (June, 1681) or in his postscript to Maimbourg's *History of the League* (1684). Marvell's remark in a letter to Sir John Trott in 1667 states a central theme of *Absalom*: ' 'Tis Pride that makes a Rebel. And nothing but the over-weening of our selves and our own things that raises us against divine Provi-dence.'[2] And surely Dryden would have had no quarrel with Marvell's well-known reflections on the Civil Wars:

> I think the cause was too good to be fought for. Men ought to have trusted God; they ought and might have trusted the King with that whole matter . . . The King himself, being of so accurate and piercing a judgment, would soon have felt where it stuck. For men may spare their pains where nature is at work, and the world will not go the faster for our driving. Even as his present Majestie's happy Restauration did it self, so all things else happen in their best and proper time, without any need of our officious-ness.[3]

In his dedication to the Earl of Danby of *All for Love* (1678) Dryden celebrated 'moderation' and 'steadiness of temper' as the two requisites of a minister of state 'that he may stand like an isthmus between the two lawless seas of arbitrary power and lawless anarchy.' *To my Honour'd Kinsman, John Driden* (1699) emphasizes this moderating, mediating function:

> *Well-Born and Wealthy; wanting no support,*
> *You steer Betwixt the Country and the Court.*

(127–8)

How close Dryden's position was to Marvell's appears from Wallace's summary: 'England had been blessed by its mixed or limited monarchy,

---

[1] 'To the Reader'.
[2] Quoted in Wallace, *Destiny his Choice*, 182.
[3] *The Rehearsal Transprosed,* in *Complete Works*, ed. A. B. Grosart (n.p., 1872–5), III 212–13.

and, humanly speaking, the equitable distribution of power among the estates of the realm afforded her a strength that probably could not be bettered, and which could only be endangered by the failure of the components to keep their proper place.'[1]

Granted such a fundamental agreement on political principles, how can one explain the hostility that persisted between the two leading political poets of the age? Why, in 1672, did Marvell attack Dryden, by implication, as a champion of arbitrary power in using the Laureate's nickname for the odious Samuel Parker? And why, in the same year, did he single out Dryden for obloquy as 'the town Bayes' in his poem commending *Paradise Lost*? And why, ten years later, did Dryden attack the dead Marvell in his preface to *Religio Laici* as 'a Presbyterian Scribler, who sanctify'd Libels to the use of the Good Old Cause'? Marvell's anti-prelatical bias is scarcely sufficient to motivate the antipathy of one whose feelings toward the clergy were as hostile as Dryden's. How, finally, could Dryden have justified his misrepresentation of Marvell as one of 'a pack of sectaries and commonwealths-men'?

If there is any explanation for this persistent hostility, it is to be sought in the specific interpretations Dryden and Marvell made of the main public issues and events of their time. The threat to the balance of constitutional forces which stemmed from the covert extension of royal authority, beginning with the Secret Treaty of Dover in 1670, produced the dangers that Marvell revealed in *The Growth of Popery and Arbitrary Government* (1678): Louis XIV's sweeping triumphs in Flanders, the maintenance of a standing army to cow parliamentary opposition, the bribery of MPs by French agents (among others), and Charles' short-circuiting of Parliament by repeated prorogations and by misappropriation of funds. Well before the sham Popish Plot broke out in 1678 there was a real plot, based on this secret pact with Louis, and the threat to the liberties of Englishmen was greatly exacerbated by the prospective heir to the throne, an inflexible bigot (in Scott's words) and hence, as a Catholic, all the more to be feared. By the time *Absalom and Achitophel* was written, this was common knowledge, but Dryden chose to ignore the threat of a Stuart tyranny and preferred

1 *Destiny his Choice*, 204.

o find the real danger exclusively in the activities of the opposition. While Shaftesbury's ruthless and unprincipled exploitation of the sham plot greatly aggravated the danger of another civil war, the fact remains that the King and his brother and his ministers had prepared the culture in which this poisonous plant was to flourish. From a modern perspective the surprising thing is not that Marvell should have insisted on calling attention to these dangers but that he should have done so in such a temperate way, and the surprising thing about Dryden is that, while proclaiming moderation, he constantly supported the forces of arbitrary power. While invoking the values of the traditional mixed monarchy Dryden seems to have been willing to pay almost any price for the imagined stability of an inherently autocratic régime. As Laureate and Historiographer-Royal Dryden supported Charles II and the Stuart succession with a singlemindedness that astounds anyone who accepts his pleas for moderation in virtually everything he wrote in the 1670s and 1680s: in pamphlets such as *His Majestie's Declaration Defended*, on the stage in *The Duke of Guise* and *Albion and Albanius*, in numerous prologues and epilogues, even in his translation of Maimbourg's *History of the League* and its highly partisan postscript, as well as in his explicitly political poems. In this unqualified support of the Stuarts and equally unqualified hostility to the opposition, in which loyalists and 'rebels' were huddled together, Dryden's 'moderation' turns out to be more manner than substance. Under the guise of a reasoned concern for a constitutional balance of power, as I shall try to show in the conclusion of this chapter, the Laureate belittled the all-too-real fears and grievances of the loyal opposition.

VIII

Dryden's Strategy in 'Absalom and Achitophel

Dr Johnson observed of Dryden's use of Davidic myth in *Absalom and Achitophel* that 'the original structure of the poem was defective: allegories drawn to great length will always break; Charles could not run continually parallel with David'.[1] The observation is factually correct:

---

[1] *Lives of the Poets*, ed. G. B. Hill, 3 vol Oxford 1905, III 436–7.

the final appearance of Charles, his speech and its affirmation by the Almighty, and the invocation of a 'series of new time' following Charles' re-restoration have no counterpart in the Old Testament story of David.

This departure from the Davidic model is not, however, a defect. It was essential that Dryden modify the myth to allow for Charles/ David's effective stroke against his enemies by the dissolution of Parliament at Oxford and to prophesy a final victory over them. The King's bloodless victory in the conclusion of the poem also suspends the implications of Absalom's Miltonic temptation and his movement in the direction of outright rebellion to suggest this poem is not another *Paradise Lost* but a *Paradise Restored*. The ultimate authority for the restoration, the Godlike David, is Charles II.

The absence of any violent dénouement, which Charles and Dryden alike most wished to avoid, has led to the feeling that the ending is anticlimactic. Charles' enemies and friends alike vanish without trace, as if, Dr Johnson suggests, by magic:

> The chiefs on either part are set forth to view; but when expectation is at the height the king makes a speech, and
> 'Henceforth a series of new times began.'
> Who can forbear to think of an enchanted castle, with a wide moat and lofty battlements, walls of marble and gates of brass, which vanishes at once into air when the destined knight blows his horn before it ?[1]

But the absence of a decisive contest at the end of the poem is not to be attributed solely to the fact that the necessary role of historical truth meant that 'the action and catastrophe were not in the poet's power'. Nor should we hasten to accept the explanation that the apparent anticlimax was due to discrepancies between the historical facts and the myth Dryden had employed.

As Godfrey Davies has shown, the concluding speech is modelled on Charles' *Declaration* of June 1681, defending the dissolution and presenting the King as the guardian of constitutional government which

----

[1] *Lives of the Poets,* ed. G. B. Hill, 3 vol Oxford 1905, III 436–7.

he Whigs were trying to wreck.[1] Even more significant to the issue of he appropriateness of the ending is the fact that Dryden chose to follow history in making the King reassert his authority by a speech. Since the issue at the heart of the poem is the question of legitimate monarchy and the succession, Dryden plays down the providential overtones which had been predominant earlier in order to focus attention on the King himself. For one thing, it is Godlike David, not God, who announces the new dispensation, and the approving nod of Dryden's abstract Almighty is taken from Jupiter's most perfunctory—and one is tempted to say—most trivial intervention in the *Aeneid*. 'Th' Almighty, nodding, gave Consent;/And Peals of Thunder shook the Firmament' translates literally the lines in which Jupiter agrees that Aeneas' ships (which are no longer of any use to him) shall be preserved at the request of Cybele: 'adnuit et totum nutu tremefecit Olympum' (IX. 106). The line occurs again, I should add, at X. 115 when Jupiter agrees to a hands-off policy in the war. In both cases we see the Olympian at his most detached. Furthermore, had he wished, Dryden could have emphasized the prophetic Christian overtones found in Virgil's fourth Eclogue (as he had done in *Astraea Redux*), but instead he contents himself with a nearly literal rendering of 'magnus ab integro saeclorum nascitur ordo' (I. 5): 'Henceforth a Series of new Times began.' The emphasis of the conclusion is thus doubly secular: it asserts a cyclical view of history and a view that is essentially temporal rather than spiritual. The god in the machine is Charles Stuart confirming the succession of his brother James. *Vox Regis vox Dei*.

This low-keyed secular theophany is also in tune with the historical circumstances of Charles' almost magically effective dissolution of the Whig-dominated Parliament at Oxford eight months before *Absalom and Achitophel* appeared. Trevelyan describes the scene in a terse but dramatic way:

> Meanwhile, the leaders in the Commons hurried through the Exclusion Bill. . . . On the eighth day of the session the King appeared suddenly in the House of Lords. He had come in a sedan

[1] 'The Conclusion of Dryden's *Absalom and Achitophel*', *HLQ* CX, 1946, 69–82.

chair, closely followed by another, of which the drawn curtains
presumably concealed some attendant lord. The Commons, hastily
summoned to the Upper House expecting to hear the King
announce his surrender, came rushing tumultuously across the
quadrangle, crowded up a steep and winding staircase, jostled
through a narrow door, and passed down some steps into the body
of the hall. Charles with a gay face watched his enemies defile. At
length they stood there, as many as could fight their way in,
below the throne, panting, a close-headed mob. The King was in
the robes of State—the real contents of the second sedan. In those
robes alone could he dissolve Parliament. He spoke the fatal words
and left the room, while the Commons trooped back the way they
had come with 'dreadful faces' and 'loud sighs'. . . . A panic
seized the undisciplined and braggart host that had ridden into
Oxford.[1]

By the unexpected assertion of his royal prerogative in dissolving a
Parliament bent on annulling the prerogative, the King scattered his
enemies like chaff. What the Tories regarded as an attempt to destroy
the King's authority by interfering in the succession was thwarted by
the breath of royal authority. David's apparent passivity throughout the
poem throws into relief the Godlike power of his word.

If one looks back over the poem from this perspective one can see
how cunningly Dryden prepares us for the concluding theophany of
Charles. 'Godlike David' appears at line 14 and often thereafter. At
first it strikes us as a formal heroic epithet, and only at the end do we
get the full force of the identification. The poem starts out with the
familiar typological identification of the King as God's vicegerent, but
little by little, he assumes Godlike powers in his own person. This
gradual and subtle substitution is insinuated in a number of other ways.
Royal 'grace' is identified with divine 'Grace', thus blurring the distinction between the two orders, in

> *The Jews, a Headstrong, Moody, Murmuring race,*
> *As ever try'd th' extent and stretch of grace.*

(45-46)

---

[1] George Macaulay Trevelyan, *England under the Stuarts*, 1949, 346.

Also, by representing the Monmouth party as rebel angels, Dryden implicitly identifies the King with God:

> Some had in Courts been great, and thrown from thence,
> Like Fiends, were harden'd in Impenitence.
> Some by their Monarchs fatal mercy grown,
> From pardon'd Rebels, Kinsmen to the Throne.
>
> (144–7)

As Charles grows more Godlike, he learns to shed this 'fatal mercy' and declares, like Milton's God announcing divine retribution,

> Their Belial with their Belzebub will fight;
> Thus on my Foes, my Foes shall do me Right.
>
> (1016–17)

At the climax of the temptation scene the often-noted Miltonic rhetoric emphasizes the explicit identification of Achitophel with Satan and Absalom with Adam and the implicit identification of Charles/David with God the Father:

> Him Staggering so when Hells dire Agent found
> While fainting Vertue scarce maintain'd her Ground,
> He pours fresh forces in, and thus replies . . .
>
> (373–5)

The cumulative effect of these largely subliminal and oblique identifications of Charles with God is unobtrusively to dismantle the conventional providential and supernatural framework of the Davidic and Miltonic myths and erect in its place an autonomous myth of divine right with Charles as its final cause. In the important passage which introduces the King's speech there is, to be sure, a perfunctory nod toward Heaven, but the ultimate authority is really the speaker himself:

> With all these loads of injuries opprest,
> And long revolving, in his carefull Breast,
> Th' event of things; at last his patience tir'd,
> Thus from his Royal Throne by Heav'n inspir'd,
> The God-like David spoke: with awfull fear
> His Train their Maker in their Master hear.
>
> (933–8)

The whole tendency of Dryden's adaptation of traditional myth material in this poem is to remove—or at least obscure—the orthodox distinctions between the divine Maker and the secular Master and assert the God-like authority of King Charles.

In many ways I would agree with Leon Guilhamet who, in a recent article, sees 'a revolutionary debasement of the traditional David story' in which 'the king himself becomes the most significant figure out-doing God, rather than relying on Him for support; and the Church is thrust into the background as a mere appurtenance of David-Charles' authority'.[1] On the other hand 'debasement' and 'thrust into the background' overlook, I believe, the subtlety and quietness with which Dryden has effected the change of focus.

Guilhamet also sees Dryden as 'rejecting' the David story in order to permit David-Charles 'to emerge as Charles alone,' thus 'reinterpreting' the old myth 'out of existence'.[2] While it is hard to see how Dryden could have extended the Davidic parallel to cover the conclusion of the poem, in view of historical realities, it seems nevertheless inescapable that he has at the very least de-emphasized the myth. blending Virgilian references with his *Odyssey*-like finale, Guilhamet suggests, Dryden is giving us a new secular, classical poetic style match the new political age. *Absalom and Achitophel* thus seems mark the decline of the serious use of religious myth in English political poetry and, perhaps, the beginning of the myth of secular authority that has accompanied the development of the modern state.[3]

[1] 'Dryden's Debasement of Scripture in *Absalom and Achitophel*', *SEL* IX, 1969, 395–413; 407.
[2] *Ibid.* 412.
[3] *Windsor-Forest* seems to be a very late example of a political poem with the traditional religious myth at its centre.

7: Dryden and Satire: 'Mac Flecknoe, Absalom and Achitophel, the Medall', and Juvenal

MICHAEL WILDING

'THE RIGHT of blaming bad Authors, is an ancient Right, pass'd into a custom, among all the Satirists, and allow'd in all ages,' wrote the French satirist Boileau in 1668.[1] But though following an ancient right, Dryden derived little from the ancient manner of classical satirists when he came to write his own onslaught on a bad author in *Mac Flecknoe*. Dryden may well have felt the same anger as Persius did at the corruptions of literature, but Persius employs direct moral censure:

> *First, to begin at Home, our Authors write*
> *In lonely Rooms, secur'd from publick sight;*
> *Whether in Prose or Verse, 'tis all the same:*
> *The Prose is Fustian, and the Numbers lame.*
> *All noise, and empty Pomp, a storm of words,*
> *Lab'ring with sound, that little Sence affords.*
> *They Comb, and then they order ev'ry Hair:* }
> *A Gown, or White, or Scour'd to whiteness, wear:* }
> *A Birth-day Jewel bobbing at their Ear.*
> *Next, gargle well their Throats; and thus prepar'd,*
> *They mount, a God's Name, to be seen and heard*
> *From their high Scaffold; with a Trumpet Cheek:*
> *And Ogling all their Audience e're they speak.*
> *The nauseous Nobles, ev'n the Chief of* Rome,
> *With gaping Mouths to these Rehearsals come,*

[1] Boileau, *A Discourse of Satires Arraigning Persons by Name*, tr. anon., 1730; appended to Walter Harte, *Essay on Satire* (1730), Augustan Reprint Society 132, Los Angeles 1968.

> *And pant with Pleasure, when some lusty line*
> *The Marrow pierces, and invades the Chine.*
> *At open fulsom Bawdry they rejoice;*
> *And slimy Jests applaud with broken Voice.*
> *Base Prostitute, thus dost thou gain thy Bread?*
> *Thus dost thou feed their Ears, and thus art fed?*
> *At his own filthy stuff he grins, and brays:*
> *And gives the sign where he expects their praise.*
>
> (Persius, I. 32–54 tr. Dryden)

This direct diatribe, without irony, without comedy, is characteristic
of classical verse satire. That we tend now to expect wit, humour,
obliqueness, double entendre and subtlety in satire is a result very much
of Dryden's achievement. Denunciatory satire existed in English in
such writers as Hall and Marston before Dryden. But with Dryden the
nature of English satire was markedly changed.

Dryden's attack on bad writing operates utterly differently from that
of Persius. He does not offer a personal condemnation of corruption
but through the personality and mouth of Flecknoe presents a panegyric on bad writing. The wit resides in our knowing that it is bad
writing that is being praised, in seeing the discrepancy between the
values asserted in the praise and the values adhering to the literature
itself. That Flecknoe is shown as monarch of the 'Realms of *Non-sense*'
establishes the value of his praise, makes it a cruel attack; but since
what he says about Thomas Shadwell is put into this positive context
of praise rather than of the negative destruction of Persius' railing, the
satire is given a geniality of tone. Flecknoe decides to resign his throne
of the 'Realms of *Non-sense*'

> *And pond'ring which of all his Sons was fit*
> *To Reign, and wage immortal War with Wit;*
> *Cry'd, 'tis resolv'd; for Nature pleads that He*
> *Should onely rule, who most resembles me:*
> *Sh— alone my perfect image bears,*
> *Mature in dullness from his tender years.*
> *Sh— alone, of all my Sons, is he*
> *Who stands confirm'd in full stupidity.*

> *The rest to some faint meaning make pretence,*
> *But* Sh— *never deviates into sense.*
>
> (*Mac Flecknoe,* 11–20)

What is said is as damning as anything from Persius—Shadwell's 'dullness', 'stupidity'—but it is done with a smile. And along with the smile go the subtler, crueller attacks. Insofar as Shadwell thought of himself as heir to any writer, it was to Ben Jonson, whose comedies he admired, whose enthusiasm for beer he shared, and whose physical girth he rivalled. Jonson's poetic disciples were known as the 'sons of Ben'—and Dryden retains this concept when Flecknoe considers 'all his Sons'; but Shadwell is presented as a son of Flecknoe, a prolific writer of unsuccessful works.

'Mac Flecknoe' means, of course, 'son of Flecknoe'; but the Irishness of the formula—'such barb'rous *Mac's*' Dryden calls the Irish in one of his Prologues to the University of Oxford[1]—needs explanation. The Irishness is stressed; Flecknoe gives Shadwell a realm of watery emptiness, one of whose shores is Ireland—'from *Ireland* let him reign/To farr *Barbadoes*' (139–40); and describing Shadwell's art he tells how

> *Like mine thy gentle numbers feebly creep,*
> *Thy Tragick Muse gives smiles, thy Comick sleep.*
> *With whate'er gall thou sett'st thy self to write,*
> *Thy inoffensive Satyrs never bite.*
> *In thy fellonious heart, though Venom lies,*
> *It does but touch thy* Irish *pen and dyes.* (197–202)

The art of Shadwell and Flecknoe inverts the values it might be expected to aim for. The poetry comes out back to front—tragedy provokes smiles, satires cause no offence. Such inversion of values is the peculiar quality of Irish bards. 'There is amongst the Irishe a certen kinde of people Called Bardes which are to them in steade of Poets whose profession is to sett fourthe the praises and dispraises of menne in their Poems or Rhymes,' Edmund Spenser wrote in *A View of the*

---

[1] Kinsley, I 374 (l. 27).

Present State of Ireland (1633)[1]. It is as an Irish bard that Flecknoe
presented—'the yet declaiming Bard' (213) he is called, the wo
'bard' at this date having a specifically Irish primary association. Flec
noe's praise of Shadwell is an Irish bard's panegyric. The panegyrics
Irish bards were not like conventional panegyrics, Spenser explair
'It is moste trewe that suche poetes as in theire wrightinges doe labo
to better the manners of men and thoroughe the swete bayte of thei
numbers to steale into the yonge spirites a desire of honour and vert
are worthie to be had in greate respecte, But these Irishe Bardes a
for the moste parte of another minde and so farre from instructing
yonge men in morall discipline that they themselues doe more deser
to be sharpelye discipled for they seldome vse to Chose out themselu
the doinges of good men for the argumentes of theire poems but who
soeuer they finde to be moste Licentious of life moste bolde and lawl
in his doinges moste daungerous and desperate in all partes of disob
dience and rebellious disposicion him they set vp and glorifye in th
Rymes him they praise to the people and to yonge men make an exar
ple to followe.' Irish bards praise the bad. By presenting Flecknoe in t
prophetic robes of an Irish bard, the subject of his panegyric mu
inevitably be seen as 'moste licentious of life . . .' etc., as a figure
destruction, as an outlaw from the realms of true literature like the ou
laws praised by the bards, as indeed the possessor of a 'fellonious hear

However, Dryden does not want to stress the seriousness of t
threat Shadwell poses to literature; that would be an acknowledgme
of the stature of his rival. By treating him as a comic figure, Dryden ca
still attack him yet not seem to be worried. That Shadwell's trag
Muse provokes smiles is evidence of the Irish bardic inversion of prop
values, but it is also evidence of a comic incompetence. It is a charg
that Dryden makes with some effrontery since it had previously be
levelled at him in the prologue to *The Rehearsal* (1672), the burlesq
play by which the Duke of Buckingham and others attacked Dryde

---

[1] *Spenser's Prose Works*, ed. Rudolf Gottfried, in *The Works of Edmund
Spenser: A Variorum Edition*, Baltimore 1949, 125. I am indebted to
R. M. Cummings of the University of Glasgow for this reference. The
bards are well covered by Robert C. Elliott, *The Power of Satire*,
Princeton 1960.

dramatic techniques: '*Our Poets make us laugh at Tragoedy/And with their Comoedies they make us cry.*'[1]

Shadwell of course missed the point of the Irish allusions. In the epistle dedicatory to his translation of *The Tenth Satyr of Juvenal* (1687) he complains that 'the Author of *Mac-Fleckno*' 'goes a little too far in calling me the dullest, and has no more reason for that, than for giving me the *Irish* name of *Mack*, when he knows I never saw *Ireland* till I was three and twenty years old, and was there but four Months.'[2] But Shadwell was not alone in missing the point. Poor Flecknoe is now referred to in every reference work from the *Dictionary of National Biography* to the *Oxford History of English Literature* as an *Irish* priest; a priest he seems to have been, but there is nothing to suggest he was Irish, except Dryden's joke.[3]

By the device of the Irish bard, Dryden can present something more complex than the simple railing of Persius. By setting the priestly-prophetic bard on a throne of bad literature, Dryden establishes a dramatic situation whose context allows a free run for the mock heroic. The central episode of *Mac Flecknoe* is Flecknoe's abdication from his throne and the coronation of Shadwell. For the monarchist Dryden the coronation was the central symbol of the establishment of social order. And the coronation of Shadwell draws on the dignified and heroic associations of coronations in Biblical, classical and contemporary

[1] In *Burlesque Plays of the Eighteenth Century*, ed. Simon Trussler, 1969, 5.

[2] *The Works of Thomas Shadwell*, ed. Montague Summers, 5 vol, 1927, V. 292.

[3] I am grateful to Mrs E. E. Duncan Jones of the University of Birmingham for pointing out to me that there is no evidence for believing Flecknoe was Irish: Marvell, who had met him, calls him in his poem 'an *English* Priest at Rome'. No convincing argument of why Dryden chose Flecknoe as his monarch of dullness has been given, but the suggestions include: Peter Cunningham, 'Dryden's Quarrel with Flecknoe', *Gentleman's Magazine*, NS XXXIV, 1850, 597–9; John Harrington Smith, 'Dryden and Fleckno: A Conjecture', *PQ*, XXXIII, 1954, 338–41; and Maxmillian E. Novak, 'Dryden's "Ape of the French Eloquence" and Richard Flecknoe', *Bulletin of the New York Public Library*, LXII, 1968, 499–506.

writing. But these dignified associations exist primarily so that the discrepancy between them and the new monarch of dullness, Shadwell, can be established. Samuel Butler's *Hudibras*, one of the most popular poems of the Restoration, had exploited this discrepancy for burlesque effect in his account of a Civil Wars would-be hero of epic and romance; but the Don Quixote-like adventures of Hudibras are described in burlesque verse as vulgar and comic as the hero it describes—and both are comically distant from the classical models they are aware of and constantly remind us of. Attempting to disperse a bear-baiting, Hudibras and Ralpho end up with some villagers in a brawl that is a modern degenerate version of epic warfare. Hudibras engages Talgol, no Trojan Knight but local butcher, in single combat:

> *This said, with hasty rage he snatch'd*
> *His Gun'shot, that in holsters watch'd;*
> *And bending Cock, he level'd full*
> *Against th'outside of* Talgol's *Skull;*
> *Vowing that he shou'd ne're stir further,*
> *Nor henceforth Cow or Bullock murther.*
> *But* Pallas *came in Shape of Rust,*
> *And 'twixt the Spring and Hammer thrust*
> *Her* Gorgon-Shield, *which made the Cock*
> *Stand Stiff, as if 'twere turn'd t'a stock.*

(I. ii, 775–84)

The epic penumbra to the ignoble event and the classical allusion all provide a precedent for Dryden's *Mac Flecknoe*. But Dryden rejects the burlesque octosyllabics for reasons he explains in his *Discourse Concerning Satire*: 'in any other Hand, the shortness of his Verse, and the quick returns of Rhyme, had debas'd the Dignity of Style'. To find mock heroic handled with dignity of style, Dryden turned to Boileau's *Lutrin*: 'He writes it the *French* Heroique Verse, and calls it an Heroique Poem. His Subject is Trivial, but his Verse is Noble' (Kinsley, II 663, 664).[2]

---

[1] Samuel Butler, *Hudibras*, ed. John Wilders, Oxford 1967, 51. The first part of *Hudibras* was published in 1662.

[2] I have discussed Butler's manner further in 'The Last of the Epics: The Rejection of the Heroic in *Paradise Lost* and *Hudibras*' in *Restoration Literature: Critical Approaches*, ed. Harold Love, 1972.

Butler, however, provided an English model for mock-heroic dignity in his 'To the Happy Memory of the most Renown'd Du-Val' (1671).[1] A pindaric ode, metrically it is unlike Dryden's satire, but the elegance of language, the controlled vocabulary and movement of its opening, provide a noble tone:

> *'Tis true, to compliment the Dead*
>   *Is as impertinent and vain,*
> *As 'twas of old to call them back again,*
>   *Or, like the* Tartars, *give them Wives*
>   *With settlements, for After-lives:*
> *For all that can be done, or said,*
> *Tho' ere so noble, great, and good,*
> *By them is neither heard, nor understood.*
>   *All our fine Slights, and Tricks of Art,*
> *First to create, and then adore Desert,*
>   *And those Romances, which we frame,*
>   *To raise ourselves, not them, a Name,*
> *In vain are stuft with ranting Flatteries,*
> *And such as, if they knew, they would despise.*
>
>   (1–14)

It is a beautiful opening for an elegiac poem, but its beauty is there for the ironic discrepancy with its subject Du-Val, a notorious highwayman who was hanged at Tyburn in 1669. It is with a similar dignified, slow, elegiac note, a similar heavy, sententious manner for a similar un-heroic sort of subject that Dryden opens *Mac Flecknoe*:

> *All humane things are subject to decay,*
> *And, when Fate summons, Monarchs must obey:*
> *This* Fleckno *found, who, like* Augustus, *young*
> *Was call'd to Empire, and had govern'd long:*
> *In Prose and Verse, was own'd, without dispute*
> *Through all the Realms of* Non-sense, *absolute.*
>
>   (1–6)

---

[1] Samuel Butler, *Satires and Miscellaneous Poetry and Prose*, ed. René Lamar, Cambridge 1928, 97–103.

But though the mock-heroic tone of *Mac Flecknoe* is similar to Butler's
in *Du-Val*, Dryden does not, like Butler, create his satire through the
ambiguity of a sustained suppression of his subject's nature. That
Du-Val is a highwayman emerges not by statement but from ironic am
biguities:

> He had improv'd his nat'ral Parts,
> And with his magic Rod could sound
> Where hidden Treasure might be found.

(78-80)

Whereas Flecknoe and Shadwell are explicitly established as dull
writers of nonsense by the sixth line. As Ian Jack points out, 'The ridicule is much more direct than that in *A Tale of a Tub* or *Jonathan Wild
the Great*. Qualities in fact ridiculous are nominally praised; but they are
given their true names, "dulness", "nonsense", "tautology".'[1] By the
device of the Irish bard Dryden can have the true nature of Shadwell
explicitly stated, instead of established by irony and ambiguity, and he
can praise this true nature instead of railing at it as Juvenal or Persius
would have done.

The elevation to an ideal of something explicitly stated as bad, and
the rigorous commitment to such an ideal of badness, are classically
portrayed in Milton's *Paradise Lost* (1667). 'Evil be thou my Good,
Satan declares (IV 110); and that, as James Sutherland has remarked,
is the sentiment on which Flecknoe's opening speech is based.[2] The
'immortal War with Wit' which Flecknoe looks for as on to wage is a
version of Satan's 'immortal hate' (I. 107). Dryden knew *Paradise Lost*
in close detail, having turned it into an 'opera', *The State of Innocence*
(1677). He alludes to it constantly in his poetry, finding in the rebellion
of Satan the archetype of political rebellion in seventeenth century
England.[3] The Satanic rebellion serves as a touchstone in his satires

[1] Ian Jack, *Augustan Satire*, Oxford 1952, 50.
[2] James Sutherland, *English Satire*, 1958, 56.
[3] Ronald Paulson, *The Fictions of Satire*, Baltimore 1967, 110-20, argues
for the importance of *Paradise Lost* as a model of satiric possibilities.
On Shaftesbury as Lucifer in *The Medall*, see Roper, 87-103. All quotations from *Paradise Lost* are from Milton's Poems, ed. B. A. Wright,
1956.

providing a metaphoric hinterland to illuminate Shaftesbury and his associates in *Absalom and Achitophel* and *The Medall*. Since Shadwell and Flecknoe are rebels in the realm of literature, they are placed by allusions to the Satanic materials of *Paradise Lost*.

Milton's portrayal of Satan has its own satiric dimension. Satan attempts to equal God but achieves only parody; the devils stand in semi-circles in Hell whereas the angels stand in perfect circles in heaven; Hell's gates open to a fearful sound, Heaven's to harmony; Satan's journey to earth to destroy mankind by introducing death is a parodic prefiguring of Christ's journey to earth to save man by giving his own life; the trinity of Satan, Sin and Death is a grotesque parody of the heavenly trinity. The wit of Dryden's allusions to *Paradise Lost* depends on our recognition of Milton's original parody scheme, for Dryden brilliantly exploits these different levels. When, for instance, Flecknoe states '*Sh—* alone my perfect image bears' the blasphemous implications of Flecknoe's reference to his adopted poetic son Shadwell in terms normally applied to God's relationship to His Son, readily enough establish Flecknoe's self-aggrandizing delusions and, in spite of his being a priest, his lack of decorum. His moral and literary failings are exposed. But in fact in *Paradise Lost* the Son is described by the phrase 'the radiant image of his Glory' (III. 63); Adam and Eve are not the subjects of the phrase either—'in thir looks Divine/The image of thir glorious Maker shon' (IV. 291-2). The phrase 'perfect image' does indeed come from *Paradise Lost*, but from Sin's description of how Satan fell in love with her, his daughter: 'Thy self in me thy perfet image viewing/Becam'st enamourd' (II 764-5). The blasphemous presumptions of Flecknoe are properly there; but for the reader who locates the specific source of Dryden's allusion, there is a further dimension—the further joke that Flecknoe's phrase in fact expresses his kinship to Satan, not to God; attempting to emulate divinity, he achieves only a parody of a parody of divinity. It is a two-level response that Dryden evokes. We need to recognize not only the phrase quoted, but also the expected phrases not quoted—for '*radiant* image' and 'image . . . *shon*' contain the essential quality missing from the Satanic version—light, brightness. The imagery of *Mac Flecknoe* is of fogs and glooms to express the dullness of its subjects; and part of the game Dryden plays is incorporating allusions and phrases from noble literature, but always excluding any images of light that might be contained, either excising them or substituting images of dullness. When Flecknoe is shown 'High on a Throne of his own Labours rear'd' (107) the allusion is to Satan's throne in *Paradise Lost*: 'High on a Throne of Royal State, which far/Outshon the wealth of *Ormus* and of *Ind*' (II. 1–2). Satan's throne is itself an attempted physical imitation of the spiritual glory of God's throne in 'the pure Empyrean' (III. 57). Satan attempts to imitate that realm of pure fire by studding his throne with jewels; but Flecknoe's throne does not even have a tawdry brightness; the light is replaced by the dullness of 'his own Labours', his benighted literary works.

Mac Flecknoe is packed with this sort of allusion to literary works and to the Bible; we shall see further examples when we turn to the poem's climax, and there are a number of articles that indicate something of Dryden's range of allusion.[1] What is remarkable about Dryden's allusions is their minutely specific nature, contrasting with the general echoes of heroic contexts from heroic literature that Butler used in *Hudibras*. That mock heroic use of the noble as a touchstone to illuminate the degradation of the satire's subjects is present in *Mac Flecknoe*, but with these additional rewards of specific jokes. Because of the religious meanings of a coronation and because of Flecknoe's being a priest, the religious imagery has its function; but the especial relevance of Flecknoe's blasphemous presumptions of a divine role arises from a play on the idea of God as 'creator', just as the allusions to Aeneas have a force additional to the simple provision of a heroic context for the enthronement, through a play on the word 'author', the categorization of Aeneas in those lines of the *Aeneid* alluded to in lines 106–9 of *Mac Flecknoe*:

> *Then issu'd from the Camp, in Arms Divine,*
> *Æneas, Author of the* Roman *Line:*
> *And by his side* Ascanius took his Place,
> *The second Hope of* Rome's *Immortal Race.*
>
> (*Aeneid*, XII. 251–4 tr. Dryden)

[1] A. L. Korn, '*Mac Flecknoe* and Cowley's *Davideis*', *Huntington Library Quarterly*, XIV, 1951, 99–127; Michael Wilding, 'Allusion and Innuendo in *Mac Flecknoe*.' *Essays in Criticism*, XIX, 1969, 355–70; and those discussions referred to in n. 1, p. 207, below.

Flecknoe and Shadwell are not, however, in Dryden's view authors, creators, at all but rather rebels in or outlaws from the realm of literature, destroyers. They may think they are creators, but the Satanic illusions establish their true nature; 'only in destroying I find ease' Satan declared in *Paradise Lost* (IX. 129).

This sort of specificity of allusion is not typical of Dryden's political satires. That famous Miltonic line describing Achitophel's renewed assault of temptation on Absalom, 'Him Staggering so when Hells dire Agent found' (373) imitates the general Miltonic manner but is not a specific echo or parody. The reader who had merely glanced at Milton's work would recognize the 'miltonics' and register the idea of devilish temptation. And that is all that is essential: *Absalom and Achitophel* and *The Medall* were political satires designed for a wide readership. *Mac Flecknoe*, however, was designed for a different audience. Dryden published it in 1684 only after a pirated edition had appeared in 1682.[1] It seems likely that the poem was never intended for publication and a general readership, but was written as part of a private literary feud; it is full of close literary allusions and jokes because the readership would have been primarily a literary one. It is a very in-group satire, depending on a knowledge of literary works in such detail of a kind that only someone with a professional concern with literature—writer, critic, book-seller, patron—would be likely to have. The utter literariness of the satire with practically every line and episode an allusion to some other literary work, is appropriate for its subject and milieu; the full meanings are revealed only to those who have a shared experience of reading and play-going with Dryden.

In particular, *Mac Flecknoe* is filled with allusions to Shadwell's own writings, and the discrepancy between allusions to Virgil's Ascanius and Shadwell's Prince Nicander (179) for instance, creates those disjunctions that are the basis of comedy and satire; if, of course, the reader agrees with Dryden that Shadwell's work is so bad.

[1] Harold Brooks, 'When Did Dryden Write *Mac Flecknoe?*' *RES*, XI, 1935, 74–78; G. Thorn-Drury, 'Dryden's *Mac Flecknoe*: A Vindication', *MLR*, XIII, 1918, 276–81; George McFadden, 'Elkanah Settle and the Genesis of *Mac Flecknoe*', *PQ*, XLIII, 1964, 55–72.

For fourteen years before *Mac Flecknoe* was published, Dryden and
Shadwell had been sniping at each other in the prefaces, prologues and
epilogues to their plays. Their professional rivalry expressed itself critic
ally in a debate about the nature of wit and comedy, the precedent of
Ben Jonson's comedy, and the use of rhyme in drama.[1] Shadwell, to
judge from his prefaces, must have been both remarkably naive and
remarkably self-assured. He confesses to weaknesses and utterly ex
poses himself, yet clearly was too confident and too lazy to feel impelled
to correct them. In the Preface to *Psyche* (1675), his first verse play, he
attacks other verse dramatists (Dryden foremost among them), implies
that verse drama is not worth writing, admits the inadequacies of his
own work, and yet at the same time manages to congratulate himself on
certain of its features:

> In a good natur'd Countrey, I doubt not but this my first Essay in
> Rhime would be at least forgiven; especially when I promise to
> offend no more in this kind: But I am sensible, that here I must en-
> counter a great many Difficulties. In the first place (though I ex-
> pect more Candor from the best Writers in Rhime) the more
> moderate of them (who have yet a numerous party, good Judges
> being very scarce) are very much offended with me, for leaving
> my own Province of *Comedy*, to invade their Dominion of *Rhime*:
> But methinks they might be satisfied, since I have made but a
> small incursion, and am resolv'd to retire. And were I never so
> powerful, they should escape me, as the Northern People did the
> *Romans*, their craggy barren Territories, being not worth the
> Conqu'ring. . . .
>   In a thing written in five weeks, as this was, there must needs
> be many Errors, which I desire true Criticks to pass by; and
> which perhaps I see my self, but having much bus'ness, and indulg-
> ing my self with some pleasure too, I have not had the leisure to
> mend them, nor would it indeed be worth the pains, since there are
> so many splendid Objects in the Play, and such variety of Diver-
> sion, as will not give the Audience leave to mind the Writing; and
> I doubt not but the Candid Reader will forgive the faults, when he

[1] D. M. McKeithan, 'The Occasion of *Mac Flecknoe*', *PMLA*, XLVII,
1932, 766–71; R. Jack Smith, 'Shadwell's Impact on John Dryden', *RES*,
XX, 1944, 29–44; Michael W. Allsid, 'Shadwell's *Mac Flecknoe*', *SEL*,
VII, 1967, 387–402.

considers, that the great Design was to entertain the Town with variety of Musick, curious Dancing, splendid Scenes and Machines: And that I do not, nor ever did, intend to value my self upon the writing of this Play.

(Summers, II. 279; original in italics)

Shadwell's flippant, casual attitude to playwriting provided Dryden with sufficient reason for launching his satire. And the terms in which Shadwell couched his preface—'province', 'dominion'—appear in the satire as indications of his fatuous presumptuousness; 'Of his Dominion may no end be known' Flecknoe intones (141), providing an even emptier 'Dominion' from Ireland to the Barbadoes than the 'craggy barren Territories' of the 'Dominion of *Rhime*'. The monarchical presumptions which lead to Shadwell's acceptance of coronation are implied in his own language.

In the verse Prologue to *Psyche* Shadwell establishes another range of imagery for himself which Dryden exploits:

> *As a young wanton when she first begins,*
> *With shame, and with regret of Conscience sins;*
> *So fares our trembling Poet the first time,*
> *He has committed the lewd sin of Rhime,*
> *While Custom hardens others in the Crime.*

(Summers, II. 281)

Shadwell may have intended 'the lewd sin of Rhime' to reflect on Dryden and his verse plays; but Dryden turns the images back on him and sets up Shadwell's throne in a training ground for young wantons—the actors' training school on the site of the old Barbican watchtower: 'From its old Ruins Brothel-houses rise,/Scenes of lewd loves, and of polluted joys.' (70–71). The lines are an adaptation of Cowley's description of Hell in the *Davideis* and degrade that divine epic by applying its lines to prostitution: but such is the literary degradation Flecknoe and Shadwell practice. They may presume to monarchy but their throne is in the brothel area; Flecknoe is indeed 'the *hoary* Prince' (106).

Prostitution is an appropriate image for the debasement of literary skills. Dryden was often enough accused of it himself. *The Tory Poets*, which Shadwell may have written, says of Dryden 'His *Muse* was prostitute upon the Stage,/And's *Wife* was Prostitute to all the age . . .'

(Summers, V. 279). In *Mac Flecknoe* Dryden develops the implicatio
of the image; if Shadwell thought of himself as 'a young wanton' wh
did that mean? Not the usual analogy, of simply selling his pen for hir
Dryden takes as the central aspect of prostitution here the avoidance
procreation, the avoidance of conception or birth. Once again Shadwe
himself provides the imagery. At the end of the Preface to *Psyche
Postscript notes that two of the songs had been previously publishe
including 'about eight lines in the first Act, beginning at this line, 'T
frail as an abortive Birth.' (Summers, II. 280). The singling out of such
line may well have provoked Dryden's mirth. The image recurs in th
epilogue to *The Virtuoso* (1676) where, apologizing again, Shadwe
concludes:

> *You know the pangs and many laboring throws*
> *By which your brains their perfect births disclose.*
> *You can the faults and excellencies find;*
> *Pass by the one, and be to th' other kind.*
> *By you he is resolv'd to stand or fall;*
> *What'er's his doom he'll not repine at all.*
> *And if his birth should want its perfect shape*
> *And cannot by your care its death escape,*
> *Th'abortive issue came before its day,*
> *And th' poet has miscarried of a play.*[1]

Dryden develops these images of unfruitful pregnancies and uses Sha
well's own ideas, words, images to reveal the uncreativeness of his a
He readily interprets Shadwell's fatness as pregnancy—'big with Hym
(41)—and Flecknoe declares ,'learn thou from me / Pangs without birt
(147–8). When we see Shadwell enthroned it is appropriate that h
regalia should symbolize his non-creativeness:

> *In his sinister hand, instead of Ball*
> *He plac'd a mighty Mug of potent Ale;*
> Love's Kingdom *to his right he did convey,*
> *At once his Sceptre and his rule of Sway;*
> *Whose righteous Lore the Prince had practis'd young*
> *And from whose Loyns recorded* Psyche *sprung.*   (120–

[1] *The Virtuoso*, ed. by Marjorie Hope Nicholson and David Stuart Rodes
1966, 141–2.

he particular association of drinking with the dulling of a playwright's
its is made by Flecknoe himself in his *A Short Discourse of the English
tage*, printed with *Love's Kingdom* in 1664. 'A Dramatick Poet,' Fleck-
oe wrote, was 'to be a wise as well as a witty Man, and a good man, as
ell as a good Poet; and I'de allow him to be so far a good fellow too, to
ke a chearful cup to whet his wits, so he take not so much to dull 'um,
d whet 'um quite away.' The prophetic father indeed. But as well as
ing the monarchical regalia of Shadwell's imperial presumptions to
press his habitual drinking, Dryden exploits it for sexual innuendo.
nstead of Ball' the monarch holds 'potent Ale'; calling the orb a ball
nphasizes the idea of a testicle—to make the point that these monarchs
e ball-less; whereas potent balls beget, procreate potent, ale produces
o offspring, only sleep. And instead of a sceptre the monarch holds
ove's Kingdom, Flecknoe's play, whose title readily implies a sexual
eaning; but whereas the sceptre is an image of a penis, the penis is
ually love's king; *Love's Kingdom* is the vagina—'O my America! my
w-found-land.' For these monarchs of dullness. Dryden has intro-
ced the monarchical regalia of orb and sceptre, and then super-
posed a grotesque parody of these trappings—testicle and penis; and
en for these monarchs he has shown them not even maintaining the
rody but enthroned within a parody of a parody—a mug of ale, and
e of Flecknoe's works that is the type of the female genitalia. The
ference to Shadwell's pregnancy makes more consistent sense when
e find he has the sexual characteristics of a woman—he is of the same
x as his 'young wanton' and as Milton's Sin. This, then, is the final
xual insult, the attack on Shadwell's virility (and by implication on
ecknoe who as a priest was sworn to celibacy). No wonder Shadwell
plied in *The Medal of John Bayes* to Dryden: 'An old gelt Mastiff has
ore mirth than thou' (Summers, V. 253).

Shadwell's literary impotence is expressed by giving him the sexual
aracteristics of a woman. But though his girth betokens pregnancy,
 is doomed to 'Pangs without birth, and fruitless Industry.' But if he
d Flecknoe are impotent, sterile, barren and aborting, what are those
erary works of theirs whose titles Dryden mentions? 'Love has
ched his mansion in/The place of excrement': the appropriate
agery is established early when 'Echoes from *Pissing-Ally*, Sh— call'

(47) and the context of the street name establishes the possibilities c
scatological substitution of Sh— which is exploited later:

> *From dusty shops neglected Authors come,*
> *Martyrs of Pies, and Reliques of the Bum.*
> *Much Heywood, Shirly, Ogleby there lay,*
> *But loads of Sh— almost choakt the way.*   (100–)

The fate of poems for wiping arses, the 'loads' that 'choakt the way' an
the fact that Shadwell's name alone of the writers there is abbreviated
makes the association inevitable, not only in these lines but at ever
other mention of Sh—. Flecknoe's *Business* (i.e. sexual intercourse an
defecation) and the throne of his own labours take on new meaning.

The combination of literary allusion and obscene innuendo giv
Mac Flecknoe its characteristic tone. It is not simply the co-existence
noble literature and scatology that create the surprise of wit, but th
peculiarly erudite and pedantic minutiae from which the allusions g
their effect allied with the broad strokes of vulgarity; and the more i
direct obscenities that are introduced with the subtlety and sophisticate
suggestiveness applied to literary allusions. The full effectiveness
both the literary allusions and the obscenity depends on the existence
the other. The merely obscene would have limited *Mac Flecknoe* to th
sort of lampoon often directed against Dryden—*The Tory Poets*, or h
Satire to his Muse; there would have been little humour other than th
issuing from calling somebody a rude name. Shadwell in his 'Epistle
the Tories' prefacing *The Medal of John Bayes* attacks Dryden in th
most offensive and personal way, totally without subtlety or wit: '*H*
prostituted Muse *will become as common for hire, as his Mistress* Reves
was, upon whom he spent to many hundred pounds; and of whom (to she
his constancy in Love) he got three Claps, and she was a Bawd.' And
concludes the poem

> *Pied thing! half Wit! half Fool! and for a Knave,* ⎫
> *Few Men, than this, a better mixture have:*   ⎬
> *But thou canst add to that, Coward and Slave.*   ⎭
>
>   (Summers, V 248, 26

Dryden avoids the simple abuse of simply calling someone a rude nam
by handling rudeness with subtlety, by implying rather than mere

stating. But the obscenity is strongly present: had the literary allusion alone provided his material the effect of the poem would have been reduced to relatively ineffectual literary fun.

Literary allusion and vulgar innuendo are inseparably involved in the poem's climax. The very event that concludes the poem is a literary allusion. In Shadwell's play *The Virtuoso* the two 'Gentlemen of wit and sense' Bruce and Longvill let down the long-winded orator Sir Formal (whose style Flecknoe blessed Shadwell with in line 68) through a trapdoor (III. iv, 126). It is a rather broad comic trick; and Shadwell repeats it on Sir Samuel Hearty later (III. iv, 201). And in *Psyche*, too, Shadwell has the envious sisters sink below stage at the end of act IV: 'Arise ye Furies, snatch 'em down to Hell' (Summers, II. 327)—one of the 'splendid Scenes and Machines' Shadwell proudly commented on in his Preface. The repetition of this not especially subtle dramatic trick ensures its place in *Mac Flecknoe*. But though we might have expected Shadwell to fall victim to his own bad art, the engineer hoist with his own petard, Dryden avoids that obviousness and, more sadly, makes Flecknoe who has such pride in his poetic son's skills, the victim.

The incident is the culmination of the allusions to Shadwell's plays. The religious allusions[1] in the poem are brought to a simultaneous culmination with the parodic echo of 2 Kings II. 9–13 when Elijah hands over his prophetic power and mantle to Elisha. Cowley had already made commendatory use of the episode in his poem 'On the Death of Mr Crashaw' (1656) providing a precedent for its use in literary panegyric:

> *Thou from low earth in nobler Flames didst rise,*
> *And like Elijah, mount Alive the skies.*
> *Elisha-like (but with a wish much less,*
> *More fit thy Greatness, and my Littleness)*
> *Lo here I beg (I whom thou once didst prove*
> *So humble to Esteem, so Good to Love)*
> *Not that thy Spirit might on me Doubled be,*
> *I ask but Half thy mighty Spirit for Me.*

---

[1] Baird W. Whitelock, 'Elijah and Elisha in Dryden's *Mac Flecknoe*', *MLN*, LXX, 1955, 19–20; J. E. Tanner, 'The Messianic Image in *Mac Flecknoe*', *MLN*, LXXVI, 1961, 220–3.

But whereas Elisha—and Crashaw—soared up to heaven in a whirl-wind, Flecknoe sinks downwards, in parody of the divine prophet and the noble religious poet, in imitation of the fallen angels, going Hell-ward like Psyche's sisters. The hell imagery from *Paradise Lost* and the *Davideis* is now fulfilled; having shared Satan's presumptuousness, Flecknoe now shares his fate. That it is the darkness of Hell he falls into is confirmed by the 'subterranean wind'—the last of the echoes from *Paradise Lost*. Its source is the imagery of Hell:

> *as when the force*
> *Of subterranean wind transports a Hill*
> *Torn from* Pelorus, *or the shatter'd side*
> *Of thundring Ætna, whose combustible*
> *And fewel'd entrails thence conceiving Fire,*
> *Sublim'd with Mineral fury, aid the Winds,*
> *And leave a singed bottom all involv'd*
> *With stench and smoak.*   (I, 230-7)

This cosmic defecation[1] relates to the imagery of *Mac Flecknoe*; the imagery of pregnancy—'conceiving'—develops into defecation. And the 'subterranean wind' has a precise, functional role in the poem, carry-ing the poet-priest's mantle upwards in defiance of gravity, instead of letting it sink with him. The Miltonic original defines that wind's nature and origin, issuing from 'a singed bottom all involv'd/With stench and smoak.' If we read the alliterative pattern of Dryden's final couplet correctly it is easily identified:

> *The Mantle fell to the young Prophet's part,*
> *With double portion of his Father's Art.*   (216-17)

The proper alliteration to balance and rhyme with 'Prophet's part' is, of course, 'Father's fart'; the alliterative play within the couplet empha-sizes this—'Fell . . . Prophet's part' is neatly varied into 'portion . . . Father's fart.' The fart, then, is Father Flecknoe's final utterance from the throne. Elisha said to Elijah, 'I pray thee, let a double portion of thy spirit be upon me.' But the spirit, the prophetic gust of air that Flecknoe

---

[1] J. B. Broadbent, *Some Graver Subject*, 1960, 83.

imparts is a poetic utterance in keeping with the nature of Flecknoe's and Shadwell's poetry that the anal and excretory imagery has established. No wonder when Dryden returned to Shadwell in *Absalom and Achitophel part II* he began, 'Now stop your noses Readers . . .' (457).

When *Mac Flecknoe* was first printed in a pirated edition (1682) it had as subtitle 'A Satyr upon the *True-Blew Protestant* Poet, T. S. By the Author of *Absalom & Achitophel.*' This was dropped in the authorized 1684 edition, and is generally taken as the pirate printer's addition. Presumably the printer hoped to capitalize on the success of *Absalom and Achitophel* by presenting *Mac Flecknoe* as a political satire. But though Dryden later attacked Shadwell for being one of the Whig propagandists in the lines he contributed to Nahum Tate's continuation of *Absalom and Achitophel*, *Mac Flecknoe* is not political in its concerns. Its basic image, nonetheless, reveals Dryden's political habits of thought. The concept of the monarchy of wit countered by a rebel monarchy of dullness and nonsense, indicates Dryden's authoritarian and hierarchical assumptions operating in the realm of literature as well as in the realm of England.[1]

Absalom and Achitophel was intended to influence public opinion against Shaftesbury who was about to be brought before the grand jury on a charge of high treason. However, the London grand jury rejected the bill of indictment. The Whigs rejoiced, and struck a commemorative medal. Charles II is supposed to have suggested to Dryden the plan of a poem in response[2]—though what plan *The Medall* has is hard to discern. The medal had a bust of Shaftesbury on the obverse, and a view of London Bridge with the sun rising above the Tower (where Shaftesbury had been imprisoned for over four months) dispersing a cloud on

---

[1] On the authoritarian patterns of imagery, see Hoffman; also Bernard N. Schilling, *Dryden and the Conservative Myth*, New Haven and London 1961. Attempts to see specific political concerns in *Mac Flecknoe* can be found in Samuel Holt Monk, 'Shadwell's "Flail of Sense" ', *NQ*, NS VII 1960, 67–68; Michael W. Allsid, 'Shadwell's *Mac Flecknoe*', *SEL*, VII, 1967, 387–402; line 65 is sometimes taken to refer to the Popish Plot.

[2] Joseph Spence, *Observations, Anecdotes, and Characters of Books and Men*, ed. James M. Osborn, 2 vol Oxford 1966, I. 28.

the reverse. To some extent the design of Dryden's poem can be seen as imitating that of the medal, dealing with Shaftesbury in its first half and about midway (line 167) turning to deal with London. A. E. Wallace Maurer has argued for a more schematic medallic structure: 'after the introduction in lines 1–21, the obverse takes shape in lines 22–144, and the reverse in lines 145–324.'[1] But the problem of deciding exactly where the poem moves from obverse to reverse (lines 145 or 167), and of whether lines 145–66 offer an introduction to the reverse comparable to but a line longer than the opening introduction, render unconvincing any arguments for a precise or symmetrical structure. The poem depends more for its effect on the rough vigour of its manner than on any strictly defined shape.

Perhaps Charles suggested the virulent and vindictive tone of the poem. Morally it is no worse than *Absalom and Achitophel*, which was intended to influence the jury. Dryden's political satires were political instruments. Whatever literary qualities we may admire in them, we need to remember their manipulative, political intent, their McCarthyite smearing. *Absalom and Achitophel*, however, has some wit and subtlety: 'How easie it is to call Rogue and Villain, and that wittily! But how hard to make a Man appear a Fool, a Blockhead, or a Knave, without using any of those opprobrious terms! To spare the grossness of the Names, and to do the thing yet more severely, is to draw a full Face, and to make the Nose and Cheeks stand out, and yet not to employ any depth of Shadowing.' So Dryden wrote later in his *Discourse concerning Satire*, and cited his portrait of Buckingham: 'The Character of *Zimri* in my *Absalom*, is, in my Opinion, worth the whole Poem: 'Tis not bloody, but 'tis ridiculous enough. And he for whom it was intended, was too witty to resent it as an injury. If I had rail'd, I might have suffer'd for it justly: But I manag'd my own Work more happily, perhaps more dextrously' (Kinsley, II. 655). But there is little witty geniality in *The*

[1] A. E. Wallace Maurer, 'The Design of Dryden's *The Medall*', *Papers on Language and Literature*, II, 1966, 296; see also Samuel A. Golden, 'A Numismatic View of Dryden's "The Medal" ', *NQ*, NS, IX, 1962, 383–84. As I observe later, Roper, 87–103, argues unconvincingly in my view for the poem's unity by virtue of its 'divine analogy' and forensic ordering.

Medall. The scatological imagery of *Mac Flecknoe* operates as a joke: but the image of Shaftesbury infecting the nation with syphilis in *The Medall* is devoid of comedy:

> *Religion thou hast none: thy* Mercury
> *Has pass'd through every Sect, or theirs through Thee.*
> *But what thou giv'st, that Venom still remains;*
> *And the pox'd Nation feels Thee in their Brains.*
> *What else inspires the Tongues, and swells the Breasts*
> *Of all thy bellowing Renegado Priests,*
> *That preach up Thee for God: dispence thy Laws;*
> *And with thy Stumm ferment their fainting Cause?*
> *Fresh Fumes of Madness raise; and toile and sweat*
> *To make the formidable Cripple great.*
>
> (*The Medall*, 263–72)

The disease images that recur through *The Medall*—the 'fester'd Sore' of the jurors (151), 'the swelling Poyson of the sev'ral Sects' (294)—are designed to nauseate, not amuse. And though the imagery is a metaphor of what Dryden sees as the disease of sedition infecting the nation, the specific associations of the disease are meant to reflect personally on Shaftesbury, implying that he is syphilitic; just as the earlier passage on his breaking with the Commonwealth uses sexual imagery that works both metaphorically and personally:

> *But, as 'tis hard to cheat a Juggler's Eyes,*
> *His open lewdness he cou'd ne'er disguise.*
> *There split the Saint: for Hypocritique Zeal*
> *Allows no Sins but those it can conceal.*
> *Whoring to Scandal gives too large a scope:*
> *Saints must not trade; but they may interlope.*
>
> (*The Medall*, 36–41)

K. H. D. Haley has considered the assertions concerning Shaftesbury's sexual adventures in his biography[1] but has found no support for them. They seem to have been the product of Tory propagandists who

---

[1] K. H. D. Haley, *The First Earl of Shaftesbury*, Oxford 1968, 211–15.

attempted to discredit Shaftesbury in the 1680s and after; none of the stories dates from before his sixtieth year. Dryden had made no attack on Shaftesbury's sexuality in *Absalom and Achitophel*; his sudden assertion in *The Medall* that 'His open lewdness he cou'd ne'er disguise' (37) is a newly discovered weapon; he uses it skilfully, and the personal applications of the sexual metaphors give the satire its unadmirable power. The emphasis on Shaftesbury as 'Cripple' (272), 'Pigmee' (27), the dwelling on his high-pitched voice, his being a eunuch—'the lowdest Bagpipe of the squeaking Train' (35)—all these have a virulence that the insults of *Mac Flecknoe* avoided:

> Oh, cou'd the Style that copy'd every grace,
> And plough'd such furrows for an Eunuch face,
> Cou'd it have form'd his ever-changing Will,
> The various Piece had tir'd the Graver's Skill!
> A Martial Heroe first, with early care,
> Blown, like a Pigmee by the Winds, to war,
> A beardless Chief, a Rebel, e'r a Man:
> (So young his hatred to his Prince began.)
> Next this, (How wildly will Ambition steer!)
> A Vermin, wriggling in th' Usurper's Ear.
>
> (*The Medall*, 22–31)

The emphases are personal and derogatory; whereas when Dryden used the pigmy image in *Absalom and Achitophel* it was not merely an easy jibe at Shaftesbury's smallness but, allied with the generalizing phrase 'Tenement of Clay' a comment on all mankind, on the propensity of the human mind to drive the body mercilessly, on the restless ambition of man, on the hunger of the imagination:

> A fiery Soul, which working out its way,
> Fretted the Pigmy Body to decay:
> And o'r inform'd the Tenement of Clay . . .
> Great Wits are sure to Madness near ally'd;
> And thin Partitions do their Bounds divide:
> Else, why should he, with Wealth and Honour blest,
> Refuse his Age the needful hours of Rest?

> Punish a Body which he could not please;
> Bankrupt of Life, yet Prodigal of Ease?
> > (*Absalom and Achitophel*, 156–8, 163–8)

For all the dislike of Shaftesbury in *Absalom and Achitophel*—and the dislike and destructiveness in the portrait must not be minimized—there was an understanding of the psychological type of person to which he belonged. But *The Medall* does not have this abstracting, this conceptualizing treatment of Shaftesbury; it depends on specific, abusive attack. There is never any sense of Shaftesbury as a type or as a character in *The Medall*—nothing comparable with the character of Shadwell in *Mac Flecknoe*, nothing of the types of Zimri or Achitophel in *Absalom and Achitophel* or of the portraits of Settle and Shadwell written for Tate's continuation. Insofar as there is any character analysis of Shaftesbury other than abuse, it is contradictory. Dryden is torn between wanting to stress Shaftesbury's utter fickleness, changeableness, and consequent treacherous unreliability, and at the same time wanting to stress an unchangeable consistency of corruption. If changeable, then Shaftesbury would sometimes be on the side of the 'good'—and Dryden added some lines in the second edition of *Absalom and Achitophel* praising his probity as a judge.[1] But by the time of *The Medall* Dryden was unable to make such concessions: 'Ev'n in the most sincere advice he gave/He had a grudging still to be a Knave' (57–58). The sincere advice Shaftesbury gives because of his changeableness cannot be admitted to be unadulteratedly sincere. Dryden balances on his contradiction skilfully, and Dr Johnson wrote admiringly of lines 50–64 of *The Medall*: 'The picture of a man whose propensions to mischief are such that his best actions are but inability of wickedness, is very skilfully delineated and strongly coloured.'[2]

Although various images and metaphors—such as those of disease

---

[1] These are, however, the only known references to Shaftesbury's probity as a judge, and H. T. Swedenberg has raised the possibility of their being ironic: 'Challenges to Dryden's Editor' in *John Dryden, Papers Read at a Clark Library Seminar*, Los Angeles 1967.

[2] Samuel Johnson, *Lives of the English Poets*, ed. G. B. Hill, 3 vol Oxford 1905, I. 438.

and of Satanic rebellion—recur through the poem, attempts to see them as creating structurally unifying patterns, rather than as *ad hoc* touch-stones and illustrations, are unpersuasive.[1] The images provide moment-ary vigour, but the satire is too urgent to allow the leisurely, cumulative development of organizing metaphors. The literary convention which determines the manner of *The Medall* is one of avoiding obvious literary conventions: sustained literary allusion or developed metaphoric analo-gies would smack distractingly of the library in the serious struggle of matters of life and death Dryden was taking sides in. Nor does *The Medall* work primarily by the establishment of character, or by the nar-rative of some central event. Dryden in his *Discourse on Satire* (Kinsley, II. 637) classed both *Mac Flecknoe* and *Absalom and Achitopel* as Var-ronian satires: satires organized round a particular narrative and em-ploying comedy. But with *The Medall* events are too pressing to allow the detachment of comedy or of character creation. *The Medall* is closer to Juvenalian satire: it depends on the vigour of its denunciation and draws a stream of examples and arguments to attack the topic of sedition in Shaftesbury and his supporters in the city of London. Dr Johnson noted the limited appeal of the poem: '*The Medall*, written upon the same principles with *Absalom and Achitophel*, but upon a narrower plan, gives less pleasure, though it discovers equal abilities in the writer. The superstructure cannot extend beyond the foundation; a single character and incident cannot furnish as many ideas as a series of events or multi-plicity of agents. This poem therefore, since time has left it to itself, is not much read, nor perhaps generally understood, yet it abounds with touches both of humorous and serious satire' (Hill, I. 437–8).

Dryden's sheer verbal skill, nonetheless, gives his diatribe a tremend-ous vigour. His great suspicion of the crowd, his fear of the uncontrolled power of the people[2] provokes him to some of his finest alliterative in-

---

[1] See for instance Roper, 87–103.

[2] There is a scene in *Don Sebastian* where the corrupt Mufti declares the voice of the *mobile* to be the voice of God, a nice parody of vox *populi*, *vox dei*; yet the rabble does in fact prove to be one of two agencies that overthrow the bad characters and re-establish the good. Dryden be-lieved the energy or vitality of the rabble its important feature—gener-ally to be feared, but not *always* bad in its effect.

vective, achieving a marvellous consonantal contempt. The evil of Shaftesbury is that

> *He preaches to the Crowd, the Pow'r is lent,*
> *But not convey'd to Kingly Government;*
> *That Claimes successive bear no binding force;*
> *That Coronation Oaths are things of course;*
> *Maintains the Multitude can never err,*
> *And sets the People in the Papal Chair.*

(The Medall, 82–87)

The verbal play on People/Papal produces its devastating political message. And the idea of the elevation of the crowd to infallibility—to divinity, even—produces some of Dryden's most biting wit, in which the parodic skills of *Mac Flecknoe* are allied in the apostrophe with a moving indictment of the crowd's fickleness:

> *Almighty Crowd, thou shorten'st all dispute;*
> *Pow'r is thy Essence; Wit thy Attribute!*
> *Nor Faith nor Reason make thee at a stay,*
> *Thou leapst o'r all eternal truths, in thy Pindarique way!*
> *Athens, no doubt, did righteously decide,*
> *When Phocion and when Socrates were try'd:*
> *As righteously they did those dooms repent;*
> *Still they were wise, whatever way they went.*
> *Crowds err not, though to both extremes they run;*
> *To kill the Father, and recall the Son.*

(The Medall, 91–100)

The account is masterly and it is easy to forget its onesidedness. The arbitrary judgments of the crowd Dryden presents truly enough; the arbitrariness of monarchy and aristocracy he fails to mention. And even if we react to his satire and argue that fickle as the crowd is, it is at least better than arbitrary monarchy, we are still accepting Dryden's version of events. We tend to respond to his identification of Whig policies with republicanism and the formenting of civil war by saying what is wrong with republicanism, rather than inquiring whether it is a true identification. Some of the responses to *Absalom and Achitophel*, such as Samuel Pordage's *Azaria and Hushai* (1682) deny Dryden's analysis. Replying to Dryden's charge that 'No King could govern, nor no God could please' the English (*Absalom and Achitophel*, l. 48), Pordage asserted

> *No people were more ready to obey*
> *Their Kings, who rul'd them by a gentle Sway*
> *Who never sought their Consciences to curb,*
> *Their Freedom or Religion to disturb. . . .*
> *Tho' Kings they lov'd, and for them Reverence had,*
> *They never would adore them as a God.*
> *God's Worship, and their Laws they did prefer,*
> *They knew, them men might by bad Councils Err.*
> *Tho' Loyal, yet oppress'd, they did not fear*
> *To make their heavy Grievances appear.*
>
> (1682 ed., 12)

Dryden's implication that the Whigs were *all* violent, bloodthirsty republicans is clearly not true. Certainly Pordage concedes 'And some perhaps there were, who thought a King/To be of Charge, and but a useless thing' (23). But Dryden's strategy of presenting all his opposition as identified with republicanism—and hence advocates of Civil War for the achievement of republicanism—can be seen as the device of a political propagandist. He is engaged in the dispute, he is not a detached, literary observer. It was a strategy Pordage exposed in his reply to *The Medall, The Medall Revers'd. A Satyre against Persecution* (1682):

> *With piercing Eyes he does the Medal view*
> *And there he finds, as he has told to you,*
> *The Hag Sedition, to the life display'd,*
> *Under a States-man's Gown; fancy'd or made,*
> *That is all one, he doth it so apply;*
> *At it th'Artillery of his Wit lets fly;*
> *Lets go his Satyr at the Medal straight,*
> *Whorries the Whiggs, and doth Sedition bait.*
> *Let him go on, the Whiggs the Hag forsake;*
> *Her cause they never yet would undertake,*
> *But laugh to see the Poets fond mistake.*
> *But we will turn the Medal; there we see*
> *Another Hag, I think as bad as she:*

> *If I am not mistaken 'tis the same,*
> Christians *of old did* Persecution *name:*
> *That's still her Name, tho now grown old and wise,*
> *She has new Names, as well as new disguise.*
> *Let then his Satyr with* Sedition *fight,*
> *And ours the whilst shall* Persecution *bite:*
> *Two Hags they are, who parties seem to make;*
> *'Tis time for Satyrs them to undertake.*

(1683 ed., 3–4)

Pordage is no match as a writer for Dryden. And the danger is that Dryden's poetic skill will persuade us of the truth of the case he puts in *The Medall*. But the Whigs no more wanted another civil war than the Tories. As Pordage writes of the Whigs:

> *We dread the effects of a new Civil War.*
> *We dread* Romes *yoak, to us 'tis hateful grown*
> *And Rome will seem a Monster in our Throne.* (9)

Certainly there were the violent extremists amongst Shaftesbury's supporters. But it was the Tories' particular technique to use the scare of civil war as a weapon against all the Whigs, as Pordage tells us:

> *They will not let the Graves and Tombs alone,*
> *But Conjure up the Ghost of Fourty One.*
> *With this they try the ignorant to scare,*
> *For men are apt the worst of things to fear,*
> *Tho that Ghost is no liker Eighty two,*
> *Than a good* Christian *like a* Turk *or* Jew. (12)

Despite its subtitle 'A Satyre Against Sedition', *The Medall* is not a general satire on a general vice. The diatribe is directed against a specific occasion—the jury's verdict of 'Ignoramus' to the attempted indictment of Shaftesbury. Today we see the classical satires of Juvenal and Persius as primarily interesting for their general indictments of general vices. But the seventeenth century habit was to look for specific historical references in their work. Persius, Dryden wrote in his 'Argument of the prologue to the first satyr' *'liv'd in the dangerous Times of the Tyrant* Nero; *and aims particularly at him, in most of his Satyrs'*. The specific railing of *The Medall* would have appeared to contemporaries as a satire very much in the classical tradition.

Barten Holyday's translation of Persius appeared in 1616, and his Juvenal in 1673; Sir Robert Stapylton's translation of *The first six satyrs of Juvenal* appeared in 1644, and the complete work in 1647. There were numerous other translations of individual satires of Juvenal.[1] There was no point in Dryden's attempting another scholarly, close translation; that had been done and, in his view, done badly:

> If rendring the exact Sense of these Authors, almost line for line, had been our business, *Barten Holiday* had done it already to our hands: And, by the help of his Learned Notes and Illustrations, not only of *Juvenal*, and *Persius*, but what yet is more obscure, his own Verses might be understood.
>
> But he wrote for Fame, and wrote to Scholars: We write only for the Pleasure and Entertainment, of those Gentlemen and Ladies, who tho they are not Scholars, are not Ignorant.
>
> (Kinsley, II. 668)

The extreme alternative to the attempted 'rendring the exact sense' was the imitation, in which writers were able to use a considerable latitude of paraphrase, to expand, 'to supply the lost Excellencies of another *Language* with new ones in their own';[2] and once the principle of introducing new excellencies of language was accepted, new excellencies of allusions, settings, incidents and modern references were readily incorporated. Dr Johnson wrote of *London*, his imitation of Juvenal's third satire, 'part of the beauty of the performance (if any beauty be allow'd it) [consists] in adapting Juvenal's Sentiments to

---

[1] Quotations are from *Juvenals Sixteen Satyrs or, A Survey of the Manners and Actions of Mankind* by Sir Robert Stapylton, 1647; and *Decimus Junius Juvenalis, And Aulus Persius Flaccus Translated* by Barten Holyday, Oxford 1673. Other translations are also discussed by G. L. Broderson, 'Seventeenth Century Translations of Juvenal', *The Phoenix, The Journal of the Classical Association of Canada*, VII, 1953, 57–76.

[2] Abraham Cowley in the preface to *Pindarique Odes*, 1656, cited in Harold F. Brooks, 'The Imitation in English Poetry', *RES*, XXV, 1949, 124–40.

modern facts and Persons'.[1] The strength of such imitations lay in the vitality of their verse, unrestricted to 'the exact sense', and in the relevance and ironies of their modernizations. Thomas Wood's *Juvenalis Redivivus. or the First Satyr of Juvenal taught to speak plain English* (1683) included the Latin text at the foot of each page, but updated Juvenal's attack on classical bad poets to attack those who were Dryden's own targets:

> But of all plagues Mack Fleckno *is the worst,*
> With Guts and Poverty *severely curst:*
> Large is his Corps, *his mighty works do swell,*
> Both carefully fill'd up, *and stuff'd from Hell:*
> Eternal Sot, *all o're a publick Ass,*
> Is cypher'd in the *margin of his Face.*

(1683 ed., p. 2)

Juvenal and Persius had achieved currency in late seventeenth-century English satire not through the painstaking translations of Stapylton or Holyday, but through such imitations. In his satires, first published in 1666, the French poet Boileau drew largely on those of Horace and Juvenal; he did not offer translations or even modernized paraphrases, but would draw on more than one satire for material for one of his own. His 'imitations' were in turn imitated by such English satirists as Rochester, Butler, and Oldham. In this way Juvenal and Persius reached English writers and readers—but reached them only indirectly. By 1687 when Dryden began his translations,[2] there was need for a version that would attempt to render the content of what Juvenal and Persius had written, that would attempt a translation rather than an imitation of what they might have written had they lived in seventeenth-century Europe; but at the same time, a version that would have the vigorous manner of the original Latin, that would have a satiric bite comparable to that of contemporary satire and the free imitations. Stapylton and Holyday gained precision but lost fluency, lost poetry—and hence lost

---

[1] *The Letters of Samuel Johnson*, ed. R. W. Chapman, Oxford 1952, I. 11.

[2] Harold F. Brooks, 'Dryden's Juvenal and the Harveys', *PQ*, XLVIII, 1969, 12–19.

relevance; unless translations work as poems, their critiques and moralities will not engage the reader. It was on the achievement of a vigorous and lively style that Dryden put his stress for the relevance of the satires, rather than on any modernizations of reference or any seeking out of contemporary equivalents for the allusions they made. Such attempts to make Juvenal 'express the Customs and Manners of our Native Country, rather than of *Rome*' occur rarely in Dryden's translations: 'the Manners of Nations and Ages, are not to be confounded: We shou'd either make them *English* or leave them *Roman*' (Kinsley, II 669–70). The very generality of the vices and delusions Juvenal and Persius denounced, the timeless recurrence of their themes, ensured their continuing relevance.

In avoiding the pursuit of 'the exact sense', Dryden also avoids the archaeological perpetuation of classical detail. By tactfully excluding obscure references, he allows the satires to have a contemporary applicability. In the 'Argument of the First Satyr' of Juvenal he admits to having '*omitted most of the Proper Names, because I thought they wou'd not much edifie the Reader*'. Clearing away the accretions of time—he explains he has also '*avoided as much as I cou'd possibly the borrow'd Learning of Marginal Notes and Illustrations*' (Kinsley, II. 671)—he allows the enduring moral and satirical relevance of the satires to shine through unimpeded. In Stapylton's version of the danger of collapsing houses and fires in cities, from Juvenal's third satire, the proper names create a distance from the English reader that the packed, cumbersome verse can never bridge:

> *Who feares or ever fear'd in country townes*
> *Their bane, at moist* Preneste, *where wood crownes*
> *The* Volsian *cliffs, among the simple sort*
> *Of* Gabians, *or in bending* Tibur's *fort?*
> *We fill a towne shoard-up with slender poles*
> *Brought by the Boore, who th'old wide-gaping holes*
> *Dawbes over,* and then bids us sleepe secure,
> When we to sleep for ever, may be sure.
> *Let me live where no night-shrieks terrify,*
> *Here one, fire fire, here others water cry,*
> Vcalegon *tuggs out his lumber there;*
> *Below they've chimneys, therefore fire may feare,*

> But thou three stories high unwarn'd art took,
> That couldst for no mischance but drowning look,
> The raine from thy loft being kept away
> Only by tiles, where eggs soft pidgions lay.

(III 221–36)

Dryden, however, drops the limitingly classical references so allowing for the drawing 'of Analogy, betwixt their Customes and ours' (Kinsley, I. 670). He retains the well known Cumae as the country town alternative to Rome, but delays mentioning Rome itself, introducing it initially by the paraphrastic 'the World's Metropolis', a phrase so applicable to London for Dryden's readers that the analogies are immediately established; with the result that the fire takes on associations with the Great Fire of London. The entire vocabulary allows for such an analogy in its contemporary naturalness and specificity—gutters, cock-lofts, garrets:

> Who fears, in Country Towns, a House's fall,
> Or to be caught betwixt a riven Wall?
> But we Inhabit a weak City, here;
> Which Buttresses and Props but scarcely bear:
> And 'tis the Village Masons daily Calling,
> To keep the World's Metropolis from falling.
> To cleanse the Gutters, and the Chinks to close;
> And, for one Night, secure his Lord's Repose.
> At Cumae we can sleep, quite round the Year:
> Nor Falls, nor Fires, nor Nightly Dangers fear;
> While rolling Flames from Roman Turrets fly,
> And the pale Citizens for Buckets cry.
> Thy Neighbour has remov'd his Wretched Store
> (Few hands will rid the Lumber of the Poor)
> Thy own third Story smoaks; while thou, supine,
> Art drench'd in Fumes of undigested Wine.
> For if the lowest Floors already burn,
> Cock-lofts and Garrets soon will take the Turn.
> Where thy tame Pidgeons next the Tiles were bred,
> Which in their Nests unsafe, are timely fled.

(III 312–31)

Dryden's version becomes immediately intelligible to his seventeenth century readers, by relating to their own experiences and myths. At th same time Dryden remains faithful to the original, avoiding, the add tion or substitution of contemporary equivalents; he has cleared awa the inhibitingly academic so that the contemporary can suggest itself.

In the later recommendation to leave the city and live modestly i the country, Dryden does substitute the theatre for the Roman circu but this is not a substitution of something foreign to Roman life; fc Juvenal himself writes of the theatre elsewhere in his third satire. It is substitution that makes the same point as the original—of abandonin urban pleasures—removes distancing detail; and at the same time Dryde omits the distancing detail of the possible country districts round Rom to retire to. Holyday's version opens

> *Could'st thou but leave the* Circus, *and woudst go*
> *To* Fabrateria, Sora, Frusino . . .

But Dryden immediately creates a world that could be either Juvenal Rome or Dryden's England; nothing in his version is inappropriate t either:

> *But, cou'd you be content to bid adieu*
> *To the dear Play-house, and the Players too,*
> *Sweet Country Seats are purchas'd ev'ry where,* ⎫
> *With Lands and Gardens, at less price, than here* ⎬
> *You hire a darksom Doghole by the year.* ⎭
> *A small Convenience, decently prepar'd,*
> *A shallow Well, that rises in your yard,*
> *That spreads his easie Crystal Streams around;*
> *And waters all the pretty spot of Ground.*
> *There, love the Fork; thy Garden cultivate;*
> *And give thy frugal Friends a* Pythagorean *Treat.*
> *'Tis somewhat to be Lord of some small Ground;*
> *In which a Lizard may, at least, turn round.*

(II 363-7

When Dr Johnson treated this passage in *London*, he provided somethir as specifically limited to England as Holyday's version was to Rom Like Dryden, Johnson replaces the circus by the playhouse; but unli

Dryden he does not simply remove the proper names, he provides English substitutes:

> Could'st thou resign the park and play content,
> For the fair banks of Severn or of Trent;
> There might'st thou find some elegant retreat,
> Some hireling senator's deserted seat;
> And stretch thy prospects o'er the smiling land,
> For less than rent the dungeons of the Strand;
> There prune thy walks, support thy drooping flow'rs,
> Direct thy rivulets, and twine thy bow'rs;
> And, while thy grounds a cheap repast afford,
> Despise the dainties of a venal lord:
> There ev'ry bush with nature's musick rings,
> There ev'ry breeze bears health upon its wings;
> On all thy hours security shall smile,
> And bless thine evening walk and morning toil.
>
> (210–22)[1]

Dryden's version allows us to make such interpretations of the Strand, or the River Severn or Trent; Johnson's restricts his poem to them. Yet Johnson oddly retains a Roman senator—not an English political title at all; and continually mixes the English specificities of his version with Latin names for characters—Orgilio, Thales, Clodio. This is an inconsistency Dryden scrupulously avoids, except for his substitution of Shadwell for the bad poet Cluvienus who appears in Juvenal's first satire. Dryden reduces the classical specificities but nonetheless keeps them consistent; he offers a reduced classical model from which we can draw contemporary analogies. Johnson presents a classicized contemporary England.

Johnson's two imitations of Juvenal have always been interpreted as moral critiques of eighteenth-century life; they have been read as original poems, and their episodes often given personal interpretation. Richard Savage has been seen as the original of Thales in his farewell

---

[1] Samuel Johnson, *Poems*, ed. E. L. McAdam, Jr., with George Milne, Yale edition of *The Works of Samuel Johnson*, New Haven and London 1964, VI. 58.

to London; the famous line in *The Vanity of Human Wishes*, 'slow rise
worth by poverty depressed', has been taken as a restrained expression
of Johnson's youthful experiences. Dryden's translations of Juvenal
however, have generally been considered as simple, workaday, translations; even when they have been recognized as good translations
they have not often been read as poetic creations. But though not as
free as Johnson's imitations, they have a poetic integrity lacking in the
close renderings of Stapylton and Holyday. Dryden is carefully handling his material to give a true and lively account of Juvenal—but he is
vitally concerned to make his versions relevant to the seventeenth century, to make them live as contemporary poems. By removing obstacles
to contemporary acceptance he produces translations that are faithful
and yet have a renewed personal meaning:

> *No Profit rises from th'ungrateful Stage,*
> *My Poverty encreasing with my Age;*
> *'Tis time to give my just Disdain a vent,*
> *And, Cursing, leave so base a Government.*

(III. 41-4

The details are equally applicable to Juvenal's Umbricius in Rome and
to Dryden's personal experience in seventeenth-century London. In
the vivid accounts of the corruptions of the theatre, the dangers of being
beaten up in the city, the oppressive noise and traffic of the metropolis
Dryden has found in Juvenal a voice that readily becomes his own. And
a further depth is added to Dryden's sceptical conservatism by not imitating or modernising. The idea of the Restoration as England's Augustan
age gave the dignity of classical precedent; but here we see a classical
precedent for the corruptions, for the decline of society. London is
merely repeating the errors of Rome. That a satire on second-century
Rome should apply so readily to seventeenth-century London, with no
modifications, is the most depressing realization of all.

If the corruptions of Rome provided a type of the corruptions of
London, then the attack on those corruptions could provide the mode
manner of attack for the seventeenth century. In his translations of
Juvenal and Persius Dryden is offering a procedure for contemporary
satirists. He is offering in effect a cultural programme. The long, prefatory

Discourse concerning the Original and Progress of Satire fulfils an educational role in supplying a history and definition of the genre, carefully distinguishing between the varieties of satire—Varronian, Horatian and Juvenalian. Dryden considers, and rejects, the two main English streams of satire, the roughness of Donne and the burlesque of Butler: '*Donn alone, of all our Countrymen, had your Talent*', he writes to his dedicatee, the Earl of Dorset; 'but was not happy enough to arrive at your Versification. And were he Translated into Numbers, and *English*, he wou'd yet be wanting in the Dignity of Expression' (Kinsley, II. 603). Dryden stands out from the English Elizabethan and Jacobean satirists in his avoidance of the obscurities and metrical roughness they deliberately cultivated. To imply that Donne did not write English is perhaps a little excessive. But Donne, Hall, and Marston did believe that the obscurity of Juvenal and Persius was appropriately and properly emulated in a crabbed, tortured and rough manner encouraging the reader in the belief that matters of importance were concealed, appealing to an élite of readers who could take trouble with the obscurities.[1] Dryden departed from this tradition; and though his style varies in *Mac Flecknoe*, *Absalom and Achitophel* and *The Medall*, it is a variation within the limits of clarity and fluency. His praise of his contemporary Oldham's satires is ambiguous in its reaction to their notorious roughness. He says that satire does not *need* fluency and ease, rather than saying it should *avoid* them as the Elizabethans and Oldham believed, and he implies that Oldham's roughness was a result of his youth, his poetic immaturity:

> *O early ripe! to thy abundant store*
> *What could advancing Age have added more?*
> *It might (what Nature never gives the young)*
> *Have taught the numbers of thy native Tongue.*

[1] Raymond MacDonald Alden, *The Rise of Formal Satire in England Under Classical Influence* University of Pennsylvania Series in Philology, Literature, and Archaeology VII, No. 2, Philadelphia, 1899; Arnold Stein, 'Donne's Obscurity', *ELH*, XIII, 1946, 98–118; R. Selden, 'Roughness in Satire from Horace to Dryden,' *MLR*, LXVI, 1971, 264–72.

> *But Satyr needs not those, and Wit will shine*
> *Through the harsh cadence of a rugged line.*
> *A noble Error, and but seldom made,*
> *When Poets are by too much force betray'd.*
> (*To the Memory of Mr Oldham*, 11-18)

Wit will shine through, but the harsh cadence and rugged line are an error all the same. Oldham's 'Satire in imitation of the third of Juvenal' shows his characteristics—the deliberately discordant half rhymes, the harsh elisions and crammed lines, the slang and familiar phrases, all contributing to the easy colloquial manner:

> '*Whoe'er at Barnet, or St Albans, fears*
> *To have his lodging drop about his ears,*
> *Unless a sudden hurricane befal,*
> *Or such a wind as blew old Noll to hell?*
> *Here we build slight, what scarce outlasts the lease,*
> *Without the help of props and buttresses;*
> *And houses now-a-days as much require*
> *To be ensured from falling, as from fire.*
> *There, buildings are substantial, though less neat,*
> *And kept with care both wind and water tight;*
> *There, you in safe security are blessed,*
> *And nought, but conscience, to disturb your rest.*
> '*I am for living where no fires affright,*
> *No bells rung backward breaks my sleep at night;*
> *I scarce lie down, and draw my curtains here,*
> *But straight I'm rous'd by the next house on fire;*
> *Pale, and half dead with fear, myself I raise,*
> *And find my room all over in a blaze;*
> *By this't has seized on the third stairs, and I*
> *Can now discern no other remedy,*
> *But leaping out a window to get free;*
> *For if the mischief from the cellar came,*
> *Be sure the garret is the last takes flame.*'[1]

Oldham's harshness and roughness were avoided in the translations of

[1] *The Poems of John Oldham*, ed. Robert Bell, 1960, 197-8.

Juvenal's tenth and thirteenth satires by Henry Higden. Higden made Juvenal fluent and genial, and Dryden praised him for tempering Juvenal's savagery—'You make him Smile in spight of all his Zeal' (Kinsley, I. 466). But Higden's was again not a manner Dryden followed. Higden drew on Butler's burlesque octosyllabic *Hudibras* for his model—a tradition Dryden rejected, praising Butler, but remarking in his *Discourse* on satire:

> in any other Hand, the shortness of his Verse, and the quick returns of Rhyme, had debas'd the Dignity of Style. And besides, the double Rhyme, (a necessary Companion of Burlesque Writing) is not so proper for Manly Satire, for it turns Earnest too much to Jest, and gives us a Boyish kind of Pleasure. It tickles aukwardly with a kind of pain . . .
>   I wou'd prefer the Verse of ten Syllables, which we call the *English* Heroique, to that of Eight. This is truly my Opinion. For this sort of Number is more Roomy. The Thought can turn it self with greater ease in a larger compass. When the Rhyme comes too thick upon us, it streightens the Expression; we are thinking of the Close, when we shou'd be employ'd in adorning the Thought. It makes a Poet giddy with turning in a Space too narrow for his Imagination. He loses many Beauties without gaining one Advantage.   (Kinsley, II. 663, 664)

Higden's description of Sejanus' fall in *A Modern Essay on the Tenth Satyr of Juvenal* (1687) is vigorous, readable and lively, but certainly lacking 'the Dignity of Style':

> *The Founders Fournace grows red hot,*
> Sejanus *Statue goes to pot:*
> *That Head lately ador'd, and rekond*
> *In all the Universe the Second,*
> *Melted new forms and shapes assumes,*
> *Of Pisspots, Frying-pans, and Spoons . . .*
>   (1687 ed., p. 13)

Dryden retains the pisspot—something Johnson would certainly have thought improper and undignified—but he uses it as the anti-climactic, shocking conclusion to the marvellous amplitude, the measured dignity, of the preceding lines:

> *The Smith prepares his Hammer for the Stroke,*
> *While the Lung'd Bellows hissing Fire provoke;*
> Sejanus *almost first of* Roman *Names*
> *The great* Sejanus *crackles in the Flames:*
> *Form'd in the Forge, the Pliant Brass is laid*
> *On Anvils; and of Head and Limbs are made,*
> *Pans, Cans, and Pispots, a whole Kitchin Trade.*

(X. 91–7)

It is not simply that Dryden avoids the roughness of Oldham and the burlesque of Higden. The new style he establishes is one of much greater range and flexibility than the limited manners of those two. Dryden is able to achieve the effects of harshness and of burlesque comedy, without sacrificing his tone utterly to those modes. Dr Johnson complained that Dryden's Juvenal lacked dignity—a complaint that has persisted, particularly when Johnson's own solemn versions are compared: 'The general character of this translation will be given, when it is said to preserve the wit, but to want the dignity of the original. The peculiarity of Juvenal is a mixture of gaiety and stateliness, of pointed sentences, and declamatory grandeur. His points have not been neglected; but his grandeur none of the band seemed to consider as necessary to be imitated, except Creech, who undertook the thirteenth *Satire*.'[1] But if we see Dryden's version in the context of the scurrilous satiric lampoons written against him, of the rough, informal manner of Oldham, of the burlesque of *Hudibras*, we can get a better sense of what its impact was on the seventeenth-century reader.

Probably Dryden's commendatory poem 'To my Ingenious Friend, Mr. Henry Higden, Esq; On his Translation of the Tenth Satyr of Juvenal's is to be seen not as an advocacy of Higden's poetic manner, but as another round in the feud with Shadwell. Higden tells in his preface how having completed the translation '*Mr.* Shadwell *did me the Favour to peruse it, keeping it for a considerable Time by him: At the Return he*

---

[1] Johnson, *Lives*, ed. Hill, I 447–8. A similar verdict is given in William Frost, *Dryden and the Art of Translation*, New Haven 1955, pp. 67–69. However, H. A. Mason has argued that Dryden is often 'more faithful to Juvenal's *tone*' in 'Is Juvenal a Classic?' in *Critical Essays on Roman Literature: Satire*, ed. J. P. Sullivan, London 1963, 107–15.

old me, He had a mind to Translate it for his Diversion.' Then Shadwell's translation appeared first—stealing Higden's potential readership. Shadwell used the preface to his own translation to attack Dryden; he complained about *Mac Flecknoe*, and attacked the very idea of translation as a fit occupation (Dryden's *Sylvae* with its translations and preface on translation having appeared in 1685, two years earlier). So Dryden may well have been happy enough to offer Higden some support.

Shadwell's translation is a convenient way of showing the strength of Dryden's, of showing not just Shadwell's overall lack of elegance and flexibility, but also the ineptness a bad translation can fall into, and the opportunities it can miss. The famous conclusion to Juvenal's tenth satire with its declaration of *mens sana in corpore sano* as the best and most worthwhile hope man can have appears in Shadwell's translation not simply in its original pagan context, but with the disqualifying absurdities of certain comic combinations of words:

> *Yet—*
> *That you may ask, and offer at some* Shrine ⎫
> *Or* Holy place, *your* Sausages Divine. ⎬
> *And the choice* entrails *of a pure* white Swine. ⎭
> Pray for a healthful body, a sound mind
> That's never to the fear of death inclined . . .

(Summers, V. 320)

At least Holyday's 'With a white Hoggs pure sasages, still crave/In a sound Body, a sound Mind, so Brave/That Death ne're daunt it' (1673 ed., p. 192) avoids the clumsy 'Sausages Divine', which appears like a fine oxymoron from a burlesque poem. Shadwell, moreover, emphasizes the dangerously comic aspect of the pagan ritual by putting his inept phrases in the stressed position at the line's end, and then grotesquely rhyming 'divine' with 'swine'. So striking is the discord that the reader expects that some witty or ironic or satiric point is being made by the rhyme. But it is not; Shadwell is using rhyme simply to hold the lines together, not to make points. Dryden's version of these lines reduces the pagan aspects in order to emphasize the permanent morality of Juvenal's positive. '*This Divine Satyr*' Dryden calls it in the Argument, following many ecclesiastics in seeing in it a Christian morality, and he glosses it

in Christian terms: '*All we can safely ask of Heaven, lies within a ver,
small Compass. 'Tis but* Health of Body and Mind.' His translatio.
describes the pagan altars in terms suitable for Christian ceremonies:

> *Yet, not to rob the Priests of pious Gain,*
> *That Altars be not wholly built in vain;*
> *Forgive the Gods the rest, and stand confin'd*
> *To Health of Body, and Content of Mind:*
> *A Soul, that can securely Death defie,*
> *And count it Nature's Priviledge, to Dye* . . .

$$(\text{X. } 547{-}5 \text{ 1})$$

An avoidance of the invalidatingly archaeological, the allowance of con,
temporary application, dignity—these positive achievements of Dryden*
shine in contrast with the incompetent way in which Shadwell handle
verse. In his account of Hannibal, for instance, Shadwell produces th
amazing couplet 'To *Æthiopian* Inhabitants,/And to a different kind c
Elephants' (Summers, V. 308). Juvenal's other elephants have been
perpetual scholarly crux and Holyday and Stapylton produce compar
able absurdities—all of them detracting from Juvenal's fine point abou
human morality. Dryden, with his poet's sense of language, copes wit
the crux and removes the difficult elephants from a stressed position—
'Which Ethiopia's double Clime divides,/And Elephants in other Moun
tains hides' (X. 240–1). But he brilliantly exploits the comic potential c
elephants as a stressed rhyme word in a context where it is appropriate
few lines later when he comes to Hannibal's empty glory:

> *Ask what a Face belong'd to this high Fame;*
> *His Picture scarcely wou'd deserve a Frame:*
> *A Sign-Post Dawber wou'd disdain to paint*
> *The one Ey'd Heroe on his Elephant.*

$$(\text{X. } 252{-}5)$$

The grotesque that Shadwell and Holyday unintentionally and absurdl;
achieved in the earlier lines, is functionally and powerfully placed here
The lines have an epigrammatic bitterness Stapylton, Holyday an,
Shadwell utterly failed to approach: 'O how did th' one-ey'd Generall'
picture look,/Riding on his *Getulian Elephant* took' (Stapylton, X. 179
80); 'O goodly Face and Picture! A one-Eyed/Gen'ral does a *Getulia*

Beast bestride!' (Holyday 188); 'Rare Visage, what a Picture 'twould appear,/When the *Getulian* Beast does th'one Ey'd *General* bear!' (Shadwell, Summers, V. 308).

The immeasurable superiority of Dryden's version of Juvenal and Persius to those of his predecessors and contemporaries lies in his creating his translations as poetry. He is not simply turning Latin into English and tagging the lines with rhymes. He is thinking through the rhyme, using it for meaning; he is using the verse movement, the stresses, the combinations of words and phrases, the choice of vocabulary, to make his satiric and moral points. And he is brilliantly able to modulate from tone to tone within a passage. The opening of Juvenal's sixth satire finely encompasses dignity and vulgarity, nostalgic amplitude and satiric bitterness: 'In *Saturn's* Reign, at Nature's Early Birth,/There was that Thing call'd Chastity on Earth . . .' (VI. 1–2). The exploitation of discrepancy, high expectation and debased actuality, is at its most successful in Dryden's account of the cuckolding of Emperor Claudius (denoted by the burlesque periphrasis 'the good old Sluggard') by his wife Messalina, 'th'Imperial Whore'—a powerful oxymoron. The two phrases establish the tonal range of the passage:

> *The good old Sluggard but began to snore,*
> *When from his side up rose th'Imperial Whore.*

> (VI. 163–4)

Messalina's desperate session disguised as a prostitute provokes some of Dryden's most powerful verse. There is not just the disgusted censure of the moralist—'Ropy Smut', 'foul'; certainly he captures her hypocrisy—'the modest Matron'; and with a cold, numbly objective periphrasis all the more powerful for its seeming avoidance of the emotional or descriptive, shows her betrayal—'brings him back the Product of the Night'. But Dryden captures also her desperate yearning, her hopeless sadness:

> *Prepar'd for fight, expectingly she lies,*
> *With heaving Breasts, and with desiring Eyes:*
> *Still as one drops, another takes his place,*
> *And baffled still succeeds to like disgrace.*
> *At length, when friendly darkness is expir'd,*
> *And every Strumpet from her Cell retir'd,*

> *She lags behind, and lingring at the Gate,*
> *With a repining Sigh, submits to Fate:*
> *All Filth without and all a Fire within,*
> *Tir'd with the Toyl, unsated with the Sin.*
> *Old* Caesar's *Bed the modest Matron seeks;*
> *The steam of Lamps still hanging on her Cheeks*
> *In Ropy Smut; thus foul, and thus bedight,*
> *She brings him back the Product of the Night.*

(VI. 176–8₉

The sadness of Messalina is expressed in the language of sensation, th
'heaving Breasts', 'desiring Eyes', 'lingring', 'repining Sigh', 'submits t
Fate'. Dryden's treatment of her dealings with her customers diffe
from that of his predecessors: she 'Smil'd upon all that came' Stapylto
translates (VI. 133), and Holyday offers 'Kind words she gave/To the
that came, and the Reward did crave!' (p. 93). But Dryden emphasiz
here not her hypocrisy or betrayal, but her wretchedness, her inabilit
to find the satisfaction she sought: 'Still as one drops, another takes h
place,/And baffled still succeeds to like disgrace.' To a lesser writ
'disgrace' would have been reserved for Messalina; but Dryden boldl
applies it to the customers who have failed to give her satisfaction; ju
as he strikingly applies 'submits to Fate' not to an inevitable submissic
to degradation, but to her having to accept that the brothel has finishe
business for the night. Dryden's strength comes not only from h
superior craftsmanship, but from his sense of the emotional potential
the material, his drawing out of the emotional meanings, and the powe
ful ambiguities of feeling that make his satires so rich. He does n
provide simple diatribe or simple disgust; his world picture is muc
more complex than that.

The translation of Persius' satires is less interesting. His work wa
well known to Dryden; in the argument to the third and to the fif
satires Dryden recalls how he had translated them at school, and w
can see how satire six, on the use of riches, informed the portrait
Shimei in *Absalom and Achitophel*. But Dryden fails to make Persi
especially interesting for us, despite the clarity of the translation. The
are passages that achieve a lively vigour, like that of the glutton wh
persists in drinking, eating and bathing until 'he vomits out his Sou

(III. 205), and like that on impotence—'bid'st arise the lumpish *Pendulum*' (IV. 119). And Dryden evidently enjoyed the parodies of pompous and dated verse styles in the first satire (I. 185–204). But though we can find striking passages, fragments and epigrams, overall Persius is much less interesting than Juvenal and Dryden does not do much with his material.[1]

The remarkable feature of Dryden's satires is that he never repeated himself. In *Mac Flecknoe* he achieved a monstrously witty mock heroic whose vulgar comedy still provokes ribald laughter: but it was left to Pope's *Dunciad* to extend the onslaught on dullness with its scatological imagery and literary allusions. Dryden achieved his satiric aim in brief, and never went back. With *Absalom and Achitophel* he proceeded with dignity, and the brilliant character sketches, sharp and devastatingly witty as they can be, retain that tone. The sketches he wrote for Tate's continuation of *Absalom and Achitophel* have a broad humour, a more visual and a more genial quality than the analytical, conceptual characterizations of part I. *The Medall* differs again in being written in a tone of barely controlled fury—or a cunning feigning of such a tone: there is none of the comedy or the dignity of the other works, but instead a sustained, virulent diatribe. And having achieved success in all of these varieties, Dryden does not lamely return to attempt a repetition. Never niggardly about his gains, he was always moving on to something else. Having had his own say in satire, when he returned to the form later it was to familiarize his readers with the achievements of the classical past, rather than to repeat himself. The translations draw on his particular satiric practices, but draw, too, on a whole career of poetic and dramatic writing, to give a fluency, a clarity and a tonal range that made his translations a model for the next hundred years.[2]

---

[1] For a lively discussion of translations of Persius, including Dryden's, see William Frost, 'English Persius: The Golden Age', *Eighteenth-Century Studies*, II, 1968–9, 77–101.

[2] I am grateful to the Senate of the University of Sydney for granting me study leave, during which this chapter was completed, and to Professor T. J. B. Spencer of the University of Birmingham for allowing me to use the facilities of the Shakespeare Institute in the course of my work.

8: Forms and Motives of Narrative Poetry

EARL MINER

I

Historical and Critical Canons

IT WAS in Paris in 1650 that Sir William Davenant published his prefatory remark about *Gondibert*. Although English wits had a few days sport in commenting on a preface unaccompanied by a poem, the 'Preface' was not published alone. The 'Answer' by Thomas Hobbes to whom the forthcoming poem was dedicated, still has things to tell us about what narrative meant to the seventeenth century and to that renaissance of narrative poetry beginning in 1642 with the *Psychozooie* of Henry More and the *Leoline and Sydanis* of Sir Francis Kynaston and crowned by the poems of Butler, Milton, Dryden, and Pope. Hobbes and Davenant were part of a general shift in taste, of a reordering of literary genres. They were part of the Caroline court on what Charles II later termed his travels, and like the Marian exiles they were to bring back a new learning adaptable to English uses. The Marian exiles returned to bring England up to date with Protestant reformation. The royalists returning from France, the Low Countries, and Spain would help to bring England up to the standard of continental civilization and by the next century, make it the leader of Europe. War, trade, printing, science, music, theatre, criticism, and such other things as classical scholarship made up the story of the new learning and the new experience that was moving toward revival of narrative. Hobbes is always a prophet in the guise of a describer, and he is always worth attending to particularly when one feels disagreement.

Hobbes starts from a common seventeenth-century distinction be tween 'the three Regions of mankinde, Court, City, and Country'.

> From hence have proceeded three sorts of Poesy, *Heroique,*
> *Scommatique* [comic], and *Pastoral.* Every one of these is dis-
> tinguished again in the manner of *Representation,* which some-
> times is *Narrative . . .* and sometimes *Dramatique . . .* For the
> Heroique Poem narrative . . . is called an *Epique* Poem. The
> Heroique Poem Dramatique is *Tragedy.* The Scommatique Narra-
> tive is *Satyre,* Dramatique is *Comedy.* The Pastorall narrative is
> called simply *Pastorall,* anciently *Bucolique;* the same Dramatique,
> *Pastorall Comedy.*[1]

Such critical geometry is supported by Aristotle's distinction between
narration and drama and by his dictum that writers depict men better,
like, or worse.[2] For all his simplifying, Hobbes remains useful for our
purposes in assuming without doubt that satire and pastoral may be as
narrative in kind as epic.

Such assumptions affect the way we regard many of Dryden's poems
whose generic status seems otherwise uncertain. Following Hobbes, we
would accept *Mac Flecknoe* as a narrative. And there exist altogether
respectable definitions of narrative that permit us to include *Religio
Laici* as well. The best known Roman treatises of rhetoric distinguished
three kinds of *narratio.*[3] At one extreme there was *fabula,* 'which is not
merely not true but has little resemblance to the truth' ('truth' being
actual fact in these formulations). At the other pole lay *historia,* 'exposition of actual fact'. The ground between was occupied by *argumentum,* 'which, though not true, has yet a certain verisimilitude'. Those
of Dryden's non-lyric works that cannot be admitted to the class of

[1] Hobbes, *The Answer,* Spingarn, II 55. As Gerald F. Else shows in
Aristotle's Poetics=The Argument, Cambridge, Mass. 1967, ch. 24, (especially 609–11) Aristotle recognized the radical differences between
epic and narrative plots, and although the evidence of Dryden's plays
is important, I shall omit it here.

[2] *Poetics,* III 1; II 1. The traditional interpretation as to likeness was
followed by Dryden and has only recently been challenged by Else.

[3] The kinds, and the rhetoricians, are discussed in more detail in Miner,
290–1. Chapter viii also relates to the discussion of *Fables* that concludes
this chapter, just as chs. i and v relate respectively to *Annus Mirabilis*
and *The Hind and The Panther.*

narrative by Hobbes's scheme stand every chance of entering as *argumentum*. As Dr Johnson said, in his note at the end of *Romeo and Juliet*, Dryden's genius was 'acute, argumentative, comprehensive, and sublime'. Those virtues belong not to lyricism but to the genres traditionally thought highest.[1]

The difficulties of generic theory become more apparent with a writer like Dryden than with a Milton or a Marvell. Unlike the one, Dryden often mixes genres in very un-neoclassic ways; unlike the other, his *oeuvre* is so large and varied that numerous dissimilar examples of each genre can be found. In addition to plays and lyrics, Dryden wrote a goodly number of longer poems for which 'narrative' in the strictest sense (whatever that may be) may not be the best definition but yet remains the only ready means of characterization. Moreover, our problems are not new. Hobbes's interest in defining narrative so broadly, as one of two principal literary modes, responds to Aristotle in the light of the emergence of a new poetic practice in Europe. Similarly, Roman rhetoricians defining *narratio* were conscious of varieties of kinds practised by their contemporaries in oratory, history, and other forms. In the end the problem is apt to lead us to admit many examples into the gross category of narrative and then to discriminate the differences between individual versions.

Contrary to the Romans, Hobbes, and some modern theorists, many readers define a narrative as that kind of work that tells a 'story'. Unfortunately, that is another name for the same problem of narrative, and 'story' may mean in one guise an excuse, and in another history (*storia*). It would seem that narratives possess certain *symptoms* that we observe in varying combinations in different works which we may loosely term narrative. Although very difficult to define, most of us recognize a 'plot', and probably regard it as the prime symptom of narrative. What Dryden often gives us is quasi-narrative, or narrative perspective, and what plot there is does not bear full responsibility for the sense of movement his

---

[1] Even in advanced German criticism today the narrative, drama, lyric triad is accepted (e.g., Eberhard Lämmert, *Bauformen des Erzählens* 2nd printing, Stuttgart 1967); so does Northrop Frye accept them, *Anatomy of Criticism*, Princeton 1957, adding 'prose'.

poems undeniably possess. These other symptoms of narrative suppress or displace the function of concatenated *episodes* by providing other forms of sequence. Although some of these elements in Dryden are so small as almost to seem of little importance, and others so large as to be lifelong concerns, they are not difficult to identify. As Pope and Dr Johnson recognized, Dryden's poetry possesses an energy of thought and drive of style that are extraordinary. Like Milton, Dryden pushes us constantly forward, and only by act of will does a reader slow the pace to observe details that are there but are often passed by so quickly that they are not observed. Along with that drive of mind goes another symptom, Dryden's unusual stress on active verbs. A principal function of his couplet is to give special stress to the last word of the line, which very often turns out to be a verb, and an active one at that, so giving a verse paragraph intermittent acceleration. Another symptom of great importance is Dryden's almost universal tendency to give his poems a temporal sequence: past, present, future. Anything presented as happening along that sequence carries the strongest of narrative presumptions. Such temporal movement finds reinforcement in a number of devices that recur in his poetry, affording yet other symptoms.

Dryden often uses the progress piece, or *translatio studii*, an account of the historical development of a given art or branch of knowledge (painting, navigation, science, music, poetry, or even translation as rendering into another language). In effect, the progress piece functions to emphasize the underlying presumption of temporal sequence in the whole poem. Dryden also employs panegyric and satiric perspectives that look back on a past or project a future, giving a sense of narrative to lyric poems like the Anne Killigrew Ode or *Threnodia Augustalis*, or even to the character of Shaftesbury-Achitophel which, as Coleridge recognized, is not a static but a moving, developing thing. One last example of such symptoms of narrative must not be omitted, Dryden's constant allusiveness and comparison. By giving a sense of Milton's epics and of historical writing (from 2 Samuel, after all) in *Absalom and Achitophel*, or by founding *Mac Flecknoe* on the supposition of a play, a coronation, and an important religious event, Dryden creates the sense of narrative. It seems highly likely that he went to such lengths because he yearned to write a narrative, and in particular an

epic: 'A heroic poem, truly such, is undoubtedly the greatest work which
the soul of man is capable to perform.'[1] Denied support for his epic, he
found some satisfaction late in life by translating Virgil and other narrative poets. But throughout his career the heroic tone and narrative
effects obsessed Dryden and helped shape his most important poems.
Rather than examine Dryden's major narratives in search of their
several symptoms, I shall try to present validation of what I have said
from Dryden's critical writings and then discuss the ways in which
Dryden's narratives change in form in order to respond to his changing
aims and needs.

In his Preface to *Fables*, Dryden speaks of *Palamon and Arcite*
(Chaucer's Knight's Tale) as a poem 'of the epic kind'.[2] On the other
hand, he termed his own *Annus Mirabilis* a 'poem historical, not epic'
because of its 'broken action', which 'is not properly one'.[3] In the
same 'Account' of *Annus Mirabilis*, in speaking of well wrought
descriptions or images, he says that images may be thought

> the adequate delight of heroic poesy; for they beget admiration,
> which is its proper object; as the images of the burlesque, which
> is contrary to this, by the same reason beget laughter . . . But
> though the same images serve equally for the epic poesy, and for
> the historic and panegyric, which are branches of it, yet a several
> sort of sculpture is to be used in them.[4]

If panegyric and historical poetry are 'branches' of epic, then they must
necessarily be narrative in mode. Not only they: 'In the character of an
hero, as well as in an inferior figure, there is a better or worse likeness
to be taken: the better is a panegyric, if it be not false, and the worse a
libel [satire].'[5] The critical commonplace of the time, which held that

---

[1] Dedication of Virgil's *Aeneis* (Watson, II 223). See also 'The Author's
Apology for Heroic Poetry' and 'A Discourse . . . of Satire' (Watson,
I 198; II 96); and n. 1, p. 240.
[2] Watson, II 290.
[3] 'An Account', Watson, I 95. This preface is one of Dryden's most significant critical moments, especially for anticipating his poetic career.
[4] Watson, I 101.
[5] *A Parallel Betwixt Poetry and Painting*, Watson, II 202.

panegyric and satire are counterparts, brings satire into the fold of narrative and makes it a cousin to epic itself. By rhetorical principle and Hobbesian mode, satire had a claim to be a species of narrative.

Some few critics, unwilling to linger with Dryden's more complex views or unable to attend to his poetry, have made much of a line from *To Sir Godfrey Kneller*: 'But Satire will have room, where e're I write' (l. 94). The immediate contexts of that line cannot concern us here,[1] but in the larger context of Dryden's characteristic procedures we must say that satire does enter as a control mingling the moral, the affective, and the rhetorical ('amplification'). It is equally true that panegyric came to him as second nature and as a control. Readers may long debate whether the praise of Achitophel in verses added to the second printing of *Absalom and Achitophel* heightens the satire or brightens the portrait, or both. But so much is clear: no other satirist so lauds his central villain, or founds one of his two thoroughgoing satires, *Mac Flecknoe*, on praise. Dryden's 'art of praise' was not left, like David's sword, in rest except for rare occasions.

Much the same proves true of the historical element he related to epic. One could read the productions of very many writers without learning that most of mankind's adult concerns turn on war and peace, government and family, specific achievements and disasters, the rise and disappearance of personalities, and the unending drama between men, events, and principles. Much of what we need as human beings belongs to Donne's intimate 'little roome', but one will not find there the world of epic nor those mutant forms that Dryden had warrant to consider akin to the epic. Dryden almost always sought 'a better or worse likeness'. And of what? we may ask. Very often of *historia*, of what had actually happened. At other times, of things hoped for, giving evidence of things not seen. When he so treats of what had not happened but what faith (or hope) led him to aspire to, he turns more lyrical and eschatological, as in *A Song for St Cecilia's Day* or in the vision of Christ's Spouse, the Church, in *The Hind and the Panther* (II. 499–525).

---

[1] It is one of my concerns in 'Dryden's *Eikon Basilike: To Sir Godfrey Kneller*' in *Seventeenth-Century Imagery*, ed. Earl Miner, Berkeley, Los Angeles, and London 1971, 151–67.

Above all, the epic beckoned Dryden, because it seemed to combine history and faith, the exemplary hero and the supernatural. Whether or not the heroic play reflects what is central to human experience, it certainly grows from ideals that animated Dryden and the Renaissance. The heroic (or epic) provided Dryden with much more than Hobbes's version, narrative and dramatic. To Dryden great satire required the mixture of epic with venom. The heroic was a tone or mood; it was a standard of ethical and artistic worth. Because it was so supremely important, the greatest thing the soul of man could aspire to, he found it seemingly everywhere.[1] As Virgil's epic dealt with the founding of the new Troy, Dryden's ideal artistic and human city consists in the heroic struggle to achieve the highest goals. In that *civitas verbi*, with that Homeric sense of great deeds and great words, the intimate is replaced by character and passions. The emphasis falls almost exclusively upon what men and women share as a civilized heritage, and the rejecters or anarchists are branded by satire, while the aspirers and winners are lauded with panegyric. Epic plays captain in that enterprise, with history, panegyric, and satire lieutenants. They rule the court, town, and country of narrative, and not infrequently make incursions into drama and lyric.

As W. B. Yeats remarked, however, in literature we would all be parvenus without models. The Renaissance and seventeenth century knew that axiomatically, the axiom being a prime humanistic article. When in 1667 Dryden had *Annus Mirabilis* published, he could not have known that a few months would bring *Paradise Lost*. But he was about thirty-six and by then had acquired a full experience of narrative poetry before Milton. English aside, Latin and French were Dryden's first languages. He was especially admiring of Italian, and he read Greek and no doubt Spanish. Whether he made much of an effort to learn 'Dutch' may be doubted, but in those days before editions of Chaucer had glossaries and notes he picked up Middle English as a matter of course. After Homer and Virgil in his estimation came Ovid, Lucan, Statius, and Silius Italicus, with some lesser wights. For Dryden,

---

[1] See H. T. Swedenberg, Jr., 'Dryden's Obsessive Concern with the Heroic', *SP*, ES, 4, 1967, 12–26.

as for everybody, Dante, Tasso, Ariosto, and Boccaccio were the Italian masters of narrative. The French narratives that he read had not the distinction of the Italian, but they were immensely more popular. Such lengthy, complicated, and rarified romances suggest that readers then had unexampled memories and patience in sitting down to Georges de Scudéry's epic *Alaric* or Honoré d'Urfé's prodigiously influential romance, *L'Astrée*. From the epic Dryden took that nobility of spirit that inspires wonder, 'admiration', along with the sense of personal and national destiny to be achieved by concerted effort. From the romance he took some fool's gold of language, some quicksilver of personality, and the staples of love and valour. But it must be asked after all this, which of these explains *Annus Mirabilis*?

Of course it must be recognized that Dryden admired narrative poets in his own language, particularly Chaucer, Spenser, and later Milton. Near the end of his life, writing his 'Preface' to *Fables* Dryden suggests that he admires but does not belong to what might be termed the line of wit and refinement he characterizes in Fairfax (translator of Tasso's *Jerusalem Delivered*), Edmund Waller, and Sir John Denham. No, for him it is the 'poetical house' of Chaucer, Spenser, and Milton: the line of narrative and genius. Dryden knew the real article as quickly as any critic, and recognized that *Paradise Lost* was a classic as soon as it appeared. As a classic, it could be alluded to, and so could *Paradise Regained* when it appeared. But in 1667 they had not appeared and Dryden had to put his models respectfully on the shelf as he sought to fashion out of the momentous events of contemporary life something that was indebted to epic and romance but that possessed a character of its own.

II

Annus Mirabilis

When Dryden sat down to write his first longish poem, his reputation was that of a playwright. He had shown that he could create characters and events in dramatic plots. Like other poets before him he might have tried to translate drama into narrative. Kynaston, Chamberlayne, and Davenant attempted the structural analogy between a narrative poem and a five-act play.[1] Dryden was wise to choose another alternative, as had Butler in the first part of *Hudibras*, and as Milton would in *Paradise Lost*. Again, he might have chosen, like Cowley, to paraphrase a biblical story at length. Since Milton was at the moment closing up his papers for *Paradise Lost*, Dryden was wise for other reasons to have eschewed Cowley's example. As almost always with Dryden, anyone taking the trouble to observe what his contemporaries and immediate predecessors were doing will discover that he, who was temperamentally conservative in many ways, was experimental and radical as a poet. Rejecting available models—including also allegory and the verse romance—he wrote about his own time, the 'year of wonders', 1666. Those wonders included early portions of the second Anglo-Dutch naval war and the terrible Great Fire of London, with a glance at the 'spotted Deaths' of the Great Plague.

Dryden wrote, as he claimed, a historical poem. The Puritans had taught Englishmen that the events of their own day constituted history every bit as much as the great events of Greece and Rome. And as Butler's instalment of *Hudibras* had taken a mordantly worse 'likeness' of the men of the Interregnum, Dryden set about presenting a better likeness of men and of events still fresh in men's minds. Choosing the 'heroic quatrain' that Davenant had employed in *Gondibert*, Dryden returned to an older tradition of stanzaic narrative in order to write of achievement and death, destruction and renewal.

His 'Account' makes clear that he recognized that the poem suffered from its double subject. Much has been said, and more can be, on the ways in which he relates the two episodes of war and fire. The political purpose, the imagery, and above all that unprecedented intellectual drive of the style do create a single milieu.[2] His experience as a drama-

---

[1] On Chamberlayne's practice, see the note by George Saintsbury, *Minor Caroline Poets*, 3 vol Oxford 1905, 1921, I. 7. He reprints Sir Francis Kynaston's vigorous but not wholly serious *Leoline and Sydanis* in Vol. II. Davenant spelled out in greatest detail what the play-narrative analogy meant structurally in his 'Preface' to *Gondibert*, ed. David F. Gladish, Oxford 1971, 11. 506–23, or Spingarn, I. 17–18.

[2] See *Works* I; and Steven Zwicker, *Dryden's Political Poetry, The Typology of King and Nation*, Providence, R. I. 1972, ch. iv.

ist assisted him in drawing parallels between the two actions: it is the king who crucially directs the repair of the fleet so that it may return to victory, and it is the king whose prayers obtain divine release from fire. The fire is led up to by a section labelled 'Transitum', which is itself prepared for by the last naval action, an English squadron's burning of Dutch ships in the Vlie. Much else might be mentioned about Dryden's integrative procedure, but the fact remains that every reader experiences a relation of two things that have been rendered kindred but not one single thing.

To be sure, narrative is in some ways a more capacious or looser form than others, and the discerning critic will call less for tidiness than for movement toward significant ends. The most telling justification of the poem's structural integrity is negative: Dr Johnson, who was so sensitive to such matters, enters no strictures on that head. He thought the poem stylistically uneven, as it certainly is, but that is another matter. *Annus Mirabilis*, Johnson says, 'is one of his greatest attempts. He had subjects equal to his abilities, a great naval war, and the Fire of London.'[1] If anything, Johnson seems to have appreciated the formal art of the poem, remarking that the digression on the Royal Society provided 'an example seldom equalled of seasonable excursion and artful return'.[2] What, then, is it that has led Johnson and everyone else to prefer *Absalom and Achitophel*? 'The general fault,' Johnson said of the poem of wonders, 'is that he affords more sentiment than description, and does not so much impress scenes upon the fancy [imagination] as deduce consequences and make comparisons.'[3] There is truth in that, although the same thing may be said yet more appropriately of poems Dryden was to write in the next two decades, including *Absalom and Achitophel*. Unlike them, however, *Annus Mirabilis* takes its entire being from the presumption that it is something like essential narrative. All experience of genuine narrative possesses a significant movement. We apprehend the relevant and directive accumulation of past episodes,

[1] *Lives of the English Poets*, ed. George Birkbeck Hill, 3 vol. Oxford, 1905, I. 430.
[2] *Ibid.* I. 434.
[3] *Ibid.* I. 431.

following a continuous narrative present toward fulfilment. We discover the movement to be intelligible, not only as action itself, as a 'good story', but as a significant intellectual and affective process. *Annus Mirabilis* satisfies such requirements unevenly, even as its style shows other kinds of uncertainty. In the end, our judgments are apt to be comparative. By comparison with most English attempts at narrative poetry in the preceding seven or eight decades, *Annus Mirabilis* proves not only novel in conception but whole, complete. But *Annus Mirabilis* is fine enough to invoke higher comparisons, and its merits are sufficiently attractive for us to feel more than indifference to its flaws.

So much said, we owe it as much to ourselves as to Dryden to inquire about his aim. Like Dante, Dryden always pursues remarkably clear ends, clear at least when discovered. If his means proved uneven in *Annus Mirabilis*, his end was clear. He sought a special version of the state that Hobbes the critic would have appreciated more than Hobbes the philosopher. Dryden emphatically wished to show the Court and the City at one (with occasional glances at the Country in similes) in pursuing a high national destiny. Negatively, he had to argue against such views that the '666' or 'the number of the beast' in 1666 heralded divine judgment and the end of the world. Positively, he understood, as did Charles II and his brother, that England's future lay in trade. He knew that the war with Holland was a battle over the future, and he knew that London, 'this fam'd Emporium', was the necessary focus of such effort. His royalism comes as no cause for surprise, but it is truly significant that he should show so emphatically that the king needed the City as much as the City the Court. With hopes that are immemorially human, Dryden wished the struggle of war and disaster at home to end so that human effort could be directed to achievement in the arts of peace.

Among the obstacles to realizing such hopes was the threat posed by France under Louis XIV, for whom Dryden never had a good word.

> *Such deep designs of Empire does he lay*
> *O're them whose cause he seems to take in hand:*
> *And, prudently, would make them Lords at Sea,*
> *To whom with ease he can give Laws by Land.*   (33–36)

This capacity for seeing into things provides more 'sentiment' than 'description', although at some moments Dryden imagines the experience of battle under sail brilliantly: 'Silent in smoke of Canons they come on' (l. 329). But Dr Johnson is right to suggest that Dryden commonly proves more memorable for his inferences than for his descriptions of battle.

> *Such are the proud designs of human kind,*
> *And so we suffer Shipwrack every where!*
> *Alas, what Port can such a Pilot find,*
> *Who in the night of Fate must blindly steer!*   (137–40)

It turns out that in narrating the uncertain, unhistorical *future* Dryden is able to combine action and vision into a much wished for whole.

> *Instructed ships shall sail to quick Commerce;*
> *By which remotest Regions are alli'd:*
> *Which makes one City of the Universe,*
> *Where some may gain, and all may be suppli'd.*   (649–52)

English imperialism of the next two centuries has been envisioned and its deals provided. Anticipating and transcending the later charge of the English as a nation of shopkeepers, Dryden makes the trading world into a universal city. The model for the city-superstate is of course London, and the paean to that city towards the close of the poem is therefore wholly appropriate.

> *Before, she like some Shepherdess did show,*
> *Who sate to bathe her by a River's side:*
> *Not answering to her fame, but rude and low,*
> *Nor taught the beauteous Arts of Modern pride.*
>
> *Now, like a Maiden Queen, she will behold,*
> *From her high Turrets, hourly Sutors come:*
> *The East with Incense, and the West with Gold,*
> *Will stand, like Suppliants, to receive her doom.*
>
> *The silver* Thames, *her own domestick Floud,*
> *Shall bear her Vessels, like a sweeping Train;*
> *And often wind (as of his Mistress proud)*
> *With longing eyes to meet her face again.*   (1181–92)

Annus Mirabilis suffers from treating two distinct episodes, from unevenness of style, and from attempting too much in a new kind. Yet it is a narrative poem of numerous merits and dignified ends. It startled its contemporaries by its originality and vigour. If too much of Dryden's scaffolding seems to have been left standing, the narrative edifice is the more remarkable for showing poets that there existed a new design, a 'fabric' as Dryden would say, possessing that combination of beauty and strength esteemed in the century. For the next portion of his career, Dryden had proved that he could command narrative resources if he chose, and above all that to him as by right of discovery belonged one kind of historical, public poetry such as England had not seen. For this poem and for *Of Dramatick Poesie*, 1667 was itself Dryden's first year of wonders. Whether accidental or not, after *Paradise Lost* appeared as the greatest poetic wonder of that or any English year, Dryden turned to a new direction. For years he would forsake the pure narrative mode in order to develop highly adapted forms such as the wide Roman sense of *narratio* allowed.

III

Crisis and New Forms: 1675–83

The years immediately following *Annus Mirabilis* were calm ones for Dryden and for England. His career as playwright developed quickly, premised by the theoretical foundation in *Of Dramatick Poesie*. That essay deserves a moment's consideration in this chapter, because in spite of its being centrally a 'sceptical' dialogue[1] and a critical debate, it is also a semi-fiction with many endearing touches of narrative about it. Sir Philip Sidney had been thwarted in his handsome *Defence of Poesy* by the lack of any considerable dramatic or narrative achievement in modern English. Having the great dramatists of 'the last age', the examples of French, Spanish, and classical drama, and the aspirations animating himself and his contemporaries, Dryden did not have to de-

---

[1] On the nature of Dryden's scepticism, see Phillip Harth, *Contexts of Dryden's Thought*, Chicago 1968, ch. i; for the classical, Academic tradition of scepticism and the dialogue, see *Works*, XVII, on *Of Dramatick Poesie*.

fend poetry itself. Once that issue was resolved, Dryden could become, in Dr Johnson's phrase, the father of English criticism. In prose as well as drama, the needs of the age and the talents of the man coincided so that what was new could be natural, and so that a man of profoundly conservative temperament could prove more innovative than any of his contemporaries, Milton included.

As the 1670s wore on, the gentlemanly terms of literary debate in Dryden's essay began to change towards more personal gestures. No one has ever been able to account for Dryden's possessing his soul in patience, as he liked to advise others, for some long season and then for his astonishing flashes in verse. Dryden's contemporaries were mystified that a man so diffident and shy in personal contact could prove to possess as a poet such Olympian detachment and Jovian thunderbolts. *Mac Flecknoe* is the creation of that disputatious period and of that man who had never revealed any inclination, much less talent, for satire. Its date is uncertain, although John Oldham had set down parts of it in 1678. Some evidence suggests that in an earlier version it crowned Elkanah Settle Prince of Dulness.[1] Whatever uncertainties remain, the result is clear. Dryden had introduced into satire a withering gaiety and a detached finality that did what satire seldom does, reduce its object, Thomas Shadwell, into the incoherence of which he was accused.

Mac Flecknoe affords delight in its spirits, its wit, and its tight fabric. Everyone seems to remember it as far longer than it is, merely 217 lines. That length and other characteristics make its status as a narrative dubious, but it may provide a test case of Hobbes's conception of satire as the narrative form of the comic. The poem relates the verbose attempt of the essentially dull poet, Flecknoe, to abdicate from the throne of dullness in favour of that son most like himself. The abdication proceedings at last end abruptly when the chosen prince (a poet who says not a word during the proceedings) deposes his father by sending him down a stage trapdoor. The declamations of Flecknoe I upon Flecknoe II represent a praise of folly in the tradition of Erasmus (whom Dryden family tradition held as a friend of an ancestor). What

[1] George McFadden, 'Elkanah Settle and the Genesis of *Mac Flecknoe*', *PQ*, XIII, 1964, 55–72.

narrative there is to move *Mac Flecknoe* forward derives from numerous sources: from analogy with a play and a coronation, from temporal sequence, and from the artful mixing of *fabula*, *argumentum*, and *historia*.[1] The action itself is minimal, much more given to deducing consequences and making comparisons, as Dr Johnson said of the earlier poem. The liveliest movement of the poem takes place not in the narrative action at all but in the operations of the mind with that 'wonderful velocity of thought' that Jane Austen was to speak of. Dryden's thought attain movement by constant interaction (which is not the same as simple narrative action). Depending on the observer, what is going on may be described as a network of images, a process of analogy, or making of metaphor.[2]

In other words, *Mac Flecknoe* uses, rather than is, narrative. Narrative is important in the total effect, but only subordinately effective. The air of narrative about to begin hovers over the poem from its outset.

> *All humane things are subject to decay,*
> *And, when Fate summons, Monarchs must obey:*
> *This* Fleckno *found . . .*

And as always, Dryden gains much of a sense of narrative perspective (as opposed to movement) by looking forward to what might be done, as in Flecknoe's praise of his princely son towards the end.

> *Like mine thy gentle numbers feebly creep,*
> *Thy Tragick Muse gives smiles, thy Comick sleep.*
> *With whate'er gall thou sett'st thy self to write,*
> *Thy inoffensive Satyrs never bite.*
> *In thy fellonious heart, though Venom lies,*
> *It does but touch thy* Irish *pen, and dyes.*
> *Thy Genius calls thee not to purchase fame*
> *In keen Iambicks, but mild Anagram:*
> *Leave writing Plays, and chuse for thy command*
> *Some peacefull Province in Acrostick Land.*   (197–206)

[1] See n. 3, p. 235 above.

[2] 'Imagery' was the term preferred by Hoffman, who first revealed the importance and complexity of the matter; Roper preferred 'analogy', and I 'metaphor'. Dryden himself uses no term that will cover all his various larger figurative procedures.

Never had satire been at once so good humoured and so final. Although the opposition is utterly demolished, the world shared by the poet and the reader miraculously escapes demeaning.

Dryden employs somewhat greater narrative resources in creating *Absalom and Achitophel*. We are made to feel that momentous events impend: revolution and counter-revolution threaten, and England agonizes over a Popish Plot. The papists were said to be plotting against the life of Charles II and the nation. At a time when Charles had to exercise the power of veto for the first time and take a stand alone merely to save his queen from unjustified accusations of homicide, the roughs were going about London with 'Protestant flails', and each week there were unexplained murders and new frights. Even Dryden must have struggled to maintain that air of calm, that meaningful but straight-faced wink with which he begins, 'In pious times . . .' when Israel's monarch 'Scatter'd his Maker's Image through the Land'. The poem affords in such matters a curious inversion of *Mac Flecknoe*, which had, as we have seen, begun a hilarious poem with solemnity. Unlike Flecknoe, Charles II would not abdicate and would not choose his bastard son (Absalom-Monmouth) as his true heir. And by an accident of history, the meaningful narrative of non-actions in the satire turns into a narrative whose plot is a Plot that essentially does not exist. In the end, unlike Mac Flecknoe, Achitophel-Shaftesbury is unable to depose that 'Idol Monarch', Charles. The king cleverly outmanoeuvred his enemies by calling Parliament to meet in Oxford, where his father had held out against his enemies during the Civil Wars. Dismissing the Oxford Parliament with a speech like that by David at the end of the poem, Charles acted with great resoluteness, then shrugged, and pocketed money (as had his opposition in Parliament) from Dryden's hated Louis XIV.

Dryden was as well informed as any man living about the growth of popery and arbitrary government, as Marvell put it on the other side. What he did not know he darkly suspected about the growth of knavery and anarchy. Summoning his prejudices and his wisdom, he joined to them satiric, panegyric, and epic strains to write a poem ostensibly at least devoted to what Cowley had termed 'the troubles of David'. As with the numerous 'comparisons' of *Mac Flecknoe*, the biblical parallel provided Dryden with a partial narrative. One secret of *Absalom and Achitophel* rests inimitably in Dryden's capacity to create a sense of the whole experience of crisis and forestalled revolution by presenting, and controlling, selected aspects of events. By limiting the full pressure of anything at each moment, but by seeing everything and everybody in at least double guises, and by having a clearly thought out political theory himself, Dryden wrote his most widely esteemed poem.

Annus Mirabilis concerned London and England's imperial destiny. *Mac Flecknoe* concerned the kingdom of letters and its destiny.[1] *Absalom and Achitophel* concerned itself with the present kingdom of England, its constitution, and its destiny. Dryden certainly recognized the imperfections of men and their institutions. 'Peace itself is War in Masquerade.' 'That Change they covet makes them suffer more.' The conservative *dicta* and the brilliant verse paragraphs drive home a sober message: you can ruin a working state, but until men differ from what they are, you will only bring greater misery by sudden change. All this is said or shown with the air, and somewhat more, of fair-mindedness such as can be exampled elsewhere only in Marvell's Horatian Ode on Cromwell. But Dryden is firmer and better able to convey the wider scene. No earlier nondramatic poem had conveyed the sheer variety and swirl of opinion at a historical crisis. None other had conceded so much (in order to claim yet more) by taking off so wittily in its opening the central figure of the poem. And none had been able to rise above the role of angry opposition to the role of thoughtful authority. Dryden begins his personal statement of political principle (ll. 759-810) by asking, 'What shall we think!' and by considering the major alternative polities understood in his day.

The initial wit earns the right to the increasingly sober tone govern-

[1] For 'The Kingdom of Letters', see Roper, 136–84. A valuable proof that *Mac Flecknoe* does possess narrative energy will be found by comparing it with 'To My Dear Friend, Mr Congreve', which is very like in subject and motif but without plot pressure. Even the *Congreve* possesses others of the narrative 'symptoms' mentioned earlier, however, and well represents that shift from 'dramatic' to 'narrative' emphasis in the century that I sought to show in *The Metaphysical Mode from Donne to Cowley*, Princeton 1969, 66–99.

ng the poem. What governs its conduct is something similar, a narra-
ive stance in a poem that is not any more, or less, purely narrative than
t is epic, satiric, panegyric, or political. As is revealed by the echoes of
Paradise Lost and, more importantly, of the temptation of the kingdoms
in *Paradise Regained*, Dryden had learnt from Milton that the relation
of events in terms of an immutable moral order puts details and charac-
ers firmly in place. Although in his preface 'To the Reader', Dryden
akes both the narrative and satiric stance, he denies that he is the
'Inventour' of a story: he is its 'Historian'. He seems always to be say-
ng, 'I could a tale relate', and always to be about to do so as he recalls
certain present and future possibilities of momentous event. But much
as the poet's and the reader's minds move over great tracts, their feet
move by inches, and the poem ends with the king 'restored' before he
had been in fact deposed.

In the next year (1682), Dryden published his second full-scale
satire, *The Medall*. A Whig jury had acquitted Shaftesbury, whose rejoicing followers had a medal struck for their hero. The London of
Annus Mirabilis is still 'the great *Emporium* of our Isle' (l. 167). The
declamation of *Mac Flecknoe*, remains, but is spoken as a philippic by
the satiric orator: In the name of Heaven, Shaftesbury, how long will
you abuse our patience ? And the poem in some sense continues the historical sequence treated by *Annus Mirabilis*. But the tone and the stance
of the earlier poems yield to anger, even in reflective passages. Although still voiced by authority, the white-lipped satire employs a
degree of steady invective that Dryden never again sought to sustain.
Except for a very effective passage of reflection (123–144) Dryden re-
linquishes the narrative stance in order to stigmatize as a judge the sins
of his age. In the crisis of 1682, Dryden appeared to abandon the more
spacious plain of narrative for the furious spot of time.

IV

Religious Confession

The closely related forces of religion, politics, and social movements
combined throughout the seventeenth century to induce in thoughtful

people 'cases of conscience' or periods of doubt. We infer that th
writers of the century were especially prone to such inner conflicts
because most of them changed their religion at least once. There is
Restoration story of two brothers, one Anglican and one Catholic, wh
entered one of those 'conferences' designed to convert each other: both
succeeded. Dryden stands apart from the other major poets of th
century in two matters relating to religion. Although others were con
verted to Catholicism (Jonson, Marvell, Wycherley, for example)
Dryden alone was imprudent enough to remain steadfast in his new
faith. And he alone was impelled to two confessions of faith. The forme
of these, *Religio Laici* (1682), followed *The Medall* in time and in cer
tain literary emphases. 'The Religion of a Layman' is a wonderfully
cool, charitable, clear exposition of faith, seeking a moderate position
among rival claims of the faiths. In that it is unlike *The Medall*, bu
after the plangent music and the imagery of its opening lines it turns to
almost pure 'discourse of reason', becoming progressively less imagis
tic.[1] The poem was eagerly taken up by Anglican divines and laymen
and it has a historical importance seldom commented on in crowning
long process of change within Anglican thought. From the time of the
return of the Marian exiles, Anglicanism had become more and more
affected by Calvinist thought—even George Herbert was Calvinist
even James I believed in predestination. The conflict of ideas and
separation into parties represented by the Civil Wars gradually re
turned Anglicans to the position of their 'Churches Champion', Richard
Hooker, and to what has been called 'the axiom of knowledge'.[2] To the
poet himself, however, it was a statement of personal belief.

> *Thus have I made my own Opinions clear:*
> *Yet neither Praise expect, nor Censure fear:*
> *And this unpolish'd, rugged Verse, I chose;*
> *As fittest for Discourse, and nearest Prose.*   (451–4)

[1] Hoffman, ch. iii.
[2] The first phrase is Charles Cotton's in his poem on Walton's new
edition of his *Lives*; the second is Herschel Baker's in *The Wars of Truth*,
Cambridge, Mass. 1952. For reviews of scholarship on Dryden's religi
ous poems, see *Works*, II, III.

One of the same points is made by the epigraph: 'The topic refuses to be adorned, for it is content with being explained.'[1]

That is too simple, except by way of contrast with Dryden's other poetry. One need only read the long prose preface, covering the very topics of the poem, to see the difference between that prose and this verse. With a clarity and a style that recall Horace's *Art of Poetry*, Dryden raises the two crucial questions for the century's religious debate: what constitutes a 'rational faith' and what should be 'the rule of faith'. As the opening lines show, Dryden adhered as he always would to the position of Aquinas and Hooker. Faith alone could deal with mysteries and lead a man to salvation through divine grace; but certain aspects of faith could be understood and even guided by reason, which should govern all else. In 1682 Dryden held to the Anglican position that the Bible was in itself a clear and sufficient rule of faith (see ll. 364–9).

Religio Laici is the one poem substantiating the claim that Dryden's is the poetry of statement. (T. S. Eliot admired Dryden in ways that would have sunk a lesser poet.) While rejecting the Epicureanism and dogmatism of Lucretius, Dryden showed that he could discuss that which moved him most without the narrative mode or the narrative stance. Seeking maximum clarity, Dryden divagated farther from narrative than he was ever to do again in extended non-dramatic poetry.

Paradoxically, when Dryden turned to Lucretius to translate parts of *De Rerum Natura* for *Sylvae* (1685) he effected a kind of narrative out of the least narrative parts of the poem. Each selection leads to the next, and each opens a major view onto the human condition. The selection from the fourth book, for example, deals with love and procreation. Appropriately the selection from the fifth begins with a result from sexual union.

> *Thus like a Sayler by the Tempest hurl'd*
> *Ashore, the Babe is shipwrack'd on the World:*
> *Naked he lies, and ready to expire;*
> *Helpless of all that humane wants require:*
> *Expos'd upon unhospitable Earth,*
> *From the first moment of his hapless Birth.* (1–6)

[1] Manilius, *Astronomicon*, III 139: '*Ornari res ipsa negat; contenta doceri.*'

The narrative approach to the discursive Lucretius presents us with the converse of *Religio Laici* (and recalls *Annus Mirabilis*). The same holds true philosophically. The Christian poem offered personal testimony, affirmation of faith and hope, indeed charity as well. The selections from Lucretius are greatly heightened in their paganism and their bleakness.[1] The pagan philosophy is not allowed to put all in doubt. Rather it fails completely to answer Christian needs and proves its own destitution. Pan is dead.

The Hind and the Panther shares a surprising number of concerns with his first *confessio*, and especially attention to a rational faith and, yet more, the rule of faith. His idea of the former has changed little. His idea of the latter—the need for an infallible Church to interpret the Bible and guide the believer—has changed radically. Perhaps it is appropriate that the differing answer should assume a novel form. The best known passage of the poem, the *confiteor*, uses the imagery of the opening of *Religio Laici* wrought to higher grandeur.

> *But, gratious God, how well dost thou provide*
> *For erring judgments an unerring Guide?*
> *Thy throne is darkness in th' abyss of light,*
> *A blaze of glory that forbids the sight;*
> *O teach me to believe thee thus conceal'd,*
> *And search no farther than thy self reveal'd;*
> *But her alone for my Directour take*
> *Whom thou hast promis'd never to forsake!*
> *My thoughtless youth was wing'd with vain desires,*
> *My manhood, long misled by wandring fires,*
> *Follow'd false lights; and when their glimps was gone,*
> *My pride struck out new sparkles of her own.*
> *Such was I, such by nature still I am,*
> *Be thine the glory, and be mine the shame.*
> *Good life be now my task: my doubts are done.*   (I. 64–79)

---

[1] A classicist, Norman Austin, has established the point in what is perhaps the finest analysis of Dryden as a translator of the classics: 'Translation as Baptism: A Study of Dryden's Lucretius', *Arion*, VII, 1968, 576–602.

his is Dryden's answer to that question which troubled the whole cen-
ury: What shall I do to be saved? And it is also answer sufficient to any
f his smaller critics. Those who are suspicious of converts to Catho-
cism have seemed to feel their doubts confirmed by the extraordinary
east fable of *The Hind and the Panther*. In the first part, the Catholic
Hind and the Anglican Panther are introduced in 'characters', along
vith descriptions of the Presbyterian Wolf, the Independent Bear, and
esser ecclesiastical beasts. The Hind and the Panther meet at the close
f Part I. In the second part they debate the present issues of religion in
England, with the Hind getting the longer arguments and the role of the
rue church, while the Panther, with her malicious grins and affected
awns, gets the wit. The debate continues in the third part, with atten-
ion turning to the future of religion in England. Each of two sections
f debate is followed by a fable of birds within the larger beast fable.
he Panther leads off with the fable of the foolish Catholic Swallows
vho think the false spring of the reign of James II is a true one and who
re (that is, will be) killed off for their mistake. The Hind's fable, which
ll but concludes the poem, presents a much more complicated avian-
cclesiastical situation on the 'Estate' of that 'Plain good Man', *alias*
ames II. In spite of the greed of the Anglican Pigeons, in spite of their
alling in the predatory Buzzard (modelled on both William of Orange
nd Gilbert Burnet), the 'good Man' saves them and his other fowl by
ssuing a *fiat*, assigning each species to its proper free realm. At this
oint, the Anglican Pigeons dwindle (that is, will dwindle) away.

Dryden had more fun with his beast fable than have many of his
ritics, who wish for a tidy beast allegory, something more like Orwell's
Animal Farm, something less like one of Dryden's declared models,
Aesop in seventeenth-century guises. (How unkind of Dryden to for-
;et that he is a Neoclassical poet!) Dryden's fun comes from raising the
east allegory here, dropping it there, or playing off its one term against
he other, as we shall see. By the same token he draws on numerous
orms of narrative mode or stance without ever committing himself to
:omplete narrative. In one sense the poem offers the ecclesiastical his-
ory of England from early times to the future. That history is told in the
;uise of one branch of natural history. But natural history is itself treated
acredly, partly as in such sacred zoögraphies as the *Historia Animalium*

Sacra of Franzius, and partly by analogy with the intermittent tropolo-
gical glossings of the divine word, or biblical history. In addition to such
sources—as well as Aesop, Spenser, and Chaucer's Nun's Priest's Tale
—Dryden drew upon the heated religious issues of the day and his own
personal biography.

Unlike *Absalom and Achitophel*, whose biblical parallel is unbroken
except for a wink or two, the fable of *The Hind and the Panther* is a
multiple, ever-varying thing, just as the Catholic interpretation of
scripture might now be moral, now allegorical, now anagogical, or now
simply literal. Dryden forces the question on us: Is this not absurd?
Here (II. 714–20) is the Panther, bewildered at the Hind's simple and
'lonely cell'.

> *The silent stranger stood amaz'd to see*
> *Contempt of wealth, and wilfull poverty:*
> *And, though ill habits are not soon controll'd,*
> *A while suspended her desire of gold:*
> *But civily drew in her sharpn'd paws,*
> *Not violating hospitable laws,*
> *And pacify'd her tail, and lick'd her frothy jaws.*

Cannot Dryden make up his mind whether he is telling the story of a
church (which he accuses of greed) or an animal (with sharp claws)?
That feline church becomes more feline than ecclesiastical by the end,
a great predatory cat soothing herself for the night. Of course it is
absurd, because that is just what Dryden wishes us to think of the Anglican church. The Hind is 'sober', never described absurdly, and except
for her passages of high poetry (e.g. II 499ff. and III 279ff.) is a humour-
less Mother Superior not averse to strong language (e.g. III 144–68).
The giddy Panther, who lately features in scandalous reports about a
liaison with the Presbyterian Wolf, is every way more amusing. I shall
not argue that Dryden was of the Panther's party without knowing it,
but I believe that she was his favourite character in the poem.

For all that, critics worry over what Dr Johnson termed the 'constitutional absurdity' of the fable, its depiction of beasts who not only
represent churches but who talk about matters ecclesiastical. Given
tidier eighteenth-century standards, and given Dr Johnson's reluctance

have matters divine treated at all, Dryden is simply Baroque. He ay mean much and he may mean in a brilliant style (as even Macaulay cognized), but to many readers he means a perverse religion in a erverse fable. Ironically, the most esteemed longer passages of the oem are precisely the fables of the Swallows and of the Pigeons. In a oem that continually gives over its narrative impulses, here are two istained narratives. Here, also, is the beast fable at its Baroque height. easts representing certain churches and talking to beasts representing ie rival churches tell stories of birds that represent the very same chur- ies. And yet the critics who object to the fable in general praise these assages in particular.

One suspects that such critics are really bothered less by the ele- ent of fable than by two other things. The objection to Dryden as a atholic and advocate of Catholicism is their problem, not Dryden's id 'none of my own'. The second matter, the arousal constantly of irrative needs which are answered too often with debate—this I re- ird as Dryden's problem and my problem with him. In *Hudibras*, itler does the same thing, and although his art does not approach ryden's, he is in a sense more successful. He means us to become irri- ted with action frustrated by harangue, and he means us to feel ever ore uneasy with his characters and their world. Dryden only saves mself by the maturity of his style, by the clarity and integrity of his eas, and by a sense of humour. On this occasion, Dryden's disciplined ind took either a lark or some great risks. In musical terms, he plays at ill a polyphony, a monody, and a diatonic scale. The result is at once edieval and *avant-garde*, a seventeenth-century quasi-narrative (and iasi- much else) compounding of a Dante and an Ezra Pound. There is o need for everyone to share my enthusiasm for the three high as- ounding tales of the seventeenth century—William Chamberlayne's tle read but wonderfully fantastic *Pharonnida*, Butler's *Hudibras*, and he *Hind and the Panther*. A taste for such also admits Quarles (in nallish doses) and much else that was more popular in the seventeenth intury than today. But every reader today must surely admire a pas- ge that a narrative poet in theory should deny himself as a digression, passage whose too liberal views were not only suspected but actively iught by almost all sides in Dryden's century.

> *Of all the tyrannies on humane kind*
> *The worst is that which persecutes the mind.*
> *Let us but weigh at what offence we strike,*
> *'Tis but because we cannot think alike.*
> *In punishing of this, we overthrow*
> *The laws of nations and of nature too.*
> *Beasts are the subjects of tyrannick sway,*
> *Where still the stronger on the weaker prey.*
> *Man onely of a softer mold is made;*
> *Not for his fellows ruine, but their aid.*
> *Created kind, beneficent and free,*
> *The noble image of the Deity.*
>
>   *One portion of informing fire was giv'n*
> *To Brutes, th' inferiour family of heav'n:*
> *The Smith divine, as with a careless beat,*
> *Struck out the mute creation at a heat:*
> *But, when arriv'd at last to humane race,*
> *The god-head took a deep consid'ring space:*
> *And, to distinguish man from all the rest,*
> *Unlock'd the sacred treasures of his breast:*
> *And mercy mix'd with reason did impart;*
> *One to his head, the other to his heart:*
> *Reason to rule, but mercy to forgive:*
> *The first is law, the last prerogative.*   (I. 239–6:

Dryden has interrupted the narrative to plead for moderation, but th
very plea soon becomes another narrative of God's differing creation c
the beasts and of man. That difference clashes with his characterizatic
in his fable, where beasts represent churches, and it clashes with h
narrative of those beasts. Or so it may seem to many, who may thir
that one such poem is enough. I value *The Hind and the Panther* for i
self and for its ventilating effect on certain theories about Dryden ¡
poet and man. No estimation of him in either guise can be thougl
proven until it applies to him in his plays, in his lyrics, in *The Hind ar
the Panther*, and in the *Fables*.

V

Fables Ancient and Modern

A decade after *The Hind and the Panther*, Dryden brought out his translation of Virgil (1697). Having lost his official posts and severed his connection with the theatre, despairing of support for the epic he wished to write, Dryden turned to translation. In that lay not only hopes for profit, but also of rapprochement with an age from which he was increasingly estranged by religion and by the important changes in sensibility accelerating after the Revolution of 1688. All men share the past, providing it can be renovated, and Dryden set himself the task of doing just that. His translation of the *Georgics*, 'the best poem by the best poet', as he said, probably approaches perfection as nearly as perfection can be judged. But his *Aeneis* remains the test case. It realizes his aim of rendering Virgil both in the Virgilian spirit and as if Virgil were his contemporary. The two aims conflict at many points, but by submitting fully to Virgil's language and by exploring the genius of English, Dryden achieved a responsible and yet independent result. Taken as a whole, or in those centuries-old favourites, Books IV and VI, the *Aeneis* shows that a great poet has given us the finest poetic version of one of the classics. It need only be enjoyed.

Most readers take to the *Fables* because its warm and spacious quality offers a sense of liberation.[1] The collection frees one from the oppressive yet contingent meaninglessness of our lives. It could not do so if it did not also free itself from the fears and rigours of seventeenth-century experience and from that merger of complexity and intellectual drive that marks Dryden's achievement in *Mac Flecknoe* and during the 1680s. The sense of freedom derives as well from the diversity of the works included. Two of Dryden's finest poems of complimentary address appear more or less at the beginning: *To the Dutchess of Ormond* and *To My Honour'd Kinsman, John Driden of Chesterton*. Two poems written

---

[1] The *Fables* have long been especially popular. Considering the length of the collection, publication at least a dozen times in the eighteenth century—apart from appearance in editions of Dryden's poems—must be taken as a remarkable proof of popularity. Since then, from Byron to our day, popular and critical estimation has remained high.

earlier appear more or less toward the end: *Alexander's Feast* and 'The
Monument of a Fair Maiden Lady'. The rest consists of translations
the first book of the *Iliad*, three stories from Boccaccio, five Chaucerian
poems (including *The Flower and the Leaf*, a charming but un-Chau
cerian poem then still thought canonical), and eight selections from
Ovid's *Metamorphoses*. In all, in the original handsome folio, the poems
extend to 558 (misnumbered) pages.

Such conspicuous variety contributes, as does Spenser's seeming
casualness, to our sense of liberation. Dryden was long past the age of
casualness, however, and although he eschewed the allegory that he
might have used, he found in Ovid, Boccaccio, and Chaucer examples
of masterpieces made up from borrowed material. Boccaccio and Chaucer order their works with 'framing' devices, as Ovid and Dryden do
not, except for touches at the beginning and end of each. Dryden's
long interest in Ovid puts him at one with his century in poetic preferences.[1] Fittingly, Ovid provides not only the largest number of stories
but also he and he alone the order of the stories taken. Recent study of
Ovid has done much to clarify his art, in particular the kind of epic he
wrote and the meanings he expressed in it.[2] Dryden's title attempts to
include the changes recounted by Ovid, the novelle of Boccaccio, and
the tales by Chaucer. Of the three kinds of *narratio* defined toward the
beginning of this discussion (*fabula, argumentum,* and *historia*) one finds
all three in *Fables* as easily as in the *Metamorphoses*. Comparing *Fables*
with Dryden's earlier poems, we discover however that the element of
historia has greatly decreased; that change must also have assisted in
giving Dryden and the reader a new freedom.

The *Fables* affords, then, that sense of variety moving toward
creative order that Dryden sought all his life and to which his favourite

[1] Of all poets first appearing before 1660 and published between 1600
and 1700, Ovid is second in popularity after Quarles—if popularity can
be judged by frequence of publication (recorded in Pollard and Red-
grave's *Short-Title Catalogue*, and Wing's continuation). Dryden himself
comes third and others follow these three at considerable distance.

[2] In *Ovid as an Epic Poet,* Cambridge, Mass., 1966, Brooks Otis makes
clear what had not been so in Ovid, and in much of Dryden's approach
to Ovid. It is a pity that Otis does not discuss Dryden's version.

…ord, harmony, is best applied.[1] He and his publisher, Jacob Tonson, …ad gained experience of assembling poetic miscellanies from the first … 1684 to the most recent, *Examen Poeticum* in 1693. The second, how-…ver, the *Sylvae* of 1685, offers the best precedent for *Fables*, both in the …lassical associations of the *silvae* or poetic 'Forrest' as Jonson put it, …nd in its effort to supply by editorial ordering a coherence of subject …nd theme. It will be recalled that the selections from Lucretius (in *…ylvae*) tell a story unintended by the original poet. In order to convey …esh things about human hope and experience, then, Dryden selected …ie works for *Fables* carefully, joined them with linking devices, and …rdered them into a varying but unified view of life.

The linking of one work with another in *Fables* has been discussed …reviously in such detail that a purely formal example will serve here. …n the full title of the first poem we are invited to move to the next: *…o the Dutchess of Ormond, With the following Poem of Palamon and Arcite, …om Chaucer.* Or, to convey again by formal example the larger rela-…ons, the last poem, *Cymon and Iphegenia, from Boccace* begins with an …xcursus spoken by the poet, a *poëta loquitur* addressed to the Duchess …f Ormonde and commenting on love and its place in poetry: 'Love's …ie Subject of the Comick Muse.' In the first Iliad, valour is the sub-…ct; in *Palamon and Arcite*, love and valour are the subject of the comic-…eroic muse. We seem to be taken back to the world of romance as de-…ned by Dryden's heroic plays, or indeed by his whole dramatic world.

Something happens to the earlier concerns as they are revisited in *…ables*. To take the poem most like a play, that cantata *Alexander's …east*, we recognize valour *a priori* in Alexander the Great. Before long …e also recognize the presence of 'The Comick Muse'. After Alexander …as drunk himself maudlin, the '*Lydian* Measures' struck by the musician …imotheus enable the beauty of the courtesan Thais to smite the con-…ueror.

---

[1] Dryden's 'harmony' is inclusive of a trope popular in the seventeenth century, *discordia concors*, and of ideas of the *musica humana* and *musica mundana* in speculative music. See the commentary on *A Song for St Cecilia's Day* (*Works*, III). That ode well shows how ordered vitality or dynamism constitutes harmony: the four elements 'In *order* to their stations *leap*' (l. 9, my stress).

> The Prince, unable to conceal his Pain,
>   Gaz'd on the Fair
>   Who caus'd his Care,
>   And sigh'd and look'd, sigh'd and look'd,
>   Sigh'd and look'd, and sigh'd again:
> At length, with Love and Wine at once oppress'd,
> The vanquish'd Victor sunk upon her Breast.   (109–15)

A principal note of the comedy here and throughout *Fables* is that of limitation, of what lies beyond the power or nature of man. Before considering other major emphases, the narrative expression of such limitation deserves clarifying.

Since dialogue is required of plays, it is no wonder that Dryden's dramatic characters talk. What is remarkable is their tendency to debate issues and to generalize about life. With some few exceptions, general debate and comment about life is exactly what Dryden does not allow the central characters of *Fables*. The protagonists generally act (Alexander is never quoted), and even their words are action, as in most plays. The generalizations exist indeed, but they are given to what may be termed the *raissoneurs*, the narrator's surrogates in the individual works. Here, for example, is Timotheus' comment in the passage just before the last quoted.

> War, he sung, is Toil and Trouble;
> Honour but an empty Bubble.
>   Never ending, still beginning,
> Fighting still, and still destroying,
>   If the World be worth thy Winning,
> Think, O think, it worth Enjoying.
>   Lovely Thais sits beside thee,
>   Take the Good the Gods provide thee.   (99–106)

The counterparts of Timotheus include Theseus in *Palamon and Arcite* (especially III. 1024–1134), the Nun's Priest in *The Cock and the Fox*, good King Numa in *Of the Pythagorean Philosophy*, and Dryden *in persona poëtae* in the poems to the Duchess of Ormonde and John Driden, as also elsewhere. As a result of the new technique, we readers are not drawn in so closely to the feverish concerns of Aureng-Zebe

Antony, Don Sebastian, or Alcmena (in *Amphitryon*). We gain perspective and ease. Also, the predominance of action proves simpler than the tightly woven design of idea and metaphor in Dryden's earlier non-dramatic poetry.

The *Fables* gradually assumes before us the shape of a highly episodic verse novel. The linkings and the narrative line lead us forward, but the return to subjects treated earlier gives a spiralling effect. *Alexander's Feast* again provides the suitable microcosm: in the middle five stanzas (II–VI) Timotheus speaks and Alexander does in five acts. Dryden amusedly comments on Alexandrian repetition,

> *Sooth'd with the Sound the King grew vain;*
> *Fought all his Battails o'er again;*
> *And thrice he routed all his Foes; and thrice he slew the slain.*
>
> (66–68)

Seven years before, Dryden had rendered the opening lines of Ovid's epic of changing forms.

> *Of Bodies chang'd to various Forms I sing:*
> *Ye Gods, from whom these Miracles did spring,*
> *Inspire my Numbers with Coelestial heat;*
> *Till I, my long laborious Work compleat:*
> *And add perpetual Tenour to my Rhimes,*
> *Deduc'd from Nature's Birth, to* Caesar's *Times.*

Since Ovid's span reached 'ab origine mundi/ad mea . . . tempora', Dryden's '*Caesar's* Times' is a characteristic historical emphasis. But when he came to adapt *Metamorphoses*, XV, for *Fables*, he stopped short of the paean to the Caesars. Not only does history now come in single spies and smaller battalions, but more importantly Dryden for once does not begin at the beginning and work forward to the future by means of a chronological or temporal order. Instead, he provides a cycle of search for the good life, a search successful only in the rare instances of the Good Parson and the Fair Maiden Lady.

The ultimate values remain as Christian as ever. Other values prove partial, whether they be valour, love, or the Pythagorean search for wisdom. The comic value of love stresses limitations, because the best exemplars of charity (the Parson, the Maiden Lady) and of conjugal

love (Baucis and Philemon, Ceyx and Alcyone) constitute a minority
however attractive. The inclusion of such ideal figures leads Dryden
from the more radically limited and insufficient single examples (the
incestuous Cinyras, for example) over the whole spectrum from temporal to eternal. Once seen by being read in its entirety, the spectrum
yields not merely the comedy of love but the *comédie humaine* with
glimpses of the *divina commedia*.

One of the donnish pleasures afforded by *Fables* is the comparison
of Dryden's poems with their originals, the long way about to the less
scholarly reader's conviction of unusual stylistic capacity. In *The Cock
and the Fox*, for example, Dryden actually expands on Chaucer's interest in dreams, as in the foolish merchant's rejection (twenty-three lines
to Chaucer's ten) of the validity of dreams. How well he puts it.

> *When Monarch-Reason sleeps, this Mimick wakes:*
> *Compounds a Medley of disjointed Things,*
> *A Mob of Coblers, and a Court of Kings.* (326–8)

We are drawn, as is Dryden, to assent. Yet the expounder is proved
wrong, at least in his small context. Dryden draws us in contrary ways
as does life. Such implicit dilemmas become explicit when the Nun's
Priest speaks of 'Predestination' (507–64). Somehow, God is omniscient,
prescient, and omnipotent—and yet man is free. Such a dilemma and
such a solution provide at once the basis for limitation and affirmation in
Fables. In the end, human imperfections endear us to humanity, proving at the same time the necessity for a higher immutable order. An
idyll here poises with tragedy there, heroism there matches illusion
here.

Humour, dissonances, and threats sustain a larger harmony. The
last fable, *Cymon and Iphigenia*, is introduced idealistically in the old
trope of love as education. It is told beautifully, but at the end there is
stealing of brides and murder—and final reconciliation. The endearing
or threatening imperfections of humanity require the consolation of
philosophy. Perhaps the finest moment of many in the *Fables* comes with
Theseus' consolation for the death of Palamon (III. 1024–1118). Dryden
accentuates the paganism of Chaucer's milieu by introducing neo-
Epicureanism: 'The Cause and spring of Motion' and 'the jarring Seeds

(Lucretius' favourite *semina* for Epicurean atoms).[1] And yet Dryden echoes the opening of *De Rerum Natura* in a Christian voice largely absent from Chaucer.

> *Then since those Forms begin, and have their End,*
> *On some unalter'd Cause they sure depend:*
> *Parts of the Whole are we; but God the Whole;*
> *Who gives us Life, and animating Soul.*   (1040–3)

That Christian God is not in Chaucer, but rather the divine principle ('the Movere') and the pagan equivalent, if in context it be equivalent ('Juppiter').

In a later portion of Theseus' speech, Dryden gives his hostages to change and human limitation.

> *So wears the paving Pebble in the Street,*
> *And Towns and Tow'rs their fatal Periods meet.*
> *So Rivers, rapid once, now naked lie,*
> *Forsaken at their Springs; and leave their Channels dry.*
> *So Man, at first a Drop, dilates with Heat,*
> *Then form'd, the little Heart begins to beat;*
> *Secret he feeds, unknowing in the Cell;*
> *At length, for Hatching ripe, he breaks the Shell,*
> *And struggles into Breath, and cries for Aid;*
> *Then, helpless, in his Mothers Lap is laid.*
> *He creeps, he walks, and issuing into Man,*
> *Grudges their Life, from whence his own began.*
> *Retchless of Laws, affects to rule alone,*
> *Anxious to reign, and restless on the Throne:*
> *First vegetive, then feels, and reasons last;*
> *Rich of Three Souls, and lives all three to waste.*   (1062–77)

At such, and indeed at greater length, since it is a characteristic of *Fables*, Dryden bids us face the deficiencies of human nature. It is vanity, but not all is vanity. The reconciliation Theseus at last offers recognizes tragedy by finding a larger harmony.

---

[1] For the philosophical import of these few words (and Dryden's entire passage), see Robert Hugh Kargon's excellent account, *Atomism in England from Hariot to Newton*, Oxford 1966.

> *What then remains, but after past Annoy,*
> *To take the good Vicissitude of Joy?*
> *To thank the gracious Gods for what they give,*
> *Possess our souls, and while we live, to live?*
> *Ordain we then two Sorrows to combine,*
> *And in one Point th' Extremes of Grief to join;*
> *That thence resulting Joy may be renew'd,*
> *As jarring Notes in Harmony conclude.*   (1111–18)

'From Harmony, from heav'nly Harmony / This universal Frame began' (*Song for St Cecilia's Day*, 1–2). And in harmony, *Palamon and Arcite* concludes.

Sufficient 'jarring Notes' sound in the *Fables*, but the harmony arises from larger concords. Dryden no more than any other poet creates here Milton's seamless web of fact (*factum*, the done) and mythic significance. In *Annus Mirabilis* 'fact' itself is not wholly one, and in his most important subsequent poems, action is more presumed than shown. In them possibly discordant worlds are harmonized not so much by plot as by the other symptoms of narrative I have described, as well as by Dryden's unusual powers of comparison, by his intellectual drive, and by his capacity to envision several things at once. No other English poet has Dryden's obsession with, or power over, that form of analogy more sustained than syntactic metaphor but less strict than allegory. And yet, nearing seventy, his always developing poetic powers found in *Fables* what is in some ways their maturest element. In a miscellany that is not miscellaneous, and in translations that yield original poems, Dryden created yet again something new. In its harmony of jarring notes the *Fables* offer a last testament to the much jarring integrity of seventeenth-century experience. Dryden relates at length the sorry and ennobling transactions among men and women, and periodically no little of the transactions between the temporal and the eternal. He had reason to depict the 'Annoy' that too often seems to dominate our lives as he reached the end of his life sick and an exile in his own loved *patria*. But his vision of 'Joy' did not falter, and the harmonious music includes that 'beyond the stars heard'. In no work is Dryden more the narrative poet or the *vir generosus*, in all the Latin senses of 'generous', than in his timeless *Fables Ancient and Modern*.

9: *Dryden and the Classics: With a look at His 'Aeneis'*

WILLIAM FROST

The days are, or ought to be, long past in which any well-informed critic could take the couplet poets of our 'Augustan' school at their own valuation as 'classical' writers.

C. S. LEWIS

[Dryden] was a good Latinist, well read in the Latin orators and poets, from whom he learnt compactness and force.

A. W. VERRALL

I

DRYDEN'S classicism, an enormous topic, includes two features of obvious initial interest: a constant series of minute technical problems to challenge the investigation of detective-scholars; and the larger dramatic spectacle of antiquity intelligently confronted by a period at once post-medieval and pre-Victorian. For example, a bibliographical discussion of an ancient author for whose reappearance Dryden wrote an introduction[1] tells us the following:

The earlier date of the second volume arose probably because the work was laid out in assignments, and the second volume was ready before the first. Woodward [the bookseller] was located in St Christopher's churchyard before he moved to Scalding-Alley. There is a break in the pagination of the second volume which skips from page 188 to page 359. The pagination of Volume I stops

[1] Hardin Craig, 'Dryden's Lucian', *Classical Philology*, XVI, 1921, 154.

with page 347, and it may be that the second volume, which was probably begun first, was filled out with matter in excess from the first volume. A second break in Volume IV, where the pagination drops back from 238 to 141, is less easily explained.

One may turn from this to a page of the new translation Dryden introduced:[1]

> We shall soon see, says she to me, whether you are the man you brag you are; for as my name is *Palaestra*, so was I never worsted in *Cupid's* Field. I accepted the Challenge, and she undress'd, telling me, Now the Stage is clear, prove your Manhood; and if I find you a capable vigorous young Man, I'll teach you some curiosities in these matters; Come strip, and to it. While you exert your Courage I'll be Umpire, and will give you Directions what to do; be you sure to obey my Orders. Sound the Charge, (says I then) and take care that our Engagement be warm and fierce, and show equally Conduct and Gallantry. At this, she being stark naked, Come, Sir, strip, strip, and take heed to the Word of Command. Anoint your Body with those Perfumes, and make ready. Advance my Thighs. Ground me on the Bed. Draw your Baggonet of Generation. Put it in the Muzzle of the Piece. Mount the Breach. Maintain your Ground. Push your Baggonet. Again. Again. Again. Briskly, my Lad. Courage. Advance. Make good your Footing. Attack again; but preserve your Fire. Now, now, now; Give fire! Oh, ye Gods! cry'd she, all in Rapture, how I expire in Extasie and Delight. The Fantasticalness of her Expressions made me less moved with the tumultuous Bliss, and without any Concern, when the Parly was sounded, My charming Lady, (says I to *Palaestra*), you see now how dextrous I am at my Arms, tho' you hudled over your Words of command with so much Precipitation.

One may turn (to repeat) from bibliography to contents with the reflection that, although Dryden's interest in Lucian may have been in part ideological ('The gist of Dryden's Defense [of Lucian's skepticism] is that Lucian was not Christian or an apostate, that Christianity probably

---

[1] *The Works of Lucian, Translated from the Greek by Several Eminent Hands*, 1711, Vol I, 117–19. Baggonet=bayonet. It is not clear whether Dryden actually saw the translation; but he knew Lucian.

appeared to him in a base form, and that he is after all not satirizing Christianity as such, but humbuggery and fanaticism'),[1] Dryden was also the classicist who had once defended his own explicitly phallic versions of Lucretius:

> *Endearments eager, and too brisk a bound,*
> *Throws off the Plow-share from the furrow'd Ground* . . .
>
> (IV. 282–3)

on the grounds that:

> without the least Formality of an excuse, I own it pleas'd me: and let my Enemies make the worst they can of this Confession.[2]

In what periods except our own and that of Dryden would such a confession have been even imaginable?

II

But the topic has many facets. Dryden's circumstances were also special in ways not necessarily shared with the late twentieth century; and he and Pope were not, of course, the only classicizing authors of our tongue. How deeply rooted in Greece and Rome more than one illustrious practitioner of English or American literature has been it takes but

---

[1] Craig 156.

[2] See *Works*, III 65, 12. There are currently two theories about what Dryden was doing in such Lucretian passages. The more complicated is that of Norman Austin ('Translation as Baptism', *Arion*, VII 1968, 595): 'In Lucretius IV Dryden diverges considerably from the original to render the clinical style of his author into a more "luscious English." We may suspect that his motive for the transformation was . . . to indict Epicureanism by exaggerating the salacious.' The simpler is that of Mary Gallagher ('Dryden's Translation of Lucretius', *Huntington Library Quarterly*, XXVIII, 1964, 23): 'Although he was no Lord Rochester, Dryden shared the Restoration taste for explicitly sexual poetry and drama.' According to T. F. Mayo, *Epicurus in England, 1650–1675*, Dallas, 1934, 186, 'Both Creech's edition of Lucretius and his translation [which preceded Dryden's Lucretius] were reissued several times, the translation assuming its final form in 1722, when Dryden's verses were used to fill the gaps left by Creech's pudency.'

a few scholarly titles to remind us.[1] Dryden and Pope, however, beyond all English or American writers, stand out, in this regard, for their special relation to that early European past. With them, antiquity was more than roots, it was the continuing basis of their careers, and they remained the spokesmen of its values all their lives. From the *Pastorals* to the *Epilogue to the Satires*, Pope was never less than an active classicist. For Dryden, much the same is true of his several professional careers: as a dramatist, an original poet,[2] a critic,[3] and a translator.[4]

To see the variety and specificity of Dryden's lifelong classical concern, one need only run rapidly through a roster of his plays and the prose pieces with which he introduced them to a wider public. At the beginning, in 1663 or thereabouts, Dryden's poem 'To the Lady Castlemaine, Upon her Incouraging His First Play' compares the King's mistress, Dryden's supporter, first to Cato siding with the losers in Lucan's *Pharsalia* and then to a *deus ex machina* descending upon the stage in ancient Greece and thus preserving the ill-made play by a final

[1] *Chaucer and the Roman Poets* (Edgar Finley Shannon, Cambridge, Mass., 1929). *Shakespeare and the Classics* (J. A. K. Thomson, London, 1952). *Milton and the Roman Elegists* (Stanley Koehler, Princeton, 1941). *Wordsworth's Reading of Roman Prose* (Jane Worthington, New Haven, 1946). *The Platonism of Shelley* (J. A. Notopoulos, Durham, N. C., 1949). *Thoreau: The Quest and the Classics* (Ethel Seybold, New Haven, 1951). *Matthew Arnold and the Classical Tradition* (Warren D. Anderson, Ann Arbor, 1965).

[2] See my *Selected Works of Dryden*, 2nd ed. New York 1971, 6–7 (on *Mac Flecknoe*); Lillian Feder's article (n. 1, p. 275); her unpublished dissertation 'Dryden's Interpretation and Use of Latin Poetry and Rhetoric', Minnesota, 1951 (particularly ch. v, on Juvenal, Persius, and Dryden); Roper 44–47; F. Olivero, 'Virgil in XVII and XVIII Century English Literature', *Poetry Rev.*, XXI, 1930, 171–192; and especially Miner, *passim* (for example, at all the entries referred to in the index under 'Virgil').

[3] See below, Section III.

[4] The importance of Dryden's translations to his career is noticed in my *Dryden and the Art of Translation*, New Haven 1955, 1969, 1–3; and, for his Virgil in a very practical sense, in John Barnard's 'Dryden, Tonson, and the Subscriptions for the 1697 Virgil' *Papers of the Bibliographical Society of America*, LVII, 1963, 129–51.

coup de théâtre. In 1664, his Dedication of *The Rival Ladies* to Roger Boyle, Earl of Orrery, compares that nobleman to Xenophon and Augustus Caesar in his effort to combine a literary career with a military or political one; and one scene of the play itself takes its situation and some of its dialogue from the *Satyricon* of Petronius.[1] For *The Indian Queen* (acted 1664), not obviously a classical play, important plot parallels have nevertheless been detected in Homer, Virgil, and Heliodorus.[2] To *The Indian Queen's* sequel, *The Indian Emperour*, Dryden prefixed an essay defending his recent *Of Dramatick Poesie*, and including citations of Seneca, Julius Caesar, Lucan, Horace, Homer, and Aristotle. The play itself shows influences of Virgil and ancient stoicism.[3] Again, the preface to *An Evening's Love*, or *The Mock Astrologer* (1668) discusses poetic justice in comedy and tragedy, mingling examples drawn from Plautus, Terence, and Euripides. In the preface to *Tyrannic Love* a year later, Dryden defends a line in one of his prologues by citing Horace, and a line in *The Indian Emperour* by quoting Virgil.

Dryden's essay, 'Of Heroic Plays', printed with *The Conquest of Granada, Part I*, in 1672, discusses the theory of epic poetry,[4] with quotations, including some from Homer's Greek. In 'The Defense of the Epilogue' to the same play, Dryden applies Horace's generalizations about new and old words to Jonson and to himself. An Elizabethan (according to Dryden) may be as serviceable to a Restoration writer as Lucilius was to Horace a century later. Dryden compares the retirement of older English writers (without the social life characteristic of the Restoration) to that of Epicurus in his garden, a theme continued a

---

[1] See *Works*, VIII 96, 268–9, 276, 281.

[2] See A. B. Parsons, 'The English Heroic Play', *MLR*, XXXIII, 1938, 9, cited in *Works* VIII, 283 and 289.

[3] Reuben A. Brower, 'Dryden's Epic Manner and Virgil', *PMLA*, LV, 1940, rptd in H. T. Swedenberg, *Essential Articles for the Study of John Dryden*, Hamden, Conn., 1966, 469–70; and John A. Winterbottom, 'Stoicism in Dryden's Tragedies', *JEGP*, LXI, 1962, 868–883; both cited in *Works*, IX 327–30.

[4] The extent of Dryden's reading, traditionalism, and originality on this topic has been well clarified by H. T. Swedenberg, Jr., in his *Theory of the Epic in England 1650–1800*, Berkeley and Los Angeles 1944, 54–57.

year later in the epistle dedicatory to Dryden's *Assignation*. Dedicating
the play to Sir Charles Sedley, Dryden parallels his own association with
literary and titled friends to the happy conversation and friendship
shared by Horace, Virgil, Ovid, Tibullus, and Maecenas.

For the propaganda play *Amboyna* next year (1673) Dryden supplied
an epilogue beginning and ending with reminiscences of Greek and
Roman history. His Apology prefixed to the quasi-Miltonic *State of
Innocence* (1674) is full of passages and citations from the masters of
ancient criticism, Aristotle, Horace, and Longinus, as well as references
to Apollonius, Theocritus, and other ancient poets. The epistle dedicating *Aureng-zebe* to Mulgrave (1676) contains much Lucretius, also
other ancients, and a long quotation from Cicero at the end.

In the preface to *All for Love* (1678), Dryden, besides contrasting
Nero and Maecenas, compares Racine's *Phèdre* to its original in Euripides, making the famous witticism about Racine having turned Euripides's heroic Hippolytus into the elegant and amorous Monsieur
Hippolyte. The *Oedipus* of Dryden and Lee (printed 1679) has been
regarded by some—Scott, for one—as more modelled on Sophocles than
on either Seneca or Corneille. Dryden's Preface to *Troilus and Cressida*
(1679) parallels Shakespeare with Aeschylus as a pair of elder, difficult
dramatic poets; cites Euripides's *Iphigenia* as a precedent for some of
Dryden's own versions of Shakespeare; quotes Longinus (in translation but with a bit of Hesiodic Greek); and paraphrases Aristotle on
'The Grounds of Criticism in Tragedy'.

In 1690, Dryden supplies *Don Sebastian* with a dedication to Leicester explicitly composed in the vein of Cicero writing to Atticus. In the
same year his epistle dedicatory to *Amphitryon* (a play modelled on
Plautus and Molière) draws a comparison between Dryden writing to
Sir William Gower, and Ovid writing a lamentable epistle from Pontus.
(Under William III, Dryden felt as though he were in exile.) The
Preface to *Cleomenes* (1692) points to Dryden's sources in Plutarch and
perhaps Polybius; Creech's translation of Plutarch's life of Cleomenes
was printed with the play. For *Love Triumphant* (1693–4) Dryden wrote
an epistle dedicatory to Salisbury in which he cites Menander and
Terence. And, finally, the next year, when his son John's play *The
Husband His Own Cuckhold* was printed, Dryden supplied, in Latin, a

Virgilian title-page motto—'Let both his father Aeneas and his Uncle Hector spur him on' (*Aeneid*, III, 343)—associating himself and Howard with the same two Roman heroes he had many years earlier invoked for comic purposes in *Mac Flecknoe*:

> *Let Father* Flecknoe *fire thy mind with praise*
> *And Uncle* Ogleby *thy envy raise.* (ll. 174-5)

Everywhere one looks one finds evidence that for three decades as a practising dramatist Dryden continually put his plays, himself, and his dedicatees into a kaleidoscopic variety of classical contexts.

III

The same is also true, and needs no demonstration, of his critical prose, his original poems, and above all his translations, to one of which, his *Aeneis*, we shall soon be turning. But first, what are we to make of such enduring preoccupation with an ancient past? In connection with any work of Dryden's, or any ancient writer relevant to Dryden—in connection with Dryden's whole concept of his profession—a series of questions seems naturally to arise, and has provoked investigation on several fronts.

First—the characteristic academic question—how much did Dryden actually *know*, how first-hand is his classicism (could he read Greek, for example?); and where did he acquire his expertise? Not a sabre-toothed classical scholar in the full-blown Miltonic sense[1] Dryden is yet a

---

[1] Sketched by John Wain in Frank Kermode's *The Living Milton*, 1960, 2: 'Milton belonged to the first generation of fully-qualified, card-carrying classical scholars, as Housman did to the last; he had the literary tastes and interests of that powerful enclave who dominated Western European education unbrokenly from his day to ours. Given a little time to catch up with the latest work, he could have walked straight into a classical professorship in Jowett's day. (There is an emendation of Milton's in the received text of the *Bacchae* of Euripides.) He was the first, and immeasurably the greatest of the 'scholar-poets,' as that term was delimited and defined by the eighteenth and nineteenth centuries.' Dryden wrote no original poetry in Latin or Greek; Milton remains one of the best Anglo-Latin poets.

sounder working Latinist, or even Hellenist, than his off-hand manner has sometimes led incautious critics and editors to assume;[1] and he evidently moved easily in the learned literary discussions conducted by writers like Dacier and Rymer during his day.[2] His controversial preface to *All for Love*, for example, has been described as 'a piece of epideictic rhetoric devoted to a censure of Rochester' in which Dryden takes his cue 'from Juvenal's eighth satire on the subject of true and false members of the peerage' and uses it 'as a framework to reprove the Earl for calling things by their wrong names'.[3] The classics both in

[1] The classic study of this matter is J. McG. Bottkol's 'Dryden's Latin Scholarship', *MP*, XL, 1953, 241–55, rptd in H. T. Swedenberg's *Essential Articles*; cf. also my *Dryden and the Art of Translation*, 34–36, and 'More about Dryden as a Classicist' in *N & Q* for January, 1972. For the sources of Dryden's knowledge, see G. F. Russell Baker's *Memoir of Richard Busby* (Dryden's schoolmaster), 1895; and for his use of Boileau's translation of Longinus, Alfred Rosenberg, *Longinus in England*, Berlin 1917, 21. On his Virgil, see Arvid Løsnes, 'Dryden's *Aeneis* and the Delphin Virgil' in Maren-Sofie Røstvig, *The Hidden Sense*, Oslo 1963.

[2] Editing his Dedication to *Examen Poeticum*, I was startled to find that a very pointed Virgilian quotation tossed back and forth between Rymer and him—*quantum mutatus* ('how changed')—at the end of the dedication's first paragraph [cf. *Paradise Lost*, I. 84]—had been annotated by none of Dryden's several previous editors. [But cf. C. A. Moore, *Restoration Literature*, New York 1934, 555, an exception discovered since this note was written.] So striking and so relevant is the passage in the *Aeneid* [II 274], when once discovered, that I formed the theory that Malone, Scott, Saintsbury, and Ker must have refrained from a note only for fear of insulting their readers' intelligence; but *tempora mutantur*. In Dryden's day, certainly, no annotation was needed: he knew well enough that Rymer, in a two-word jibe, was comparing the Dryden-Lee *Oedipus* (in contrast to Sophocles's) to the mutilated body of Hector after Achilles has dragged it around Troy: 'torn by the car . . . and black with gory dust, his swollen feet pierced with thongs' (Loeb translation).

[3] Frank L. Huntley, 'Dryden, Rochester and the Eighth Satire of Juvenal', *PQ*, XVIII, 1939, 269–84; quoted from Swedenberg, *Essential Articles*, 104.

quoted bits and as longer structures were counters in a game in which Dryden could more than hold his own.

Second, beyond his philological competence and his ease in referring to specific passages, how well did Dryden understand the classics he worked from? Obviously not a blind 'slavish adulation' or mere copying, to what extent was his relation to them really flexible and rich in nourishment for his age and ours? The beginning of an answer to this question is to be found, I think, in what we know of Dryden as critic, and in Dryden's interest in, and use of, literary genres.

If by literary critic we understand a writer whose chief original work is continually accompanied by explicit analysis and discussion of literary procedures, Dryden is the first English critic, the predecessor and inspiration of Johnson, Arnold, and Eliot; but he does not invent criticism—his own work has its origins in the first European critics, Aristotle, Cicero, Horace, Quintilian, and Longinus; in their French followers during the seventeenth century; and in such English forerunners as Sidney and Jonson. With the ancient tradition Dryden's criticism re-establishes living continuity.[1] From Aristotle Dryden takes the very idea of criticism, as a valid or probable series of abstract notions deduced from literary creations;[2] and from Horace he takes the model of a practising critic who is also an original poet. It has been said that if Horace's *Ars Poetica* were to be lost, it could almost be reconstructed from quotations in Dryden's essays: 'to trace the influence of Dryden on subsequent literary criticism is, to a large extent, to trace the influence of Horace'.[3] And Dryden of course does more than recapitulate or re-enact: he pushes beyond, incorporates new problems—for ex-

---

[1] Dryden's criticism has been studied in relation to Aristotle by Hoyt Trowbridge, 'The Place of Rules in Dryden's Criticism', *MP*, XLIV, 1946, 84–96, reprinted in Swedenberg, *Essential Articles*, 112–34; to Horace by Amanda Ellis in 'Horace's Influence on Dryden', *PQ*, IV, 1925, 39–60; to Longinus by Rosenberg in *Longinus in England*, 19–29; and to Cicero and Quintilian by Lillian Feder in 'John Dryden's Use of Classical Rhetoric', *PMLA*, LXIX, 1954, 1258–78, reprinted in Swedenberg, *Essential Articles*, 493–518.

[2] The topic of Trowbridge's essay, cited in the preceding note.

[3] Ellis 57.

ample, the place of riming speech in drama or the position of a new luminary, Chaucer, in literary history.

As for genre, Dryden is at once a practitioner, analyst, and deviser of new ones. Not only do his original verse epistles, for example, follow classical models even to recapturing their tone;[1] but (together with Jonson) he has been credited with using the verse epistle as a basis for what becomes in his hands virtually a new genre, characteristically Restoration but of enduring value: the stage prologue-and-epilogue.[2] In satire, he not only writes the first and the finest English theoretical statement to take full account of the meaning of 'satire' in antiquity and in his own century, but he also devises, in *Mac Flecknoe* and *Absalom and Achitophel* two new 'satiric' genres: the mock coronation poem, later developed by Pope; and the satirical heroic brief epic, an achievement transcending formal categories and never successfully imitated by any one.[3]

This creative element constantly at work in Dryden's traffic with the classics prompts two final questions about his dealings with them: what is his effect on them (how does he change our image or understanding of antiquity?); and what is theirs on him? Dryden affected later con-

---

[1] See, e.g., the comments of Hoffman on the 'middle style' of the epistles to Congreve and to John Driden, 133ff.; and Jay A. Levine, 'The Status of the Verse Epistle Before Pope', *SP*, LIX, 1962, 658–684 and 'John Dryden's Epistle to John Driden', *JEGP*, LXIII, 1964, 450–74.

[2] Reuben A. Brower, 'An Allusion to Europe: Dryden and Poetic Tradition' in *Alexander Pope: The Poetry of Allusion*, reprinted in Bernard N. Schilling's *Dryden: A Collection of Critical Essays*, Englewood Cliffs, N J, 1963, 46: 'The prologue, as used by Jonson to give instruction in literary taste, is a theatrical form of the Roman epistle.' Hoffman, 39ff., discusses classical influences on Dryden's work in this form.

[3] Mary Claire Randolph in her 'Formal Verse Satire' (*PQ*, XXI, 1942, 368–84) makes the point that although Dryden wrote no original satires in the classical sense, he was the first Englishman to relate his theoretical statement to continental thought, especially that of Casaubon and his epitomizer Dacier. Cf. my 'Dryden's Theory and Practice of Satire' in Bruce King, Dryden's *Mind and Art*, Edinburgh, 1969; and 'Dryden and "Satire"', *SEL*, XI, 1971, 401–16.

eptions about classical authors most directly by translating ancient
poets.[1] Dryden's Persius, for example, is one of a group of Restoration
and eighteenth-century poetic versions, extending from his own time to
that of Gifford, which have given English-speaking readers an extraordinarily lively and inventive simulacrum of that difficult poet's resources.[2] Dryden's *Aeneis*, to take a more complex project, has been
seen as subtly transforming the Aeneas of Virgil into a more virile, less
flattering, less sensitive epitome of the ideal prince, more fully embodying Dryden's royalist ideals.[3] As for the effect of the classics on Dryden's
original verse, this begins with the heroic couplet itself, now understood
to have descended to Dryden through a long line of English versifiers
as a naturalization of the Latin elegiac distich;[4] and includes much of
Dryden's characteristic vocabulary for poems[5] as well as his sense of
how to construct a verse paragraph in the Virgilian manner.[6]

[1] For three Greek prose writers, Lucian, Polybius, and Plutarch, Dryden
served rather as sponsor than direct translator: see L. R. M. Strachan,
'Dryden's character of Polybius', *N & Q*, 11th ser., IX, 1914, 103–105;
and Hardin Craig, 'Dryden's Lucian', above, n. 1, p. 267. Craig also cites
Dryden's enthusiasm for the translation his biography of Plutarch introduced, as a reason for his labours on Lucian.

[2] Cf. my 'English Persius: The Golden Age', *Eighteenth-Century Studies*,
II, 1968–69, 77–101.

[3] Cf. T. W. Harrison, 'Dryden's *Aeneid*' in Bruce King's *Dryden's Mind
and Art*, 143–67.

[4] See Ruth Wallerstein, 'The Development of the Rhetoric and Metre
of the Heroic Couplet', *PMLA*, L, 1936, 166–209, rptd in Bernard N.
Schilling, *Essential Articles for the Study of English Augustan Back-
grounds*, Hamden, Conn., 1961, 198–250; and George Williamson, 'The
Rhetorical Pattern of Neoclassical Wit', *MP*, XXXIII, 1935, 55–81.

[5] See Reuben Brower, 'Dryden's Poetic Diction and Virgil', *PQ*, XVIII,
1939, 211–17.

[6] See Brower, 'Dryden's Epic Manner and Virgil', *PMLA*, LV, 1940,
113–138, reprinted in Swedenberg's *Essential Articles*, 466–492; Brower
includes an example of a 'long and rather beautiful reworking of
Virgil's description of Venus' in Dryden's *Tyrannic Love*; and a splendid parallel between a passage in *Aeneid* II and *All for Love* (Swedenberg, *Essential Articles*, 471, 476).

IV

Dryden's most direct relationship to the classics was through verse translating, an activity he embarked on in mid-career (1680) with his contributions to *Ovid's Epistles*; by the last decade of his life it was his main preoccupation and source of sustenance, not even coming to an end with the 1700 *Fables* (containing *Iliad* I and large parts of the *Metamorphoses*), for his Ovid's *Art of Love*, Book I, and two elegies were published posthumously. The central achievement was his *Works of Virgil* (written 1693–7; published 1697; second edition 1698).

In composing his Virgil Dryden consulted, of course in Latin, the most recent European scholarship; and in addition studied the work of a number of earlier English Virgil translators and at least one French predecessor[1]—studied them and felt free, in the usual Renaissance manner, to incorporate parts of their results. To know how Dryden arrived at his version of a particular line or even phrase of Virgil, it is clear that we may have to reconstruct, as far as possible, a considerable library of learning.

There is, finally, the question of the value of his efforts—for us, for seventeenth-century enthusiasts, for classicists, for anyone who reads poetry. Dryden's preface was characteristically modest—

> Lay by *Virgil*, I beseech your Lordship . . . when you take up my Version [he wrote to Mulgrave]; and it will appear a passable Beauty when the Original Muse is absent: But like *Spencer's* false *Florimel* made of Snow, it melts and vanishes, when the true one comes in sight.[2]

Twentieth-century readers—and there have been a series of editions in

[1] On this matter, see Helene M. Hooker, 'Dryden's *Georgics* and English Predecessors', *Huntington Library Quarterly*, IX, 1945, 273–310; J. McG. Bottkol's comments on her article in *PQ*, XXVI, 1947, 118–19; L. Proudfoot, *Dryden's Aeneid and Its Seventeenth Century Predecessors*, New York 1960 (mainly about Book IV); my review of Proudfoot in *Classical Philology*, LVII, 1962, 118–21; and Arvid Løsnes, 'Dryden's *Aeneid* and the Delphin Virgil'. These partial attacks on an unwieldy topic nevertheless indicate the outlines of what remains to be known.

[2] Dedication of *Aeneis*, Kinsley, III 1059.

our century[1]—have generally responded more warmly. Perhaps the qualities, strengths, and weaknesses of what Dryden could do can be suggested very concretely by some extracts from the opening books of the *Aeneid*, in which the earliest verse translation Dryden theoretically could have studied,[2] that of Gavin Douglas into Middle Scots (completed by 1513) may serve as a foil, parallel, and contrast to his own work.[3] The fact of Douglas's version being in Scots rather than English seems to have made no difference to subsequent translators, for the two languages were, then as now, often very close. To take only one example, Surrey's blank verse renditions of Books II and IV, first printed in the 1550s, are heavily influenced by Gavin Douglas.[4]

To start, then, with the storm with which the *Aeneid* itself commences (in each case, I will give Douglas first)[5]

[1] I know of the following: *Works of Virgil*, London and New York, Chandos Classics, 19—?; *Works of Virgil*, World's Classics 1903; *Aeneid* Selections, ed. Bruce Pattison, Scholar's Library 1938; *Aeneid*, New York 1944; *Works of Virgil*, introd. by James Kinsley, 1961; *Aeneid*, ed. Robert Fitzgerald, New York 1965. Dryden translated the *Eclogues*, *Georgics*, and *Aeneid*; not the minor poems.

[2] There is a theory that Dryden 'does not appear to have known Douglas's work' (Robert Fitzgerald, Dryden's *Aeneid of Virgil*, 18); but no study of the question seems to have been undertaken.

[3] Douglas's version is the only one to have been preferred to Dryden's by any competent judges, so far as I know, in the last quarter-century. See C. S. Lewis, *History of English Literature in the Sixteenth Century*, Oxford 1954, 84–86; Douglas Bush, *Mythology and the Romantic Tradition in English Poetry*, Cambridge, Mass. 1937, 6, 17; and Robert Bridges, *Ibant Obscuri*, Oxford 1916, 139. E. M. W. Tillyard, *The English Epic and its Background*, London 1954, 340, calls it 'probably the best translation of one of the great epics till Dryden and Pope'.

[4] See the detailed analysis in Emrys Jones's edition of Surrey's poems, Oxford 1964, 134–40; and Florence Ridley, 'Surrey's Debt to Gavin Douglas', *PMLA*, LXXVI, 1961, 25–33.

[5] Text of Dryden from Kinsley; of Douglas from the edition of John Small, Edinburgh, 1874. 'Now the stout ship of Ilioneus, now of brave Achates, and that wherein Abas sailed and that of aged Aletes, the storm has mastered; with side-joints loosened, all let in the hostile flood and gape at every seam' (Loeb translation of *Aeneid*, I 120–4).

> . . . *and the strang barge tho*
> *Bair Ylioneus, and scho that bair also*
> *Forcy Achates, and scho that bair Abbas,*
> *And scho quhairin ancyant Alethes was*
> *The storme ourset, raif ruvis and syde semis;*
> *Thai all leckit, and salt water stremis*
> *Fast bullerand in at every ryft and boir.*[1]

> *The stoutest Vessel to the Storm gave way,*
> *And suck'd through loosen'd Planks the rushing Sea.*
> Ilioneus *was her Chief:* Alethes *old,*
> Achates *faithful,* Abas *young and bold*
> *Endur'd not less: their Ships, with gaping Seams,*
> *Admit the Deluge of the briny Streams.*   (I. 170–5

Dryden has departed from the *fides Achates* school of translation here
to achieve his effect of rapid forward motion, touching quickly on per
son after person, rather in the manner of a pointer moving accurately
from spot to spot on a map. The four men in his second couplet, with
their static attributes of leadership, moral qualities, and age-placement
are centred in the midst of two swirling inanimate seascapes. Douglas
like Virgil withholding his subject and predicate ('the storme ourset')
piles up a gradual initial accumulation of direct objects in the form of
relative clauses (non-Virgilian) to be overset by the storm in his fifth
line. These clauses come to a climax in line four, whose orotund
Biblical sound, due partly to the medial trochaic substitution, gives a
suitably exalted tone. The Bishop,[3] perhaps translating with a slightly

---

[1] Douglas follows Virgil's rhetorical pattern, except for using more lines.
'Forcy' Achates imitates Virgil's *fortis Achatae.*
[2] His 'faithful' in the third line is not any more literally faithful than
are his separation and rearrangement of parts. However, he does get
two men into each line, like Virgil in 125–6: *Jam validam Ilionei navem,
jam fortis Achatae; | Et qua vectus Abas, & qua grandaevus Alethes* (text
from Ruaeus's second edition: see Løsnes, 'Dryden's Aeneis', 119).
Dryden's 'briny' in the last line quoted could be a reminiscence of
Douglas's not easily forgotten wind-up here; none of Dryden's other
predecessors mention the unVirgilian 'salt' at this point.
[3] Douglas was Bishop of Dunkeld.

Old Testament touch, is impressed by the tempest, and more contempla-
ive than Dryden. The onomatopoeia of the last couplet is the sort of
thing which has helped give Douglas's version its lasting popularity.

During the Aeneas-Venus interview later in Book I (Venus has asked
Aeneas's identity), Douglas's Aeneas[1]

> *Said, O thou goddes, gif I sall begin*
> *And tell our labour frome the formest end,*
> *To heir our storeis set thou wald attend,*
> *Or I maid end, Vesper the evin sterne brycht*
> *Suld close the hevin and end the dais lycht.*
> *We are of ancyant Troye, gif euir ʒe*
> *The name of Troye hes hard in this cuntre* . . .

In Dryden, the hero

> . . . *replyes:*
> *Cou'd you with Patience hear, or I relate,*
> *O Nymph! the tedious Annals of our Fate!*
> *Thro' such a train of Woes if I shou'd run,*
> *The day wou'd sooner than the Tale be done!*   (I. 510–15)

In Gavin Douglas (once again closer to specific details of the Latin,
although giving five lines for Virgil's three), the narrative voice dwells
lovingly on the act of narration itself; gradually twilight descends (as
his Aeneas imagines the possible scene) while the woes are still unfold-
ing. For Dryden,[2] any suggestion of garrulity is *out*. What is to be un-
folded is so important that each detail must be lucidly and energetically
explicated; otherwise 'the day wou'd sooner than the Tale be done',
and what a pity!

Soon Aeneas encounters the splendours of Dido's palace:[3]

[1] 'O goddess, should I, tracing back from the first beginning, go on to
tell, and thou have desire to hear the story of our woes, sooner would
heaven close and evening lay the day to rest (*Ante diem clauso componet
Vesper Olympo*)': Loeb *Aeneid*, I. 372–4.

[2] Who drops Vesper but follows Sandys, Ogilby, and Lauderdale in im-
porting 'Annals' from Virgil's *annales* in l. 373.

[3] 'Brazen was its threshold uprising on steps; bronze plates were its
lintel-beams, on doors of bronze creaked the hinges':—Loeb *Aeneid*,
I 628–31.

The entre rais with hie stagis of bras,
With brass also the cupplis fesnyt was;
The brasin durris iargis on the marble hirst.

On Brazen Steps the Marble Threshold rose,
And brazen Plates the Cedar Beams inclose:
The Rafters are with brazen Cov'rings crown'd,
The lofty Doors on brazen Hinges sound.   (I. 628–31)

To bring about his fourfold 'brazen' arrangement Dryden has doubled
Virgil's lintel-beams, providing both beams and rafters. His four lines
with the repeated adjective moving backward in position in the second
couplet suggest a row of beams themselves, the placing on the page
being architectural, visual, and geometric. Douglas, more oral-aural
here, tries for the creek: 'iargis on the marble hirst'. An excellent palace
in each translator.

Earlier in Book I, Jupiter had reassured Venus that Rome would
actually be founded in due course:[1]

Away sic dreid, Citheria, be nocht afferd,
For of thi lynage vnchangit remanis the weird.
As thou desiris, the cietie thou sall se,
And of Lavyne the promist wallis he;
Eik thou sall rais abufe the sterrit sky
The manfull Eneas, and him deify.

Daughter, dismiss thy Fears: To thy desire
The Fates of thine are fix'd, and stand entire.
Thou shalt behold thy wish'd Lavinian *Walls,*
And, ripe for Heav'n, when Fate Aeneas *calls,*
Then shalt thou bear him up, sublime, to me; . . .
                                                                    (I. 350–4)

Douglas is an especially apt foil to Dryden here, where he not un-
characteristically shows his strong sense of the integrity of the indi-

[1] 'Spare thy fear, Lady of Cythera; thy children's fates abide un-
moved. Thou shalt see Lavinium's city and its promised walls; and thou
shalt raise on high (*sublimem*) to the starry heaven great-souled
Aeneas': Loeb *Aeneid*, I 257–60.

vidual line, couplet, or passage of his own verse—a sense undoubtedly inherited from his master, Chaucer. In this passage Dryden's heavy line-by-line alliteration at the start, followed by the complex distortion of normal word order in his fourth line, helps make Zeus's words to Aphrodite almost sculptural in his rendition. In Douglas, other methods serve a comparable purpose. The fine sentence-inversion in line two, for example, makes its syntax a contrast with that of Dryden's simpler, more direct first couplet. Strong accents on the key words *rais, sky, Aeneas,* and *deify* undergird Douglas's third couplet.

The four preceding instances have shown some of the ways in which Dryden and Douglas, each an excellent practitioner of the couplet, nevertheless differ markedly in style and translating method. Here are two further illustrations, the first from the initial encounter of Aeneas and Dido:[1]

> *How, say me, ʒonkeris, saw ʒe walkand heir,*
> *By aventure ony of my sisteres deir,*
> *The cace of arrowis taucht by hir syde,*
> *And cled into the spottit linx hyde,*
> *Or with lowde cry followand the chace*
> *Eftir the fomy bair, in ther solace?*
> *Thus said Venus. And hir sone agane*
> *Answeris and saide: Trewlie, maidin, in plane*
> *Nane of thi sisteris did I heir ne se;*
> *Bot, O thou virgine, quham sall I call the?*
> *Thi visage semis na mortale creature;*
> *Nor thi voce soundis nocht lik to humane nature* . . .

> *Ho! Strangers! have you lately seen, she said,*
> *One of my Sisters, like my self array'd;*
> *Who crost the Lawn, or in the Forest stray'd?*

[1] ' "Ho!" she cries, "tell me, youths, if haply ye have seen a sister of mine here straying, girt with quiver and a dappled linx's hide or pressing with shouts on the track of a foaming boar." Thus Venus; and thus in answer Venus' son began: "None of thy sisters have I heard or seen— but by what name should I call thee, O maiden? for thy face is not mortal nor has thy voice a human ring . . ." ': Loeb *Aeneid*, I. 321–8.

> *A Painted Quiver at her Back she bore;*
> *Vary'd with Spots, a* Linx's *Hide she wore:*
> *And at full Cry pursu'd the tusky Boar?*
> *Thus* Venus: *Thus her Son reply'd agen;*
> *None of your Sisters have we heard or seen,*
> *O virgin! or what other Name you bear*
> *Above that stile; O more than mortal fair!*
> *Your Voice and Meen Celestial Birth betray!*   (I. 443–53)

Unlike Dryden, Douglas occasionally prefers to blur the edges of his couplets by an unemphatic opening ('By aventure') or close ('in ther solace'). Dryden's geometrical planning, shown in his twice placing the 'Sisters' phrase at the beginning of a line, gives him here an almost ballad-like echo effect ('One of my Sisters . . . None of your Sisters'), a clear contrast to Douglas's 'ony . . . Nane' and his use of 'deir' (another light couplet-ending) in the first phrase.[1]

Despite the contrast, however, it seems to me likely that Douglas is the predecessor whom, if anyone, Dryden is translating 'against' in this passage. Douglas is the only one except Phaer to translate Virgil's *tegmine* (l. 327) as 'hyde' rather than 'skin'; the only one except Ogilby to end a line with anything like Dryden's 'heard or seen' in his fourth couplet; and the only one (without exception) to render Virgil's *Sic Venus: at Veneris contra sic filius orsus* (325) by a line beginning with 'Thus' and 'Venus,' and ending with 'agane'. I believe the working model, the prototype Dryden revised in creating his version of this famous encounter, was almost surely Douglas.

A further reason for so thinking is the similar length of the two versions, eleven lines in Dryden to Douglas's twelve. Douglas is often

---

[1] Douglas's 'cace of arrowis' may illustrate one of the things Dryden perhaps had in mind when he spoke of Chaucer's 'want of Words in the Beginning of our Language' (Preface to *Fables*, Kinsley, III 1457); for Douglas is Chaucerian here (cf. *Knight's Tale*, ll. 2080, 2058). 'Quiver', though dating from 1300 or earlier, never gets into Chaucer. Compare Douglas's 'arrow caice' for *pharetram* in *Aeneid* I 504; and the complex periphrases he is forced into for lack of the word 'trident' (no *OED* instance before 1599) at *Aeneid* I 142 and 149 (see below, the first example in section V).

longer. Though each poet is copious, Douglas has 1326 lines (roughly iambic pentameter) to Dryden's 1065 in Book I. A short passage from early in Book II (Hector's charge to Aeneas) suggests a reason:[1]

> *In thi keiping committis Troy, but les,*
> *Hir kindly goddis clepit Penates;*
> *Tak thir in fallowschip of thi faitis all,*
> *And large wallis for thame seik thou sall,*
> *Quhilk at the last thi self sall beild up hie,*
> *Eftir lang wandring and errour our the see.*

> *Now Troy to thee commends her future State,*
> *And gives her Gods Companions of thy Fate:*
> *From their assistance happyer Walls expect,*
> *Which, wand'ring long, at last thou shalt erect.*

(II. 389–92)

The contrast of fallen Troy and Rome-to-be implied by Dryden's 'happyer' walls is not in Douglas's version; his 'but les' (without lies) seems an oddly unemphatic kind of emphasis in its riming position; and though the translation of Virgil's *pererrato . . . ponto* by both 'wandring' and 'errour' is perhaps a welcome, even Virgilian, expansion, the redundancy of 'large' and 'beild up hie' seems more flaccid than faithful. Douglas's methods, though often sensitive to Virgilian nuances, here lack something crisply epic that has got into Dryden.

V

I now want to compare the two translators in their handling of several sorts of situations, tropes, rhetorical patterns, or emotional effects. To begin with the epic simile, in one of its greatest classical examples Virgil parallels the alleviation of natural and civic disorders:[2]

[1] 'Troy commits to thee her holy things and household gods; take them to share thy fortunes: seek for them the city—the mighty city which, when thou hast wandered over the deep, thou shalt at last establish!': Loeb *Aeneid*, II 293–5.
[2] . . . the god himself upheaves them with his trident, opens the vast quicksands, allays the flood, and on light wheels glides over the top-

The god himself can hesing thame behind,
With his big sceptre haifand granis thre;
Oppinnis schald sandis, and temperis wele the see.
Our slidand lychtlie the croppis of the wallis.
And as ʒe se, oft amang commonis fallis
Stryfe and debait, in thair wod fulich ire,
Now fleis the stanis, and now the broyndis of fire,
Thair greife and fury ministeris wappinis plentie;
Bot than percaice, gif thai behald or se
Sum man of great authoritie and efferis,
Thai ceis, and all still standand gewis him eris;
He with his wordis can slaik thar moide and swage.
On the samyn wise fell all the seis rage.
Efter that the fadir of the fluidis Neptune
Had on sic wise . . .

   The God himself with ready Trident stands,
   And opes the Deep, and spreads the moving sands;
   Then heaves them off the sholes: where e're he guides
   His finny Coursers, and in Triumph rides,
   The Waves unruffle and the Sea subsides
   As when in Tumults rise th'ignoble Crowd,
   Mad are their Motions, and their Tongues are loud;
   And Stones and Brands in ratling Vollies fly,
   And all the Rustick Arms that Fury can supply:
   If then some grave and Pious Man appear,
   They hush their Noise, and lend a list'ning Ear;
   He sooths with sober Words their angry Mood,
   And quenches their innate Desire of Blood:
   So when the Father of the Flood appears,
   And o're the Seas his Sov'raign Trident rears,
   Their Fury falls . . .   (I. 208–23)

most waters. And as, when oft-times in a great nation tumult has risen,
the base rabble rage angrily, and now brands and stones fly, madness
lending arms; then, if haply they set eyes on a man honoured for noble
character and service, they are silent and stand by with attentive ears;
he with speech sways their passion and soothes their breasts; even so,
all the roar of ocean sank, soon as the Sire . . .': Loeb *Aeneid*, I 145–55.

Here Dryden's predictable epic signallers, 'As when . . .' and 'So when . . .', each opening its couplet, contrast, as we might expect, with Douglas's seemingly casual, throw-away sidle into the simile: 'And as ye see, oft . . . fallis/Stryfe . . . On the samyn wise fell all the seis rage.' In Douglas, there is in fact a quiet link-up between the entrance and exit to the image by means of the 'fallis . . . fell' pun, which lines up political and oceanic disturbances beside each other. The pun would not have been available to Dryden, who seems to have taken his 'Their Fury falls' from George Sandys,[1] and who would not have used such subliminal methods anyway. But if one can judge from such evidence as his 'The God himself', 'opes', 'shoals', 'fury',[2] 'ear' as rhyme word, and 'Father of the Flood' for Virgil's *genitor* (l. 159), he studied Douglas as carefully here as in the Venus–Aeneas interchange just examined. The point has been made, in both the eighteenth century and today, that 'innate desire of blood' is a pretty strong anti-populist addition to Virgil's sense,[3] but it seems to me that Dryden has absorbed his perhaps Hobbesian excrescence into the fabric of a passage impressively well unified in all three poets, Virgil and his two translators.

No less characteristic of Virgilian epic than the extended simile are certain kinds of supernatural manifestations, as when the dead Sichaeus revisits Dido:[4]

> *Bot of hir husband bigravit the image*
> *To hir aperis in sleip, with paill visage*
> *On mervalus wise, and can at lynth declair*
> *How he was cruellie slane at the altair:*
> *He schew the knyfe out throw his breist threst,*
> *And all the hid cryme of hir house manifest . . .*

[1] Sandys published his version of Book I with his *Ovid's Metamorphoses* in 1632 (*Short Title Catalogue*, 18966) and 1640 (*Short Title Catalogue*, 18968). He begins a line 'Their fury fell.'

[2] Also in Stanyhurst, however.

[3] See Harrison, 167, quoting the preface to Joseph Trapp's version (1718–20).

[4] 'But in her sleep came the very ghost of her unburied husband; raising his face pale in wondrous wise, he laid bare the cruel altars and his breast pierced with steel, unveiling all the secret horror of the house': Loeb *Aeneid*, I 353–6.

> At length, in dead of Night, the Ghost appears
> Of her unhappy Lord: the Spectre stares,
> And with erected Eyes his bloody Bosom bares.
> The cruel Altars, and his Fate he tells,
> And the dire Secret of his House reveals.   (I. 486–90)

Because, perhaps, of a misunderstanding of Chaucerian rhythms after the lapse of more than a century, Douglas's theoretically iambic couplet is designedly flexible and unpredictable, a fact which enables him to clothe grotesque physical detail in meter of a suitably violent irregularity ('the knyfe out throw his breist threst'); but if Dryden's 'bloody Bosom' glosses over something from *trajectaque pectore ferro*, his 'cruel Altars' periphrasis is closer to Virgil than Douglas's second couplet is. Virgil, parent of so much, fathers forth in one age the Chaucerian narrative manner, in another the proto-gothic.

With some of Virgil's subhuman monsters, the contrast of translations is even stronger. Laocoon tries to rescue his sons from the serpents as follows:[1]

> Syne thai the preist invadit, baith twane,
> Quhilk with his wappins did his besy pane
> His childrene for to helpin and rescew;
> Bot thai about him ⌐wpit in wympillis threw,
> And twyse circulit his myddle round about,
> And twyse faldis thair spurtlit skynnis, but dowt,
> About his hals . . .

> The wretched Father, running to their Aid
> With pious haste, but vain, they next invade:
> Twice round his waste their winding Volumes rowl'd,
> And twice about his gasping Throat they fold.
> The Priest, thus doubly choak'd, their Crests divide,
> And tow'ring o're his Head, in Triumph ride.   (II. 284–9)

---

[1] 'Then himself too, as he comes to their aid, weapons in hand, they seize and bind in mighty folds; and now, twice encircling his waist, twice winding their scaly backs around his throat, they tower above with head and lofty necks.': Loeb *Aeneid*, II 216–19.

n Douglas, the doublets ('twyse . . . twyse') combine with jouncing
rythms and picturesque vocabulary[1] ('twyse faldis thair purtlit skynnis,
ut dowt') to carry the message of weird disaster; whereas in Dryden
he doubling in 'Twice . . . twice . . . double . . . divide' seems to
npose an order of its own. Dryden's medium, counteracting chaos,
:nds constantly to organize the folklore material and hence adapt it to
Dryden's form of epic elevation and flow.[2]

Each in his own way, both translators are excellent at action pas-
sges. Take the following scene just after the Greek troops pour out of
ie horse and fighting begins within Troy:[3]

> *Sum cumpanyis, with speris, lance and targe,*
> *Walkis wachand in rewis and narrow streitis;*
> *Arrait battellis, with drawin sweirdis at gletis,*
> *Standis reddy for to styk, gore and sla . . .*[4]

> *To sev'ral Posts their Parties they divide;*
> *Some block the narrow Streets, some scour the wide.*
> *The bold they kill, th' unwary they surprise;*
> *Who fights finds Death, and Death finds him who flies.*

(II. 447–50)

Dryden's brilliant binary methods, extending beyond Virgil to the in-
:ented witticism of his fourth line, foreshadow Pope's picture of the
unce invasion in the *Epistle to Arbuthnot* (ll. 7–10)—'They pierce my
hickets, thro' my Grot they glide,' etc.[5] Douglas's triplets—'speris,

---

[1] For the theory that Scots poetry of Douglas's school adapted vocabulary to situation (as with an increase of Doric forms in the lyric parts of
a Greek tragedy), see C. S. Lewis, *English Literature in the 16th Century*,
79–80.

[2] Dryden's 'invade' in the first couplet seems not to come directly from
Douglas, since Lauderdale rhymes 'invade' and 'aid' here; but 'invade'
is unusual for the passage and may derive ultimately from Douglas.

[3] '. . . others with confronting weapons have barred the narrow ways;
a standing line of steel, with flashing point unsheathed, is ready for the
slaughter': Loeb *Aeneid*, II 332–4.

[4] *rewis* = streets; *at gletis* = glittering.

[5] Text of Pope from his *Poems*, ed. John Butt, 1963, 598.

lance and targe' and 'styk, gore and sla'—also not very literal, have
their own monosyllabic punch. A characteristic of good verse transla
tion is that the practitioner is set on fire by his original, and produces his
own special effects.[1]

Since an epic is apt to be a mosaic made up of a series of relatively
short poetic units, transitional passages often need special care, and are
therefore likely to be good indicators of a poet's procedures. In the
middle of Book I, Aeneas's attention turns from the Trojan War mural
in Dido's palace to the approach of the queen herself:[2]

> Quhill as the manful Troiane Eneas
> To se thir nyce figuris thocht wounder was,
> And as he musit, studeand in ane stair
> Bot on ane sycht quharon he blenkit thair,
> The quene Dido, excellent in bewtie,
> To temple cummis with ane fair men ʒie
> Of lustie ʒonkeris walking hir about.

> Thus, while the Trojan *Prince employs his Eyes,*
> *Fix'd on the Walls with wonder and surprise;*
> *The Beauteous* Dido, *with a num'rous Train,*
> *And pomp of Guards, ascends the sacred Fane.*   (I. 695–8)

Each poet begins one couplet with the hero and another with the
heroine; but Douglas has devoted a whole couplet to each of Virgil's
first two lines:

> Haec dum Dardanio Aeneae miranda videntur,
> Dum stupet, obtutuque haeret defixus in uno . . .

As Dryden's 'Fix'd', echoing *defixus*, shows, he has not neglected to pay
the Latin some close attention, but what interested Douglas was
obtutuque . . . in uno. Douglas slows the action down, dramatizing the
inwardness of Aeneas's rapt contemplation; Dryden speeds it up, to

---

[1] Cf. *Dryden and the Art of Translation*, 27–32.
[2] 'While these wondrous sights are seen by Dardan Aeneas, while in
amazement he hangs rapt in one fixed gaze, the queen, Dido, moved
towards the temple, of surpassing beauty, with a vast company of youths
thronging around her': Loeb *Aeneid*, I 494–7.

bring on the encounter with the queen. Douglas is more psychological, Dryden more theatrical; each, in his way, very Virgilian.

This sort of contrast—emphasis on mental states in Douglas, on patterns of action in Dryden—ultimately produces, in effect, two quite different Aeneases. Having been told by Hector in a vision that Troy is falling, and ordered to escape and set forth to found Rome, Aeneas nevertheless prepares to enter the final battle within the doomed city:[1]

> *Wpsprang the cry of men and trumpis blist;*
> *As out of mynd, myne armour on I thrist,*
> *Thocht be na resoun persaife I mycht, but faile,*
> *Quhan than the force of armes culd availe;*
> *3 it, hand for hand, to thryng out throw the preis*
> *With my feris, and rynnand or we ceis*
> *To the castell, our hartis brynt for desyr;*
> *The fury cachit our myndis hait as fyir,*
> *So that we thocht maist semelie in a feild*
> *To dee fechtand, enarmit wnder scheild.*

> *New Clamours, and new Clangors now arise,*
> *The sound of Trumpets mix'd with fighting cries.*
> *With frenzy seiz'd, I run to meet th' Alarms,*
> *Resolv'd on death, resolv'd to die in Arms.*
> *But first to gather Friends, with them t' oppose,*
> *If Fortune favour'd, and repel the Foes.*
> *Spurr'd by my Courage, by my Country fir'd;*
> *With sense of Honour, and Revenge inspir'd.* (II. 421–8)

The whiff of irrationality in Virgil's *nec sat rationis in armis* (rendered by Douglas's second couplet) has almost evaporated (despite 'With frenzy seiz'd') in Dryden's version. Douglas's Aeneas—not inappropriately in the world of Virgil's Book II—is berserk, or something very near it:

[1] 'Then rise the cries of men and the blare of clarions. Frantic I seize arms; yet little purpose is there in arms, but my heart burns to muster a force for battle and hasten with my comrades to the citadel. Rage and wrath drive my soul headlong and I think how glorious it is to die in arms': Loeb *Aeneid*, II 313-16.

> . . . *our hartis brynt for desyir;*
> *The fury cachit our myndis hait as fyir* . . .

In Dryden on the other hand we have an example of the rationally
heroic, an advance over the original to which Douglas was more faithful:

> Courage as the conquest and control of fear is plainly preferable to
> courage as unthinking wrath. Dryden's hero proceeds almost
> meticulously with conscious purpose and not through fear, rage,
> or desperation, or any of the more usual goads to military courage.[1]

To all this effect Dryden's style—the 'turn' in 'Resolv'd on death,
resolv'd to die in arms', the chiasmus and parallelism in the last couplet
quoted—has made its organic contribution.[2]

VI

Dryden's classicism, exemplified in the fullness of his career by such
magnificent sustained achievements as his 'Discourse on Satire' and his
works of Virgil in the 1690s, dominated the succeeding decades. For the
generation of Pope (born 1688) and Richardson (born 1689), it is hardly
too much to say that Dryden's conception of satire *was* satire, or even
that Dryden's Virgil *was* Virgil. When Clarissa's insulting brother
James wishes to imply that insatiable lust for the handsome Lovelace is
the only reason she has turned down marriage with the toadlike miser
Soames, it is to Dryden's Virgil that he refers his sister[3]—'Virgil's *Amor
omnibus idem* (for the application of which I refer you to the Georgic,
as translated by Dryden) is verified in you'; for James knows, as does
Clarissa and no doubt Richardson's audience in general, that Dryden,
with his Restoration taste for sexual explicitness, had infused a special

---

[1] Harrison, 157.

[2] Despite his rewriting the script, the most obvious influence on
Dryden's language in the passage is Virgil's Latin: *clamorque* . . .
clangorque in 313 and *in armis* at the end of both 314 and 316. 'Fir'd' in
Dryden's 427 could be a reminiscence of Douglas's 'hait as fyir'; no
other predecessor has the image, either at a line's end or elsewhere.
What Dryden diverged from he diverged from deliberately.

[3] *Clarissa*, ed. John Butt, 4 vol London and New York 1962, I. 256.

earthiness into Virgil's simple word *Amor* by means of the second line of the couplet James alludes to:[1]

> *Thus every Creature, and of every Kind,*
> *The secret Joys of sweet Coition find . . .*

And when Pope, in the fullness of *his* career, forty-two years after the publication of Dryden's *Aeneis,* writing a private poem in response to a gift from a beautiful younger neighbour of his at Twickenham,[2] wishes to allude in self-mocking regret to the recent conclusion of his series of Horatian satires, he elaborately coils the allusion around both the illustrations and text of what was no doubt (along with Ogilby's well-known Homer) one of his remembered childhood delights, the 1697 Virgil.[3] Written in the style, mood, and stanza of Prior's fine earlier poem 'To a Child of Quality of Five Years Old, the Author Suppos'd Forty,' Pope's 'On Receiving from the Right Hon. the L A D Y F R A N C E S S H I R L E Y A S T A N D I S H A N D T W O P E N S' begins with the poet's mistaken presumption (as he tells the story) that the gift exemplifies the descent of Athena—sober Minerva, goddess of wisdom—for the purpose of equipping Pope for renewed assaults on the vices and follies of his day:

> *Yes, I beheld th' Athenian Queen*
> *Descend in all her sober charms;*
> *'And take (she said, and smil'd serene)*
> *'Take at this hand celestial arms.'*   (ll. 1–4)

How wrong he is in his self-admiring rapture the donor of the utensils speedily makes plain:

> *'Athenian Queen! and sober charms!*
> *'I tell ye, fool, there's nothing in't:*
> *' 'Tis Venus, Venus gives these arms,*
> *'In Dryden's Virgil see the print.'*   (ll. 25–29)

[1] *Georgics,* III 375–6. Dryden's version is not out of harmony with the passage in Virgil as a whole, one of the latter's more Lucretian moments.
[2] She was probably thirty-three at the time (1739) and has been (or was to be?) Chesterfield's mistress; Pope was over fifty.
[3] See Twickenham edition, VI 378–80.

It is Petrarchan poetry of courtly compliment he is expected to supply
the bantering lady informs him—let him only abandon epic or satiric
ambitions and she stands ready to

> '. . . *list you in the harmless roll*
> '*Of those that sing of these poor eyes.*'   (ll. 31-32)

A modern reader may turn at once to Dryden's Virgil, page 458
where, illustrating the couplet[1]

> *Proud of the Gift, he rowl'd his greedy sight*
> *Around the Work, and gaz'd with vast delight,*

there appears (created by W. Hollar in 1653 and now dedicated to
Godfrey Kneller for having contributed his five guineas to Dryden's
enterprise)[2] one of the more touchingly preposterous heroic visualiza-
tions ever to have graced a printed epic: Aeneas's goddess-mother
presenting to him the famous pictorial shield at the foot of a tree in
whose branches three *putti* are suspending a helmet and breastplate just
above the hero's head. Aeneas, eyes gleaming with delight at the elaborate ornamentation of the shield, scarcely notices these assistants, or
his mother, or the spear leaning against the tree just behind her, or the
sword and scabbard hung from one branch just above him, or the pair
of military boots dangling from another a bit farther back.

The point I want to make about all this, a matter which so far as I
know has hitherto escaped notice, is that, appropriate though the print
is to Pope's excellent little poem, it is not only the *print* he draws on:
he has the text in mind too, and not just the text of this particular passage. At the very end of Dryden's *Aeneis*, three couplets from the conclusion of the twelfth and last book, Aeneas, almost yielding to his chief
enemy Turnus's entreaties to spare Turnus's life on the battlefield, suddenly notices that Turnus is clad in the spoils of a friend and ally, young
Pallas, Evander's son, Aeneas's earliest comrade in the wars in Italy.
The hero's wrath is aroused:

[1] Book VIII ll. 824-5.
[2] The plates were 'sold' to a variety of sponsors at this figure. The same
plates had originally appeared in Ogilby's folio Virgil translation a
generation earlier.

> Traytor, dost thou, dost thou to Grace pretend,
> Clad, as thou art, in Trophees of my Friend?
> To his sad Soul a grateful Off'ring go;
> 'Tis Pallas, Pallas gives this deadly blow.   (XII. 1370–4)

Feeling as though he were nearing the end of his own life of wit, a warfare upon earth, Pope glances swiftly at this climatic scene; and, as though the line had referred to Pallas Athena rather than the Pallas who was Aeneas's friend, transforms it into

> 'Tis Venus, Venus gives these arms.

Dryden's Virgil, fountain of epic allusion and mythopoeic splendour, takes him back to that fine first world, the world of Belinda and *The Rape of the Lock*.

VII

Despite the six or more reprints of his *Aeneis* in the twentieth century, Dryden's lifelong symbiotic association with the classics is probably little felt by most readers today, if only because attention has been so long focused mainly on the poet's original works, and on only a few of these at that: the major satires and a handful of shorter poems. On a shelf in Room 1720 South Hall of the University of California's Santa Barbara campus, where this essay is being composed, there stand a dozen modern anthologies of Restoration or Restoration-and-eighteenth-century literature, some of poetry only, some of prose, poetry, and plays—anthologies ranging in size from two to thirteen hundred pages, but nearly all blockbusters of the thousand-page variety. Very few print any samples of Dryden's work as a translator: not one gives a single line of his Virgil. It is almost as though the modern custodians of enlightenment poetry had accepted the aberrational doctrine of C. S. Lewis quoted at the start of this discussion, and were viewing with scepticism the traditional assessment of our couplet poets as classicists. Or perhaps it is as though the classics themselves had been thrust into the shadows by some luminescence from more recent poetry. (I note at any rate that the compiler of a recent anthology of *Roman* culture includes plenty of Dryden.)[1] Yet Dryden wrote his translations and many of his original poems as part of a tradition of resumed continuity in civilization, a tradition stretching from Chaucer in the fourteenth century to Pope in the eighteenth, and well beyond. For Dryden, these bones lived. When and as they live again for us, the quality and scope of what he did will come at last to be more fully understood.

[1] Garry Wills, *Roman Culture: Weapons and the Man*, New York 1966; a reader might well turn at once to Plate 24, with its caption from Ovid, well rendered by Dryden.

10: *Dryden and Seventeenth-Century Prose Style*

K. G. HAMILTON

DRYDEN'S chief work, according to Bonamy Dobrée, consisted in creating a language 'fit for civilized Englishmen to use'.[1] And for T. S. Eliot 'it is hardly too much to say that Dryden found the English speechless and he gave them speech . . . the language which we can refine, enrich, distort or corrupt as we may, but which we cannot do without'.[2] Dryden, of course, wrote a great deal more verse than he did prose, and remarks such as these do not necessarily refer to his achievement as a prose writer. Nonetheless, whether deriving from his prose or his verse, it has been on prose that his lasting influence has been felt—thus George Saintsbury maintains that 'if, as some critics have inclined to think, the influence of Dryden tended to narrow the sphere and cramp the efforts of English poetry, it tended equally to enlarge the sphere and develop the energies of English prose'.[3]

But important as Dryden's role in it may have been, the process by which the modern tradition of English prose developed was an essentially historical one; a process which though it had much earlier origins reached its climax in the later seventeenth century. The aim in what follows will be to examine Dryden's prose style in its seventeenth-century context—the context, that is, both of ideas about prose style and of actual practice.

The analysis of prose style is extremely difficult because the factors involved are often intangible and difficult to isolate. However, particularly in the seventeenth-century context, the pattern of sentence struc-

[1] Bonamy Dobrée, *Variety of Ways*, Oxford 1932, 9.

[2] T. S. Eliot, *John Dryden*, New York 1932, 24.

[3] George Saintsbury, *Dryden*, 1881, 131.

ture—the kind of sentences a writer uses and the way he puts them together—is one basic element in style, and we shall begin by looking at a passage of Dryden's prose from this point of view. Lacking any accepted method of stylistic analysis, and in order to facilitate an examination of sentence structure, a particular method of setting out has been adopted: a method aimed at revealing the pattern of relationships between the various parts, or members, of the passage, particularly the pattern of grammatical co-ordination and sub-ordination. To this end members have been arranged in ranks, ranging from Rank A containing members not sub-ordinate to any other member (those normally referred to as principal clauses), through Rank B containing members subordinate immediately to those in Rank A, and so on. Where a member is interrupted before completion by the interposition of another member this is shown by brackets, thus $\rangle$ . . . $\langle$, around the interposed member, and the linking of members with each other in co-ordinate or paratactic structure is indicated by bracketing.

The division into members has been made on the basis of grammatical clauses containing a finite verb, irrespective of the actual punctuation. One reason for this is the uncertainty regarding seventeenth-century punctuation. So far as I am aware, it is not possible on the evidence available to decide, at least for any practical purpose, how far Dryden's punctuation is his own and what his printers have contributed to it; nor can we be certain just what function the punctuation was intended to perform—no doubt it was primarily grammatical, but at least some of the older rhetorical concept of punctuation probably still remained. No particular grammatical or other formal linguistic significance, however, is intended by this arrangement: it is adopted simply as a convenient means of examining the structure of complex sentences.

One other matter should perhaps be raised at this point. Already I have spoken of Dryden's prose 'style', and shall continue to do so, with, however, certain reservations. Firstly Dryden's prose style obviously does not remain unchanged throughout the whole period of his writing. More important, prose, like verse, is for Dryden required to meet the demands of decorum, and consequently style is likely to vary according to the writer's intention. An essay such as the Preface to the *Fables* may require a different style from that of, say, a complimentary letter. For these reasons it would be more accurate to speak of Dryden's 'styles'. My belief, however, is that even though Dryden himself would have accepted without question this need for differing styles, his importance for the history of English prose is such that in his own writing he rose above, as it were, the concept of style in this sense. Underlying almost all his prose, and dominating most of it, is a basic style which seems simply fresh and spontaneous, which achieves distinction, achieves indeed 'style', without appearing to do so. It is this basic quality in Dryden's writing that separates him from his predecessors, and that I am concerned with when I speak of his style.

The passage chosen for this initial inspection is the opening of the Preface to the *Fables*, as an example of Dryden's most successful and most mature prose:

A1	'Tis with a poet as with a man
B1	who designs to build
B2	and is very exact⟩
C1	as he supposes
	⟨in casting up the cost beforehand
B3	but generally speaking he is mistaken in his account
B4	and reckons short of the expense
C2	he first intended
B5	he alters his mind
C3	as the work proceeds
B6	and will have this or that convenience more
C4	of which he had not thought
D1	when he began
A2	So has it happened to me
A3	I have built a house⟩
B7	where I intended but a Lodge
	yet with better success than a certain nobleman
B8	who beginning with a dog-kennel never lived to finish the palace
C5	he had contrived
A4	From translating the First of Homer's *Iliads*⟩
B9	which I intend as an essay to the whole work
	⟨ I proceeded to the translation of the twelfth book of Ovid's *Metamorphoses*

        B10   because it contains among other things the causes the beginning and ending of the Trojan War

A5   Here I ought in reason to have stopped

A6   but the speeches of Ajax and Ulysses lying next in my way I could not balk 'em

        B11   When I had compassed them

A7   I was so taken with the former part of the fifteenth book

        B12   which is the master'piece of the whole *Metamorphoses*

        B13   that I enjoined myself the pleasing task of rendering it into English

A8   And I now found by the number of my verses

        B14   that they began to swell into a little volume

        B15   which gave me an occasion of looking backward on some beauties of my author in his former books

A9   there occurred to me the Hunting of the Boar, Cinyras and Myrrha the good'natured story of Baucis and Philemon with the rest

        B16   which I hope

                C6   I have translated closely enough

                C7   and given them the same turn of verse

                        D2   which they had in the original

A10   and this⟩

        B17   I may say without vanity

    ⟨is not the talent of every poet

A11   He⟩

        B18   who has arrived nearest to it

    ⟨is the ingenious and learned Sandys the best versifier of the former Age

        B19   if I may properly call it by that name

                C8   which was the former part of this concluding century

A12   For Spenser and Fairfax both flourished in the reign of Queen Elizabeth great masters in our language

        B20   and who saw much further into the beauties of our numbers

                C9   than those who immediately followed them

A13   Milton was the poetical son of Spenser and Mr. Waller of Fairfax

        B21   for we have our lineal descents and clans as well as other families

A14   Spenser more than once insinuates

        B22   that the soul of Chaucer was transfused in his body

⎡   B23   and that he was begotten by him two hundred years
⎣   after his decease[1]

This should be long enough for any possibly emerging pattern at least to begin to show itself. Two things are clear enough. Firstly the sentence structure is almost entirely what might be described as trailing, or cumulative—that is, the dominant idea is stated first and the rest of the sentence develops or accumulates on this basis. Only once (B11) is the principal clause, or for that matter any clause, preceded by another that is dependent on it. This is in contrast to the 'suspended' structure of the so-called Ciceronian period, deriving from Latin prose, in which the main idea is held in abeyance until well into the sentence and until various kinds of qualifications have been introduced. Look, for instance, at this sentence from Milton in which the principal clause is barely introduced before being suspended to allow for the introduction of some fourteen qualifying and amplifying subordinate clauses:

A1 Wherein⟩
        B1   although I have not doubted to single forth more then
              once such of them
               C1   as were thought the chiefe and most nomin-
                     ated opposers on the other side
                     D1   whom no man else undertooke
   ⎡ B2   if I have done well either to be confident of the truth⟩
               C2   whose force is best seene against the ablest
                    resistance
       ⟨or to be jealous and tender of the hurt
               C3   that might be done among the weaker by the
                    intrapping authority of great names titl'd to
                    false opinions
        B3   or that it might be lawfull to attribute somewhat to
             guifts of Gods imparting
 ⎨   C4   which I boast not
               C5   but thankfully acknowledge
               C6   and feare also
                     D2   lest at my certain account they be
                         reckon'd to me many rather than few

---

[1] Watson, II 269-70.

B4   or lastly if it be but justice not to defraud of due esteeme
      the wearisome labours and studious watchings
          C7   wherein I have spent
          C8   and tir'd out almost a whole youth
⟨I shall not distrust to be acquitted of presumption knowing
    B5   that⟩
              C9   if heretofore all ages have receav'd with good
                    acceptance the earliest industry of him
                        D3   that hath been hopefull
              ⟨it were but hard measure now
          C10   if the freedome of any timely spirit should be
                 opprest meerely by the big and blunted fame
                 of his elder adversary
          C11   and that his sufficiency must now be sentenc't
                     D4   not by pondering the reason he shewes
                     D5   but by calculating the yeares he brings[1]

This sentence just quoted from Milton will serve to indicate the
second obvious characteristic of the Dryden passage which also dif-
ferentiates it from Ciceronian prose. In the latter a single principal
clause is likely to support a complex structure of subordinate clauses,
some of which may be as many as seven or eight ranks removed from
it. The single principal clause in the Milton sentence, for instance, sup-
ports a total of 21 subordinate clauses, although in this case the extent
of removal from the principal clause is not great. Of the 48 clauses in
the Dryden passage 14 are in Rank A—that is, are not dependent on
any other clause—and these together have a total of 34 clauses directly
or indirectly dependent on them, an average of only 2·5 dependent
clauses for each Rank A clause. Of the 34 dependent clauses, 23 are in
Rank B—that is, directly dependent on Rank A clauses, 9 in Rank C
and only 2 in Rank D. The passage, therefore, from the point of view
of clause structure, is simple rather than complex, consisting largely of
principal clauses with only a relatively limited degree of subordination.

Such integration as there is tends to be loose, both grammatically
and logically. B5, for instance, actually begins a new sentence, although
logically it still refers back to 'man' in A1 and is part of the pattern of

[1] Milton, *An Apology against a Pamphlet*, ed. Merritt Y. Hughes, *The
Complete Prose Works of John Milton*, New Haven 1953-, I 869.

co-ordinate clauses. The 'this' of A10 is logically an extension of the proposition contained in B6–7 and C2, and strictly should carry on the train of subordination, except that it also provides the lead into the 'he who' of A11 and B18, and through this to all the remainder of the passage. Also the force of the connective 'for' beginning A12 is not altogether clear, logically or grammatically. In the closely integrated periods of the kind illustrated from Milton, where syntax and logical development are closely co-ordinated, this sort of looseness would not occur.

Most of the clauses in Dryden's passage—37 out of 48—are in Ranks A and B. The opportunity for a conscious pattern of co-ordination or parataxis within this accumulation of clauses of equal rank has not been exploited to any degree. Most of the co-ordinate groups consist of only two clauses joined by 'and', or in one case by 'but'. Even in the relatively more extensive groups (A1–3 and 12–14, and B1–6) the variation of simple connectives and the occasional omission of the connective ensure that no obtrusive pattern is set up. Dryden's periods do not have, as Dr Johnson has said, 'the formality of a settled style, in which the first half of the sentence betrays the other',[1] and again in this respect his prose is at the opposite end of the scale, this time from the highly stylized patterning of balanced clauses in the so-called euphuistic prose seen in its most exaggerated form in the *Euphues* of John Lyly. Notice, for instance, the last three Rank A clauses (A12–14). These express more or less parallel ideas—each is an illustration of the proposition put forward in the preceding sentence—and with its dependent clauses each forms a roughly similar structure. But no more than roughly similar—there is no attempt to achieve any symmetry or harmonious balance, either between or within the periods. We might compare this part of the passage with a sentence from Browne's *Religio Medici* which expresses something of the same idea: 'To see our selves againe wee neede not looke for *Platoes* yeare, every man is not onely himselfe; there hath beene many *Diogenes*, and as many *Tymons*, though but few of that name; men are lived over againe; the world is now as it was in

---

[1] Johnson, 'Dryden', in *Lives of the English Poets*, ed. G. B. Hill, 3 vol, Oxford 1905, I 418.

ages past; there was none then, but there hath been some one since that parallels him, and is, as it were, his revived selfe.'[1] Only perhaps in its closing stages does Dryden's passage approach the finely controlled harmony achieved by the asymmetrical balance, if it might be called that, of these lines.

There is little else in the passage that bears remarking on. The diction is neither aggressively 'English' nor overladen with foreign words—the words are either Anglo-Saxon in origin or have already been thoroughly assimilated into the language. The sentence structure is basically of the subject-verb-object kind, with just enough variety to avoid monotony. There is only slight dependence on participial phrases or absolute constructions characteristic of prosë modelled on Latin—notice, for example, the way in which the last seven clauses in the passage quoted earlier from Milton form an extended participial construction. The sentences are mainly too long to conform with the seventeenth-century fashion for brevity, to be found, for example, in Bacon's *Essays* or in the work of 'character' writers like Bishop Hall. But they are still not unduly long, at least by some earlier standards.

Indeed, it is becoming apparent that Dryden's style, particularly in the sixteenth- and seventeenth-century context, is to be defined primarily by negatives. He is, as we know from Mathew Arnold, one of the 'classics of our prose', a statement which most critics would be prepared to accept at its face value—although this may not be quite what Arnold intended. His standing as a prose writer has not been seriously questioned in the way his position as a poet sometimes has. And yet, having said that he is one of the key figures in the development of modern English prose, it is not easy to say a great deal more about Dryden's prose style—much less easy than it is to discuss the style of the outstanding writers who preceded him—Hooker, Browne, Burton, Milton —whose brilliance was more individual and obvious. One is tempted, indeed, simply to agree with F. P. Wilson that 'if one hesitates to call it "modern" that is only because it is so good',[2] and leave it at that. But

[1] Browne, *Religio Medici, The Works of Sir Thomas Browne*, ed. Geoffrey Keynes, 4 vol Oxford and Chicago 1964, I 16.
[2] F. P. Wilson, *Seventeenth Century Prose*, Cambridge 1960, 11.

this in itself is significant. For Dryden's modernity, and his consequent importance, is essentially a matter of the relatively unobtrusive and anonymous quality of his style. As Dr Johnson has said, he does not appear 'to have any other art than that of expressing with clearness what he thinks with vigour. His style could not easily be imitated, either seriously or ludicrously; for, being always equable and always varied, it has no prominent or discriminative characters'.[1] And for Saintsbury, too, Dryden's style was 'singularly destitute of mannerisms'.[2]

It was essential that English prose achieve such a style before its use could be fully developed. It might, for instance, be validly argued that the failure of the novel form to emerge finally before the eighteenth century, despite the earlier predilection for story telling, was largely owing to the lack of a prose style sufficiently flexible and unobtrusive to meet its needs. This does not mean that the prose of the later seventeenth century was necessarily superior to any that had been written previously. On the contrary, there were many writers before Dryden who wrote prose that was superior in its own particular way to his. It may indeed have been in prose as Dryden himself saw it in drama, when he wrote in 1693, in a verse epistle to Congreve celebrating *The Double Dealer*:

> *Our age was cultivated thus at length,*
> *But what we gain'd in skill we lost in strength.*
> *Our builders were with want of genius curst;*
> *The second temple was not like the first.*   (ll. 11–14)

But whether or not the earlier prose was superior, it was less consistently 'useful'. The modern reader may find earlier writers whom he can admire more than Dryden, writers whom he would prefer to read; but not, I think, writers whom he would be more desirous of emulating, except perhaps for some rather special purpose.

The great prose writers of the sixteenth and earlier seventeenth centuries each developed an individual style, more or less admirably suited to the end in view, but limited in its suitability for other ends. Magnificent as it is, the prose of the *King James Bible*, of Hooker's *Laws of Ecclesiastical Polity* or Browne's *Religio Medici*, is in each case a special-

[1] Johnson, 'Dryden', I 418.
[2] Saintsbury, *Dryden*, 129.

ized prose; and it is, moreover, a prose that may draw as much or more attention to itself as to its subject matter—one has only to compare the *King James Bible* with a modern translation to see how much of the particular grandeur that can be its dominant impression is derived from its style. It is in the second half of the seventeenth century, and most consistently in Dryden's essays, that English prose develops finally as a means of discourse flexible and unobtrusive enough to meet adequately a wide variety of demands without itself requiring wide variations.

Kenneth Clark in his *Civilisation* (1969, 219-20) says something the same as this, but with a wider reference. Speaking of the hostility of the Royal Society to things of the imagination he says that

> '. . . there was a compensation: the emergence of a clear, workable prose. Even then, of course, something was lost. Compare a piece of Thomas Browne and Dryden. Here is Browne, full of metaphor and allusion—an almost Shakespearean richness of language: "Though Somnus in Homer be sent to rouse Agamemnon, I find no such effects in these drowsy approaches to sleep. To keep our eyes open longer were but to act our antipodes. The huntsmen are up in America, and they are already past their first sleep in Persia." And here is Dryden: "If by the people you understand the multitude; 'tis no matter what they think; they are sometimes in the right, sometimes in the wrong: their judgement is a mere lottery." Perfectly good sense, but the verbal magic, the incantation, of the Thomas Browne is on a higher plane. Still we must allow that what Dryden himself called "the other harmony of prose" was a civilizing force. It was the tool of the new philosophy almost as much as Stevin's decimal system was a tool of the new mathematics. . . . It is arguable that the non-existence of a clear, concrete German prose has been one of the chief disasters of European civilization.'

This, however, while it emphasizes the great value of Dryden's contribution, is I think to go too far in stressing the purely workmanlike qualities of his prose. His prose is different from Browne's, but it is nonetheless literary; it has value beyond the purely utilitarian.

This emergence of English prose as an 'all purpose' medium, however, was not, as I said earlier, the achievement of a single individual or of a particular period. It was something that had been going on, or was being prepared for, at least since the beginning of the sixteenth century, and to some extent from the beginnings of English prose itself. The native English prose of King Alfred and the Anglo-Saxon *Chronicle*, with its succession of clauses joined by simple connectives like 'and', 'but', etc., was excellent for narrative purposes, but for not much else, because its nature prevented it from doing anything more complicated than moving forward in a straight line. During the fourteenth and fifteenth centuries, mainly under French influence and using more complicated connectives, the English sentence retained the general forward movement of Anglo-Saxon, but instead of progressing in a relatively straight line tended to ramble every which way as the ideas coming into the writer's head dictated. Thus, while gaining in the range and complexity of ideas and relationships it could express, it lost the simple shapeliness of Anglo-Saxon prose. At the same time the introduction of a great number of new words, mainly from French and Latin, many of them imperfectly integrated into the language, added to the generally chaotic effect frequently achieved by writers like Caxton in the late fifteenth and early sixteenth centuries.

The reaction to this chaos was a period of self-conscious seeking after form—a form that would lend distinction to what by comparison with French and Latin was thought of as still an essentially barbarous language. This self-consciousness, though for the time being it subjected English prose to influences not entirely natural to it, may be seen as an essential preliminary to the final emergence of the unselfconscious, natural shapeliness of a prose such as Dryden's. The process, which was the dominant influence on prose style during the period 1500–1650, was a complicated one of action and reaction, and only the barest outline of it can be attempted here.[1] Underlying it was the influence of classical rhetoric and of the example provided by classical writers, particularly Cicero. This influence resulted in the development of two more or less distinct attempts towards the achievement of form. On the one hand

[1] The subject is given detailed treatment in George Williamson, *The Senecan Amble: A Study in Prose Form from Bacon to Collier*, 1951, and in various articles by Williamson, M. W. Croll and R. F. Jones. A recent study is Robert Adolph, *The Rise of Modern Prose Style*, Cambridge Mass., 1968.

there was the endeavour to impose on English prose the suspended, tightly subordinate sentence structure of classical Latin. On the other were the 'figures of speech'—of sound and of meaning—which were the staple material of classical rhetoric, and which emphasized particularly balance and antithesis based on syntactical co-ordination or parataxis. Of these two influences towards form, the first is to be seen most completely in the heavily Latinate, periodic style of Hooker, and less perfectly in Milton; and the second in the highly stylized prose of Lyly's *Euphues*, the so-called Euphuism. The latter was, and has continued to be, the dominant influence, and it seems likely that, as a basis for style, co-ordination is closer to the natural genius of a largely uninflected language such as English than is sub-ordination. Both are essential, however, if the full potentialities of the language are to be exploited, and these extremes of style in the sixteenth century may be seen as complementary parts of the process by which men educated themselves in the handling of English prose.

Two other sixteenth-century movements need to be mentioned. First there was the dispute between those who like Sir John Cheke believed that English should retain its native purity, free from the taint of importations from other tongues, and others who believed that it needed to be enriched from the resources of more civilized languages. Of these the latter were, of course, the ones who eventually prevailed, but in the sixteenth century the excesses both of the vocabulary builders and of those who sought an Anglo-Saxon word for every purpose showed the need for both influences before a successful compromise could be reached. Then there was the so-called anti-Ciceronian movement, almost as old as Ciceronian imitation itself, which, however, had as its aim the elimination not only of specifically Ciceronian style but of all elaboration of style of any kind. This movement, most closely associated first with Erasmus and then with Francis Bacon, gained in strength during the first half of the seventeenth century and led to the emphasis on 'plain' style of the kind demanded of its members by the newly-formed Royal Society of London. However, a self-conscious plainness can be as obtrusive as overelaboration, and the so-called 'curt' or 'obscure' styles of some earlier seventeenth-century writers were almost as stylized and unnatural as those they sought to replace. There was, for example, Milton's complaint concerning Bishop Hall, that he wrote 'sentences by statute, as if all above three inches long were confiscate'.

Crites, near the beginning of Dryden's *Of Dramatick Poesie*, gives a description of extremes of style which, although it refers to poetry may, for reasons that will be discussed later, be equally well applied to prose. Crites wonders if the one writer does not 'perpetually pay us with clenches upon words, and a certain clownish kind of raillery? if now and then he does not offer at a catachresis or Clevelandism, wresting and torturing a word into another meaning . . .'. The other is one whose 'style and matter are everywhere alike; he is the most calm, peaceable writer you ever read: he never disquiets your passions with the least concernment . . .'.[1] The achievement in prose of the second half of the seventeenth century, and of Dryden in particular, was to establish a balance between extremes like these; to develop a prose that was neither over elaborate nor self-consciously plain, which emphasized neither the tight sub-ordination of Ciceronian style nor the obtrusive patterning of balance and antithesis of Euphuism, which sought neither an extreme native purity of diction nor borrowed with unnecessary extravagance from other languages. What was attained, in fact, was an apparently natural style in which the demands of what was being said rather than of some external criterion of style seems to be in control, while at the same time there is still retained the feeling for form and harmony acquired by English prose from the influence of rhetoric.

The earlier rambling kind of prose had been 'natural', in that it tended to follow the train of thought wherever it might lead, untrammelled by any stylistic demands. It did not, however, consistently achieve any recognizable form of its own; nor, what is more important, did it lend any feeling of form to what was being said. Rhetoric, with its emphasis on form—on the *way* a thing should be said—provided what was lacking, but it went too far. 'Ye know not what hurt ye do to learning, that care not for words but matter',[2] declared Roger Ascham around 1568. For Francis Bacon, some thirty years later, the first vanity of learning arose

---

[1] Watson, I 21.
[2] Roger Ascham, *The Scholemaster*, ed. A. M. Wright, *The English Writings of Roger Ascham*, Cambridge 1904, 265.

when 'men began to hunt more after words than matter'.[1] For Dryden, redressing the balance, what is required is a 'propriety of thoughts and words'.[2]

Speaking of Ben Jonson in *Of Dramatick Poesie* he says, 'If there was any fault in his language, 'twas that he weaved it too closely and laboriously . . . he did a little too much romanize our tongue, leaving the words which he translated almost as much Latin as he found them: wherein, though he learnedly followed their language, he did not enough comply with the idiom of ours'.[3] Dryden was obviously much concerned with good English. In his very first essay—the Preface to the *Rival Ladies*—he declared that he had 'endeavoured to write English',[4] and his opinion of the language was higher than had been that of those earlier writers like Ascham who had felt a duty to use English while still regarding it as inferior to Greek or Latin. 'Our language is noble, full, and significant; and I know not why he who is master of it may not clothe ordinary things in it as decently as the Latin, if he use the same diligence in his choice of words.'[5] In the Dedication of *Troilus and Cressida* he said that 'I am often put to a stand considering whether what I write be the idiom of the tongue, or false grammar or nonsense couched beneath that spacious name of *Anglicism*'.[6] His remedy, incidentally, which reveals how much more at home the seventeenth-century writer was still inclined to feel in Latin than in English, was to translate 'my English into Latin, and thereby trying what sense the words will bear in a more stable language'. 'There are many', he says, 'who understand Greek and Latin, and yet are ignorant of their mother-tongue. The properties and delicacies of the English [tongue] are known to few . . .'.[7] The test of idiom, together with necessity, he also

[1] Francis Bacon, *De dignitate et augmentis scientiarum*, ed. J. Spedding and R. H. Ellis, 5 vol 1861, IV. 443.
[2] 'The Author's Apology for Heroic Poetry and Poetic Licence', Watson, I. 207.
[3] Watson, I 70.
[4] Watson, I 51.
[5] Dryden, 'Defence of an Essay on Dramatic Poesy', Watson, I 116.
[6] S–S, VI 251.
[7] Dryden, Preface to *Sylvae*, Watson, II 20.

applies to the introduction of new words. "Tis true that, when I find an English word significant and sounding, I neither borrow from the Latin or any other language; but when I want at home, I must seek abroad . . . Upon the whole matter, a poet must first be certain that the word he would introduce is beautiful in Latin, and is to consider, in the next place, whether it will agree with the English idiom.'[1] In Dryden's own writing the idiom of English prose, as a 'stable language' was finally established.

This idiom, as Dryden rightly judged, was essentially a conversational one. The 'last and greatest advantage of our writing', he declared, in comparing the work of his own day with that of the previous age, 'proceeds from conversation'.[2] And arguing for the use of verse in the drama he claims paradoxically that 'one great reason why prose is not to be used in serious plays is because it is too near the nature of converse'.[3] Prior to the sixteenth century men, when they wrote in English, had, with some notable exceptions, written more or less as they spoke. The more elaborate forms of prose writing were reserved for French and Latin. Much sixteenth-century prose, on the other hand, was 'unnatural' because in striving for rhetorical effect it was led to differ from the way in which men ordinarily speak. Dryden's aim was to bring writing, in both prose and verse, back towards a conversational norm, as he does so skilfully in the casually off-hand opening of the Preface to the *Fables*. His words in this passage illustrate to perfection the quality he requires of prose by implication when he demands that rhyme strikes us as artificial only 'when the poet either makes a vicious choice of words, or places them, for rhyme sake, so unnaturally as no man would in ordinary speaking; but when 'tis so judiciously ordered that the first word in the verse seems to beget the second, and that the next, till that becomes the last word in the line which, in the negligence of prose would be so; it must then be granted rhyme has all the advantages of prose besides its own'.[4]

---

[1] Dryden, Dedication of the *Aeneis*, Watson, II 252.
[2] Dryden, 'Defence of the Epilogue', Watson, I 180.
[3] Dryden, 'Defence of an Essay', Watson, I 11f.
[4] Dryden, Epistle Dedicatory to *The Rival Ladies*, Watson, I 7.

The emphasis here is not that verse—or prose—should *be* negligent, but that it should *seem* to be so. Much earlier prose outside the influence of rhetoric had actually been negligent, to the extent that little or no attention had been paid to the form of the words as such. But while Dryden required that the sentence structure should not have the kind of obvious movement that would reveal what was to come, so that he praises Plutarch's style for being 'easy and flowing', he also admires the same writer for his 'continuance, with . . . propriety'.[1] And after defining wit as a 'propriety of thoughts and words', he adds 'or, in other terms, thoughts and words elegantly adapted to the subject'.[2] Here again there is the requirement that style should be determined by thought, but with the added requirement of elegance. Addison, in maintaining that Dryden's definition was less of wit than of 'good writing in general' conveniently omitted the word 'elegantly' from his quotation of it.[3] But for Dryden the elegance of the adaptation was an essential element of the wit. His aim was not simply, to use Bishop Sprat's words in his advocacy of plain style on behalf of the Royal Society, that of 'bringing all things as near the Mathematicall plainness as they can; and preferring the language of Artizans, Countrymen, and Merchants, before that of Wits and Scholars'.[4] Rather he wished to use the language of ordinary conversation, not quite as it actually takes place, but not so differently as to seem artificial or stylized. The problem is that discussed by Aristotle in the *Rhetoric* (III. iii) where he maintains that both clarity and distinction are required, distinction arising from what is uncommon but still being subject to propriety in order to seem natural.

This point needs to be stressed if justice is to be done to Dryden's achievement. A recent study of seventeenth-century prose style claims that 'in the preface to *Annus Mirabilis* Dryden is postulating for poetry the same criteria everyone else has been postulating for prose'.[5] And

---

[1] Dryden, *Life of Plutarch*, ed. Malone, *Prose Works of Dryden*, 1800, II 419.

[2] Dryden, 'Author's Apology for Heroic Poetry', Watson, I 207.

[3] Addison, *Spectator*, No. 62.

[4] Sprat, *The History of the Royal Society of London* 1667, 113.

[5] Robert Adolph, *The Rise of Modern Prose Style*, Cambridge Mass., 1968, 226.

Douglas Bush has said that 'plain prose was the natural medium for most kinds of utilitarian writing and most writing was utilitarian . . . Dryden and his fellows represented a culmination rather than a beginning'.[1] These things are true to the extent that plain prose had been advocated and practised more or less widely throughout the seventeenth century and earlier, and insofar as it was simply plain, Dryden's prose was a culmination of this movement. But it was a culmination that was also a beginning. As evidence that Dryden does not, like the Royal Society followers of Francis Bacon, seek to deliver so many things in an equal number of words, I could perhaps follow F. P. Wilson and quote this tribute to *On Dramatick Poesie*: 'How artfully the plot of this critical drama is related to the scenic background, so that the very swallows which skim the water ahead of the barge are pressed into service to give a simile for the literary points of some poet under discussion! And by-and-by the watermen are bidden to turn the barge and row softly, that the party may take the cool of the evening in their return; and the talk flows on, as abundant and as richly laden as the river itself.'[2] Or, to let Dryden speak for himself, this passage from the Preface to the *Fables*:

> By the mercy of God, I am already come within twenty years of this number; a cripple in my limbs, but what decays are in my mind the reader must determine. I think myself as vigorous as ever in the faculties of my soul, excepting only my memory, which is not impaired to any great degree; and if I lose not more of it, I have no great reason to complain. What judgement I had, increases rather than diminishes; and thoughts, such as they are, come crowding in so fast upon me that my only difficulty is to choose or to reject, to run them into verse or to give them the other harmony of prose: I have so long studied and practiced both that they are grown into a habit, and become familiar to me. In short, though I may lawfully plead some part of the old gentleman's excuse, yet I will reserve it till I think I have greater need, and

[1] Douglas Bush, *English Literature in the Earlier Seventeenth Century*, Oxford 1962, 192.
[2] A. B. Walkley, quoted by F. P. Wilson, *Seventeenth Century Prose*, 11.

ask no grains of allowance for the faults of this my present work,
but those which are given of course to human frailty.[1]

This is plain prose in the sense that its structure is loose and uncompli-
cated, its periods and clauses short without being obtrusively so, its
words familiar and its figures muted. But it is not the plainness that one
responds to. It is the ease, the harmony, the propriety, the elegance;
yet these things are so much the more effective in being achieved in a
context of apparent simplicity. Dryden's prose is essentially a literary
one, and his achievement was to take the plain, utilitarian prose of
writers like Tillotson, to whom he acknowledged a debt, and put it to
the service of literature. It can be interesting from this point of view to
compare the letters of Dryden with those of a more obviously self-
conscious stylist like Sir Thomas Browne. Both write letters with no
other apparent aim than saying what they have to say and both employ
a fairly similar, straightforward style. The difference between them
arises when they write with a more definitely literary purpose.

The qualities that Dryden looked for to provide distinction in writing
were primarily those to be found in the conversation of gentlemen.
'Thus Jonson did Mechanique humour show/When men were dull,
and conversation low,'[2] and Beaumont and Fletcher were to be preferred in some respects before Shakespeare and Jonson because 'they
understood and imitated the conversation of gentlemen better'.[3] If a
single criterion were to be used it would be 'ease', for this is what
Dryden finds to be the difference between the conversation of his own
time and that of the previous age. Thus speaking of the example of the
Court after the Restoration he declares that the 'desire of imitating so
great a pattern first wakened the dull and heavy spirits of the English
from their natural reservedness, loosened them from their stiff forms of
conversation, and made them easy and pliant to each other in discourse'.[4] His confession that his own 'conversation is slow and dull; my
humour saturnine and reserved: in short, I am none of those who en-

[1] Dryden, Watson, II 272–3.
[2] Dryden, Epilogue to *The Conquest of Granada*, second part, ll. 3–4.
[3] Dryden, *Of Dramatick Poesie*, Watson, I 68.
[4] Dryden, 'Defence of the Epilogue', Watson, I 181–2.

deavour to break jests in company, or make repartees . . .'[1] suggests that he himself would have found this reformation difficult in actual speaking; yet he believes that 'wit is best conveyed to us in the most easy language'[2] and he cannot understand why 'some men should perpetually stumble in a way so easy, and inverting the order of their words, constantly close their lines with verbs, which though commended sometimes in writing Latin, yet we were whipped at Westminster if we used it twice together'.[3]

In order to understand what 'ease' came to mean in Dryden's own practice, we might compare the passage already analyzed from the Preface to the *Fables* with the opening of *On Dramatick Poesie*—a useful comparison since the two essays are his major prose works and are separated by some thirty-two years. To facilitate comparison the passage will be set out in the same way as the one looked at earlier:

A1 It was that memorable day in the first summer of the late war⟩

    B1   when our navy engaged the Dutch

⟨a day

    B2   wherein the two most mighty and best appointed fleets⟩

           C1   which any age had ever seen

          ⟨disputed the command of the greater half of the globe the commerce of nations and the riches of the universe

          B3   While these vast floating bodies on either side moved against each other in parallel lines

          B4   and our countrymen under the happy conduct of his Royal Highness went breaking by little and little into the line of the enemies

A2   the noise of the cannon from both navies reached our ears about the City

       B5 so that all men being alarmed with it and in dreadful suspense of the event⟩

            C2   which we knew was then deciding

       ⟨every one went following the sound

            C3   as his fancy led him

[1] Dryden, 'Defence of an *Essay*', Watson, I 116.
[2] Dryden, *Of Dramatick Poesie*, Watson, I 40.
[3] Dryden, Epistle Dedicatory to *The Rival Ladies*, Watson, I 6.

> and leaving the town almost empty some took towards
> the park some cross the river others down it all seeking
> the noise in the depth of silence[1]

In this passage of approximately 180 words there are 2 grammatically autonomous periods; in the first 180 words from the Preface to the
Fables there are 6 such periods. In this passage there is a total of 11
clauses, while in the other there are 22 clauses. In other words, in the
Dramatick Poesie passage the period has an average length of 90 words,
the clause an average length of 16·3 words, and there is an average of
4·5 dependent clauses for each Rank A clause. In the *Fables* passage the
average length of the period is 30 words, of the clause 8·2 words, and
there is an average of 2·7 dependent for each Rank A clause. Thus, at
least at this fairly mechanical level, there is between the two passages
an obvious movement towards a simpler, less closely integrated sentence structure.

This greater complexity in the *Dramatick Poesie* passage is associated,
too, with a greater formality, a more obvious striving for effect than is
apparent in the *Fables* passage—in the build-up of phrases like 'command of the greater half of the globe, the commerce of nations, and the
riches of the universe', or 'some took towards the park, some cross the
river, others down it'. There is also the relatively long delaying of the
main idea in the second period to allow for the introduction of qualifying clauses (B3–4), which has no parallel in the *Fables* passage; and
similarly a more obvious use of parentheses in the form of participial
phrases. Finally the diction is more elevated—'vast floating bodies',
'dreadful suspense', and so on. The difference between the two passages, indeed, is rather similar in a number of respects to the difference
between *Annus Mirabilis*, written at around the same time as *Of Dramatick Poesie*, and the poetry of Dryden's maturity. I would not claim
that the difference between the two passages is not partly fortuitous, or
that precisely the same differences would be found if any two passages
from his early and late prose were compared. However the comparison
between the passages does I think indicate that the general direction
taken by Dryden's own prose was towards the same easier, more natur-

[1] Dryden, *Of Dramatick Poesie*, Watson, I 18.

al, more conversational style that he has been seen to have advocated in his comments on the subject.

An important aspect of the seventeenth-century movement towards a plain style of prose was a distrust of figurative language, and this is frequently reflected in Dryden's own remarks. Thus he criticizes Shakespeare because, he says, his 'whole style is so pestered with figurative expressions, that it is as affected as it is obscure'.[1] In the Preface to *Religio Laici* he distinguishes between the 'Plain and Natural, and yet Majestic,' style at which he is aiming in the poem, and the 'Florid, Elevated and Figurative' way that is 'for the Passions'. 'A Man,' he says, 'is to be cheated into Passion, but to be reason'd into Truth.'[2] And again, writing ironically of the prose of Sir Robert Howard, he declares that 'I cannot but give this testimony of his style, that it is extreme poetical, even in oratory; his thoughts elevated, sometimes above common apprehension; . . . that they are abundantly interlaced with variety of fancies, tropes, and figures, which the critics have enviously branded with the name of obscurity and false grammar.'[3] Nonetheless Dryden's aim is not, as we have seen, the kind of 'mathematical plainness' that would avoid all figurative language. Here is a passage from the Dedication to *The Spanish Fryar*, which in its consistent but unobtrusive resort to similitudes and other forms of figurative language is certainly not untypical of Dryden's prose as a whole. If it is not exactly, as Johnson described his style, 'sparkling with illustrations' neither is it by any means free of them:

> When I first designed this play, I found, or thought I found, somewhat so moving in the serious part of it, and so pleasant in the comic, as might deserve a more than ordinary care in both. Accordingly, I used the best of my endeavour, in the management of two plots, so very different from each other, that it was not perhaps the talent of every writer to have made them of a piece. Neither have I attempted other plays of the same nature, in my opinion, with the same judgment; though with like success. And though many poets may suspect themselves for the fondness and

[1] Dryden, Preface to *Troilus and Cressida*, Watson, I 239.
[2] Dryden, Preface to *Religio Laici*, Kinsley, I 311.
[3] Dryden, 'Defence of an *Essay*', Watson, I 118.

partiality of parents to their youngest children, yet I hope I may stand exempted from this rule, because I know myself too well to be ever satisfied with my own conceptions, which have seldom reached to those ideas that I had within me; and consequently, I presume I may have liberty to judge when I write more or less pardonably, as an ordinary marksman may know certainly when he shoots less wide at what he aims. Besides, the care and pains I have bestowed on this, beyond my other tragicomedies, may reasonably make the world conclude, that either I can do nothing tolerably, or that this poem is not much amiss. Few good pictures have been finished at one sitting; neither can a true just play, which is to bear the test of ages, be produced at a heat, or by the force of fancy, without the maturity of judgment. For my own part, I have both so just a diffidence of myself, and so great a reverence for my audience, that I dare venture nothing without a strict examination; and am as much ashamed to put a loose indigested play upon the public, as I should be to offer brass money in a payment. For though it should be taken (as it is too often on the stage), yet it will be found in the second telling; and a judicious reader will discover in his closet that trashy stuff whose glittering deceived him in the action. I have often heard the stationer sighing in his shop, and wishing for those hands to take off his melancholy bargain which clapped its performance on the stage. In a playhouse, everything contributes to impose upon the judgment: the lights, the scenes, the habits, and, above all, the grace of action, which is commonly the best where there is the most need of it, surprise the audience, and cast a mist upon their understandings; not unlike the cunning of a juggler, who is always staring us in the face, and overwhelming us with gibberish, only that he may gain the opportunity of making the cleaner conveyance of his trick. But these false beauties of the stage are no more lasting than a rainbow; when the actor ceases to shine upon them, when he gilds them no longer with his reflection, they vanish in a twinkling.[1]

This Dedication was written in 1681 when Dryden was at the height of his powers as a poet, and its use of figurative language also reflects his poetic practice. Dryden does, on several occasions emphasize the desirability of figurative language, and indeed speaks of 'imaging' as

---

[1] Dryden, Dedication of *The Spanish Fryar*, Watson, I 274–5.

'in itself, the very height and life of poetry'.[1] But the image he then provides from his *State of Innocence* to illustrate his own powers of image making suggests that he would have done well to remember his more frequently expressed view that the imagination needs to be kept firmly under the control of the reason. However, the typical image in his poetry—his more successful poetry, that is—is not of the kind that he seems to have in mind in this discussion. Rather it is explicit, immediately perceived, yet strictly subservient to the thought it is intended to embellish: while it vitalizes the prose content it does not itself become palpable or sensuous: it is not necessarily simple, but it works not to transcend the thought but to illuminate, to reinforce, to enrich it.[2] It is an image similar in function to what is perhaps the best known image in his prose—his illustration in the *Discourse on Satire* of the distinction between fine raillery and vulgar abuse:

> Neither is it true that this fineness of raillery is offensive. A witty man is tickled while he is hurt in this manner, and a fool feels it not. The occasion of an offence may possibly be given, but he cannot take it. If it be granted that in effect this way does more mischief; that a man is secretly wounded, and though he be not sensible himself, yet the malicious world will find it out for him; yet there is still a vast difference betwixt the slovenly butchering of a man, and the fineness of a stroke that separates the head from the body, and leaves it standing in its place. A man may be capable, as Jack Ketch's wife said to his servant, of a plain piece of work, a bare hanging; but to make a malefactor die sweetly was only belonging to her husband. I wish I could apply it to myself, if the reader would be kind enough to think it belongs to me.[3]

This kind of image gives vitality to the statement without being of its essence. It could be done without if plainness and perspecuity were all that was required, but it serves to give the richness, the complexity to the idea that makes us attend to it.

Dryden's use of imagery, in fact, is only one facet of the relationship

---

[1] Dryden, 'Author's Apology for Heroic Poetry', Watson, I 203.
[2] For a discussion of Dryden's use of imagery in his poetry see K. G. Hamilton, *John Dryden and the Poetry of Statement*, St Lucia 1967, 91–123.
[3] Dryden, *Original and Progress of Satire*, Watson, II 137.

between his poetry and prose, an understanding of which can assist in the appreciation of both. Writing of the degree of licence to be allowed in the use of figurative language, he rules that 'if this licence be included in a single word, it admits of tropes; if in a sentence or proposition, of figures; both of which are of a much larger extent, and more forcibly to be used in verse than prose'.[1] Tropes and figures are thus not excluded from prose but their range and force is more limited than in verse. At times he may go so far as to allow in poetry what would not be permissible in prose. Of new words, for example, he writes 'you have taken notice of some words which I have innovated (if it be too bold for me to say *refined*) upon his Latin; which as I offer not to introduce into English prose, so I hope they are neither improper, nor altogether unelegant in verse'.[2] Generally speaking, however, good verse for Dryden is likely to have much the same qualities of style as good prose. Prose is the norm by which poetry, at least in point of style, is to be measured and it is for this reason that, while what he has to say is mostly with direct reference to verse, it can also be referred by implication to prose.

But while his remarks on style are concerned more directly with verse, it is nonetheless true that Dryden's ideal of a natural conversational style is more consistently achieved in his prose than in his poetry. There are a number of reasons for this. In the first place, the very nature of poetry as a more formal, more exalted, more intense form of expression means that 'naturalness' in verse will not be quite the same as it is in prose. And, too, Dryden in his poetry is sometimes less apt to practise what he preaches than he is in his prose. Thus, though he praised Chaucer for his representation of the death of *Arcite*, and criticized Ovid for the 'false wit' he would have used on such an occasion, when he himself comes to render this particular passage from *The Knightes Tale* he is apparently unable to avoid such stylized elaboration as:

> . . . *but I close my Breath*
> *Near Bliss, and yet not bless'd before my Death.*   (ll. 798–9)

[1] Dryden, 'Author's Apology for Heroic Poetry', Watson, I 206.
[2] Dryden, 'Account' prefixed Preface to *Annus Mirabilis*, Watson, I 100–101.

It would be hard to find in his prose an example of the kind of unnatural stylization that the couplet form has led him into here. More importantly, although prose is the norm by which the style of poetry is to be judged there is still a difference. The licence that we have seen him allow to verse as against prose is towards a slightly more extravagantly rhetorical use of language. And coupled with this Dryden as a poet tends to speak not as in everyday conversation but with an essentially public voice, the voice of the orator; compared, for instance, with Donne, whose poetic voice is a private, personal one, and Pope who, particularly in his *Satires*, achieves the kind of easy conversational style that seems in theory to have been Dryden's ideal. Van Doren originally described Dryden's poetry as the 'poetry of declamation', and though he later changed this to the better known 'poetry of statement' it remains an apt description.

Even the 'unpolish'd rugged verse' of *Religio Laici*, which Dryden regarded as 'fittest for Discourse and nearest Prose', he nonetheless describes as 'plain and natural and yet majestic'. It is a lack of this 'majesty' that separates prose from poetry—as Samuel Wesley sums it up in 1700, in *An Epistle to a Friend concerning Poetry*:

> A different Style's for Prose and Verse requir'd
> Strong Figures *here, Neat Plainnes there desir'd:*
> A different Set of Words to both belong,
> *What* shines *in Prose, is flat and mean in Song.*
>
> (ll. 154–7)

John Dennis, who was not always so complimentary to Dryden, draws attention both to the qualities of his prose and to what distinguishes it from his poetry, in a comparison of Dryden's poetry with that of Edmund Waller. 'Yet if any one is of Opinion,' he says, 'that either his [Waller's] Language or Numbers are always perfect, he errs: For as there are sometimes improprieties in his Expressions, so there is a great deal of Prose in his Verse. *Mr Dryden,* who had the good luck to come after him, has the honour to have finish'd what the other so happily begun. For as we have nothing to show, e'en in Prose, which has greater purity than some of his blank Verse, and particularly that of the *Spanish Fryar* (tho at the same time that it has the purity and easi-

ness of Prose, it has the dignity and strength of Poetry), so I cannot
imagine anything more perfect than his Equal numbers in Heroic
Verse . . .'[1] And Dryden himself considered that, though prose may be
more natural, it is 'by common consent deposed, as too weak for the
government of serious plays', which, though they represent Nature
'but 'tis nature wrought up to an higher pitch. The plot, the characters,
the wit, the passions, the descriptions, are all exalted above the level
of common converse.'[2] Blank verse on the other hand, which in this
context meant much the same thing for Dryden as prose—'measured
prose', as he called it—is 'acknowledged to be too low for a poem, nay
more, for a paper of verses'.[3] This distinction between the 'heightened'
nature of poetry and the 'low' nature of prose is certainly not new but it
is made rather more explicit than it had hitherto tended to be. It may
account for some aspects of Dryden's poetry, particularly in the
heroic plays and in the *Aeneid*, which are less popular today; but it was
also one factor in furthering the development of a straightforward,
unadorned, neutral type of literary prose, by helping to free it from the
impulse toward excessive ornament.

Despite this distinction, however, it remains true that Dryden is at
his best as a poet when he combines, as he does in poems like *Absalom
and Achitophel* and *Mac Flecknoe*, the essential imaginativeness of
poetry with the qualities of good prose. In lines like these, for example
from the classic description of Shadwell as *Og* in *The Second Part of
Absalom and Achitophel*, Dryden makes the utmost use of the couplet
form—of the full pattern of lines and half-lines, of every rhyme, of
almost every one of the five stresses in each line—constantly reinforcing
the metrical stress with some emphasis of sound, or meaning, or association, without at the same time sacrificing any of the natural force of
prose:

> *Now stop your noses Readers, all and some,*
> *For here's a tun of Midnight-work to come,*
> *Og from Treason Tavern rowling home.*

[1] John Dennis, *The Impartial Critic*, 1693; ed. E. N. Hooker, *The Critical
Works of John Dennis*, 2 vol Baltimore 1939, I 14.
[2] Dryden, *Of Dramatick Poesie*, Watson, I 87.
[3] Ibid. 87.

> *Round as a Globe, and Liquor'd ev'ry chink,*
> *Goodly and Great he Sayls behind his Link;*
> *With all this Bulk there's nothing lost in* Og,
> *For ev'ry inch that is not Fool is Rogue:*
> *A Monstrous mass of foul corrupted matter,*
> *As all the Devils had spew'd to make the batter.*
> *When wine has given him courage to Blaspheme,*
> *He curses God, but God before Curst him;*
> *And if man cou'd have reason none has more,*
> *That made his Paunch so rich and him so poor.*

(ll. 457–69)

George Young, in his *English Prosody on Inductive Lines* (Cambridge 1928) says of Dryden that his mastery in the heroic couplet 'is due to his mastery as a writer of prose; prose of a time when the language had newly reached its present level of adaptability to the requirements of modern thought' (244). But this, I think, might be to get things in the wrong order. In reading Dryden's prose one is continually reminded of his poetry, and it may be that it was the discipline he learned from writing poetry that enabled him to move with such ease and assurance in prose. The restrictions of the couplet in the form and length of the period, and the added demands of rhyme, could lead to artificiality and unnatural ordering of words. When it avoided these things, however, and achieved the 'negligence of prose' it had 'all the advantages of prose besides its own'—its own advantages from this point of view being primarily that it discouraged digressiveness and longwindedness. Pope, for instance, in writing the *Essay on Man* in verse found that he could express his ideas 'more *shortly* this way than in prose itself; and nothing is more certain than that much of the *force* as well as *grace* of arguments or distinctions, depends on their conciseness'.[1] Dr Johnson has pointed out that blank verse, by comparison with the couplet, is 'too often found in description exuberant, in argument loquacious, and in narration tiresome', and for Dryden it was something 'into which the English tongue so naturally slides that, in writing prose, 'tis hardly to be avoided'.[2] It may well be that given the

[1] Pope, Preface to *Essay on Man.*
[2] Dryden, Preface to *The Rival Ladies*, Watson, I 6.

essentially prose virtues of clarity, directness, and conciseness which neo-classicism demanded of poetry, the heroic couplet provided the final training in form that prose required. Having learned 'to manoeuvre with precision', within the couplet, Dryden could then with safety manoeuvre as freely and naturally as he does in the Preface to the *Fables* without the dangers of an old man's garrulity that he himself alludes to.

Selected Bibliography and List of Abbreviations

Most titles included are of books and articles of recent times, with a few important exceptions made for eighteenth-century titles, and rather more for nineteenth-century titles. Entries in literary histories, encyclopedias, etc. are omitted. For a checklist of Dryden's canon in chronological order and a fuller bibliography (by John Barnard), see *CBEL*, rev. ed., II (1971), cols. 439–63.

All titles have been entered under their authors' or editors' names. Place of publication is London unless otherwise specified.

I. PRIMARY TEXTS AND LIST OF ABBREVIATIONS

Kinsley James Kinsley, ed. *The Poems of John Dryden*, 4 vol 1958
S-S Sir Walter Scott and George Saintsbury, eds. *The Works of John Dryden*. 18 vol Edinburgh 1888–92 (Scott's life of Dryden in vol I has much good critical judgment).
Watson George Watson, ed. *John Dryden: Of Dramatic Poesy and Other Critical Essays* 2 vol 1962.
Works Edward N. Hooker, H. T. Swedenberg, Jr., *et al.*, eds. *The Works of John Dryden*, Berkeley, Los Angeles, and London 1956 (To be complete in 20 vol).

Critical Studies Frequently Cited

Hoffman Arthur W. Hoffman, *John Dryden's Imagery*, Gainesville, Fla. 1962.
King Bruce King, ed. *Dryden's Mind and Art*, Edinburgh 1969 (Essays

in this book are entered in the relevant place in the Bibliography, and those previously published are cited in first printing).

Miner Earl Miner, *Dryden's Poetry*, Bloomington and London, corr. ed. 1968.

Roper Alan Roper, *Dryden's Poetic Kingdoms*, 1965.

Periodicals

CL *Comparative Literature;* EC *Essays in Criticism;* ELH *English Literary History;* ECS *Eighteenth-Century Studies;* HLQ *Huntington Library Quarterly;* JEGP *Journal of English and Germanic Philology;* JWCI *Journal of the Warburg and Courtauld Institutes;* MLN *Modern Language Notes;* MLR *Modern Language Review;* MP *Modern Philology;* PMLA *Publications of the Modern Language Association of America;* PLL *Papers on Language and Literature;* PQ *Philological Quarterly;* RES *Review of English Studies;* RLC *Revue de littérature comparée;* SEL *Studies in English Literature;* SP *Studies in Philology;* TSLL *Texas Studies in Language and Literature.*

2. EDITIONS, BIOGRAPHY, BIBLIOGRAPHIES

Beaurline, L. A. and Fredson T. Bowers, eds., *John Dryden: Four Tragedies. Four Comedies,* 2 vol Chicago 1967.

Benson, Donald R. 'Theology and Politics in Dryden's Conversion.' *SEL* IV, 1964, 393–412.

Bowers, Fredson T. 'Current Theories of Copy-Text, with an Illustration from Dryden', *MP* XLVIII, 1950–51, 12–20.

— 'The 1665 Manuscript of Dryden's *Indian Emperour*', *SP* XLVIII, 1951, 738–60.

Bredvold, Louis L., *The Best of Dryden*, New York 1933.

— 'Notes on John Dryden's Pension', *MP* XXX, 1933, 267–74.

Christie, W. D., ed., *Poetical Works* [of Dryden], 1870.

— *Select Poems* [of Dryden], 5th ed., rev. C. H. Firth., 1911.

Congreve, William, ed., *The Dramatick Works of John Dryden, Esq.* 6 vol 1717.

Day, Cyrus Lawrence, ed., *The Songs of John Dryden*, Cambridge, Mass. 1932.

Derrick, Samuel, ed., *Miscellaneous Works of John Dryden, Esq.*, 4 vol 1760.

Dobell, Percy J., *John Dryden: Bibliographical Memoranda*, 1922.

Frost, William, ed., *Selected Works of John Dryden*, New York 1971.

Gardner, William Bradford, 'John Dryden's Interest in Judicial Astrology', *SP* XLVII, 1950, 506–21.

— ed., *The Prologues and Epilogues of John Dryden*, New York 1951.

Gatto, Louis, 'An Annotated Bibliography of Critical Thought Concerning Dryden's *Essay of Dramatic Poesy*', *Restoration and 18th-Century Theatre Research* V, 1966, 18–29.

Johnson, Samuel, 'Dryden' in *The Lives of the English Poets*, ed George Birkbeck Hill 3 vol Oxford 1905, Vol I; see also 'Pope', Vol III.

Ker, W. P., ed., *Essays of John Dryden*, 2 vol Oxford 1926.

Kinsley, James, *The Poems and Fables of John Dryden*, Oxford 1962.

Kinsley, James and Helen, eds., *Dryden: The Critical Heritage*, 1971.

Legouis, Pierre, tr. and ed., *Poèmes Choisis*, Paris 1946.

Macdonald, Hugh, 'The Attacks on Dryden', *Essays and Studies of the Association* XXI, 1936, 41–74.

— *Dryden: a Bibliography of Early Editions and of Drydeniana*, Oxford 1967.

Malone, Edmond, ed., *The Critical and Miscellaneous Prose Works of John Dryden*, 3 vol in 4, 1800.

Miner, Earl, ed., *Selected Poetry and Prose of John Dryden*, New York 1969.

Monk, Samuel Holt, *Dryden: A List of Critical Studies . . . 1885–1950*, Minneapolis 1950.

— 'Dryden Studies: A Survey, 1920–1945', *ELH* XIV, 1947, 46–63.

Montgomery, Guy, *et al.*, *Concordance to the Poetical Works of Dryden*, Berkeley and Los Angeles 1957.

Noyes, George R. and George Reuben Potter, eds., *Hymns Attributed to John Dryden*, Berkeley 1937.

— ed., *The Poetical Works of John Dryden*, Cambridge, Mass. 1950.

— ed., *Selected Dramas of John Dryden*, Chicago and New York 1910.

Osborn, James M., *Dryden: Some Biographical Facts and Problems*,

Gainesville, Fla. 1965.
— 'Macdonald's Bibliography of Dryden: An Annotated Check List of Selected American Libraries', *MP* XXXIX, 1941–42, 69–98, 197–212, 313–19.
Saintsbury, George, *Dryden*, 1881.
— ed., *Selected Plays*, 2 vol [1904].
Summers, Montague, ed., *Dryden: The Dramatic Works*, 6 vol 1931–32.
[Todd, H. J., ed.,] *Poetical Works* [of Dryden], 4 vol 1851.
Ward, Charles E., ed., *The Letters of John Dryden*, Durham, N. C. 1942.
— *The Life of John Dryden*, Chapel Hill, N. C. 1961.
— and H. T. Swedenberg, Jr., *John Dryden: Papers Read at a Clark Library Seminar, February 25, 1967*, Los Angeles 1967.

3. POETRY AND GENERAL CRITICISM

Adams, Percy G. ' "Harmony of Numbers": Dryden's Alliteration, Consonance, Assonance', *TSLL* IX, 1967, 333–43.
Alssid, Michael W., 'Shadwell's *Mac Flecknoe*', *SEL* VII, 1967, 387–402.
Anselment, Raymond A., 'Martin Marprelate: A New Source for Dryden's Fable of the Martin and the Swallows', *RES* n. s., XVII, 1966, 256–67.
Austin, Norman, 'Translation as Baptism: Dryden's Lucretius', *Arion* VII, 1968, 576–602.
Ball, Albert, 'Charles II: Dryden's Christian Hero', *MP* LIX, 1961, 25–35.
Barnard, John, 'Dryden, Tonson, and the Subscriptions for the 1697 Virgil', *Papers of the Bibliographical Society of America* LVII, 1963, 129–51.
Benson, Donald R., 'The Artistic Image and Dryden's Conception of Reason', *SEL* XI, (1971), 427–35.
— 'Platonism and Neoclassic Metaphor', *SP* LXVIII, 1971, 340–56.
— 'Who "Bred" Religio Laici?', *JEGP* LXV, 1966, 238–57.
Blair, Joel, 'Dryden on the Writing of Fancifull Poetry', *Criticism* XII, 1970, 89–104.

— 'Dryden's Ceremonial Hero', *SEL* IX, 1969, 379–93.

Blondel, J., 'The Englishness of Dryden's Satire in *Absalom and Achitophel*', *Travaux du Centre d'Etudes Anglaises et Américaines* I, Aix en Provence 1962.

Boys, Richard C., 'Some Problems of Dryden's Miscellany', *ELH* VII, 1940, 130–43.

Brennecke, Ernest, Jr., 'Dryden's Odes and Draghi's Music', *PMLA* XLIX, 1934, 1–36.

Brodwin, Leonora Leet, 'Miltonic Allusion in *Absalom and Achitophel*: Its Function in the Political Satire', *JEGP* LXVIII, 1969, 24–44.

Brooks, Harold F., 'Dryden's Juvenal and the Harveys', *PQ* LXVIII, 1969, 12–19.

— 'The "Imitation" in English Poetry, especially in Formal Satire, before the Age of Pope', *RES* XXV, 1949, 124–40.

Brower, Reuben A., 'An Allusion to Europe: Dryden and Tradition', *ELH* XIX, 1952, 38–48.

— 'Dryden and the "Invention" of Pope', *Restoration and Eighteenth-Century Literature*, Chicago 1963, 211–33.

— 'Dryden's Epic Manner and Virgil', *PMLA* LV, 1940, 119–38.

— 'Dryden's Poetic Diction and Virgil', *PQ* XVIII, 1939, 211–17.

Budick, Sanford, *Dryden and the Abyss of Light*, New Haven 1970. (The religious poems).

Cable, Chester H., '*Absalom and Achitophel* as Epic Satire', *Studies in Honor of John Wilcox*, ed. A. Doyle *et al.*, Detroit 1958, 51–60.

Cameron, Allen Berry, 'Donne and Dryden: Their Achievement in the Verse Epistle', *Discourse* XI, 1968, 262–56.

Chiasson, Elias J., 'Dryden's Apparent Scepticism in *Religio Laici*', *Harvard Theological Review* LIV, 1961, 207–21.

Corder, Jim W., 'Rhetoric and Meaning in *Religio Laici*', *PMLA* LXXXII, 1967, 245–49.

Davies, Godfrey, 'The Conclusion of Dryden's *Absalom and Achitophel*', *HLQ* X, 1946–47, 69–82.

Diffenbaugh, Guy Linton, *The Rise and Development of the Mock Heroic Poem in England*, Urbana, Ill., 1928 (*Mac Flecknoe*).

Dearing, Vinton A., 'Dryden's *Mac Flecknoe*: The Case for Authorial Revision', *Studies in Bibliography* VII, 1955, 85–102.

Dobbins, Austin C., 'Dryden's "Character of a Good Parson": Background and Interpretation', *SP* LIII, 1956, 51–59.

Dobrée, Bonamy, *John Dryden*, 1956.

— 'Milton and Dryden: A Comparison and Contrast in Poetic Ideas and Poetic Method', *ELH* III, 1936, 83–100.

Dyson, A. E. and Julian Lovelock, 'Beyond the Polemics: A Dialogue on the Opening of *Absalom and Achitophel*', *The Critical Survey* V, 1971, 133–45.

Eade, Christopher, 'Some English Iliads: Chapman to Dryden', *Arion* VI, 1967, 336–45.

Ellis, Amanda, 'Horace's Influence on Dryden', *PQ* IV, 1925, 39–60.

Eliot, T. S., *Homage to John Dryden*, 1925.

— *John Dryden: The Poet, the Dramatist, the Critic*, New York 1932.

— *Selected Essays*, 1951.

Empson, William, 'Dryden's Apparent Scepticism', *EC* XX, 1970, 172–81 (also ensuing discussion, *ibid.*, 446–50, 492–95; *XXI*, 111–15; 410–11).

Emslie, McD., 'Dryden's Couplets: Wit and Conversation', *EC* XI, 1961, 264–73.

Evans, George Blakemore, 'The Text of Dryden's *Mac Flecknoe*', *Harvard Library Bulletin* VII, 1953, 32–54.

Feder, Lillian, 'John Dryden's Use of Classical Rhetoric', *PMLA* LXIX, 1954, 1258–78.

Ferry, Anne Davidson, *Milton and the Miltonic Dryden*, Cambridge, Mass. 1968.

Fitzgerald, Robert, 'Dryden's *Aeneid*', *Arion* II, 1963, 17–31.

Fowler, Alastair and Douglas Brooks, 'The Structure of Dryden's "Song for St Cecilia's Day, 1687"', *EC* XVII, 1967, 434–47.

Freedman, Morris, 'Dryden's Miniature Epic', *JEGP* LVII, 1958, 211–19.

— 'Milton and Dryden on Rhyme', *HLQ* XXIV, 1961, 337–44.

French, A. L., 'Dryden, Marvell and Political Poetry', *SEL* VIII, 1968, 397–414.

Frost, William, 'Dryden and Satire'. *SEL* XI 1971, 401–416.

— *Dryden and the Art of Translation*, New Haven, 1955.

— 'Dryden's Theory and Practice of Satire', *King*, 189–205.

— 'English Persius: The Golden Age', *ECS* II, 1968–69, 77–101.

Fujimura, Thomas H., 'Dryden's *Religio Laici*: An Anglican Poem', *PMLA* LXXVI, 1961, 205–17.

Gallagher, Mary, 'Dryden's Translation of Lucretius', *HLQ* XXVIII, 1964, 19–29.

Garnett, Richard, *The Age of Dryden*, 1895.

Gerevini, Silvano, *Dryden e Teocrito: Barocco e neoclassicismo nella Restaurazione inglese*, Milan 1966.

Guilhamet, Leon M., 'Dryden's Debasement of Scripture in *Absalom and Achitophel*', *SEL* IX, 1969, 395–413.

Ham, Roswell G., 'Some Uncollected Verse of John Dryden', *London Mercury* XXXI, 1930, 421–26.

Hamilton, K. G., *John Dryden and the Poetry of Statement*, St Lucia [1967].

— *The Two Harmonies: Poetry and Prose in the Seventeenth Century*, Oxford 1963.

Hamm, Victor M., 'Dryden's *The Hind and the Panther* and Roman Catholic Apologetics', *PMLA* LXXXIII, 1968, 400–415.

— 'Dryden's *Religio Laici* and Roman Catholic Apologetics', *PMLA* LXXX, 1965, 190–98.

Harth, Phillip, *Contexts of Dryden's Thought*, Chicago 1968.

Harrison, T. W., 'Dryden's *Aeneid*', *King*, 143–167.

Hart, Jeffrey, 'John Dryden: The Politics of Style', *Modern Age* VIII, 1964, 399–408.

Heath-Stubbs, John, 'Baroque Ceremony: A Study of Dryden's *Ode to the Memory of Mistress Anne Killigrew*', *Cairo Studies in English* 1959, 76–84.

— 'Dryden and the Heroic Ideal', *King*, 3–23.

Hemphill, George, 'Dryden's Heroic Line', *PMLA* LXXII, 1957, 863–79.

Hoffman, Arthur W., 'An Apprenticeship in Praise', *King*, 45–64.

— 'Dryden's To Mr. Congreve', *MLN* LXXV, 1960, 553–56.

Hollander, John, *The Untuning of the Sky*, Princeton 1961.

Hollis, Christopher, *Dryden*, 1933.

Hooker, Edward N, 'Dryden and the Atoms of Epicurus', *ELH* XXXIV, 1957, 177–90.

— 'The Purpose of Dryden's *Annus Mirabilis*', *HLQ* X, 1946, 49–67.

Hooker, Helene Maxwell, 'Charles Montagu's Reply to *The Hind and the Panther*', *ELH* VIII, 1941, 51–73.

— 'Dryden's *Georgics* and English Predecessors', *HLQ* IX, 1945–46, 273–310.

Huntley, Frank L., 'Dryden, Rochester, and the Eighth Satire of Juvenal', *PQ* XVIII, 1939, 269–84.

Jefferson, D. W., 'Aspects of Dryden's Imagery', *EC* IV, 1954, 20–41.

Jones, Richard F., 'The Originality of *Absalom and Achitophel*', *MLN* XLVI, 1931, 211–18.

Jünemann, Wolfgang, *Drydens Fabeln und ihre Quellen*, Hamburg 1932.

King, Bruce, '*Absalom and Achitophel*, A Revaluation', *King*, 65–83.

— 'Absalom and Achitophel: Machiavelli and the False Messiah', *Etudes Anglaises* XVI, 1963, 251–54.

— 'Wordplay in *Absalom and Achitophel*: An Aspect of Style', *Language and Style* II, 1969, 330–38.

Kinsley, James, 'Dryden and the Art of Praise', *English Studies* XXXIV, 1953, 57–64.

— 'Dryden and the *Encomium Musicae*', *RES* n. s. IV, 1953, 263–67.

— 'Historical Allusions in *Absalom and Achitophel*', *RES* n. s. VI, 1955, 291–97 (and ensuing discussion, *ibid.*, VII, 410–414; 414–15).

— 'The "Three Glorious Victories" in *Annus Mirabilis*', *RES* n. s. VII, 1956, 30–37.

Korn, A. L., '*Mac Flecknoe* and Cowley's *Davideis*', *HLQ* XIV, 1951, 99–127.

Legouis, Pierre, 'Dryden plus Miltonien que Milton ?', *Etudes Anglaises* XX, 1967, 370–77.

Levine, George R., 'Dryden's "Inarticulate Poesy": Music and the Davidic King in *Absalom and Achitophel*', *ECS* I, 1968, 219–312.

Levine, Jay Arnold, 'Dryden's *Song for St. Cecilia's Day, 1687*', *PQ* XLIV, 1965, 38–50.

— 'John Dryden's Epistle to John Driden', *JEGP* LXIII, 1964, 450–74.

— 'The Status of the Verse Epistle Before Pope', *SP* LIX, 1962, 658–84.

Lewalski, Barbara K., 'David's "Troubles Remembered": An Analogue to "Absalom and Achitophel"', *Notes and Queries* CCIX, 1964, 340–43.

— 'The Scope and Function of Biblical Allusion in *Absalom and Achitophel*', *English Language Notes* III, 1965–66, 29–35.

Lowell, James Russell, 'Dryden', *The Writings of James Russell Lowell*. 11 vol Boston 1890, III. (Often reprinted in smaller collections.)

Løsnes, Arvid, 'Dryden's *Aeneis* and the Delphin Virgil', *The Hidden Sense*, ed. Maren-Sofie Røstvig, Oslo 1963, 113–57.

Macaulay, Thomas Babington, 'Dryden', *Edinburgh Review* XLVII, 1828, 1–36.

Mace, D. T., 'Musical Humanism, the Doctrine of Rhythmus, and the St Cecilia Day Odes of Dryden', *JWCI* XXVII, 1964, 251–92.

Maurer, A. E. Wallace, 'The Design of Dryden's *The Medall*', *PLL* II, 1966, 293–304.

— 'The Structure of Dryden's *Astraea Redux*', *PLL* II, 1966, 13–20.

— 'Who Prompted Dryden to Write *Absalom and Achitophel*?', *PQ* XL, 1961, 130–38.

McFadden, George, 'Dryden and the Numbers of His Native Tongue', *Essays and Studies in Language and Literature*, ed. Herbert H. Petit, Duquesne 1964, 87–109.

— 'Dryden, Boileau, and Longinian Imitation', *Proceedings of the 4th Congress of the International Comparative Literature Association*, ed. F. Jost, Fribourg 1964; Hague 1966, 751–55.

— 'Dryden's "Most Barren Period"—and Milton', *HLQ* XXIV, 1960–61, 283–96.

— 'Elkanah Settle and the Genesis of *Mac Flecknoe*', *PQ* XLIII, 1964, 55–72.

McKeithan, Daniel Morely, 'The Occasion of *Mac Flecknoe*', *PMLA* XLVII, 1932, 766–71.

Mary Eleanor, Mother, '*Anne Killigrew* and *Mac Flecknoe*', *PQ* XLIII, 1964, 47–54.

Middleton, Anne, 'The Modern Art of Fortifying: *Palamon and Arcite* as Epicurean Epic', *The Chaucer Review* III, 1968, 124–43.

Miner, Earl, 'Chaucer in Dryden's *Fables*', *Studies in Criticism and Aesthetics, 1660–1800*, ed. Howard Anderson and John S. Shea, Minneapolis 1967, 58–72.

— 'Dryden and the Issue of Human Progress', *PQ* XL, 1961, 120–29.

Miner, Earl, 'Dryden's *Eikon Basilike: To Sir Godfrey Kneller*', *Seventeenth-Century Imagery* ed. Earl Miner, Berkeley and Los Angeles 1971, 151–67.

— 'Dryden's Ode on Mrs Anastasia Stafford', *HLQ* XXX 1967, 103–11.

— 'The Significance of Plot in *The Hind and the Panther*', *Bulletin of the New York Public Library* LXIX, 1965, 446–58.

— 'Some Characteristics of Dryden's Use of Metaphor', *SEL* II, 1962, 309–320.

Moore, John Robert, '*Alexander's Feast*: A Possible Chronology of Development', *PQ* XXXVII, 1958, 495–498.

Murakami, Shikō, 'Reverence for Human Nature: The Poetry of Dryden and Pope'. *The Journal of the Faculty of Letters, Osaka University* X, 1963, i–vi, 1–84.

Myers, Robert Manson, *Handel, Dryden, & Milton*, 1956.

Myers, William, 'Politics in *The Hind and the Panther*', *EC* XIX, 1969, 19–34.

Nänny, Max, *John Drydens rhetorische Poetik: Versuch eines Aufbau aus seinem kritischen Schaffen*, Bern 1959.

Newdigate, B. H., 'An Overlooked Ode by John Dryden', *London Mercury* XXII, 1930, 438–42.

Nichol Smith, David, *John Dryden*, Cambridge 1950.

Nicoll, Allardyce, *Dryden and His Poetry*, 1923.

Novak, Maximillian E., 'Dryden's "Ape of the French Eloquence" and Richard Flecknoe', *Bulletin of the New York Public Library* LXXII, 1968, 499–506.

Parkin, Rebecca Price, 'Some Rhetorical Aspects of Dryden's Biblical Allusions', *ECS* II, 1968–69, 341–69.

Peterson, R. G., 'Larger Manners and Events: Sallust and Virgil in *Absalom and Achitophel*', *PMLA* LXXXII, 1967, 236–44.

Phillips, James E. and Bertrand H. Bronson, *Music and Literature in the Seventeenth and Eighteenth Centuries*, Los Angeles 1954.

Pinto, Vivian de Sola, 'Rochester and Dryden', *Renaissance and Modern Studies* V, 1961, 29–48.

Proffitt, Bessie, 'Political Satire in Dryden's *Alexander's Feast*', *TSLL* XI, 1970, 1307–1316.

Proudfoot, L., *Dryden's 'Aeneid' and its Seventeenth-Century Predecessors*, Manchester 1960.

Pughe, Francis Heveningham, *John Dryden's Übersetzungen aus Theokrit*, Breslau 1894.

Raleigh, Sir Walter, 'John Dryden and Political Satire', *Some Authors*, Oxford 1923.

Ramsay, Paul, *The Art of John Dryden*, Lexington, Ky. 1969.

Randolph, Mary Claire, 'The Structural Design of Formal Verse Satire', *PQ* XXI, 1942, 368–84.

Ricks, Christopher, 'Dryden's Absalom', *EC* XI, 1961, 273–89.

Roper, Alan, 'Dryden's *Medal* and the Divine Analogy', *ELH* XXIX, 1962, 396–417.

— 'Dryden's *Secular Masque*', *MLQ* XXIII, 1962, 29–40.

Rosenberg, Bruce A., '*Annus Mirabilis* Distilled', *PMLA* LXXIX, 1964, 254–58.

Rudd, Niall, 'Dryden on Horace and Juvenal', *University of Toronto Quarterly* XXXII, 1963, 155–69.

Schilling, Bernard, ed., *Dryden: A Collection of Critical Essays*, Englewood Cliffs, N. J. 1963. (The essays are given in this bibliography under their authors' names and original publications.).

— *Dryden and the Conservative Myth*, New Haven, 1961.

Selden, R., 'Roughness in Satire from Horace to Dryden', *MLR* LXVI, 1971, 264–72.

Shawcross, John T., 'Some Literary Uses of Numerology', *Hartford Studies in Literature* I, 1969, 50–62. (Killigrew Ode).

Sloman, Judith, 'An Interpretation of Dryden's *Fables*', *ECS* IV, 1970–71, 199–211.

Smith, R. Jack, 'Shadwell's Impact on John Dryden', *RES* XX, 1944, 29–44.

Späth, Eberhard, *Dryden als Poeta Laureatus*, Nürnberg 1969.

Steadman, John M., 'Timotheus in Dryden, E. K., and Gafori', *Times Literary Supplement* 16 Dec. 1960, 819.

Sutherland, James, 'Dryden: The Poet as Orator', (W. P. Ker Memorial Lecture) Glasgow 1963.

Sutherland, W. O. S., Jr., 'Dryden's Use of Popular Imagery in *The Medal*', *University of Texas Studies in English* XXXV, 1956, 123–34.

Swedenberg, H. T., Jr., 'Dryden's Obsessive Concern with the Heroic' *SP*, e.s., 4, 1967, 12–26.

— 'England's Joy: *Astraea Redux* in Its Setting', *SP* L, 1953, 30–44.

— *Essential Articles for the Study of John Dryden*, Hamden, Conn. 1966 (The essays are given in this bibliography under their authors' name and original publications.)

— *The Theory of the Epic in England, 1650–1800*, Berkeley and Lo Angeles 1944.

Taylor, Aline Mackenzie, 'Dryden's "Enchanted Isle" and Shadwell' "Dominion"', *SP* LXIV, 1967, e.s. 4, 39–53.

Thale, Mary, 'Dryden's Unwritten Epic', *PLL* V, 1969, 423–33.

Thomas, W. K., 'The Matrix of *Absalom and Achitophel*', *PQ* XLIX 1970, 92–99.

Tillyard, E. M. W., *Five Poems, 1470–1870*, 1948 (Killigrew Ode).

Towers, Tom H., 'The Lineage of Shadwell; An Approach to *Ma Flecknoe*', *SEL* II, 1963, 323–34.

Van Doren, Mark, *John Dryden: A Study of His Poetry*, New York 194((Originally *The Poetry of John Dryden*, New York 1920.)

Verall, A. W., *Lectures on Dryden*, Cambridge 1914.

Vieth, David M., 'Concept as Metaphor: Dryden's Attempted Stylisti Revolution', *Language and Style* III, 1970, 197–204.

— 'Irony in Dryden's Ode to Anne Killigrew', *SP* LXII, 1965, 91 100.

Wallerstein, Ruth, 'The Development of the Rhetoric and Metre of th Heroic Couplet', *PMLA* L, 1936, 166–209.

— 'On the Death of Mrs Killigrew: The Perfecting of a Genre', *S* XLIV, 1947, 519–28.

— *Studies in Seventeenth-Century Poetic*, Madison 1950.

— 'To Madness Near Allied: Shaftesbury and His Place in the Desig and Thought of *Absalom and Achitophel*', *HLQ* VI, 1943, 445–71.

Wasserman, Earl R., 'Dryden's Epistle to Charleton', *JEGP* LV, 195(201–12.

Wilding, Michael, 'Allusion and Innuendo in *Mac Flecknoe*', *EC* XIX 1969, 355–70.

Williams, W. H., ' "Palamon and Arcite" and the "Knightes Tale" *MLR* IX, 1914, 161–72, 309–23.

Williamson, George, 'The Rhetorical Pattern of Neoclassical Wit', *MP* XXXIII, 1935, 55–81.

Wright, Herbert G., *Boccaccio in England from Chaucer to Tennyson*, 1957.

— 'Some Sidelights on the Reputation and Influence of Dryden's *Fables*', *RES* XXI, 1945, 23–37.

Zwicker, Steven, *Dryden's Political Poetry, The Typology of King and Nation*, Providence, R. I., 1972.

— 'The King and Christ: Figural Imagery in Dryden's Restoration Panegyrics', *PQ* L, 1971, 582–98.

4. DRAMA

Allen, Ned Bliss, *The Sources of John Dryden's Comedies*, Ann Arbor 1935.

Alssid, M. W., 'The Design of Dryden's *Aureng-Zebe*', *JEGP* LXIV, 1965, 452–69.

— 'The Perfect Conquest: A Study of the Theme, Structure, and Characters in Dryden's *The Indian Emperour*', *SP* LIX, 1962, 539–59.

Banks, Landrum, 'Dryden's Baroque Drama', *Essays in Honor of Esmond Linworth Marilla*, ed. Thomas Austin Kirby and William John Olive, Baton Rouge, La., 188–200.

Barbeau, Anne T., *The Intellectual Design of Dryden's Heroic Plays*, New Haven 1970.

Bernhardt, W. W., 'Shakespeare's Troilus and Cressida and Dryden's *Truth Found Too Late*', *Shakespeare Quarterly* XX, 1969, 129–41.

Bleuler, Werner, *Das heroische Drama John Drydens als Experiment dekorativer Formkunst*, Bern 1958.

Bredvold, Louis I., 'Political Aspects of Dryden's *Amboyna* and *The Spanish Fryar*', *Essays and Studies in English and Comparative Literature* (University of Michigan) VIII, 1932, 119–32.

Broich, Ulrich, 'Libertin und heroischer Held: das Drama der englischen Restaurationszeit und seine Leitbilder', *Anglia* LXXV, 1967, 34–57.

Caracciolo, Peter, 'Dryden and the *Antony and Cleopatra* of Sir John Sedley', *English Studies* L, 1969, 50–55.

Clark, William S., 'The Definition of the "Heroic Play" in the Restoration Period', *RES* VIII, 1932, 437–44.

— 'The Platonic Element in the Restoration Heroic Play', *PMLA* XLV, 1930, 623–24.

— 'The Sources of the Restoration Heroic Play', *RES* IV, 1928, 49–63.

Danchin, Pierre, 'Le public des théâtres londoniens à l'époque de la Restauration d'après les prologues et les èpilogues', *Dramaturgie et société: Rapports entre l'oeuvre théâtrale*, ed. Jean Jacquot *et al.*, 2 vol Paris 1968, II 847–88.

Deane, Cecil V., *Dramatic Theory and the Rhymed Heroic Play*, New York 1968.

Dent, Edward J., *Foundations of English Opera*, New York 1965 (*Albion and Albanius*).

Dobrée, Bonamy, *Restoration Comedy—1660–1720*, Oxford 1924.

— *Restoration Tragedy—1660–1720*, Oxford 1929.

Freedman, Morris, 'Milton and Dryden on Tragedy', *English Writers of the Eighteenth Century*, ed. John Middendorf, New York 1972.

Fujimura, Thomas H., 'The Appeal of Dryden's Heroic Plays', *PMLA* LXXV, 1960, 37–45.

Gagen, Jean, 'Love and Honor in Dryden's Heroic Plays', *PMLA* LXXVII, 1962, 208–20.

Goggin, L. P., 'This Bow of Ulysses', *Essays and Studies in Literature*, ed. Herbert H. Petit, Duquesne 1965, 49–86 (*All for Love*).

Guffey, George Robert, *After The Tempest*, Los Angeles 1969.

Harris, Bernard, 'The Dialect of Those Fanatic Times', *Restoration Theatre*, ed. John Russell Brown and Bernard Harris, 1965, 11–40.

Hartmann, Carl, *Der Einfluss Molières auf Drydens komisch-dramatische Dichtungen*, Leipzig 1885.

Hartsock, Mildred E., 'Dryden's Plays: A Study in Ideas', *Seventeenth Century Studies, Second Series*, ed. Robert Shafer, Princeton 1937, 71–176.

Hathaway, Baxter, 'John Dryden and the Function of Tragedy', *PMLA* LVIII, 1943, 665–73.

Holzhausen, Paul, 'Dryden's heroisches drama', *Englische Studien* XIII, 1889, 414–45; XV, 1891, 13–52; XVI, 1892, 201–229.

Hughes, Derek W., 'The Significance of *All for Love*', *ELH* XXXVII, 1970, 540–63.

Jefferson, D. W., ' "All, all of a piece throughout": Thoughts on Dryden's Dramatic Poetry', *Restoration Theatre*, ed. John Russell Brown and Bernard Harris, 1965, 159–76.

— 'The Significance of Dryden's Heroic Plays', *Proceedings of the Leeds Philosophical and Literary Society* V, 1940, 125–39.

King, Bruce, '*Don Sebastian*: Dryden's Moral Fable', *Sewanee Review* LXX, 1962, 651–70.

— 'Dryden, Tillotson, and *Tyrannick Love*', *RES*, n. s., XVI 1965, 364–77.

— *Dryden's Major Plays*, Edinburgh 1966.

— 'Dryden's *Marriage a la Mode*', *Drama Survey* IV, 1965, 28–37.

— 'The Significance of Dryden's *State of Innocence*', *SEL* IV, 1964, 371–92.

Kirsch, Arthur C., 'Dryden, Corneille and the Heroic Play', *MP* LIX, 1962, 248–64.

— *Dryden's Heroic Drama*, Princeton 1965.

— 'The Significance of Dryden's *Aureng-Zebe*', *ELH* XXIX, 1962, 160–75.

Legouis, Pierre, 'Quinault et Dryden: une source de *The Spanish Fryar*', *RLC* XI, 1931, 951–62.

Loftis, John, 'Dryden's Criticism of Spanish Drama', *The Augustan Milieu*, ed. Henry Knight Miller *et al.*, Oxford 1970, 18–31.

— ' "El Principe Constante" and "The Indian Emperour" ', *MLR* LXV, 1970, 761–67.

— 'Exploration and Enlightenment: Dryden's *The Indian Emperour* and Its Background', *PQ* XLV, 1966, 71–84.

— 'The Hispanic Element in Dryden', *Emory University Quarterly* XX, 1964, 90–100.

Lynch, Kathleen, 'Conventions of Platonic Drama in the Heroic Plays of Orrery and Dryden', *PMLA* XLIV, 1929, 456–71.

— 'D'Urfé's *L'Astrée* and the "Proviso" Scenes in Dryden's Comedy', *PQ* IV, 1925, 302–308.

Lynch, Kathleen, *The Social Mode of Restoration Comedy*, New York 1926.

MacMillan, Dougald, 'The Sources of Dryden's *The Indian Emperour*', *HLQ* XIII, 1949–50, 355–70.

Monk, Samuel Holt, 'Dryden and the Beginnings of Shakespearean Criticism in the Augustan Age', *The Persistence of Shakespeare Idolatry*, ed. Herbert M. Schueller, Detroit 1964, 47–75.

Moore, Frank Harper, 'The Composition of *Sir Martin Mar-All*', *SP* LXIV, 1967, e.s. 4, 27–38.

— 'Heroic Comedy: A New Interpretation of Dryden's *Assignation*', *SP* LI, 1954, 585–98.

— *The Nobler Pleasure: Dryden's Comedy in Theory and Practice*, Chapel Hill 1963.

Muir, Kenneth, 'The Imagery of *All for Love*', *Proceedings of the Leeds Philosophical and Literary Society* V, 1940, 140–47.

Nelson, James E., ' "Drums and Trumpets"', *Restoration and 18th Century Theatre Research* IX, 1970, 46–55.

Newman, Robert S., 'Irony and the Problem of Tone in Dryden's *Aureng-Zebe*', *SEL* X, 1970, 439–58.

Nicoll, Allardyce, *Dryden as an Adapter of Shakespeare*, 1922.

Novak, Maximillian E., *The Empress of Morocco and Its Critics,* Los Angeles 1968.

— 'Political Plays of the Restoration', *MLR* XVI, 1921, 224–42.

Osborn, Scott, 'Heroical Love in Dryden's Heroic Drama', *PMLA* LXXIII, 1958, 480–90.

Pati, P. K. 'Dryden's Heroic Plays: A Study of Their Theory and Practice', *Indian Journal of English Studies* IX, 1968, 87–95.

Pendlebury, B. J., *Dryden's Heroic Plays: A Study of Their Origins*, 1923.

Perkins, Merle L., 'Dryden's *The Indian Emperour* and Voltaire's *Alzire*', *CL* IX, 1957, 229–37.

Prior, Moody, *The Language of Tragedy*, New York 1947 (*All for Love*).

Reinert, Otto, 'Passion and Pity in *All for Love*: A Reconsideration', *The Hidden Sense* ed. Maren-Sofie Røstvig, Oslo 1963, 159–95.

Rothstein, Eric, 'English Tragic Theory in the Late Seventeenth Century', *ELH* XXIX, 1962, 306–23.

— *Restoration Tragedy*, Madison and Milwaukee 1967.

Rundle, James U., 'The Sources of Dryden's "Comic Plot" in *The Assignation*"', *MP* XLV, 1947, 104–111.

Russell, Trusten Wheeler, *Voltaire, Dryden and Heroic Tragedy*, New York 1946.

Shergold, N. D. and Peter Ure, 'Dryden and Calderón: A New Spanish Source for "The Indian Emperour"', *MLR* LXI, 1966, 369–83.

Smith, John Harrington, 'The Dryden-Howard Collaboration', *SP* LI, 1954, 54–74.

— *The Gay Couple in Restoration Comedy*, Cambridge, Mass. 1948.

Sorelius, Gunnar, *'The Great Race Before the Flood': Pre-Restoration Drama on the Stage and in the Criticism of the Restoration*, Studia Anglistica Upsaliensa 4, Uppsala 1966.

Teeter, Louis, 'The Dramatic Use of Hobbes's Political Ideas', *ELH* III, 1936, 140–69.

Tisch, J. H., 'Late Baroque Drama—A European Phenomenon?' *Proceedings of the International Comparative Literature Association*, Amsterdam 1969, 125–36.

Tupper, James W., 'The Relation of the Heroic Play to the Romances of Beaumont and Fletcher', *PMLA* XX, 1905, 584–621.

Wain, John, 'Restoration Comedy and its Modern Critics', *EC* VI, 1956, 367–85.

Waith, Eugene M., *The Herculean Hero in Marlowe, Chapman, Shakespeare and Dryden*, New York 1962.

— *Ideas of Greatness: Heroic Drama in England*, 1971.

— 'The Voice of Mr Bayes', *SEL* III, 1963, 335–43.

Ward, Charles E., 'Massinger and Dryden', *ELH* II, 1935, 263–66.

Weinbrot, Howard D., 'Alexis in *All for Love*: His Genealogy and Function', *SP* LXIV, 1967, 625–39.

Wilkinson, D. R. M., *The Comedy of Habit: An Essay on the Use of Courtesy Literature in a Study of Restoration Drama*, Leiden 1964.

Wilson, John Harold, *The Court Wits of the Restoration*, Princeton 1948.

Winterbottom, John, 'The Development of the Hero in Dryden's Tragedies', *JEGP* LII, 1953, 161–73.

— 'The Place of Hobbesian Ideas in Dryden's Tragedies', *JEGP* LVII, 1958, 665–83.

Winterbottom, John, 'Stoicism in Dryden's Tragedies', *JEGP* LXI, 1962, 868–83.

Zebouni, Selma Assir, *Dryden, A Study in Heroic Characterization*, Baton Rouge, La. 1965.

5. CRITICISM AND PROSE STYLE

Aden, John M., *The Critical Opinions of John Dryden: A Dictionary*, Nashville 1963.

— 'Dryden and Boileau: The Question of Critical Influence', *SP* L, 1953, 491–509.

— 'Dryden and the Imagination: The First Phase', *PMLA* LXXIV, 1959, 28–40.

— 'Dryden, Corneille and the *Essay of Dramatic Poesy*', *RES* n. s. VI, 1955, 147–56.

Archer, Stanley, 'The Persons in *An Essay of Dramatic Poesy*', *PLL* II, 1966, 305–14.

Barnard, John, 'The Dates of Six Dryden Letters', *PQ* XLII, 1963, 396–403. (In part a reply to Margaret P. Boddy's article, below)

Bately, Janet M., 'Dryden's Revisions in the *Essay of Dramatic Poesy*', *RES* n. s. XV, 1964, 268–82.

Boddy, Margaret P., 'Dryden–Lauderdale Relationships, Some Biographical Notes and a Suggestion', *PQ* XLII, 1963, 267–72.

Brown, David D., 'John Tillotson's Revisions and Dryden's "Talent for English Prose"', *RES* n. s. XII, 1961, 24–39.

Cameron, L. W., 'The Cold Prose Fits of John Dryden', *RLC*, XXX, 1956, 371–79.

Craig, Hardin, 'Dryden's Lucian', *Classical Philology* XVI, 1921, 141–63.

Crinó, Anna Maria, 'Uno sconosciuto autografo drydeniana al British Museum', *English Miscellany* XVII, 1967, 311–20.

Davie, Donald, 'Dramatic Poetry: Dryden's Conversation Piece'. *Cambridge Journal* V, 1952, 553–61.

Dobrée, Bonamy, 'Dryden's Prose', *King*, 171–88.

Doyle, Anne, 'Dryden's Authorship of *Notes and Observations on the Empress of Morocco*', *SEL* VI, 1966, 421–46.

Ham, Roswell G., 'Dryden as Historiographer Royal: The Authorship of *His Majesties Declaration Defended*', *RES* XI, 1935, 284–98.

— 'Dryden vs. Settle', *MP* XXV, 1928, 409–16.

— 'Dryden's Dedication for *The Music of the Prophetesse*', *PMLA* L, 1935, 1065–75.

Hume, Robert D., 'Dryden on Creation: "Imagination" in the Later Criticism', *RES* n. s. XXI, 1970, 295–314.

— *Dryden's Criticism*, Ithaca, N. Y. 1970.

— 'Dryden's "Heads of an Answer to Rymer"', *RES* n. s. XIX, 1968, 373–86.

Huntley, Frank L. 'Dryden's Discovery of Boileau', *MP* XLV, 1947, 112–17.

— 'On Dryden's "Essay of Dramatic Poesy",' *University of Michigan Contributions in Modern Phology* 16, Ann Arbor 1951.

— 'On the Persons in Dryden's *Essay of Dramatic Poesy*', *MLN* LXIII, 1948, 88–95.

— *The Unity of John Dryden's Dramatic Criticism*, Chicago 1945.

Jensen, H. James, *A Glossary of John Dryden's Critical Terms*, Minneapolis, 1969.

LeClercq, Richard V., 'The Academic Nature of the Whole Discourse of *An Essay of Dramatic Poesy*', *PLL* VIII, 1972, 27–38.

— 'Corneille and *An Essay of Dramatic Poesy*', *CL* XXII, 1970, 319–27.

Legouis, Pierre, 'Corneille and Dryden as Dramatic Critics', *Seventeenth-Century Studies Presented to Sir Herbert Grierson*, Oxford 1938, 269–91.

Mace, D. T., 'Dryden's Dialogue on Drama', *JWCI* XXV, 1962, 87–112.

Maurocorodato, Alexandre, 'Positions de la critique dramatique chez Dryden', *Société des Anglicistes . . . Actes . . ., 1966–67*, Paris 1969, 103–12.

Miner, Earl, 'Dryden and "The Magnified Piece of Duncomb"', *HLQ* XXVIII, 1964–5, 93–98.

— 'Dryden as Prose Controversialist: His Role in *A Defence of the Royal Papers*', *PQ* XLIII, 1964, 412–19.

Ramsey, Paul, *The Lively and the Just* Tuskaloosa, Ala. 1962.

Sherwood, John C., 'Dryden and the Critical Theories of Tasso', *CL*
XVIII, 1966, 351–59.
— 'Dryden and the Rules: The Preface to *Fables*', *JEGP* LII, 1953,
13–26.
— 'Dryden and the Rules: The Preface to *Troilus and Cressida*', *CL* II,
1950, 73–83.
Simon, Irène, 'Dryden's Prose Style', *Revue des langues vivantes* XXXI,
1965, 506–30.
— 'Dryden's Revision of the *Essay of Dramatic Poesy*', *RES* n. s. XIV,
1963, 132–41.
— 'Precept and Practice in Dryden's Criticism', *JEGP* LXVIII, 1969,
432–40.
Singh, Sarup, 'Dryden and the Unities', *Indian Journal of English
Studies* II, 1961, 78–90.
Smith, John Harrington, 'Dryden's Critical Temper', *Washington
University Studies* XII, 1925, 201–20.
Strang, Barbara M. H., 'Dryden's Innovation in Critical Vocabulary',
Durham University Journal LI, 1959, 114–23.
Thale, Mary, 'Dryden's Critical Vocabulary: The Imitation of Nature',
PLL II, 1966, 315–26.
— 'Dryden's Dramatic Criticism: Polestar of the Ancients', *CL* XVIII,
1966, 36–54.
Thorpe, Clarence De Witt, 'The Psychological Approach in Dryden'
The Aesthetic Theory of Thomas Hobbes, Ann Arbor, 1940, 189–220.
Trowbridge, Hoyt, 'Dryden's *Essay on the Dramatic Poetry of the Last
Age*', *PQ* XXII, 1943, 240–50.
— 'The Place of the Rules in Dryden's Criticism', *MP* XLIV, 1946,
84–96.
Walcott, Fred G., 'John Dryden's Answer to Thomas Rymer's *The
Tragedies of the Last Age*', *PQ* XV, 1936, 194–214.
Wallerstein, Ruth, 'Dryden and the Analysis of Shakespeare's Tech-
niques', *RES* XIX, 1943, 165–85.
Watson, George, 'Dryden's First Answer to Rymer', *RES* n. s. XIV,
1963, 17–23.
Williamson, George, 'The Occasion of *An Essay of Dramatic Poesy*',
MP XLIV, 1946–7, 1–9.

6. MISCELLANEOUS

Alden, Raymond MacDonald, *The Rise of Formal Satire in England Under Classical Influence*, University of Pennsylvania Series in Philology, Literature, and Archaeology VII, Philadelphia 1899.

Amarasinghe, Upali, *Dryden and Pope in the Early Nineteenth Century*, Cambridge 1962.

Bevan, Allan, 'Poetry and Politics in Restoration England', *Dalhousie Review* XXXIX, 1959, 314-25.

Born, Lester K., 'The Perfect Prince According to the Latin Panegyrists', *American Journal of Philology* LV, 1934, 20-35.

Bottkol, J. McG., 'Dryden's Latin Scholarship', *MP* XL, 1943, 241-55.

Bredvold, Louis I., 'Dryden, Hobbes, and the Royal Society', *MP* XXV, 1928, 417-38.

— *The Intellectual Milieu of John Dryden*, Ann Arbor 1934.

— 'The Tendency Toward Platonism in Neo-Classical Aesthetics', *ELH* I, 1934, 91-119.

Broderson, G. L., 'Seventeenth Century Translations of Juvenal', *The Phoenix* VII, 1953, 57-76.

Butt, John, *The Augustan Age*, 1950.

Davison, Dennis, *Dryden*, 1968.

Draper, J. W., *The Funeral Elegy and the Rise of Romanticism*, New York 1929.

Emerson, Oliver Ferrar, 'John Dryden and a British Academy', *Proceedings of the British Academy* X, 1921, 45-88.

Falle, George G., 'Dryden; Professional Man of Letters', *University of Toronto Quarterly* XXVI, 1957, 443-55.

Frye, B. J., ed, *Mac Flecknoe*, Columbus, Ohio 1970 (A 'casebook' with text, reading list, and selections from criticism given elsewhere in this bibliography)

Fujimura, Thomas H., *The Restoration Comedy of Wit*, Princeton 1952.

Hagstrum, Jean H., *The Sister Arts: The Tradition of Literary Pictorialism . . . from Dryden to Gray*, Chicago 1958.

Havens, Raymond D., 'Changing Taste in the Eighteenth Century: A Study of Dryden's and Dodsley's Miscellanies' *PMLA* XLIV, 1929, 501-36.

Hill, Herbert Wynford, *La Calprenède's Romances and the Restoration Drama, University of Nevada Studies* II, 1910; III, 1911.

Holland, Norman N., *The First Modern Comedies*, Cambridge, Mass. 1959.

Hope, A. D., *The Cave and the Spring: Essays on Poetry*, Chicago 1970.

Hughes, Merritt Y., 'Dryden as a Statist', *PQ* VI, 1927, 335–50.

Jack, Ian, *Augustan Satire*, Oxford 1942.

Johnson, James William, *The Formation of English Neo-Classical Thought* Princeton 1967.

King, Bruce, 'Dryden's Ark: The Influence of Filmer', *SEL* VII, 1967, 403–14.

Kinsley, James and Helen, ed, *Dryden: The Critical Heritage*, 1971.

Korshin, Paul J., 'The Evolution of Neoclassical Poetics', *ECS* II, 1968, 102–37.

Lloyd, Claude, 'John Dryden and the Royal Society', *PMLA* XLV, 1930, 967–76.

Loftis, John, ed. *Restoration Drama: Modern Essays in Criticism*, New York 1966.

Lord, George deForrest, *et al.*, ed. *Poems on Affairs of State*, New Haven 1963—(Vols. I–IV include satires published in Dryden's lifetime.)

Maddison, Carol, *Apollo and the Nine: A History of the Ode*, Baltimore 1960.

Maurocordato, Alexandre, *La critique en classique Angleterre de la Restauration*, Paris 1964.

Miner, Earl, *Restoration Dramatists: A Collection of Critical Essays*, Englewood Cliffs, N. J. 1966.

Moore, Robert Etheridge, *Henry Purcell and the Restoration Theatre*, Cambridge, Mass. 1961.

Nevo, Ruth, *The Dial of Virtue: A Study of Poems on Affairs of State in the Seventeenth Century*, Princeton 1963.

Nicoll, Allardyce, *A History of English Drama, 1660–1900*, 6 vol Cambridge 1935–59. (Vol. I, *Restoration Drama*).

Paulson, Ronald, *The Fictions of Satire*, Baltimore 1967.

Price, Martin, *To the Palace of Wisdom: Studies in Order and Design from Dryden to Blake*, New York 1964.

Rosenberg, Alfred, *Longinus in England*, Berlin 1917.

Shuster, G. N., *The English Ode from Milton to Keats*, New York 1940.

Smith, John Harrington, 'Some Sources of Dryden's Toryism, 1682–1684', *HLQ* XX, 1956–7, 233–43.

Steger, Hugo, *David Rex et Propheta. Erlanger Beiträge zur Sprach- und Kunstwissenschaft* VI, Nürnberg 1961.

Sutherland, James, *English Satire*, 1958.

— 'The Impact of Charles II on Restoration Literature', *Restoration and Eighteenth-Century Literature*, Chicago, ed. Carroll Camden, Chicago 1963, 251–63.

Sutherland, W. O. S., Jr., *The Art of the Satirist . . . [in] Augustan England*, Austin, Texas 1965.

Underwood, Dale, *Etherege and the Seventeenth-Century Comedy of Manners*, New Haven 1957.

Turnell, G. M., 'Dryden and the Religious Elements in the Classical Tradition', *Englische Studien* LXX, 1935, 244–61.

Van Lennep, William, *et al.* eds., *The London Stage*, 11 vol Carbondale, Ill., 1960–8. (Vol. I, 1660–1700).

Waith, Eugene M., 'Tears of Magnanimity in Otway and Racine', *French and English Drama of the Seventeenth Century*, Los Angeles 1972.

Welle, J. A. van der, *Dryden and Holland*, Groningen 1962.

Wallace, John M., 'Dryden and History: A Problem in Allegorical Reading', *ELH* XXXVI, 1969, 265–90.

Williamson, George, 'The Restoration Revolt Against Enthusiasm', *SP* XXX, 1933, 571–603.

Wölfel, Kurt, 'Epische Welt und satirische Welt: Zur Technik des satirischen Erzählens', *Wirkendes Wort* X, 1960, 85–98.

Index

Compiled by Mrs Brenda Hall, MA